FICTIONS OF MODESTY

RUTH BERNARD YEAZELL

FICTIONS OF MODESTY

*Women and Courtship
in the English Novel*

The University of Chicago Press
Chicago and London

RUTH BERNARD YEAZELL is professor of English at the University of California, Los Angeles. She is the editor of *The Death and Letters of Alice James* and *Sex, Politics, and Science in the Nineteenth-Century Novel,* and the author of *Language and Knowledge in the Late Novels of Henry James,* published by the University of Chicago Press.

Published with the generous assistance of the John Simon Memorial Guggenheim Foundation.

Several pages of Chapter 9 appeared in Ruth Bernard Yeazell, "The Boundaries of Mansfield Park," *Representations* 7 (1984), 133–52. © 1984 by the Regents of the University of California.

An earlier version of Chapters 12 and 13 and the opening pages of Chapter 1 appeared in Ruth Bernard Yeazell, "Nature's Courtship Plot in Darwin and Ellis," *Yale Journal of Criticism* 2, no. 2 (Spring 1989), 33–53.

The University of Chicago Press, Chicago 60637
The University of Chicago Press, Ltd., London
© 1991 by The University of Chicago
All rights reserved. Published 1991
Printed in the United States of America
00 99 98 97 96 95 94 93 92 91   5 4 3 2 1

Library of Congress Cataloging-in-Publication Data

Yeazell, Ruth Bernard.
    Fictions of modesty : women and courtship in the English novel / Ruth Bernard Yeazell.
        p.   cm.
    Includes bibliographical references and index.
    ISBN 0-226-95096-4 (cloth)
    1. English fiction—18th century—History and criticism.
    2. English fiction—19th century—History and criticism.
    3. Courtship in literature.   4. Modesty in literature.   5. Women in literature.   I. Title.
PR858.C69Y4   1991
823.009'353—dc20   90-48888
                                                             CIP

∞ The paper used in this publication meets the minimum requirements of the American National Standard for Information Sciences—Permanence of Paper for Printed Library Materials, ANSI Z39.48-1984.

For Sandy

CONTENTS

PREFACE

People living in England in the eighteenth and nineteenth centuries seldom discoursed on women's behavior without elaborate attention to modesty. Much thinking about modesty centered on questions of middle-class marriage; and novels of the period take their most typical form as narratives of courtship. But "an in-bred sense of modesty" was bred even into the heroines of Gothic and pornographic fiction—bred so insistently that when a young woman in *The Monk* is unclothed, unconscious, and in danger of rape, the novelist pauses to remark that "there was a sort of modesty in her very nakedness, which added fresh stings to the desires of the lustful monk." This implausible monastic will not appear again in the present book, but his tastes were very much of their time. It was in the same decade that Mary Wollstonecraft took issue with just such a lurid idea of women's virtue—and argued also in the name of modesty.

The modest woman was a highly conventional figure; and like most powerful conventions, she answered to multiple and conflicting wishes. This book begins by asking what people of the time meant when they devoted so much writing to the anxious remaking of woman's "nature" and to codifying rules for her proper behavior. Not all the fictions of modesty studied here are novels. But it is the novelist, I would argue, who makes best sense of the subject's confusions and contradictions. In its most general sense, modesty is a tempering of behavior that allows individuals to meet and come to terms with one another, whether for marriage or other purposes; and in this sense what we think of as a virtue can perhaps only be understood as a story. By adopting the modest woman as a subject for narrative, the novelists were able to represent modesty not as a set of rules but as a series of changing responses—not as a fixed condition but as a passage in time. Both in the forward movement of the plot and in the persons who surround a heroine, novels could accommodate the aggressive energies and desires that her modesty might superficially appear to deny. Though novels shared with other kinds of writing the impulse to moralize the subject, at least some novelists were also capable of approaching its contradictions in a spirit of comedy or satire.

The first part of this book attempts to convey something of the popularity as well as the complexity of the subject by surveying a large number of contributions to the discussion, whether these were made by David Hume or by a certain "Harriet Diffident," as she sought advice from a popular columnist in the *Lady's Magazine*. Somewhat more space is devoted to Hume than to Diffident, but I believe we need to know what both said about matters of daily behavior, before one voice was elevated to the history of philosophy and the other forgotten—if she ever existed. Writers of conduct books and of speculative philosophy also began to explain modesty through narrative: the instance of Rousseau is only the most obvious.

The second part of the book aims to suggest some of the ways in which the English novel adopts the conventions of modesty, but I have been more interested in what individual novelists could make of a modest heroine. This part attempts no survey, therefore, but concentrates on six case histories ranging over the years from 1740 to 1866. I am taking for granted—and relying on my readers' knowledge to confirm—that modesty triumphs everywhere in classic English fiction, but I also offer the testimony of Anthony Trollope that appears as an epigraph to this part. Trollope confidently assures the readers of his *Autobiography* that the great English novelists have always taught modesty; he, too, credits six novelists, and only one of those, Jane Austen, is also one of mine. The others he names are Maria Edgeworth, Scott, Thackeray, Dickens, and George Eliot—to which list we can just as confidently add Trollope himself, since in the same work he boasts, "I do believe that no girl has risen from the reading of my pages less modest than she was before, and that some may have learned from them that modesty is a charm well worth preserving."

The six narratives studied in my pages are by Richardson, Cleland, Burney, Austen, Charlotte Brontë, and Gaskell. While Richardson's heroine is famous for her delaying action and Cleland's for her passionate accommodation, this book argues that the histories of Pamela and Fanny Hill are not so much opposites as mirror images of one another and that both works testify to the laws governing fictions of modesty. Male wishes and fantasies clearly determine the outlines of the modest heroine's story. But in taking for granted a heroine's temporary resistance to the body and its desires, novelists of both sexes were able to devote greater attention to the story of her consciousness.

If one fiction of modesty was that the lovers' passion was intensified by delay, another was that the interval of postponement allowed for female choosing; and for the women novelists in particular, the erotic plotting of modesty seems finally less important than the narrative interval afforded their heroines for observation and questioning. Tales of erotic awakening undoubtedly play an important role in every culture, but the very fact that so many English novels could concentrate their attention on the period between coming of age and marriage is one measure of how capacious were the fictions of modesty. This book deliberately concentrates on each author's most self-effacing heroine, but insofar as the history of an Elizabeth Bennet, an Emma Woodhouse, or a Margaret Hale depends on the premise that she is long unacquainted with her own heart, the stories of those bold and lively English heroines are also fictions of modesty.

In considering the women novelists here as critics and theorists of modesty, I have sometimes been tempted to classify Burney as the expert in the politics of self, Austen as the moralist, Brontë the psychologist, and Gaskell the naturalist. They are far more than this, of course, and I am not suggesting that novels acquire their value from their approximation to more abstract modes of thought. But the sequence of such a list would at least call attention to the way in which "scientific" accounts of human behavior have gradually tended to replace more openly moral and social ones: where previous generations read conduct books, we now turn to psychology or even sociobiology for models. Thus, in the third part of this book, I have briefly presented, as postscripts, some features of Darwin's theory of sexual selection and of Havelock Ellis's psychology of sex that both analyze and continue fictions of modesty. After a century of comparative neglect, contemporary scientists have recently been paying renewed attention to Darwin's account of the evolutionary role played by females selectively choosing their mates: according to one zoologist cited by the *New York Times* of 8 May 1990, female choice is "definitely the wave of the future in biology." While those who sought to codify modest behavior in previous centuries often appealed to Nature for support, our modern understanding of the natural owes at least something, I am persuaded, to the work of the novelists.

❧

For their generous support of this project over a number of years, I wish to thank the Guggenheim Memorial Foundation, the National Endowment for the Humanities, the University of California President's Research Fellowship in the Humanities, the College Institute and the Research Committee of the University of California, Los Angeles. I have gratefully relied upon the resources of the University Research Library and the English Reading Room at UCLA, and the rich collections of early women's magazines and conduct literature in the British Library and the Fawcett Library, London; and I would particularly like to thank David Doughan for his informed and friendly introduction to the Fawcett collection. Portions of this book appeared in different form in *Critical Inquiry, Representations,* and the *Yale Journal of Criticism,* and I thank the editors of these journals for permission to use the material here. For valuable suggestions and advice, I wish especially to thank Nancy Armstrong, Paula Backscheider, Ann Bergren, Ruth Bloch, Margaret Doody, Anne Mellor, Sara Melzer, Helene Moglen, Herbert Morris, Mitzi Myers, Hilary Schor, Debra Silverman, Patricia Meyer Spacks, James Turner, and Stephen Yenser. Barbara Galvin's expert and cheerful assistance made the research for the book immeasurably easier; and exchanges with a great many students have challenged and clarified my thinking. Above all, I am grateful to Alexander Welsh, who asked the hard questions, encouraged me to find the answers, and improved the argument in ways too numerous to mention. It is difficult to imagine this book without his friendship and his example.

PART ONE

Codifications

❧

Miss Prue. Well, but don't you love me as well
  as you did last Night then?

Tattle. No, no, Child, you would not have me.

Miss Prue. No? Yes but I would, tho.

Tattle. Pshaw, but I tell you, you would not—
  You forget you're a Woman, and don't know
  your own mind.

Miss Prue. But here's my Father, and he knows
  my Mind.

           —Congreve, *Love for Love*

1

The Language of Modesty

૨

In one of those notorious episodes that later generations would conventionally represent as the last waves of Victorian reaction, a bookseller named George Bedborough was arrested in 1898 for selling what the indictment called "a certain lewd, wicked, bawdy, scandalous and obscene libel, in the form of a book entitled Studies in the Psychology of Sex, volume 1: Sexual Inversion, by Havelock Ellis."[1] Though liberal opinion was briefly mobilized on Ellis's behalf, the trial itself was to prove anticlimactic: since Bedborough pleaded guilty, the merits of the work were never debated in open court; and the moral outlines of the drama were further blurred by Ellis's temporizing defense of his project in his affidavit, by his own treatment of Bedborough, and by his rather extraordinary gullibility in originally entrusting the publication of his work to a professional con man and erstwhile forger—a character who would later make an appropriately stagy exit by swallowing poison from a so-called magic ring when the police caught up with him in 1902.[2] The more immediate consequence of the Bedborough trial, however, was that Ellis turned to America rather than England to publish his *Studies* (there has never, in fact, been a complete English edition), and that he chose to alter the order in which they would appear: instead of the offending study of "Sexual Inversion," by which he of course meant homosexuality, Ellis now placed at the head of his multivolume work an extended essay entitled "The Evolution of Modesty." This, he later insisted, was where "modesty" clearly belonged. "I was pleased to be able to effect this change of order," he wrote in a foreword of 1935,

for . . . I had not originally proposed to start the *Studies* with what was inevitably regarded as an abnormal subject, and to put it at the head served to excuse

3

the not uncommon error of describing my *Studies* as "pathological." There is no real ground for such a description. . . . The original inspiration of my own work, and the guiding motive throughout, was the study of normal sexuality. I have always been careful to show that even the abnormal phenomena throw light on the normal impulse, since they have their origin either in an exaggeration or a diminution of that impulse; while, reversely, we are better able to understand the abnormal when we realise how closely it is related to the normal.[3]

Once hailed as the prophet of sexual freedom, Ellis now seems to us a more equivocal figure. Historians have begun to address the problematic consequences of the late Victorian effort to medicalize sexuality, to replace moral injunctions with an open and "scientific" labeling of sexual identities and propensities, not the least of which is the construction of the fixed identity of "the homosexual" himself.[4] But it is not the implications of Ellis's coining of the term "invert" that I wish to highlight here, nor even his effort to justify the so-called abnormal by providing it with a respectable genealogy. At the risk of seeming to reproduce his move, raising the question of "inversion" only to subordinate it to an account of the "normal impulse," I want to investigate the significance of his second thought—that normal sexuality apparently begins with the instinctive modesty of women. For Ellis and others, to think about sex was necessarily to think about female modesty and its privileged role in the sequence of events he revealingly called "courtship." No doubt the Bedborough trial and its aftermath made "The Evolution of Modesty" seem a more prudent introduction to the *Studies* than a volume on homosexuality. But the conventional wisdom of Ellis's choice is very much to the point: by understanding "normal sexuality" as above all a delaying action, a naturally scripted courtship plot whose principal motor is the instinctive modesty of women, Ellis rewrote as science the narratives that English culture had been elaborating for more than two hundred years—narratives of female resistance and female choice that I shall be calling the fictions of modesty.

Such narratives have scarcely disappeared, of course, but if they are no longer told so often or so insistently as they were in the two centuries before Ellis's work, that work was itself both a symptom and a cause of the change. Though the *Studies* began with "The Evolution of Modesty," an evolution understood to be a natural process, their comparatively frank and remarkably tolerant account of human sexual variety also began to put an end to the widespread insistence on modesty as central to the definition of female "nature." In part by making the erotic dynamics of courtship explicit, they helped to revise the culture's dominant account of sexual relations. As one of the makers of modern psychology, the man who is sometimes called the English Freud properly belongs to the end rather than the beginning of my account (and I shall in fact return to him at the end). But modern psychology also continues the conduct literature it has sometimes appeared to replace—as even the form of Ellis's *Studies* might suggest, with their loose compilation of vaguely attributed quotations, bits of anthropological data, and miscellaneous case histories; and it should not be surprising that Ellis begins where so many purveyors of conventional wisdom had begun before him. More than two centuries earlier, for example, Richard Allestree, the probable author of the immensely influential conduct book known as *The Ladies Calling* (1673), had also chosen to commence his advice to the sex by writing at length "Of Modesty."

❧

To characterize any account of modesty as conventional is not to say that it is simple. Writers of popular conduct books and philosophers alike long insisted on the importance of female modesty, even as they contradicted one another—and themselves—on the nature of the virtue.[5] It is a commonplace of the advice literature that women's modesty is instinctive, but the very existence of the literature testifies to the belief that the "instinct" must be elaborately codified and endlessly discussed: woman's "natural" modesty must be strenuously cultivated, the argument goes, lest both sexes fall victim to her "natural" lust. So *The Ladies Calling* pronounced modesty at once "natural to the sex" and "the most indispensible requisite of a woman"—and then prescriptively declared that women who lacked the "instinct" were not truly women at all: "an Impudent woman is lookt on as a kind of Monster; a thing diverted and distorted from its proper form."[6] In the centuries that followed, countless authors of printed advice for middle-class readers exhorted English-women to guard their modesty—even while insisting that true modesty is not conscious of itself and knows nothing of what might violate it. "Innocent Modesty," according to one late-eighteenth-century ladies' magazine, has an "unsuspicious look," for "it is the glory of a delicate female to be unconscious" of all "unbecoming knowledge."[7] The modest woman can be recognized by her downcast eyes, her head turned aside, and above all by the blush that suffuses her cheek—an "innocent paint" more attractive than any rouge,[8] and mysterious proof that she has neither done nor thought anything for which she genuinely need blush. Such a woman never puts herself forward, and female modesty restrains and controls the violence of masculine love; but a modestly clothed body is more seductive than a merely naked one, and modesty creates love in the very act of restraining it. As the eponymous hero of Hannah More's *Coelebs in Search of a Wife* (1808) solemnly describes his future bride, "Her nymphlike form does not appear to less advantage for being veiled with scrupulous modesty."[9] No wonder that the advice givers perpetually struggled to distinguish "true" from "false" modesty, or that radically opposed views of human nature could argue in its name.

All words so charged with value resist sharp definition, tend to surround themselves with fields of conflict and confusion. One person's good is rarely another's, and "good" has different meanings as different individuals and groups struggle for its possession. But if "modesty" seems to have been a word peculiarly apt to sustain and cover contradictions, it doubtless owes something of that power to its Latin etymology. As Ellis self-consciously recognized when he set out to analyze the problem at the end of the nineteenth century, "modesty" in his sense of the term—and, we may add, in that of the eighteenth-century conduct books—has its closest equivalent in the French *pudeur*, a word with a sufficiently complicated and baffling history of its own.[10] But while the French actively retained two words from the Latin, the humble *modestie* as well as the more erotic *pudeur*, the English settled for one—the word that originally signified moderation.[11] "Modesty, commonly mistaken for bashfulness, is a just medium in all our words and actions," declared the *Lady's Magazine* in 1775, invoking Cicero for authority; it is "the golden mean of living . . . and may be justly deemed the parent of many other virtues."[12] And insofar as the English word still carries overtones of this original sense, "modesty" at once conveys everything and nothing, a nearly universal ideal and a midpoint constantly shifting with the placement of the extremes.

Neither a prude nor a coquette, as the conduct books never tired of repeating, the modest woman occupies a mystified space between, a space largely defined by the repudiation of those imagined opposites. When Thomas Marriott exhorted the reader of *Female Conduct*, a versified "Essay on the Art of Pleasing" of 1759, to "shun, in your Behavior, each Extreme," the social map he urged her to follow was already a very familiar one:

> Safe, in the golden Mean, with Caution steer,
> Fair Nymph, nor be too gay, nor too austere;
> Distant, as far from Prude, as from Coquet,
> Form your Deportment, between both compleat.[13]

So, too, the anonymous author of *The Polite Lady*, an epistolary conduct book of the following year, unsurprisingly announced that "virtue lies in the *golden mean*," and routinely identified that mean with modesty: "modesty is the middle point betwixt coquetry and prudery, both of which are equally ridiculous and contemptible." *The Polite Lady's* formulaic contrast of those "ridiculous" types reproduces a common topos—all the more common, perhaps, because extremes are so much easier to define, and to caricature, than the elusive middle:

The prude affects an appearance of more modesty than she really has: the coquette affects an appearance of less. . . . The prude is so extremely nice and delicate, that she is offended at every thing: the coquette is so very easy and indifferent, that she is offended at nothing. The prude startles at the most innocent expressions, as rude and indecent: the coquette hears what are really the most rude and indecent, without any concern.[14]

Yet the middle ground implicitly marked out by *The Polite Lady* at once does and does not coincide with Marriott's. A conduct book that presents itself as "A Course of Female Education" in a series of letters from a mother to her daughter, it speaks for a female virtue more warily alert than his, a "modesty" not quite so subordinated to "the Art of Pleasing." While Marriott's poem urges the reader to "soft Attractions of Behavior sweet," by which, he promises, she'll "quickly catch a Lover" in her "Net," the maternal voice of *The Polite Lady* is more apt to warn young women against "such an extreme degree of complaisance, such a yielding softness of nature, as is not able to refuse any thing." True modesty, the book suggests, requires an active, and conscious, vigilance: "modesty does not consist in following the fashion, but in following reason." Having dwelt at length on the symmetrical opposition of the prude and the coquette, it significantly goes on to weight the balance, however slightly, in favor of the prude—arguing that while their characters are "equally ridiculous," they "are not equally dangerous," since the prude often manages to preserve her reputation and "at least the appearance of modesty." Though Marriott, too, warns of the dangers innocent young women face, his sympathies, it goes without saying, are hardly with the prudes: when he evokes the "slipp'ry . . . Paths, young Virgins tread," he does so only to offer his "fair" reader, imaginatively at least, his "Hand."[15]

The anonymous author of *The Polite Lady* speaks not as a potential lover but as one woman to another; and her attempt to associate female virtue with "sense" and reason partly anticipates, as we shall see, the position of rational feminists like Mary Wollstonecraft—a Wollstonecraft who in 1792 would herself extol "true" modesty as the "sacred offspring of sensibility and reason" while contemptuously dismissing the conduct-book ideal as a mere "refinement on lust." *A Vindication of the Rights of Woman* never mentions Thomas Marriott, but Wollstonecraft could well have included him among those masculine authorities on the art of pleasing who most inspire her scorn—Rousseau above all, of course, but also such English authors of advice for women as James Fordyce and John Gregory. What such writers mean by female modesty, she argued, is only "a system of cunning and lasciviousness"; and in a chapter entitled "Modesty.—Comprehensively Considered, and Not as a Sexual Virtue," she deliberately set out to wrest the word away from the "voluptuous men," to turn their self-indulgent fantasies about the "coyness" of female "ignorance" into the energetic and conscious restraint of educated women.[16]

Yet the line between the opposing camps cannot be drawn too sharply, if only because for Wollstonecraft, as for those she most fiercely resisted, the discourse of modesty continued to cover contradictions. *The Rights of Woman* angrily denounced "Rousseau's and Dr. Gregory's advice respecting modesty, strangely miscalled!"[17] but it is not altogether surprising to find a later conduct book complementing advice from Gregory with passages from Wollstonecraft's own chapter on modesty, or to see a popular ladies' magazine silently including extracts from both writers in a series of "Maxims and Sentiments Culled . . . for the Exclusive Benefit of the Fair Sex."[18] Nor is it surprising—despite the instructive contrast of Thomas Marriott and *The Polite Lady*—to find women as well as men writing on all sides of the subject. Though Hannah More would share Wollstonecraft's distrust of Rousseau's erotic sensibilities, for example, the "scrupulous modesty" which flatteringly veils the "nymphlike form" of Coelebs' bride is more than worthy of *Emile*'s Sophie, who also "does not show off her charms" but "in covering them . . . knows how to make them imagined."[19] That even as Coelebs insisted on a strict division between the sexes, the writer who spoke through him was herself a woman, and thus engaged in a form of literary cross-dressing, was not an irony that More and others like her were prepared to register.

By the time of *The Rights of Woman* at least, the idea that modesty was *not* a "sexual virtue" clearly represented a minority position— which is to say that for most users, as Wollstonecraft recognized, the word had been both highly eroticized and gendered. To think about "modesty" was automatically to think of the modest woman, and to think about this woman was above all to imagine a certain account of heterosexual relations. Indeed, "virtue" itself had largely become sexual virtue, as Pamela's valiant defense of hers should remind us.[20] At the same time, of course, such words never signify simply or univocally, and

Wollstonecraft could not have argued for a modesty "comprehensively considered" had not the term continued to carry with it other meanings and associations. For Addison and Steele earlier in the century, the smooth functioning of social life required at least some moderation of the self, some impulses of reserve and humility, in both sexes: when Steele defined modesty as "the Virtue which makes Men prefer the Publick to their Private Interest" or "the Virtue which preserves a Decorum in the general Course of our Life," he accorded it a characteristically bland approbation.[21] In Edmund Leites's words, Steele "thinks of intense feelings the way Erasmus thinks of dirt and smells"—as disagreeable intrusions, that is, on the privacy of others—and like Erasmus, he tries to cultivate a society in which each member will effectively minimize such intrusions, will restrain as much as possible the offending discharges of the self. For Steele, as Leites puts it, "I show my respect for you by limiting the extent to which you must experience me";[22] and insofar as modesty seems to mean this generalized respect for others, it means a virtue that the *Tatler* and the *Spectator* would apparently foster in men and women alike. But whenever they closely consider the gender of the modest subject, even Addison and Steele equivocate: for participants in a commercial society, they repeatedly suggest, too much self-effacement threatens to become not a virtue but a weakness. When "some Ladies" of his acquaintance commend modesty as equally "becoming" to both sexes, Isaac Bickerstaff rushes to correct them: "beautiful" as modest behavior might be in the behavior of both, he sharply observes, "yet it could not be said, it was as successful in life." Indeed, by the very next clause it apparently cannot be said to be successful for one sex at all, "for as it was the only Recommendation" in women, "so it was the greatest Obstacle to us both in Love and Business"—a distinction immediately underscored by another gentleman in the company, who just happens to be, as Bickerstaff tells us, "of my Mind" on the subject. "We must describe the Difference between the Modesty of Women and that of Men," this useful gentleman explains, "or we should be confounded in our Reasonings upon it; for this Virtue is to be regarded with Respect to our different Ways of Life." The gendering of modesty, in other words, follows from the separation of spheres—a division of labor that will increasingly free men for the aggressions of the marketplace by assigning certain "beautiful" but inconvenient virtues to the safekeeping of women. While "Woman's Province is to be careful in her Oeconomy, and chast in her Affection," according to this account, man's is "to be active in the Improvement of his Fortune, and ready to undertake whatever is consistent with his Reputation for that End."

Modesty in the woman means "a certain agreeable Fear in all she enters upon," in the man merely "a right Judgment of what is proper" for him to attempt. If "Every man"—by which the *Tatler* obviously does not mean any woman—"is the Maker of his own Fortune," then "what is very odd to consider, he must in some Measure be the Trumpet of his Fame." And though centuries of Christian doctrine do make it "very odd to consider," he apparently must not wait for the meek to inherit: "Modesty in a Man is never to be allow'd as a good Quality, but a Weakness, if it suppresses his Virtue, and hides it from the World."[23]

Modesty in a man is never "to be allow'd" an unqualified good by the *Spectator* either: men must not permit "a spiritless Sheepishness" or "unmanly Bashfulness" to hinder the workings of "honest Ambition," as Steele argues in one number, nor let what Addison in another calls a "false" and "vicious" modesty keep them from defying the fashionable depravity of the crowd. Especially when they consider how a man might fail to present himself successfully in public, both writers hasten to distinguish "a just and reasonable Modesty" from "an Excess" that "obstructs"—as Addison does, for example, after declaring it "impossible that a Person should exert himself to Advantage in an Assembly, whether it be his part either to sing or speak, who lies under too great Oppressions of Modesty."[24] Though *The Polite Lady* would later distinguish "true" modesty from a dangerous "sheepishness" in terms that have clearly been borrowed from Addison,[25] neither the *Tatler* nor the *Spectator* itself seems much inclined to worry the question where women are concerned—their authors apparently finding "a certain agreeable fear" in the other sex all too agreeable to analyze further.

But a related anxiety to discriminate between the "false" virtue and the "true" persistently troubles the discourse of female modesty, and troubles it for reasons that the *Spectator*'s concern with public performance helps to make clear. "Modesty," according to one frequently repeated maxim, is "the point of honor among women,"[26] and matters of honor characteristically turn on public appearance and performance: to be modest means to take up a particular stance toward others, and to signal them accordingly. Indeed, for *The Ladies Calling* at the end of the seventeenth century, as for the many conduct books that routinely echoed it, modesty was first of all *"the Science of decent motion"*—"that which guides and regulates the whole behavior. . . . steers every part of the outward frame," and "so impresses it self" in the face "that it seems thence to have acquir'd the name of shamefacedness."[27] Like honor, that is, modesty was first and foremost a question of face—even if such writers characteristically presumed that the female face ought to be averted rather than turned toward others. And like all questions of face, it kept threatening to prove a mere matter of appearances, which is one reason that praise of modesty so quickly yielded to anxious distinctions between the "true" virtue and the "false," as praise of chastity, for example, did not. Especially for those Christians trained most strictly to distrust appearances and outward show, there was always the worry that the modest woman's virtue was only a seeming.

"A low voice and soft address are the common indications of a well-bred woman," Hannah More typically noted in an essay on "True and False Meekness" in 1777, "but they are only the outward and visible signs"—not "meekness itself." "Nothing is more common than to mistake the sign for the thing itself," More sternly warns.[28] Yet if writers persist in taking modesty as "the thing itself," one might respond, mistaking of several kinds is inevitable. For the more that they struggle to distinguish surfaces from depths, the "true" virtue from its affectation, the more problematic the distinctions become. Particularly when a woman's modesty is understood as a sexual virtue, the lingering fear that she has merely veiled over the original immodesty of her sex continues to trouble those who sing her praises—and to trouble them most insistently, as we shall see, just when they most insist that she is modest by "nature."

2

Nature and Convention

❧

Ever since Eve, after all—or at least ever since the early Church fathers had begun to interpret her—Western culture had been inclined to tell another story about the nature of woman; and the idea that hers was in fact the more animal-like and lustful sex, as well as the more aggressively curious one, hardly disappeared even as writers increasingly pronounced female modesty "an instinct of nature." *The Ladies Calling* might contend that natural modesty defined the very essence of the sex, but approximately a decade later an anonymously published satire, *Love Given O're* (1682), could still denounce women's "natural aversness to Vertue" and "their dearest darling Vices, Lust, and Pride" in terms that centuries of misogynist invective had made familiar. "Thus if they durst, all Women wou'd be Whores," the satirist sums up one rant against their secret lusts—interrupting his text just long enough to apologize for its own potential affront to modesty before he breaks in again to question the very existence of the virtue:

> Forgive me Modesty, if I have been
> In any thing I've mention'd here, Obscene;
> Since my Design is to detect their Crimes,
> Which (like a Deluge) overflow the Times:
> But hold—why shou'd I ask that Boon of thee,
> When 'tis a doubt if such a thing there be?
> For Woman, in whose Breasts thou'rt said to raign,
> And show the glorious Conquests thou dost gain,
> Despises thee, and only courts the Name.

Having shown that the modest sex is anything but, the satirist professes himself justified in doubting that modesty itself has any existence—a

12

perversely logical tribute, one might argue, to the already commonplace association of the virtue with women:

> Thus led by what delusive Fame imparts,
> We think thy Throne's erected in their Hearts;
> But we'are deceiv'd; as faith we ever were,
> For if thou art, I'me sure thou art not there:
> Nothing in those vile Mansions does reside,
> But rank Ambition, Luxury, and Pride.[1]

Of course, any work that frankly announces itself as "a satyr against woman" asks to be read within a tradition that goes back at least to Juvenal; and there are particular reasons to believe that this example of the genre may owe more to literary convention than to the poet's own convictions.[2] But *Love Given O're* also takes its part in the contemporary debate about woman's nature, and similar suspicions of her "boundless Lust"[3] have a way of making themselves felt in works apparently very far removed from misogynist satire. Even *The Ladies Calling* does not so much deny the existence of the lascivious female as deny that she deserves the name of woman:

And if we consider Modesty in this sense, we shall find it the most indispensible requisite of a woman; a thing so essential and natural to the sex, that every the least declination from it, is a proportional receding from Womanhood, but the total abandoning it ranks them among Brutes, nay sets them as far beneath those, as an aquir'd vileness is below a native. I need make no collection of the verdicts either of the Philosophers or Divines in the case, it being so much an instinct of nature, that tho too many make a shift to suppress it in themselves, yet they cannot so darken the notion in others, but that an Impudent woman is lookt on as a kind of Monster; a thing diverted and distorted from its proper form.[4]

Note how this passage works to naturalize woman's modesty by performing a bit of rhetorical magic with the old lustful animal—briefly evoking her in the formulaic pronouncement that a woman who abandons modesty is to be ranked "among Brutes," only to make her quickly disappear when the abandoned woman is said to be as far beneath the brutes "as an acquir'd vileness is below a native." By insisting that an "Impudent woman" is not even a "Brute" but "a kind of Monster," in other words, *The Ladies Calling* tries to deprive female lust of the associations of naturalness that attach to animals, to turn it into a wholly artificial and "acquir'd" trait. Yet the strain of redefinition is all too evident—if only in those "too many" immodest ones who have to be tautologically excluded from the sex. As in the variation of this formula that

Fielding later adopts in *Amelia* (1751)—"when Women once abandon that Modesty which is the Characteristic of their Sex, they seldom set any Bounds to their Assurance"[5]—the virtue that is said to define women typically keeps rhetorical check on its opposite; and the force with which the latter repeatedly threatens to break through suggests just how much of her nature woman's modest "instincts" were felt to deny.

Most attempts to define woman's "nature" eventually founder in double-talk, though they do not always betray their difficulties as openly as does *The Ladies Calling*. When an anonymous "Friend to the Fair Sex" offered another version of Allestree's circular rhetoric in the *Lady's Magazine* of 1774, for instance, he at least took care to keep the number of women-who-are-not-women statistically small: "It is a great happiness that we see but a very small number of females divest themselves of their native modesty," he announced; "it is only by frequent and repeated falls, that they arrive to that degree of depravation, as to destroy this precious instinct. Such persons ought not to be reckoned as belonging to the sex."[6] Yet if the "too many" women said to lack the instincts of true "Womanhood" in *The Ladies Calling* make the earlier text seem more unguarded in its contradictions, Allestree's preface suggests that his use of language was far from innocent—and that rather than naively contradicting himself, he was in fact deliberately attempting to change women's behavior by changing the prevailing definition of their nature. Too many men choose to see only what accords with their own "unworthy ends on women," the preface argues, while too many women behave less virtuously than they should because they are busy living down, in effect, to men's estimation of them:

the world is much governed by estimation; and as applause encourages and exalts, so a universal contemt debases and dejects the Spirit. If it can once pass into a Maxim, that women are such silly or vicious creatures, it may put fair for the making them so indeed. Themselves may imbibe the common opinion, charge all their personal faults on their Sex, think that they do but their kind, when indeed they most contradict it, and no more aspire to any thing worthy, then a man can pretend to the excellencies of an Angel. And indeed this seems to be the practical inference of som women, who could hardly have descended to such dishonors, had they not before bin as vile in their own eies, as they have afterwards rendered themselves in others.

Arguing that most female vices originate in "the inadvertence, or malice of a great part of mankind" who "deduce Generals from Particulars, make every woman . . . an Eve . . . and because there are foolish and scandalous women, will scarce allow there are any other," the gallant author of *The Ladies Calling* sets out to "rescu the whole Sex" by reversing the process, keenly aware that definitions of human nature tend to become self-fulfilling prophecies:

It may therefore upon this account be a necessary Charity to the Sex, to acquaint them with their own valu, animate them to som higher thoughts of themselves; not to yield their suffrage to those injurious estimates the World hath made of them, and from a supposed incapacity of nobler things to neglect the pursuit of them; from which God and Nature have no more precluded the Feminine, than the Masculine part of mankind.[7]

As even these passages make clear, Allestree is far from believing that language creates the reality it purports to describe, or from claiming that sexual difference is merely a man-made invention. *The Ladies Calling* takes for granted that "God and Nature" have made woman's "kind"— and made inherent in her kind a capacity for good. (So the silly or vicious "think that they do but their kind, when indeed they most contradict it.") "Generals" are not to be deduced from "Particulars," nor Womanhood from the behavior of actual women: since too many do still "contradict it," knowledge of the kind presumably derives from revelation rather than from observing any individual specimens. In this sense, at least, calling modesty both "natural and essential to the sex" is not so much paradoxical as redundant, since woman's "nature" *is* her divinely given form or essence.

Yet for all this reaching after Neoplatonic kinds and essences, *The Ladies Calling* deploys its rhetoric with a measure of caution that tends to disappear from many subsequent pronouncements on woman's "nature," even as the relative candor with which it sets out to remake that nature is also forgotten or effaced. Like other attempts to reform human manners by encouraging habitual reactions of embarrassment and shame, the campaign to naturalize female modesty effects its own omissions and silences as it advances.[8] Later works plunder freely from the text of *The Ladies Calling* itself, but not, of course, from Allestree's comparatively frank and self-conscious preface; they plagiarize substantial sections of the chapter on modesty, but typically omit the careful qualifications of sexual difference with which that chapter begins: "All Ages and Nations have made *som distinction* between masculine and feminine Vertues . . . that being comely for the one Sex which *often* is not (*at least in the same degree*) for the other. . . . even those which are equally inclusive of both, by the divine command *may have som additional weight* on the female side" (emphasis mine).[9]

Later conduct books also enforce their arguments with historical precedent, but they prefer to rest their case on the brief and unequivocal advice that Pericles allegedly offered the Athenian women: "Aspire only to those Virtues that are peculiar to your Sex; follow your natural Modesty, and think it your greatest Commendation not to be talked of one way or other"—a translation that quietly assists the Athenian ruler to talk conduct-book English, since a more literal rendering of the Greek would urge the women not to be inferior to their existing nature rather than to "follow" their "natural modesty."[10] No doubt all "Ages and Nations," in Allestree's phrase, have made some distinction between masculine and feminine virtues; and certainly *The Ladies Calling* is far from the first text to argue for the instinctive modesty of women.[11] But between Allestree's relatively open attempt to make women more virtuous by speaking of them as such and Hannah More's emphatic capitalizing of Pericles' advice a century later—"aspire only to those virtues that are PECULIAR TO YOUR SEX; follow your natural modesty"[12]—the line between the sexes is more sharply drawn, the naturalness of female modesty more thoroughly mystified.

This clear tendency by the end of the eighteenth century to find modesty natural, and especially natural to women, owed much to Rousseau's influence—for all that Hannah More and a wide spectrum of English writers would wish to deny it. But the question also antedated Rousseau's writings, as we have seen, and the very insistence with which he set out his influential arguments for the natural modesty of the sex was partly an attempt to counter other, more skeptical analyses of the subject. In Rousseau's partisan staging of the debate between Nature and custom, those who speak for custom are rarely dignified with a name, but the voices of Bernard Mandeville and David Hume are nonetheless present in their absence; and neither the anxiety with which the apostle of Nature sought to answer them nor the history of the modest woman herself can be understood without some account of their arguments. While Mandeville and Hume approach the modest woman in quite a different spirit from the conduct books—and from one another—they importantly share in a collective worrying of her story. And even as their skeptical treatments of her modest "instincts" help to demystify the idea, they also testify, sometimes inadvertently, to its attraction. Given the continuing pressure exerted by representations of woman's lustful nature, an account of her modesty as merely custom or habit may not seem to account for very much. If woman's modesty is not instinctive, then her virtue is built, as Mandeville slyly remarks in his *Modest Defence of Publick Stews* (1724), "upon a very *ticklish* Foundation."[13]

Cheerfully, sometimes crudely explicit in its discussion of sexual organs and their functions, *A Modest Defence of Publick Stews* may seem an odd place to look for an analysis of female modesty, despite the ironic wordplay of its title. Mandeville's tract is a satiric defense of whoring against the excessive zeal of the reformers, and its physician-author pursues his argument with a deliberately anatomical wit. But its joking account of female appetite and female virtue does not really exaggerate by very much Mandeville's more sober views of the subject in *The Fable of the Bees* (1714) or *An Enquiry into the Origin of Honour* (1732); nor do its ironies essentially differ from those of his earlier, if somewhat more elusive satire, *The Virgin Unmask'd* (1709). And for all its subversive cynicism, its brutally reductive taxonomies of female character, there is a sense in which *A Modest Defence* is indeed a defense of modesty—anticipating the argument advanced in considerably less candid terms by at least a few Victorian moralists, that England's brothels provided the necessary safeguards of her domestic purity.[14] For if women owe their modesty only to custom and education, so Mandeville argues, then even the most virtuous are engaged in a constant struggle with their fundamentally appetitive nature. Unless some of the sex are expressly set aside for the purpose, any woman may be besieged—and any woman will eventually succumb. Mandeville has no doubt that when honor opposes nature, nature must finally prove the stronger, especially since repression only intensifies desire, while a single lapse of modest vigilance concludes the war:

in the Course of a long *Civil War,* it is Odds but Love one Time or other obtains a Victory, which is sure to be decisive: for Inclination has this unluckly Advantage over Honour, that, instead of being weaken'd, it grows stronger by Subjection; and, like *Camomile,* the more it is press'd down and kept under, the sturdier it grows; or, like *Antaeus,* it receives fresh Vigour from every Defeat, and rises the Brisker the oftener it is thrown. Whereas Honour once routed never rallies; nay, the least *Breach* in Female Reputation is irreparable; and a *Gap* in Chastity, like a *Chasm* in a young Tree, is every day a *Widening.*[15]

Even as the institution of the public stew supports that of the modest woman, according to Mandeville's argument, so the *Modest Defence* itself bears a kind of mirror relation to other fictions of modesty—at once subverting and reinforcing their premises. Like a good conduct book, it takes for granted that woman's sexual history is irreversible: "Honour once routed never rallies," and "the least *Breach* in Female Reputation is irreparable." And like a good courtship novel, it assumes that "Love" only "grows stronger by Subjection"—though unlike more obviously modest fictions, it simply leaps over the delaying action to the foregone conclusion. In the struggle between natural appetite and artificial restraint, "the self-appointed *agent provocateur* of the bourgeois unconscious," as Ian Watt has wittily called Mandeville,[16] would rather place his imaginative bets on the winner. And rather than efface the body, in the manner of more respectable fictions, his joke about "the least *Breach* in Female Reputation" openly acknowledges how much the woman's irreversible plot owes to a certain representation of her anatomy. It is far from coincidental, as we shall see, that when John Cleland imagines the more episodic and repetitive structure of Fanny Hill's adventures, he also imagines a heroine able to boast of her "happy habit of body"—not a "*Gap*" that is "every day a *Widening*" but a remarkable ability to recover, in Fanny's words, "that grateful stricture which is in us, to the men, the very jet of their pleasure."[17]

Despite such anatomical joking, Mandeville generally resists the temptation to read the signs of woman's modesty in her body. Whereas Rousseau would suggest that her skin is "naturally" formed for blushing, and Freud would persist in identifying the conformation of her genitals with her greater susceptibility to shame,[18] Mandeville contends that woman's inclination to cover and withdraw herself is not natural but made, and made by the relentless pressure of "Custom and Education." People only mistake custom for nature, he argues in *The Fable of the Bees*, because they fail to measure the power of early training—forgetting how constant instruction in bodily exposure and concealment turns little children into properly different men and women:

The Multitude will hardly believe the excessive Force of Education, and in the difference of Modesty between Men and Women ascribe that to Nature, which is altogether owing to early Instruction: *Miss* is scarce three Years old, but she is spoke to every Day to hide her Leg, and rebuk'd in good Earnest if she shews it; while *Little Master* at the same Age is bid to take up his Coats, and piss like a Man.[19]

The *Defence of Publick Stews* offers a similar account of female socialization—"Young Girls are taught to hate a *Whore*, before they know what the Word means"—that briefly suggests how a modest consciousness might be trained to withdraw as automatically as a leg. And both texts take for granted that "all Women are liable to these amorous Desires," which the training of some merely works to repress. But particularly in the *Defence*, Mandeville approaches sex less as an essentialist philosopher than as a classifying biologist or clinician, seeking not so much to define woman's Nature as to observe and record her natural variations;

and while all women are amorous, according to this Dr. Mandeville, some women's physiology renders them more amorous than others: "for as in some Men the *Olfactory, Auditory,* or *Optick* Nerves, are not so brisk and lively as in others, so there are some Women who have the Nerves of their *Pudenda* more lively, and endow'd with a much quicker Sensation than others." Even if such women have been raised very strictly, they will inevitably have to struggle harder to preserve their chastity than their colder sisters—who at least in this sense may be termed "naturally more Chaste." While no woman is innately modest, any individual woman's power of resistance will depend on the combined effects of both Nature and Education. Elementary permutation yields a fourfold classification of female types: those who are "naturally more Chaste, or rather, to speak properly, less Amorous than others, and at the same time have very Strict Notions of Honour" (these prove, not surprisingly, almost impossible to seduce); those who are equally strict but "naturally of a very sanguine amorous Disposition"; those who "have neither Honour nor Inclination"; and, finally, "those who have a very moderate Share of Honour, join'd to a very amorous Constitution." Though even this last type may put up some token resistance, a prospective seducer will hardly be required to exert himself before she surrenders.[20]

If this is a kind of classificatory biology, needless to say, it is a science wholly designed for masculine uses. While Dr. Mandeville acknowledges that women vary, he shares in the common masculine habit of seeing them as largely determined by their bodies or "Nerves"—and writes of the latter as if they somehow existed prior to, and apart from, the human characters they supposedly determine. The entire scheme draws heavily on the conventional trope of a battle between the sexes: the woman is an enemy town to be suddenly attacked or patiently besieged; the man is the invading party whose strategy depends largely on the strength and kind of her fortifications—and on the degree to which he can take advantage of a "Civil War" within. Though *A Modest Defence of Publick Stews* played a serious role in contemporary debates over the legality of prostitution, it is also a scabrous piece of occasional satire, and its distinctions must not be approached too solemnly. But insofar as it makes the problem of female modesty turn not on woman's Body but on women's bodies, Mandeville's tract wittily manages to elude the bipolar oppositions in which most such discussions endlessly engage—briefly complicating, at least, the conventional choices about woman's Nature.

Most writers seem unable to think of two sexes without assigning to one or the other the more amorous nature; and the proposition that women are not naturally modest typically entails the corollary that they are "naturally" more lustful than men. Yet on this question, too, Mandeville proves not quite predictable: though he argues firmly that modesty is a social invention, he does not offer the usual explanation that society is constrained to make woman virtuous because in a state of nature hers is so licentious a sex. For Mandeville, the double standard emerges not from the familiar war between Nature and Culture, Appetite and Restraint, but from a cynically accommodating agreement: "men may take greater Liberty," according to *The Fable of the Bees,* "because in them the Appetite is more violent and ungovernable." Rather than radically opposing Nature, in other words, his imaginary Culture adopted the course of least resistance, making "the Rules abate of their Rigour, where the Passion was the strongest, and the Burthen of a strict Restraint would have been the most intolerable."[21] Ironically, however, this manages to avoid the paradoxes and double-talk that characterize so many accounts of the subject only by conceding something to Nature after all: for if Mandeville's woman does not instinctively shrink from man's advances, her desires are at least naturally more moderate than his. Some ardent advocates of her modest "nature," as we shall see, could scarcely ask for more.

❦

Mandeville takes for granted that society needs to impose some curbs on the relations between the sexes—only observing, rather mischievously, that "had equal Harshness of Discipline been imposed upon both, neither of them could have made the first Advances, and Propagation must have stood still among all the Fashionable People."[22] But apart from suggesting that custom settles for restraining the woman because it is easier to do so, he never really speculates on why the double standard should have arisen in the first place: if female modesty and chastity *are* simply human conventions, as Hume will ask, what (or whose) interests do they serve? Indeed, Hume may very well have had Mandeville in mind when he impatiently dismissed those philosophers "who attack the female virtues with great vehemence, and fancy they have gone very far in detecting popular errors, when they can show, that there is no foundation in nature for all that exterior modesty, which we require in . . . the fair sex." Only a fool, Hume suggested, would think otherwise: "I believe I may spare myself the trouble of insisting on so obvious a subject," he announced at the beginning of his brief chapter on chastity and modesty in the *Treatise of Human Nature* (1739), and proposed instead to "examine after what manner such notions arise from education, from the voluntary conventions of men, and from the interest of society."[23]

Seeking to explain female modesty by the uses it serves, Hume quickly arrives at the institution of the family—or more precisely, at the need to assuage men's anxieties about the paternity of their children. As many commentators on the sexes have noted, a woman always knows that the child she bears is her own, but the bodily connection of a particular man and child always remains an inference, a belief necessarily vulnerable to mistake and deception. While both sexes identify with their offspring, only men are subject to the fear that in doing so they may commit themselves to an illusion. Hume somewhat cryptically alludes to this difference between the sexes when he traces the origins of female chastity and modesty to "the length and feebleness of human infancy" and the consequent need for extended unions between men and women to raise and educate their young:

But in order to induce the men to impose on themselves this restraint, and undergo chearfully all the fatigues and expences to which it subjects them, they must believe, that the children are their own, and that their natural instinct is not directed to a wrong object, when they give a loose to love and tenderness. Now if we examine the structure of the human body, we shall find, that this security is very difficult to be attain'd on our part; and that since, in the copulation of the sexes, the principle of generation goes from the man to the woman, an error may easily take place on the side of the former, tho' it be utterly impossible with regard to the latter. From this trivial and anatomical observation is deriv'd that vast difference betwixt the education and duties of the two sexes.[24]

If the aim of the proposed anatomical examination remains rather mysterious, the argument that follows is clear enough: "men are induc'd to labour for the maintenance and education of their children, by the persuasion that they are really their own"—and their belief in that potentially shaky hypothesis is encouraged by the culture's stern sanctions against the unchastity of women.[25]

Any woman known to have betrayed her husband will be severely shamed in consequence. But in Hume's speculative account of origins, men soon realize that keeping women in line requires more than the fear of punishment. "All human creatures, especially of the female sex, are apt to over-look remote motives in favour of any present temptation," he contends, and since "the temptation is here the strongest imaginable," women manage to persuade themselves that they can escape detection:

'Tis necessary, therefore, that, beside the infamy attending such licences, there shou'd be some preceding backwardness or dread, which may prevent their first approaches, and may give the female sex a repugnance to all expressions, and postures, and liberties, that have an immediate relation to that enjoyment.

Such "preceding backwardness" is of course modesty—though for all the calm reasonableness with which he characteristically tries to sort out the issues, Hume never appears to notice his own witty oxymoron. Indeed, whenever he defines that elusive virtue, even this most lucid of philosophers seems to find himself inadvertently reaching for paradox, as in the almost comic contortions of "a backwardness to the approaches of a pleasure, to which nature has inspir'd so strong a propensity."[26] Like those conduct books in which the modest woman instinctively trembles and withdraws before a *double entendre* can dare to be spoken, Hume represents the virtue as a sort of early warning system, an anticipatory shrinking from danger; but having dismissed the claims of instinct, he never asks how society manages to cultivate such virtuously "backward" women without producing in them an intensely "forward" consciousness, eagerly on the lookout for every hint of impropriety. Nor does he always pause to wonder whether other parts of his story have any more "foundation in nature" than the female virtues: so, for example, a man's love for his child simply appears as a "natural instinct"—though an "instinct" that could easily grow attached to the "wrong object" were it not for the conventional chastity of a wife. As for the female of the species, who ever doubted that in a state of nature she is "especially" incapable of resisting temptation?

Unlike most discussions of female virtue, however, Hume's finally suffers not so much from what it assumes as from what it leaves out of account—above all, the symbolic force of sexual difference itself. Having described woman's modesty as simply that which keeps her chaste, Hume has no way of analyzing how it simultaneously acts as a sort of erotic double agent—the sense in which the modest woman's very resistance serves to entice man as well as restrain him. Only the "preceding" of "preceding backwardness," and perhaps the "approaches" of the approaching "pleasure," hint at the buried narrative. Nor does his brief genealogy of the female virtues really explain why they are required of all women, even those well past child-bearing age. If one sex is held to a stricter standard than the other because of the risk of illegitimate children, why shouldn't that difference cease to hold when the risk has passed? Implicitly posing this question, Hume can only answer, rather lamely, by his usual recourse to the association of ideas—that once having connected modesty with women, men continue to do so, though they in fact know better: "tho' men know, that these notions are founded on the public interest, yet the general rule carries us beyond the original principle, and makes us extend the notions of modesty over the whole sex, from their earliest infancy to their extremest old-age and infirmity."[27]

Creatures of habit men certainly are, though it may be doubted whether most are as clear-eyed about the process as Hume suggests. But what seems particularly unsatisfying about his explanation today is his failure to sense how powerfully the idea of two sexes resonates through human experience, and how strong has been the impulse to draw clear boundaries between them. What is identified as "male" or "female" varies radically over time and from one group to another, but in most known cultures, as symbolic anthropologists have argued, the line of sexual difference serves as one of the fundamental means of organizing the categories of human experience, while the very need to mark out such a line, however arbitrary, intensifies in periods of anxiety and rapid change.[28] Mary Douglas has suggested that cults of virginity, for instance, tend to appear at times of social upheaval and stress—that the boundary between the dirty and the clean sharpens, and pollution ideas come to the fore, whenever the lines of a social system are precarious or threatened.[29] A modest woman may not remain a virgin forever, but her very modesty can be imagined as a kind of boundary making, a virtue especially critical to preserve at moments when other boundaries seem vulnerable; while so long as she is represented as both pure and purely feminine, her figure can thus doubly serve as a talisman against danger. Indeed, only something like this cluster of associations can begin to explain the nearly hysterical obsession with sexual difference that will surface in England in the aftermath of the French Revolution—an obsession that makes female modesty, in the words of one anti-Jacobin tract, "the last barrier of civilized society."[30] Hume's *Treatise* predates the most extravagant celebrations of the modest woman by at least half a century, yet his lucid explanations already cannot account for so overdetermined and paradoxical a figure. Perhaps only a Rousseau, one is tempted to say, could dare to contradict himself sufficiently.

☙

To those who ask why modesty *should* be peculiar to women—why that which is not shameful for one sex should be so for the other—"we would always have the same response to make," Rousseau characteristically announced at mid-century, "and it would always be without reply": "Nature wanted it so," and "it is a crime to stifle her voice." [31] In fact, as we shall see, Rousseau did not always have the same response to make—or, rather, he always had the same response to make only when he had exhausted virtually every other. Both his polemical *Lettre à M. d'Alembert* on the theater (1758), and the fifth book of his celebrated treatise on education, *Emile* (1762), took up the issue with characteristic intensity: there is scarcely an argument for woman's "natural" modesty—or against it, for that matter—that does not somewhere appear in their pages. No doubt the dizzying speeds at which Rousseau liked to shift argumentative ground, his voracious appetite for paradox and self-contradiction, were partly temperamental. Yet the relentless overdetermination of his argument was also a response to at least a halfcentury of efforts like Mandeville's or Hume's to demystify the virtue—to account for female modesty without recourse to God and Nature but merely as a social convention, subject to the requirements of a wholly human order.

That Rousseau's ideal woman was modest by "nature" did not prevent him from elaborately seeking to justify her existence. Strictly speaking, of course, his Nature endowed women with *pudeur* and *modestie* rather than the English virtue, and precisely because what seems "natural" in any culture is in part linguistically determined, the following account will leave both words untranslated. But it is no accident that Wollstonecraft should have identified the modest woman of the English conduct books with *Emile*'s Sophie, nor that Rousseau himself should have particularly singled out the English for at once sharpening the difference between the sexes and uniting them in conjugal peace and fidelity. [32] Though the opposition between French license and native modesty would provide a favorite theme for English moralizers, the author of both the *Lettre* and *Emile* writes, after all, not as a Frenchman but as "J.-J. Rousseau, Citizen of Geneva"; and in the *Lettre* he writes explicitly to prevent the city of Calvin from succumbing to the immodesty and wickedness of Paris. Despite the shifting national and religious loyalties that mark Rousseau's personal history, in other words, the Citizen of Geneva takes up an essentially Protestant position; and like his English counterparts, as we shall see, he wants to make woman "naturally" modest in order to make her fit for a Protestant ideal of marriage. The fifth and last book of *Emile* is obviously dedicated to preparing Sophie for her vocation as wife, but even the *Lettre à d'Alembert* ends with the preparation of young people for marriage—"the first and holiest of all the bonds of society." Rather than lift their ban on the theater, as d'Alembert had suggested, Rousseau urges his fellow citizens to institutionalize a form of entertainment at once more innocent and more useful by adopting the custom of a public ball: at these gatherings, "young marriageable persons will have the opportunity to take a liking to one another," while the constant gaze of the assembly will assure "reserve, *modestie*, and the most careful watching of themselves." Like the readers of so many English novels—or, for that matter, of the fifth book of *Emile*—the citizens of Geneva are to amuse themselves by watching young persons prepare for married love, as they engage in a dance of courtship. And at the end of each season, the young woman who has behaved *le plus honnêtement, le plus modestement* will be crowned as the Queen.[33]

The same man who would thus make modesty a civic institution, however, emphatically refuses to consider it a man-made virtue. Indeed, for anyone who values the modesty of women, he repeatedly manages to suggest, no real choice is possible: in Rousseau's version of the debate between nature and custom, to think of the virtue as nothing but a human invention is tantamount to thinking of it as nothing at all. So the *Lettre* briefly conjures up the objections of his enemies, unnamed spokesmen of "this philosophy of a day that is born and dies in the corner of a big city":

Popular prejudices! some cry. Petty errors of childhood! Illusion of laws and of education! *Pudeur* is nothing. It is nothing but an invention of the social laws to protect the rights of fathers and husbands, and to maintain some order in families. Why should we blush at needs that Nature has given us? Why should we find a motive for shame in an act so indifferent in itself, and as useful in its effects as that which serves to perpetuate the species? Why, the desires being equal on both sides, should the demonstrations be different? Why should one of the sexes resist more than the other inclinations which are common to both? Why should man have on this issue different laws from the animals?

These imaginary opponents ask the same questions posed less belligerently by Hume, and their scornful characterization of female modesty as "nothing but an invention of the social laws to protect the rights of fathers and husbands, and to maintain some order in families" does not differ very much from the explanation of the custom that Hume in fact provides. So far from naming his enemies, however, Rousseau refuses even to acknowledge their humanity: theirs is a philosophy, he ingeniously suggests, that would not only "smother the cry of Nature" but, still more strikingly, "the unanimous voice of mankind."[34]

Having effectively declared that no one could possibly hold such opinions, Rousseau then proceeds to answer them: shame, too, is natural—just as natural as the sexual desire it constrains. "Isn't it ridiculous that I should have to say why I am ashamed of a natural feeling, if this shame is no less natural to me than the feeling itself?" he demands. "Is it for me to render an account of what Nature has done?" But that he clearly intends these as rhetorical questions does not of course prevent him from responding. "I am afraid that these grand investigators of God's designs have weighed his reasons rather lightly," the next paragraph continues; yet "I, who don't pride myself on knowing them, I believe that I can see some that have escaped them":

In relation to sexual *pudeur* in particular, what gentler arm could this same Nature have given to the one destined to defend herself? The desires are equal! What does that mean? Are there on both sides the same capacities to satisfy them? What would become of the human species if the order of attack and defense were changed? The assailant would choose by chance times when victory would be impossible; the assailed would be left in peace, when he needed to surrender, and pursued without respite when he was too weak to succumb; in a word, the power and the will, always in disaccord, would never allow desires to be shared, love would no longer be the support of Nature, it would be the destroyer and plague.[35]

The opaque style of this passage modestly veils a rather spectacular concession: the *pudeur* of women effectively covers for men's fear of impotence. Rousseau's Nature apparently forgot to equip man with an infinite capacity for sexual performance, but kindly remembered to compensate by making woman modest. Women are always ready for sex, in other words, but must never know it, while men, as Barbara Guetti has shrewdly remarked, "must take—or be given—the initiative" lest it "become all too clear that the decision of when to start and to stop is, in fact, beyond their control."[36]

Yet the woman's resistance does more than protect the man from embarrassment: as Nature arranges her erotic plot, female modesty also serves, paradoxically, to do the real work of beginning. For without modesty, Rousseau repeatedly argues, desire itself would soon cease to exist. "If the two sexes had equally made and received advances," the *Lettre* continues,

vain importunity would never have been preserved; the passions, always languishing in a boring freedom, would never become inflamed, the sweetest of all feelings would scarcely have touched the human heart, and its object would have been badly fulfilled. The apparent obstacle, which seems to distance this object, is in reality that which brings it nearer. Desires veiled by shame only become more seductive; in hindering them, *pudeur* inflames them.[37]

To adduce Nature's "reasons" in this way is to aim at justification rather than explanation, to defend the presumed rightness of things as they are while appearing to demonstrate how they could not possibly be otherwise. Rousseau never asks why the accord between man's "will" and his "power" could not simply have been arranged better in the first place, or why the erotic capacities of the two sexes should have been distributed so unevenly. In his elegantly evasive rationalizations of Nature's design, the problem at issue keeps shifting rapidly; while at each moment his strategy depends on taking for granted—and as granted for good—all the elements in the picture but the one immediately in question. "In relation to sexual *pudeur* in particular," the passage quoted above begins, "what gentler arm could Nature have given to the one destined to defend herself?" But why did Nature destine women to defend themselves? "Are there on both sides the same capacities to satisfy them?" Rousseau sternly inquires—and then goes on to imply that since Nature made women always capable of being penetrated, and men just sometimes, and unpredictably, able to penetrate, it is only "natural" that men should seize the initiative when they can, that they will attack and women defend. And "what would become of the human species if the order of attack and defense were changed?" If women had the first move, apparently, they would always approach when men were unable to rise to the occasion, miss the moments when intercourse was possible, and "love would no longer be the support of Nature" but "its destroyer and plague."

What *would* happen if the order of attack and defense were changed? Nothing, presumably—or too much. Rousseau's language leaves the outcome nicely ambiguous: whether love would be "the destroyer and plague" of Nature because the race would fail to reproduce itself, or because the sexes would be tortured to death by unfulfilled desire, he refuses to say. All that is clear is that the natural modesty of women ensures the race against either disaster. In *Emile* he conjures up a more vivid image of the consequences:

Who could think that nature has indifferently prescribed the same advances to the one sex and the other, and that the first to form desires should also be the first to show them? What a strange depravity of judgment! The enterprise having such different consequences for the two sexes, is it natural that they would have the same audacity in indulging in it? With such a great inequality in their mutual stakes, how could one not see that if reserve did not impose on the one sex the moderation that nature imposes on the other, it would soon result in the ruin of both of them, and that mankind would perish by the means established to preserve it? Given the ease with which women can arouse the senses of men, and revive in the depths of their hearts the remains of an amorousness that is nearly extinguished, if there were some unfortunate region on earth where philosophy had introduced this practice—especially in the hot countries where more women are born than men—the men, tyrannised by the women, would finally become their victims, and would all see themselves dragged to their death without ever being able to defend themselves.[38]

In this masculine nightmare of a world without *pudeur*, Rousseau abandons the near-farce of the *Lettre*'s inopportune approaches and missed moments for an apocalyptic vision of virtual gendercide—the universal exhaustion of the one sex by the unbridled lusts of the other. Indeed, so caught up does he become in the imaginary horrors of the scene that he momentarily forgets what he has been at such pains to establish—that "reserve" and "nature" are not complementary but identical, and that it is rather by withholding themselves than by advancing that women succeed in arousing men. Even as he insists that *pudeur* is natural, in other words, Rousseau's anxious imagination keeps threatening to betray him: you may wish to believe that woman's modesty is natural, it seems to say, but I know that her voracious appetites are more natural yet.

Like other theorists of natural modesty, from Allestree to Ellis, Rousseau understandably worries the problem of animals—though no one excels him in brazening a way through the conflicting possibilities. "The argument drawn from the example of the beasts concludes nothing, and is not true," he begins one brief paragraph of the *Lettre à d'Alembert:* "man is not a dog or a wolf." No sooner has he denied the relevance of animal analogies, however, than he hastens to offer one of his own. "In spite of this," the next paragraph immediately demands, "where was it assumed that instinct never produces in animals effects similar to those that shame produces among men? Every day I see proofs to the contrary." When he observes the *amours* of animals, he sees "caprices, choices, and concerted refusals which abide very closely by the maxim of exciting the passions by obstacles." Man may not be a dog or a wolf, but the bird-watcher in Rousseau seems ready enough to imagine woman as akin to the pigeon:

At the very instant I write this I have before my eyes an example which confirms it. Two young pigeons, in the happy times of their first loves, present me with a very different picture from that stupid brutality ascribed to them by our so-called wise men. The white dove goes following her beloved step by step, and takes flight herself as soon as he turns around. Does he remain inactive? Light pecks wake him up; if he withdraws, she follows him; if he protects himself, a little flight of six steps attracts him again; the innocence of Nature arranges the provocations and the soft resistance with an art which the most skillful coquette could scarcely possess. No, the playful Galatea did not do better, and Virgil could have drawn from a dovecot one of his most charming images.[39]

Though Rousseau intends otherwise, even this tableau of pigeon *pudeur* turns into a representation of the female's desire. Indeed, with her habit of following her lover around and delivering light blows with her beak whenever he chances to fall asleep, the white dove could well serve to illustrate how easily "the order of attack and defense" *is* reversed among the birds—with just a touch of henpecking admitted into the bargain.

"Charming" as Rousseau professes to find her, the dove quickly disappears from his argument, perhaps because he senses that she is too aggressively coquettish to provide an altogether apposite model.[40] When he subsequently returns to the animal kingdom in *Emile,* he prefers instead to stress that nature has ordered these matters differently there. "If females among the animals do not have the same shame, what follows from that?" he inquires rather defensively. "Do they have, as women do, the unlimited desires to which this shame serves as a bridle?" Woman is the only animal with modesty, he goes on to suggest, because she is the only one whose desires are not otherwise limited by a cycle of heat—an argument that Ellis's *Studies* would later recast in evolutionary terms. Rather than try to find *pudeur* among the animals, in other words, Rousseau now contends that only women require it. Among animals, "when the need is satisfied, desire ceases. . . . Instinct drives them, and instinct stops them." But "what will be the substitute for this negative instinct when you have stripped women of *pudeur?*"[41]

Like his horrified vision of lovemaking with women thus stripped of their *pudeur* in the hot countries, these speculations bring Rousseau perilously close to the position he wishes to deny—that modesty is a merely human, if perhaps necessary, invention. Others would try to preserve the continuity between humans and animals by arguing that women's desires were themselves modestly limited by nature. But such a representation threatens to de-eroticize the sex; while Rousseau, as Wollstonecraft would clearly recognize, wishes above all to defend and perpetuate a system of erotic relations. Though his account of woman's modesty depends on granting her desire a logical, perhaps even a psychological, priority, he nonetheless insists on the "naturalness" of both— and boldly reaches for divine sanction in support of his paradox. "While delivering women over to unlimited desires," the Supreme Being also "joins *pudeur* to those desires in order to restrain them."[42]

Simultaneously acknowledging and seeming to master contradiction, this paradox offers a compressed instance of Rousseau's pervasive rhetorical strategy—his constant effort to forestall, by incorporating, opposition. In the *Lettre à d'Alembert*, for example, he tries to show that *pudeur* is natural rather than a "prejudice of society and education" by alleging the greater intensity of the feeling "wherever man has remained closer to the primitive state." Then he immediately appends a note, which at once anticipates a potential objection and refutes it with a further paradox: to the argument that "savage women have no *pudeur*, since they go naked . . . I answer that ours have even less; for they are dressed." If Rousseau was hardly the first moralist to discover that the teasing concealments of clothing could prove more immodest than the naked flesh, we should nonetheless recall how his terms of praise seem to reverse themselves yet again when he celebrates Sophie's dress for just such modest concealments.[43] But even within a few sentences of the *Lettre* itself, the grounds of argument can rapidly shift, as possible contradictions are at once acknowledged and absorbed, concessions seemingly granted and denied. "Everywhere women are esteemed in proportion to their modesty," one paragraph concludes ringingly:

everywhere people are convinced that in neglecting the manners of their sex, women neglect their duties; everywhere one sees that when women turn the masculine and firm assurance of the man into impudence, they debase themselves by this odious imitation and dishonor at once their sex and ours.

"I know that in some countries contrary customs prevail," the next paragraph blandly begins. "But look also at the sort of morals to which they have given rise. I require no other example to confirm my maxims."[44] "Everywhere" has its exceptions, apparently, but these only prove the rule—a rule that itself has meanwhile shifted from a universal law to the reformer's exhortation. Perhaps the most daring such turn in the argument, however, has already been negotiated at the beginning of the passage, when after finding evidence of Nature's modest designs in everything from the delicacy of women's complexions (naturally formed so that a modest blush "can be better perceived")[45] to the timidity of mountain girls and the courting of pigeons, Rousseau seems calmly to concede what he has striven so hard to deny:

Even if it could be denied that a special feeling of *pudeur* was natural to women, would it be any the less true that, in society, their lot ought to be a domestic and retired life, and that they ought to be raised in principles that suit it? If the timidity, *pudeur,* and *modestie* which are proper to them are social inventions, it is essential for society that women acquire these qualities; it is essential that they be cultivated in women, and any woman who disdains them offends good morals.[46]

If modesty should not prove natural after all—well then, it will simply have to be invented. This is such a stunning concession that at least one commentator has wondered whether it was intended very seriously, or whether it was merely tossed in as a sort of afterthought lest the full weight of the other arguments not seem altogether convincing.[47] But Rousseau's rhetoric here is hardly an aberration, only an extreme instance of his characteristic multiplying of possibilities, his readiness to sacrifice clarity and coherence to the sheer urgency of his case. Nor is this the only moment at which he seems to acknowledge female modesty as an entirely human arrangement. Just a few paragraphs after he has dismissed his opponents' contention that *pudeur* is "nothing but an invention of the social laws to protect the rights of fathers and husbands, and to maintain some order in families," he imagines their protests again, this time assimilating their Hume-like argument to purposes of his own:

"Why," they say, "should what is not shameful for the man be so for the woman? Why should one of the sexes make a crime for itself out of what the other believes itself permitted?" As if the consequences were the same on both sides! As if all the austere duties of the woman did not arise from the single fact that an infant ought to have a father.

And as if all the austere duties of the woman did *not* arise from that single fact, he immediately adds the usual mystification: "even if we lacked these important considerations, we would have always the same response to make, and it would always be without reply. Nature wanted it so, and it is a crime to stifle her voice."[48]

If Hume's account of the modest woman explains too little, it is easy to feel that Rousseau's explains too much, that her presence in his world has been relentlessly overdetermined. For the modern imagination especially, so insistent an argument demands to be read as an elaborate defense against hidden anxieties. But neither the anxieties nor the defenses are peculiar to Rousseau. Both in form and in spirit the *Lettre à d'Alembert* and *Emile* more closely resemble the conduct books—and the English novel—than does Hume's attempt at dispassionate explanation. Like Rousseau, the same authorities who seek most urgently to construct the modest woman also insist most urgently that Nature, not they, have made her. And while the novelists need never directly address the impossible question of her origins, they can eagerly exploit the very conflicts that Rousseau and others imagine her to cover. The modest woman remains the subject of paradoxes, but in the English courtship novel especially, as we shall see, she also becomes the subject of narratives. Understanding her virtue temporally, that is—as a "backwardness" to ends that are nonetheless approaching—the novelists know that the best way of making sense of the modest woman is by making stories.

3

The Matter of Courtship

❧

The modest woman was made for marriage. According to the conventional wisdom, a man might flirt with a coquette, but when he had marriage in mind he always looked for a modest woman. By the time that Hannah More sent Coelebs in search of a wife in 1808, the outcome of such quests had long been a foregone conclusion: the exemplary hero will naturally marry the blushing heroine. In 1804 the "poetical essays" section of the *Lady's Magazine* printed an anonymous little piece called "The Bachelor's Choice," a poem that claims our attention only for its formulaic statement of the commonplace. The poetical bachelor will not choose "the prude, or vain coquette / . . . the giddy romping lass; / Nor her where wealth and power are met," but—inevitably—

> . . . she whose modest mien
> Adds graces to her matchless charms;
> Who, blushing, hears a lover's pain,
> Nor seeks to triumph in alarms.

"O, Fortune!" he concludes, "grant a girl like this / May share with me connubial bliss!"[1]—his final couplet thus automatically associating the modest woman with a happy ending in marriage. Indeed, for many English writers of the period, as we shall see, it was almost impossible to separate the idea of modesty from that of "connubial bliss," or to offer an account of the virtue that was not in some sense also an account of how to marry happily. Between Allestree and Ellis, the literature of modesty was in large part a literature that sought to advise women on how best to get themselves chosen, men how best to choose, and both

parties that an affectionate marriage was itself the most satisfying goal
of life.

A figure as popular as the modest woman, it is best to assume, is not
likely to make sense too easily: the very fact that so many voices pay lip
service to her virtue suggests that no one context will suffice to explain
her. At the same time, however, it is no accident that so much talk about
modesty is also talk about courtship—or that even such radical opponents on the question as Hume and Rousseau both try to understand
the virtue teleologically, to think about female modesty as it serves the
ends of marriage. For Hume, we might recall, modesty only makes
sense in the context of paternal anxieties and the institution of the family: men want women chaste in order to assure the identity of their children, and psychologically, if not quite logically, a woman's "preceding
backwardness" seems to promise her future chastity. While Rousseau
insists that Nature rather than man has made the modest woman, such
paternal anxieties hardly seem incidental to his account: indeed, one
could argue that he only calls on Nature so strenuously because he fears
that a merely human virtue may not assure the fathers sufficient protection. But for Rousseau, as we have seen, the modest woman arouses
desire even as she promises chastity: if Nature has made her for marriage, then marriages are to be made for love. "To continue to be lovers
when one is married"—that is the "simple and easy" recipe for future
happiness that the tutor offers Emile and Sophie on their wedding day.
And to Sophie herself he specifies further, instructing her how to keep
love alive by keeping her modesty:

You will reign a long time by love if you make your favors rare and precious,
if you know how to make them valued. Do you want to see your husband
ceaselessly at your feet? keep him always at some distance from your person. But
put *modestie* in your severity and not caprice, that he should see you as reserved
and not whimsical; take care that in managing his love you do not make him
doubt yours. Make yourself cherished by your favors and respected by your refusals, that he should honor the chastity of his wife without having to complain
of her coldness.[2]

Rousseau would not always be able to sustain this vision of conjugal
care: when he came to write the further history of the married lovers in
Les Solitaires, he would find himself imagining even his carefully instructed Sophie succumbing to the temptation of adultery. But if the
effort to associate love and marriage distinguishes *Emile* and the *Lettre
à d'Alembert* from the dominant tradition of Continental literature—and
from Rousseau himself at other moments[3]—it makes them all the more

closely akin to the fictions of English Protestantism. Though *Emile* acknowledges that the intensity of desire will inevitably fade, it nonetheless ends with a vision of *l'amour conjugal* that could easily be translated into the language of many an English novel. Such a love, the tutor tells us, is "founded on an esteem which lasts as long as life, on virtues which do not fade with beauty, on a suitability of character which renders intercourse pleasant, and prolongs in old age the charm of the first union."[4]

The feelings of most people in the past are necessarily irrecoverable. But one need not believe that men and women only began to marry for love in the late seventeenth century, or that conjugal affection has a neat and unilinear history, to recognize how much writing the English in particular devoted to the subject, or how widely their ideal of a union both prudent and affectionate was disseminated.[5] The contributors to the *Spectator,* for example, waged a self-conscious campaign in favor of married love and domestic happiness—a campaign so successful that many of its assumptions rapidly became commonplaces. Under the right conditions, the *Spectator* repeatedly insisted, the married state was far to be preferred to that of a single person: "when the Affection is well placed, and supported by the Considerations of Duty, Honour, and Friendship," in the words of one paper, "there can nothing rise in the common Course of Life, or from the Blows or Favours of Fortune, in which a Man will not find Matters of some Delight unknown to a single Condition."[6] "If Love be any Refinement," another characteristically argued, "*Conjugal Love* must be certainly so in a much higher Degree"; while yet another simply pronounced marriage "an Institution calculated for a constant Scene of as much Delight as our Being is capable of" and "the State capable of the highest humane Felicity." "I have very long entertained an Ambition," Steele wrote at the beginning of that same paper, "to make the Word *Wife* the most agreeable and delightful Name in Nature."[7] Though the language of this wife-loving Nature is evidently English, the testimony of *Emile* suggests that to Rousseau, at least, she also spoke very persuasively in French: when the time comes to educate Sophie for marriage, *le Spectateur* is the sole book the tutor assigns her to read. While Emile spends two years before their wedding in travel, Sophie will prepare to be a good wife by studying *les devoirs des honnêtes femmes* according to Addison and Steele.[8]

Rousseau never tells us whether Sophie fulfills her assignment, but one of the things she might have learned from her reading is why she and Emile had thus been parted. For even as the *Spectator* urged its readers to marry, it urged them to approach the state with caution. Precisely because conjugal happiness was the greatest good life had to offer, the *Spectator* repeatedly argued, no time was more critical than that of courtship—and no decision more worth taking slowly. "Those Marriages generally abound most with Love and Constancy, that are preceded by a long Courtship," Addison announced in his famous "Essay upon Love and Marriage" of 1711, and the remarks that follow suggest that both the habit of loving and the opportunity to change one's mind are in question:

> The Passion should strike Root, and gather Strength before Marriage be grafted on it. A long Course of Hopes and Expectations fixes the Idea in our Minds, and habituates us to a Fondness of the Person beloved.
>
> There is Nothing of so great Importance to us, as the good Qualities of one to whom we join our selves for Life; they do not only make our present State agreeable, but often determine our Happiness to all Eternity.

"Before Marriage we cannot be too inquisitive and discerning in the Faults of the Person beloved," he remarks a little later, "nor after it," he adds soberingly, "too dim-sighted and superficial." Though Steele concludes a paper of the following year with "this Life" rather than the next, he, too, approaches marriage as a matter in which Last Things hang in the balance. "In a Word," he writes, "the married State, with and without the Affection suitable to it, is the compleatest Image of Heaven and Hell we are capable of receiving in this Life." As so often, the *Spectator* manages to combine strong encouragement to marry with strong reasons to hesitate. "I am verily perswaded, that whatever is delightful in humane Life, is to be enjoyed in greater Perfection in the marry'd, than in the single Condition," Steele declares, but only after he has wandered off into a cautionary account of Socrates, Xantippe, and the need for manly patience if one has tied oneself to a shrew. The essay partly tries to show that success in marriage requires a man to bring "his Reason to support his Passion"—and that a sufficiently wise man can be contented even with Xantippe.[9] But like Addison, Steele also suggests that the most assured route to marital happiness is to exercise sufficient care beforehand—a lesson that Rousseau in turn passes on through *Emile*.

"You want to marry Sophie, and it has not been five months since you have known her!" the tutor scolds when he announces the enforced separation:

> You want to marry her not because she suits you but because she pleases you— as if love were never mistaken about what is suitable, and as if those who began by loving each other never ended by hating each other. She is virtuous, I know;

but is that enough? Is being good people sufficient to suit one another? It is not her virtue that I am calling in question, it is her character. Does that of a woman reveal itself in a day? Do you know in how many situations it is necessary to see her in order to know her disposition thoroughly? Do four months of attachment answer for a whole life? [10]

In the context of *Emile* these questions seem more than a little disingenuous, since both as tutor and as author Rousseau has so obviously fashioned this young woman for this young man—and made sure that she can have no rivals. As Addison's essay on love and marriage suggests, it is usually when people choose for themselves that such questions arise, not when others make the arrangements for them. "Where the Choice is left to Friends, the chief Point under Consideration is an Estate," Addison writes; "where the Parties chuse for themselves, their Thoughts turn most upon the Person." [11] By so obviously arranging its love match, *Emile* lays bare the artifice that most novels of courtship conceal. But there is no question that the marriage between Emile and Sophie *is* intended as a love match or that Rousseau shares Addison's assumption that the happiest unions are those that are freely, if prudently, chosen.

Though most of the eighteenth-century English conduct books continued to insist on the parental right to veto a child's choice of partner, they, too, stressed that the affirmative desire must come from the parties concerned. The sing-song tetrameter of Edward Moore's popular *Fables for the Female Sex* (1744) only slightly exaggerates the conventionality of their wisdom:

> Duty demands, the parent's voice
> Should sanctify the daughter's choice;
> In that, is due obedience shewn;
> To choose, belongs to her alone. [12]

Indeed, long before Richardson's celebrated novel, the English advice literature had anticipated what might be called the Rule in Clarissa's Case: a daughter should never marry without her parents' consent, but she should never be compelled to marry when she could not love. While *The Ladies Calling* still contended that a young woman should refer all potential suitors to her parents—"virgin modesty" being more compatible with a marriage of "obedience" than of "choice"—it already put the argument for love in this negative form. [13] Though Allestree did not wish a woman to marry without love, "choice" presumably spoke too openly of desire to one so self-consciously engaged in denying female appetite. A half-century later, on the other hand, Thomas Salmon's

Critical Essay Concerning Marriage came close to advising that the prudent parent simply abdicate in favor of his children's "Inclinations," lest
an amorous Nature "have its Course" without him. "Will a Father pretend to know which Lover is like to make the most agreeable Companion for his Daughters?" Salmon inquired, adding significantly, "Nor can
it properly be called a Marriage where there is not a Union of Souls as
well as Bodies."[14] Salmon wrote more warmly of love—and more dis-
paragingly of fathers—than was typical. But he was hardly alone in assuming that "Matrimony should be the Effect of a free and previous
Choice in the Persons marrying," to quote a nearly contemporaneous
treatise by Defoe,[15] or in recognizing that parents who believed in this
ideal of marriage needed to place considerable trust in their children. As
the very conjunction of so much courtship advice with so much talk of
modesty suggests, the more "obedience" gave way to "choice," the
more fathers tried to assure themselves that they would have modest
daughters.[16]

In some "tender and sensible" speeches that Rousseau composes for
him, Sophie's father explains to her why she has complete liberty to
choose her husband for herself—and why she should use her freedom
wisely. When marriages are made by the authority of fathers, he tells
her, "it is not the persons who are married; it is rank and wealth. But all
that can change."

> The persons alone always remain, they take themselves everywhere with them.
> In spite of fortune, it is only as a result of personal relations that a marriage can
> be happy or unhappy. . . .
> It is up to the spouses to match themselves. Mutual inclination should be
> their first bond: their eyes, their hearts should be their first guides. Since their
> first duty, once united, is to love each other, and since loving or not loving is
> not within our control, this duty necessarily involves another, which is to begin
> by loving each other before uniting themselves. This is the right of nature that
> nothing can abrogate.[17]

Yet if marrying for love is a "right of nature," only after he has made
woman naturally modest does Rousseau dare to proclaim it. It was not
for nothing that Sophie's book began by establishing the nature of her
sex—or that well before the tutor introduces her to Emile, we have
been assured that woman's "unlimited desires" have been securely joined
to the *pudeur* that restrains them.[18] Were it not for their *pudeur,* in other
words, their "unlimited desires" would make the necessary delaying action impossible. As for Sophie herself, Rousseau goes on to make clear,
she deserves her freedom because she can be trusted not to act pre-

cipitately. "Let us put the thing at its worst," he says, "and give her an ardent temperament which makes a long wait painful for her. I say that her judgment, her knowledge, her taste, her delicacy, and above all the sentiments on which her heart has been nourished in her childhood, will oppose to the impetuosity of her senses a counterweight which will be enough for her to conquer them or at least to resist them a long time."[19] Rousseau may be willing to grant his model woman far more "ardent temperament" and "impetuosity" than do the English conduct books, but no more than they, obviously, does he wish to argue that good marriages are made on impulse.

If the lines just quoted suggest that Sophie owes her modest reserve more to upbringing than to nature, this would hardly be the first time we have seen Rousseau contradict himself. Just a few pages earlier, in fact, Sophie's parents are said to have raised their virtuous and lovable daughter "rather by following her taste than by thwarting it": no "counterweight" to her impulses was apparently required. But *Emile* is, after all, a treatise on education; and even as Rousseau insists that all women are naturally modest, he wants to argue that some women are more modest than others—especially, it would appear, those who are raised as Protestants. "It seems to me in general," he writes, "that in Protestant countries there is more attachment to family, and that there are more respectable wives, and more tender mothers than in Catholic countries; and if this is so, one cannot doubt that this difference is in part due to convent education." Like many critics of the Catholic system, Rousseau dismisses the convent as nothing but a breeding ground for hypocrisy and license. "Convents are veritable schools of coquetry," he declares, and "not," he hastens to add, "of that virtuous coquetry about which I have spoken." The *jeune fille* who leaves the convent and abruptly enters into noisy company, Rousseau argues, immediately feels as if she belongs there. The young woman raised at home, in contrast, learns to love "the peaceful and domestic life," while her gradual exposure to the world teaches her to resist temptation.[20] If the Protestant has thus been prepared to be both a chaste and an affectionate wife, the girl who has been artificially constrained in a convent wants a husband, Rousseau suggests, only as a cover for adultery:

An apparent constraint is imposed on girls so as to find the dupes who marry them on the basis of their deportment. But study these young persons a moment: under a constrained air they badly disguise the lust that devours them, and already one reads in their eyes the ardent desire to imitate their mothers. What they lust after is not a husband but the license of marriage. What need is there for a husband with so many resources for doing without one? But a husband is needed in order to cover up these resources. *Modestie* is on their faces, and libertinism is in the depths of their hearts; this false *modestie* itself is a sign of it. They only affect it so as to be able to get rid of it sooner.[21]

Though Rousseau goes on to condemn the dissolute women of London as well as of Paris, it is hardly surprising that the English would be quick to adapt this topos of the lustful convent girl and the modest Protestant, or that well into the next century they would vaunt their moral superiority to the Continent by contrasting the domestic virtues of a marriage made for love with the evils of the adulterous *mariage de convenance*. The young women of France "are shut up in a convent, and never taste of freedom 'till they are married," the *Lady's Magazine* informed its readers in 1782, going on to declare that "a system of education more hurtful to mortals, is scarcely within the reach of invention." The magazine's account of the problem reads like a précis of Rousseau: "unnatural confinement in a convent, makes a young woman embrace with avidity every pleasure, when she is set free," while "to relish domestic life, one must be acquainted with it."[22] In his *Remarks on the French and English Ladies* published the following year, John Andrews offered a rather more nuanced account of the contrast, but he too associated "young ladies in convents," arranged marriages, and the consequent "licentiousness" of the French, even as he argued that the English took love far more seriously. Like other such commentators, Andrews also insisted that the women of England had more "modesty" than those of France. While the fashionable Frenchwoman coquets with "a multitude of admirers" and cares for no one very much, "far different is the character of our countrywomen, in whom an appearance of affection is very seldom unaccompanied by the reality." The "consequence," Andrews solemnly explained, "is, that men usually put more trust in them, and are more taken with their plainness and sincerity, than with the brilliant attractions of the French."[23]

Whether or not men "usually" responded quite as Andrews imagined them, he would have been pleased to learn that a young French aristocrat soon to visit England would testify in very similar terms to the conjugal superiority of the natives. Married couples were closer and more affectionate in England, François de La Rochefoucauld thought, because they spent more time getting to know one another beforehand and because their women had greater liberty in courtship. "Three-quarters of the marriages are made from inclination," the eighteen-year-old wrote home with enthusiasm, "and one sees by experience that most succeed perfectly."[24] "I don't know what will happen to me in

France," he noted with a bit more caution, "but at present I would find it more to my taste to have an English wife." Perhaps not surprisingly, what would happen in France appears to have been his marriage to a Frenchwoman. Though modern historians of the family have often relied on him as a witness, "experience" everywhere was no doubt more complicated than the young La Rochefoucauld imagined.[25] But it is principally with the stories people told themselves that we are here concerned; and for some two centuries, at least, variations on the story of the extended English courtship and its "perfectly" happy conclusion were widely circulated. As the topos of the convent-immured *jeune fille* and the free-but-virtuous Protestant suggests, the English made so much of the modest woman partly because they made so much of marrying prudently for love and of taking time to get to know one's future spouse during courtship. The longer they wished to extend the passage from girlhood to marriage, in other words, the more assurance they needed that their daughters could negotiate that passage safely. Because the modest woman was, in effect, her own duenna, she could be trusted to venture out alone; and because her desires were automatically checked by her mechanism of delay, both she and her lover would have some time to look around them. "A woman, in this country," Dr. Gregory explained in his immensely popular *Father's Legacy to His Daughters* of 1774, "may easily prevent the first impressions of love, and every motive of prudence and delicacy should make her guard her heart against them, till such time as she has received the most convincing proofs of the attachment of a man of such merit, as will justify a reciprocal regard."[26] Presumably he dared not speak for the French or the Italians.

"It is even long before a woman of delicacy dares avow to her own heart that she loves," Gregory laid down the rule in another passage; "and when all the subterfuges of ingenuity to conceal it from herself fail, she feels a violence done both to her pride and to her modesty."[27] As we shall see, such an account of the modest woman's state of mind has its own problems, not the least of which is the origin of those ingenious "subterfuges" in a consciousness innocently unaware of the feeling they hide. But however she manages it, "a woman of delicacy" is obviously slow to catch fire. Even in the advanced stages of courtship, note how gradually her temperature rises:

Some agreeable qualities recommend a gentleman to your common good liking and friendship. In the course of his acquaintance, he contracts an attachment to you. When you perceive it, it excites your gratitude; this gratitude rises into a preference; and this preference perhaps at last advances to some degree of attachment, especially if it meets with crosses and difficulties; for these, and a state of suspense, are very great incitements to attachment, and are the food of love in both sexes.[28]

Like other voices in the period, Gregory at once pronounces the happiness of the married state "superior" to any other and warns against seeking it too eagerly. For a father's daughter especially, he often suggests, marriage is too important to be made on impulse. "As I look on your choice of a husband to be of the greatest consequence to your happiness," he announces solemnly, "I hope you will make it with the utmost circumspection. Do not give way to a sudden sally of passion, and dignify it with the name of love.—Genuine love is not founded in caprice; it is founded in nature, on honourable views, on virtue, on similarity of tastes and sympathy of souls." In Gregory's book, it would appear, a woman knows that she has found true love only when she doesn't know too soon: "true love is founded on esteem, in a correspondence of tastes and sentiments," as he says at another point, "and steals on the heart imperceptibly."[29]

While love at first sight needs but a glance, "tastes and sentiments" cannot correspond without time and occasion. "If you do not allow gentlemen to become acquainted with you," Gregory observes sensibly enough, "you can never expect to marry with attachment on either side." And far from hindering a young woman's opportunities for such acquaintance, he suggests, her modesty truly enables proper courtship. "You may perhaps imagine, that the reserved behaviour which I recommend to you, and your appearing seldom at public places, must cut off all opportunities of your being acquainted with gentlemen," he remarks; but "I am very far from intending this. I advise you to no reserve, but what will render you more respected and beloved by our sex." Though Dr. Gregory's daughters should indeed not venture often in public, "it is in private companies alone where you can expect easy and agreeable conversation"—and it is in such conversation alone, he implies, that you can acquire appropriate knowledge of your lover.[30] While even talk has its dangers, the truly modest woman can always manage to avoid them. Though "virgin purity is of that delicate nature, that it cannot hear certain things without contamination," the doctor's daughters should be the sort of properly modest virgins who can nonetheless venture with safety into mixed company, since their virtue will somehow forestall any hint of a *double entendre*. "There is a native dignity in ingenuous modesty to be expected in your sex," Gregory earnestly informs them, "which is your natural protection from the familiarities of the men." Indeed, well before he directly addresses the question of love and marriage, Gregory has cleared the way for courtship, by repeatedly emphasizing that it is the very reserve of his pattern young woman that enables her to talk to the opposite sex with "ease and openness." Guarded by "that dignified modesty which may prevent the approach of the most distant familiarity," as he puts it at yet another point, such a young woman can safely enter the drawing room and can linger there long enough to get to know her future mate.[31]

Gregory does not so much argue these connections, of course, as take them for granted—even, or perhaps especially, when they would most appear to require explanation. *A Father's Legacy to His Daughters* is above all an exercise in paternal wish fulfillment, and the image of the modest young woman whose innocence somehow constitutes her own protection is only one of those he would prefer not to examine too closely. Judging by the proliferation of similar representations, however—not to mention the number of times Gregory's own book was reprinted and plagiarized—this particular fantasy was widely shared. Here, for example, is the Reverend John Bennett's popular *Letters to a Young Lady* of 1789, and its pattern young woman, Louisa:

Though Louisa is the most remote from *prudery*, of any woman I know, easy and accessible to the other sex, and cheerful, lively and *unconstrained*, in her conversation with them, yet she has really so great a share of *true*, female delicacy, that the most licentious man living would not dare to use a double *entendre* in her company, or give the conversation an improper turn. Nor is it, that she has reduced rules of propriety to a system. She has really a *native* feeling, which vibrates to the most distant touch of what is proper and becoming, and would tremble, like the sensitive plant, where any thing, that could stain the delicacy of her *mind*, was conveyed in the most *distant* allusion.

In a subsequent letter, Bennett defines "true delicacy" as "nothing more, than the refinement of *modesty*," and though his ideal women tend to quiver with a rather more exquisite sensibility than Gregory's, his idea of virtue as a sort of early warning system is much the same. Like Gregory's daughters, Louisa can be "easy and accessible to the other sex" because she is automatically guarded from danger: trembling at "the most *distant* allusion" to impropriety, her "*true*, female delicacy" clears the room for polite conversation. So at least the sexes can comfortably talk together, Bennett implies, as long as they speak English. Of female delicacy on the Continent, he will only observe rather cryptically, "Let France and Italy do what they will, it is that sacred fence, which is never broken down, without melancholy consequences."[32]

Of course the young Englishwoman has need of all her modesty if she is to make a conduct-book marriage. For the longer she extends the period of courtship—the more she deliberately lingers, in effect, between her father's house and her future husband's—the more she risks losing her sexual virtue along the way. It is no accident that one of the most frequently reprinted sections of Thomas Gisborne's *Enquiry into the Duties of the Female Sex* (1797) dwells anxiously on the problem of how to see a daughter safely through this crucial transition period, even as the same book elsewhere stresses the extreme "caution" that women in particular should exercise in choosing a mate.[33] "If I was called upon to write the history of a *woman's* trials and sorrows," Bennett declared in another one of his *Letters to a Young Lady,*

I would date it from the moment, when nature has pronounced her *marriageable,* and she feels that innocent desire of associating with the other sex, which needs not a blush. If I had a girl of my own, at this *critical* age, I should be full of the keenest apprehensions for her safety; and, like the great poet, when the tempter was bent on seducing our first parents from their innocence and happiness, I should invoke the assistance of some *guardian* angel, to conduct her through the slippery and dangerous paths.[34]

Despite the allusion to "the great poet" and "our first parents," the history Bennett imagines himself writing would resemble not that of Milton's Eve but of Burney's Evelina—a "history of a *woman's* trials and sorrows" that begins at the moment when "nature has pronounced her" marriageable and ends, presumably, when someone has pronounced her married. And though he scarcely seems to recognize the fact, he has already invoked the angelic assistance he requires—only that he has tried to represent it, as might a novelist, under the guise of the young woman's own psychology. Louisa will pass safely through the "*critical* age," in other words, because she has her modesty to protect her.

❦

And it is just because Louisa has her modesty, all the authorities would agree, that the men will wish to marry her. A proper reserve, the conduct books never tired of repeating, makes a woman more, not less, desirable. In part, this was simply good economics: though the popular writers of advice for women rarely dwelled with much frankness on marriage as a market, they were very fond of pointing out that men desire most what is hardest to get—and that holding herself prudently in reserve, therefore, would only increase a woman's value. "'Tis incident to mans nature to esteem those things most that are at distance," as Allestree characteristically put it, "whereas an easie and cheap descent begets contemt." Far from making women's beauty the less prized, he insisted, "such a Reservedness" would only heighten their attractions: "so long as they govern themselves by the exact rules of Prudence and Modesty, their lustre is like the Meridian Sun in its clearness, which tho less approachable, is counted more glorious; but when they decline from those, they are like that Sun in a cloud, which tho safelier gazed on, is not half so bright." [35] Nearly one hundred years later, Dr. Fordyce would appreciatively incorporate these lines into his *Sermons to Young Women* of 1765, and after virtually another century had passed, the anonymous *Young Lady's Book of Advice and Instruction* (1859) was still repeating this extended figure of woman as the sun, while warning young ladies against the dangers of making themselves "too cheap." [36] Men may flirt with those who do so, according to the conventional wisdom, but they marry the modest ones—the formula suggesting, of course, that from a masculine perspective marriage was a high price to pay.

Despite Allestree's allusion to "the exact rules of Prudence and Modesty," however, exactly what constituted a violation of those rules seems to have varied considerably. In the *Lady's Magazine* of 1793 a "young gentleman" offered his fraternal advice on the occasion of his sister's removal from the country to the city: "I am well acquainted with the sentiments of our sex," he assured her, and "however desirous they may be that their companions of an hour, or of a day, should indulge themselves in every possible freedom, they wish to find very different manners in those whom they would chuse for the companions of their lives." Indeed, he was well enough acquainted with his own sex to conjure up quite vividly the kind of woman they didn't marry, writing with rising warmth of "fashionable ladies who obtrude themselves on us upon every occasion . . . who in public companies suffer themselves to be clasped in our arms, seated on our knees, kissed, pressed, and toyed with in the most familiar manner, with whom our hands scarce need restraint," before he dutifully turned his account, and metaphors of accounting, to the advantage of his modest sibling: "if they did but know . . . how cheap they render themselves, how they lessen our esteem, and how much we prefer your amiable diffidence, your blushing timidity, they would endeavour to be like you." A quarter century later, the magazine was still distinguishing between the companion of an hour and one chosen for life, while managing to draw the circle of "genuine modesty" considerably tighter. Again, it reflected on supply and demand by warning that "the easily obtained prize is seldom highly estimated," but now, apparently, a light touch or flip remark would suffice to identify a woman as not worth the marrying. "The youthful female who can familiarly tap a mere acquaintance upon the shoulder, or rally him upon the attention which he pays to some more favored fair, may amuse for a few hours," the magazine solemnly observed. But she "will never be the kind of companion with whom a man of sense would wish to pass whole years."[37]

For all the sobriety of such comparisons, much of the literature simultaneously managed to suggest that in choosing the modest woman, the "man of sense" also would have chosen the woman he found more amorously inspiring. Rousseau was far from the only one to praise the modest woman for what she left to the imagination—or to recognize, at least implicitly, how much human desire and love depend on such a stimulus. Most of those who sought to advise the marriageable woman, in fact, were happy not to distinguish between the economic value of a modest reserve and its erotic appeal. Some years before Sophie covered her charms so as to make them imagined, her English counterpart could have dressed to much the same effect by following the rules laid down in Moore's popular collection of *Fables for the Female Sex:*

> The maid, who modestly conceals
> Her beauties, while she hides, reveals;
> Give but a glimpse, and fancy draws
> Whate'er the Grecian Venus was.
> From Eve's first fig-leaf to brocade,
> All dress was meant for fancy's aid,
> Which evermore delighted dwells
> On what the bashful nymph conceals.

Like many such fictions, Moore's *Fable* routinely contrasts this bashful nymph to her opposite number. "The nymph, who walks the public streets, / And sets her cap at all she meets, / May catch the fool, who turns to stare, / But men of sense avoid the snare"[38]—presumably because they are prudent types who recognize a streetwalker when they see one. Yet at the same time, and also typically, Moore's erotically teasing lines manage to imply that there are sensualists in these men of sense, and that they prefer the modest woman because they know how much of pleasure is anticipation. "A fine woman shews her charms to most advantage, when she seems most to conceal them," as Dr. Gregory remarked, adding with unaccustomed bluntness, "The finest bosom in nature is not so fine as what imagination forms."[39]

That such advice effectively reversed the conduct books' usual position on nature is an irony well worth noting. Whatever the beauties Moore's bashful nymph may conceal, it still seems to her advantage that her lover should fancifully "draw" the Grecian Venus in their stead. And no natural bosom, clearly, could hope to compete with that constructed by Gregory's imagination. A man like Gregory might elsewhere suggest that the modesty of women was "natural," but in offering advice on courtship he was effectively writing an *ars*—not a *natura*—*amatoria*. When such men wrote about what made women attractive, in other words—which is to say when they wrote about what attracted them— they indirectly testified to how little "nature" alone would explain.[40] And though they often wrote as if woman were merely the artless stimulus of an imagination unmistakably masculine, they were, after all, typically addressing their advice to her, and in the very act of doing so inevitably made her a collaborator. In Marriott's *Female Conduct,* for example, the poet offers the usual instruction to his woman reader: "Modest Concealments please a Lover's Eye, / The Charms you hide, his Fancy will supply." But even as he speaks for an obviously masculine "Fancy," he goes on to draw an analogy which reverses the lines of iden- tification, turning the lover into the reader and the modest woman into the poet. Like the great "Bards," he tells her, she is an artist who arouses the imagination by holding some things back: "While *Virgil* Charms, with this concealing Art, / His Reader pleas'd supplies the hidden Part."[41] Despite the flattering allusion to classical epic, needless to say, this evoking of "hidden parts" more closely resembles the art of the soft pornographer.

The imagination that dwells on the modest woman's clothing is— obviously—visual: even as it focuses on what she keeps unseen, the the- ory of "Modest Concealments" appeals primarily to an eroticism of the eye. But the literature of modesty has also what might be called its ther- mal model of female attractions: if one of the paradoxes of modesty is that the clothed body entices more than the naked one, another is that a well-insulated vessel retains the heat that a warm surface dissipates. Though the model was not developed very explicitly—perhaps because the physics involved remained rather vague—the coquette would seem to have been imagined as an open fire, whose warmth is widely available and rapidly expended, while the modest woman was more like a de- pendable stove, whose regulated surface temperature might promise a higher heat within. When a contributor to the *Spectator* argued that the "Passion of Love to a Mistress" resembled "the Flame of a Feaver," while "that to a Wife" was like "the Vital Heat," he drew on images of health and disease rather than of physics, and focused more on the man's feeling than on the woman who inspired him.[42] But variations on the outwardly destructive "Flame" versus the inward "Vital Heat" were commonplace; and if the warmth of marriage was to be prolonged and sustaining, the modest woman had been well constructed to provide it.

Having urged the readers of his 1829 *Advice to Young Men* to marry only women of "perfect modesty," William Cobbett went on to assure the "*ardent-minded*" that they would never regret having done so:

An *ardent-minded* young man . . . may fear, that this great *sobriety of conduct* in a young woman, for which I have been so strenuously contending, argues a want of that *warmth,* which he naturally so much desires; and, if my observation and experience warranted the entertaining of this fear, I should say, had I to live my life over again, give me the *warmth,* and I will stand my chance as to the rest.

This warmth he further associates with a kind of density of being, without which nothing will stay put for long. Pleasure especially will not settle down:

levity is, ninety-nine times out of a hundred, the companion of *a want of ardent feeling*. Prostitutes never *love,* and, for the far greater part, never did. Their passion, which is more *mere animal* than any thing else, is easily gratified; they, like rakes, change not only without pain, but with pleasure; that is to say, pleasure as great as they can enjoy. Women of *light minds* have seldom any *ardent* passion; love is a mere name, unless confined to one object; and young women, in whom levity of conduct is observable, will not be thus restricted.

Cobbett adds, however, that young men should not judge the other sex too severely: manners differ, he observes, and some countries tolerate a good deal more "levity" in their women than the English do. Predictably, the other people he happens to have in mind are the French. But even as he goes on to reminisce benignly about a "gay, sprightly" *jeune fille* of his acquaintance who nonetheless married successfully, he is quick to follow with "a truth which, I believe, no man of attentive observation will deny"—the more modest a woman, the more love she promises. "As, in general, English wives are *more warm* in their conjugal attachments than those of France," so the modest Englishwoman is to be preferred to her more light-minded sisters: "those English women who are the *most light* in their manners, and who are the *least constant* in their attachments, have the smallest portion of that *warmth,* that indescribable passion which God has given to human beings as the great counterbalance to all the sorrows and sufferings of life."[43] By focusing and restraining her desires rather than lightly dissipating them, the modest Englishwoman effectively intensifies their heat. Marry such a woman, Cobbett promises, and you will be the object not of casual feeling but an "*ardent* passion"—a passion all the more ardent for having been long held in check.

Just so, we might recall, does Rousseau hint that his modest young woman will love in *Emile:* indeed, "the need to love by itself devours her"—Sophie not having the "good luck," as her creator remarks ironically, to be "an amiable Frenchwoman, cold by temperament and coquettish by vanity," the kind who wants "to glitter rather than to please." Though crowds of men importune her, this most English of Continental heroines seems to know, as Cobbett would say, that "love is a mere name, unless confined to one object." Rather than win the fleeting acclaim of the fashionable, she wants "to please one virtuous man—and to please him forever."[44] But that "forever" is the strangest of all ideas of modesty. Forever is not just a long time, but a stopping or losing of time altogether; and a love out of time is possible only in the imagination. Even as he dwells on the pleasures toward which Emile is heading, the theorist of modesty is therefore strikingly reluctant to provide them. Emile is in love with Sophie, and "he hopes for, he expects a return that he feels is due him"; yet his present happiness, Rousseau announces, will never be surpassed.

He is as happy as a man can be. Shall I at this moment shorten a destiny so sweet? Shall I trouble a pleasure so pure? Ah, the whole value of life is in the felicity he tastes! . . . Even in crowning his happiness, I would destroy its greatest charm: this supreme happiness is a hundred times sweeter to hope for than to obtain; one enjoys it better when one anticipates it than when one tastes it. O good Emile, love and be loved! Enjoy a long time before possessing . . . I shall not shorten this happy time of your life. I shall spin out for you its enchantment; I shall prolong it as much as possible.[45]

One "tastes" felicity, it seems, in the imagination of tasting—and of the two sorts of experience implied, Rousseau has no doubt which is superior. As the tutor later suggests before extending the period of anticipation yet longer in travel, "the felicity of the senses" is as nothing to that which the "imagination" promises.[46] By covering up and holding back, the modest woman inspired men to just such imaginative pleasure—which suggests why Addison thought "the pleasantest Part of a Man's Life," as he famously remarked in the *Spectator,* "is generally that which passes in Courtship." Provided "his Passion be sincere, and the Party beloved kind with Discretion"—the *Spectator*'s idea of modesty, was, as always, rather less ardent than Rousseau's—"Love, Desire,

Hope, all the pleasing Motions of the Soul rise in the Pursuit."[47] This time of which Addison spoke so fondly—this interval of imagining that Emile's tutor would have liked to "spin out" and "prolong"—became the special province of the English novel. And in exploiting the temporal dimension of female modesty, in sensing the narrative possibilities implicit in all its paradoxes of anticipation and delay, the novelists would also show how this interval of courtship gave rise to "Motions of the Soul" in both sexes.

4

The Matter of Consciousness

❦

The modest woman resists now the better to accede later: so men imagine her to serve the ends of courtship. But the more intently they wish her to serve those ends, it often appears, the more they wish her not quite to know where she is going. For the man who woos her, the woman who says "no" while consciously aware that she intends to say "yes" is worse than a hypocrite: she is actively engaged in manipulation, a manipulation all the more dangerous for being concealed. Worse still, perhaps, she may consciously intend to behave immodestly with another. Under the cover of modesty, in other words, a woman who knows her own desires always threatens to take secret charge of the scene. But if women remain modestly unaware that they love until they are asked to marry, their desires will remain safely in the keeping of their husbands. Not until young gentlemen "declare themselves," as the idiom has it, will female consciousness—and sexuality—be awakened. Though critics like Wollstonecraft observed sharply that keeping women ignorant was just what rendered them vulnerable, most authorities on the subject preferred to believe that a modest young Englishwoman would "instinctively" shrink from danger. So quickly would her modest reflexes react, they seem to have imagined, that a conscious thought would have no time to form. Needless to say, such modest unconsciousness did not bear very close examination—especially by those who were at the same time busily engaged in advising it. Despite the protests of Wollstonecraft and others, however—and despite the automatic propensity for a rule against thought to get itself broken—the pattern young lady of the conduct books does tend to exhibit an increasing blankness of mind.

51

When Allestree announced that "every indecent curiosity, or impure fancy, is a deflowering of the mind," he simultaneously imagined the virgin's consciousness as inviolate as her body and argued that one kind of deflowering would lead by imperceptible stages to the other. Though to be violated by an idea was still to be a long way from a prostitute, a woman who had lost her mental virginity had nonetheless rendered herself vulnerable. "Between the state of pure immaculate Virginity and arrant Prostitution there are many intermedial steps," but "she that makes any of them, is so far departed from her first integrity" as to begin the descent into corruption: "she that listens to any wanton discourse, has violated her ears; she that speaks any, her tongue; every immodest glance vitiates her eye, and every the lightest act of dalliance leaves somthing of stain and sullage behind it." To think of virginity as a state of absolute purity, the passage suggests, is to imagine that even an idea can begin to defile it. "For as nothing is more clean and white then a perfect Virginity," in Allestree's words, "so every the least spot or soil is the more discernible." [1]

Yet at the same time that Allestree wished to keep the virgin mind as blank as possible, he seemed to recommend a method for doing so that would inevitably involve some active consciousness on the part of the young woman herself—even a measure of deliberate deception:

> The truth is, an affected ignorance cannot be so blamable in other cases as it is commendable in this. Indeed it is the surest and most invincible guard, for she who is curious to know indecent things, 'tis odds but she will too soon and too dearly buy the learning. The suppressing and detesting all such curiosities is therefore that eminent fundamental piece of continence I would recommend to them, as that which will protect and secure all the rest. [2]

Fifteen years later, the Marquis of Halifax still more pointedly encouraged a mere pretense of unconsciousness, urged the future wife confronted by her husband's sexual crimes not to "seem to look or hear that way," and repeated the formula that "an *affected Ignorance,* which is seldom a *Vertue,* is a great one here." [3] Compared with this rather blunt advice, Allestree's rhetoric already blurred the line between behavior and consciousness, as it hovered uncertainly between encouraging "an affected ignorance" and the real thing. Of course, Allestree was trying to prolong the innocence of virgins, while Halifax was cynically anticipating the experience of wives. Though *The Lady's New-Years Gift,* as Halifax's advice to his daughter was called, continued to be reprinted and plagiarized in the century that followed, most middle-class conduct books were not inclined to share its aristocratically cynical view of marriage—or to instruct women so openly in the need to dissemble. Halifax might advise his daughter to affect ignorance, but a century later Dr. Gregory insisted that with his daughters there could be no question of affectation. "You will be reproached perhaps with prudery," he informed them. But "by prudery is usually meant an affectation of delicacy. Now I do not wish you to affect delicacy; I wish you to possess it." How they were to go about acquiring this wished-for possession he did not say. Though Gregory explicitly trusted to his daughters' "conscious virtue" to repel improper words and advances, he was reluctant to imagine such virtue as conscious of very much. If "virgin purity," as he solemnly informed them, "is of that delicate nature, that it cannot hear certain things without contamination," then he obviously could not name those "certain things" without immediately violating his definition of delicacy.[4]

Gregory's allusion to prudery recalls the familiar triad of the prude, the coquette, and the modest woman. But when it came to improper consciousness, many authorities agreed, the opposition of the prude and the coquette collapsed into an identity. As Steele had succinctly formulated the paradox at the beginning of the century, "the *Prude* and *Coquet* (as different as they appear in their Behaviour) are in Reality the same Kind of Women: The Motive of Action in both is the Affectation of pleasing Men. . . . each of them has the Distinction of Sex in all her Thoughts, Words and Actions."[5] In this particular contribution to the *Tatler,* Steele was more concerned with mocking the prude than with worrying about how to remove "the Distinction of Sex" from the thoughts of the modest woman. But by implying that the true measure of a woman's virtue lay in psychological "Reality" rather than "Behaviour," he indirectly called attention to a dilemma that would continue to trouble the literature of modesty. And it is not surprising that those who wished to imagine a woman "really" modest in this sense would increasingly figure her virtue as something closer to a natural instinct than a conscious thought, an automatic reaction so swift and sure that deliberation of any kind would not be necessary. Thus when Addison defined modesty in the *Spectator* a few years later as "a kind of quick and delicate *feeling* in the Soul, which makes her shrink and withdraw her self from every thing that has Danger in it . . . such an exquisite Sensibility, as warns her to shun the first appearance of every thing which is hurtful," he provided subsequent authorities with one of their favorite accounts of the virtue.[6] Addison's shrinking female was a personified "Soul," and not necessarily the soul of a woman—the essay had begun by considering the "Oppressions of Modesty" in a male public speaker—

but no sooner had he conjured with this essentially feminine and inte-
riorized image than a digression on "the Strength of Female Modesty"
immediately followed. The image suggests that modesty operates as
a kind of instinctive early warning system, producing reflexes more
"quick" and "delicate" than thought; and for most of those who later
chose to adopt it, "such an exquisite Sensibility" was both natural and
naturally female.

Judging by the conduct books, at least, these unconscious instincts
would appear to have been especially well developed in women toward
the close of the century and the beginning of the next. We might recall
again the scene of proper conversation in Bennett's *Letters to a Young
Lady* of 1789, and the way in which the vibrations of "*native* feeling" in
the modest Louisa automatically forestall the slightest sound of a *double
entendre*. Note that true delicacy for Bennett is not only a question of
feeling rather than of thought but of feeling that prevents thought:
trembling like a "sensitive plant" at the most distant allusion that could
"stain" the delicacy of the mind, it preserves that mind unspotted—or
would do so, were such a distant allusion ever threatening to be uttered.
So effectively does Louisa's delicacy tremble that she herself will have no
occasion to, since "the most licentious man living" would never dare to
say anything licentious in her company. "A girl should *hear*, she should
see, nothing that can call forth a blush, or even stain the *purity* of her
mind," Bennett insists; and by proleptically censoring even the most
distant hint of impropriety, Louisa's delicacy clears the room for her
presence. Assured that she will neither hear nor see what she should
not, the model young Englishwoman can be "easy and accessible to the
other sex," her conversation, "cheerful, lively and *unconstrained*." [7]

Though Bennett believes that modest vibrations have their effect
even on the most licentious, how they communicate themselves remains
something of a mystery, especially since they seem to operate at so high
a frequency that no vibration is detectable. In a subsequent letter that
returns to the trope of the sensitive plant, he is at pains to distinguish
this "refinement of *modesty*" that "trembles" at "bare *apprehension*" from
the overt gestures of the "*tremblingly* modest female"—the type who
elaborately apologizes and withdraws herself when she hears that some
gentlemen are coming to tea. While true modesty cheerfully socializes,
false modesty rushes from the room. And while Louisa "is the most remote from *prudery,* of any woman I know," the rapid retreat of the
trembling type automatically proves her the opposite: "*her* delicacy" is
"absolute *prudery and affectation*." It is also, Bennett has little doubt, a
mere cover-up: "if it had been possible to look into her heart, probably,

at the very moment, it was thrilling with joy, for the agreeable information," he confidently speculates. In fact, "we always *suspect* these prudes. We fancy, that their modesty diminishes in private, in proportion, as it appears to dilate and to magnify itself, before the publick inspection."[8] Suspicion "always" follows the retiring prude, and the logic of suspicion is inexorable: by trembling and rushing away, she reveals a heightened consciousness of sexual danger; her consciousness betrays interest; and her interest, her hypocrisy. The more obviously she shrinks from the encounter, the more she will betray her secret forwardness—and the more thoroughly she will condemn herself as hypocritical.

Such are the traps of "false" modesty, from whose relentless circles "true" modesty is imagined to escape. Thus true and false modesty often make their appearance together, and writers can scarcely endorse the virtue of the one without repudiating the affectation of the other. The same foregone conclusion governs the representation of both: a woman might rush away from some gentleman visitors for many reasons, but if "we" are intently focused on the management of desire, "we" will always suspect that she has nothing but sex on her mind. Even as Bennett immediately goes on to explain how true delicacy is compatible with "all the sweets of an intercourse betwixt the sexes,"[9] so those who imagine the modest woman almost always imagine her to serve sexual ends; and what she does not think—or does not think yet—is never very far from their consciousness. By the same law of reversal which is thought to govern the prude's own interested denials, in other words, the figure of the hyperconscious woman keeps breaking into representations of the unconscious one; and it is always easier to turn about and unmask hypocrisy than to try to examine the mental state of the modest woman too closely.

In a brief allegory published by the *Lady's Monthly Museum* for 1798, Modesty's affected double appeared as "Bashfulness" rather than a prude, but she appeared to similar purpose. While Modesty, of course, was born of Truth, Bashfulness is the child of Falsehood—from whom she presumably inherits her youthful talent for simulation: "till they arrived at a state of adolescence," the allegorist tells us, she "was the constant copier of her lovely friend," apparently able to mimic both Modesty's tears and her blushes. But at adolescence, significantly, a difference of knowing and not-knowing sharply divides them: "the sober, mild, yet unsuspicious look of innocent Modesty was powerfully contrasted by the shy, yet artful, and pretendedly retiring glance of Bashfulness, who, willing to suppose evil, where no ill was intended, betrayed an unbecoming knowledge of what it is the glory of a delicate female to be

unconscious." The adventure concludes when Bashfulness weakly succumbs to a stolen kiss that Modesty successfully resists; but lest this
seem one case in which virtue is not plotted to amorous ends, we should
note that Bashfulness learns a lesson "of the utmost importance" when
she is punished for her compliance by "the most pointed neglect" of the
aggressor![10]

Affected ignorance, it seems, is no match for the real thing, even in
an artist like Bashfulness. While for Allestree and Halifax, the pretense
of not knowing might almost be virtue enough, by the beginning of the
nineteenth century writers increasingly tended to locate modesty in the
mind, and to insist, like the allegorist of the *Lady's Monthly Museum,*
that it was "the glory of a delicate female to be unconscious" of all "unbecoming knowledge." In *Olivia's Letter of Advice to Her Daughter,* a
brief compendium of received wisdom published in 1808, Mrs. Wilmot
Serres routinely passed on the following definition: "Modesty [i]s the
companion of Virtue, it always resides in a mind naturally Pure, it prevents us from observing indelicate occurrences, it will not permit us to
listen to improper conversation."[11] And when Cobbett set out in 1829
to describe the sort of "perfect modesty" his young men should seek
in a wife, he represented a woman so unconscious as to be virtually
insensible:

Chastity, perfect modesty, in word, deed, and even thought, is so essential, that,
without it, no female is fit to be a wife. It is not enough that a young female
abstain from everything approaching towards indecorum in her behaviour towards men; it is, with me, not enough that she cast down her eyes, or turn aside
her head with a smile, when she hears an indelicate allusion: she ought to appear *not to understand* it, and to receive from it no more impression than if she
were a post.

"If *prudery* mean *false* modesty, it is to be despised," he quickly added;
"but if it mean modesty pushed to the utmost extent, I confess that I
like it."[12] Using the same routine as the other writers, Cobbett no
sooner describes his ideal of modest unconsciousness than he dismisses
the virtue's despised twin, "*false* modesty," as if to conjure away the
threat of affectation and hypocrisy. Since he has himself stipulated only
that his virtuous young woman "appear" not to understand an indelicate allusion—sounding for the moment oddly like Halifax—he perhaps has particular need of this ritual exorcism.

Even in the mid-nineteenth century, most commentators were not
about to follow Cobbett's lead and confess that they "liked" something
called "prudery." But his attempt to rehabilitate the term is nonetheless

a sign of the times—and striking evidence of the extent to which he was ready to push his ideal of the virtue. And so too is his unfortunate image of woman-as-post, a figure of such "perfect modesty" that she appears to have no feeling at all. Indeed, the idea that good women simply had no sexual feelings may well have been the final consequence of the culture's effort to assure itself that female modesty was genuine, as the woman who knew nothing of desire blurred imperceptibly into the woman who had no desire to know. If women were essentially without erotic passion, after all, then there could be no danger that their modesty was false, their restraint affected and hypocritical.[13] Of course Cobbett did not really want a wife as wooden and dead as his figure of the post would suggest, anymore than he "liked" the prude as most people imagined her.[14] Like most writers on modesty, he was attempting to manage desire, not to abolish it. This is, after all, the same letter of "Advice to a Lover" in which he would assure his readers that the more sober a woman's conduct, the more "*warmth*" she promised—and back up his claim with the declaration that he was himself the sort of man to say "give me the *warmth,* and I will stand my chance as to the rest."[15] But what he did want, clearly, was to make sure that all that warmth was thoroughly insulated and channeled in one direction. Marriage, he repeated insistently, is "to *last for life* . . . and it must, therefore, be perfect, or it had better not be at all."[16] And if this vision of perfection required him to imagine a young woman who would scarcely betray a sign of consciousness beforehand, he was apparently willing to risk it.

Because he addressed his advice to young men rather than the women they would court, Cobbett may have testified to the interests of his own sex more openly than most. But in his double insistence on female ardor and on a modesty so absolute that it verged on insensibility, he only exaggerated a tension that made itself felt whenever the issue of the modest consciousness was in question. For the young woman's unknowing, one might say, was always engaged in undoing itself—even, or especially, when she was being advised as to her own "instinctive" modesty. Though the conduct literature for women never acknowledged the problem directly, the very act of instructing an innocent consciousness would necessarily tend to undermine it. That-which-was-not-to-be-thought might only appear under the cover of a modest negative like the "indelicate" or the "improper," but to allude to the danger of an "indelicate allusion" is already to bring it one step closer. Writing in 1842, one of the most prolific and influential of early Victorian authorities on female conduct took for granted that the difference between true and false modesty was a state of consciousness—and routinely praised what amounted to mental incapacity. "Allusion has already been made," Sarah Ellis rather sternly announced in *The Daughters of England,* "to that affectation of modesty which consists in simpering and blushing about what a truly delicate mind would neither have perceived nor understood, nor would have been in the slightest degree amused by if it had."[17] Failing even to perceive, much less to understand or be amused, the "truly delicate mind" could only be an unconscious one. Yet Ellis has no sooner evoked this ideal than she compromises it, as her progressively weakening negatives convey instead a brief narrative of perception and comprehension. Seeking to define the modest consciousness, the sentence effectively tells a story—and if this story stops short of amusement, it nonetheless closes with a mind which has perceived and understood all too well.

ॐ

Not every commentator on female modesty was tempted to find any "glory" in a state of unconsciousness. While writers of both sexes routinely extolled the "delicate female" for instinctively shrinking from harm, some women sharply protested this representation of their virtue. Indeed, a virtue requiring no exertion, no struggle of or with the self, seemed to them hardly worthy of the name. Why should praise attach to a restraint exercised helplessly—and what sort of protection could an ignorant "delicacy" really afford? As Mary Wollstonecraft exclaimed sharply, "Ignorance is a frail base for virtue!"[18] And by articulating this protest at length in her *Vindication of the Rights of Woman,* she undoubtedly gave the argument for the active consciousness its fullest and most influential form. But well before the appearance of *The Rights of Woman* in 1792, other, anonymous voices anticipated its call to a rational and deliberate exercise of mind.

Writing to the *Lady's Magazine; or, Polite Companion for the Fair Sex* in 1759, a correspondent who signed herself "Elenora" sought to distinguish between two types of female virtue—an instinctive response that she identified with "modesty," and the conscious exercise of will for which she reserved the name of "chastity." While modesty depends on "a bashful awe and natural coldness in the constitution," in Elenora's words, chastity is "a noble virtue in our sex, founded on reason and religion, and having its existence in the mind." And precisely because modesty is merely an instinctive and automatic response, it is the "inferior kind" of virtue. Women should be grateful for this "gift of nature," Elenora argues, but only chastity deserves our pride—"for it is our own work, the effect of reason; strengthened by piety." And only this "rational reserve" promises to keep us from danger, for the ignorance of modesty proves all too easy to deceive:

Clelia was modest, but the cunning of her lover conquered: Antonia was chaste, and will be so for ever. A natural reserve may be wearied out with importunities; but that which is the effect of reason and religion never can. When Clelia's lover on the road to Scotland told her they might now look upon themselves as married, she trembled; but believed him: had a thousand such attempts been made upon her sister they would have failed; for hers was rational reserve, founded on the example and the precepts of her parents, and strengthened by religion.[19]

Six years after the Clandestine Marriage Act outlawed marriages made without parental consent—and thereby drove those who sought secrecy across the border into Scotland—Elenora's fable puts trembling modesty on the road to Gretna Green and seduction.[20] While her chaste sister "would have known . . . that to evade the laws . . . is to the full as criminal as it is to break them," and that "from the person who could advise her to it" she had "every thing to fear," Clelia's merely instinctive virtue entails neither the knowledge nor the power of reasoning necessary to save her.[21]

After the story of the unfortunate Clelia, shrinking modesty also appears in the familiar guise of the sensitive plant—but when Elenora draws on the image, she primarily notices how such plants are vulnerable to destruction:

The true way to escape danger is to avoid the first attacks; modesty shrinks from these with terror; but superior chastity rejects them with disdain: the first withdraws from the rude touch like the sensitive plant, which the next effort crushes: the latter armed with virtue and with truth, deters the boldest from repeated trials.

    . . . Let us thank nature which has made us modest; but to improve that frail good to a lasting virtue, let us use all our efforts to establish on it the everlasting bulwark and defence of chastity.[22]

Juxtaposing one conventional trope for female virtue with another, the passage implicitly registers their contradiction, as the shrinking plant is swiftly crushed amidst the battle for her honor. Though modesty usually figures as the "guard" of chastity in that battle, in Elenora's version of the allegory it offers far too frail a defense; while chastity, having been redefined to include conscious knowledge, thereby proves strong enough to supply its own protection. Indeed, simply by taking seriously

the familiar metaphor of a war between the sexes, she manages to remind her readers how much a struggle for power is in question—and
how little an instinctive delicacy will avail them.

Published the year after Elenora's letter, *The Polite Lady* advanced a
similar argument. If the title of this work suggests some of the assumptions it shared with other conduct books in the period, its subtitle—*A
Course of Female Education. In a Series of Letters, from a Mother to a
Daughter*—already implies that the charms of womanly ignorance were
not among them. Its fictive mother, Portia, does not make Elenora's attempt to redefine the female virtues, and modesty stands in something
more like the usual relation to chastity in this work. But when Portia
advises her daughter that "if you would wish to have a modest look, you
must endeavour to have a modest mind," she intends to cultivate a
rational and conscious reserve, not an instinctive shrinking and trembling. The latter she contemptuously dismisses as "sheepishness," associating it with "a kind of false modesty" that she firmly distinguishes
from the real thing.

A modest person will not talk too much or too high in company, because she
knows it is improper: a sheepish person will hardly talk any at all, or at least not
so as to be understood, because she is afraid. A modest lady looks with a decent
assurance: a sheepish lady looks abashed, and blushes at she don't know what. A
modest person will never contradict the general taste of the company, unless it
be inconsistent with decency and good-manners: a sheepish person will hardly
contradict it, even when it is: the one acts from principle, the other from mere
instinct: the one is guided by the rules of right reason, and therefore is consistent in her conduct; the other is guided by no rules at all, and consequently has
no uniformity of character.

This sheepishness naturally leads to, and commonly ends in, a kind of false
modesty, which is such an extreme degree of complaisance, such a yielding softness of nature, as is not able to refuse any thing.

The distinction is very like that between the two sisters in Elenora's ex-
emplum, and a sheepish woman who was "not able to refuse any thing"
would surely fare no better than Clelia on the road to Scotland. All
feminine yielding potentially leads to the same end: "from an excess of
modesty," in Portia's phrase, such a woman "perhaps might be tempted
to violate the laws of modesty itself."[23]

"But, my Dear, this is not modesty; it is weakness," she hastens to
correct herself. "Modesty does not consist in following the fashion, but
in following reason," and "true modesty . . . is meant to be the pre-
server, not the betrayer of your virtue."[24] The author of *The Polite Lady*
would rather trust to firm distinctions than to coy paradoxes, even as

she would rather trust the woman who decisively repels advances to the one who flirtatiously retreats. Because she intends her work as "a Course of Female Education," she can straightforwardly "advise" modesty, can write that a young woman "must endeavour to have a modest mind," without immediately entangling herself in contradiction, for the rational virtues she wishes to inculcate require both instruction and struggle. And because she intends to encourage an active and conscious virtue rather than an unconsciously shrinking one, she can draw her distinctions between true modesty and "sheepishness" from a paper in the *Spectator* that addressed not the courtship of daughters but "the ill Effects of a vicious Modesty" in a certain "modest young Gentleman." The young woman who guided herself by *The Polite Lady*'s "rules of right reason," in other words, would be following the same definition of "true Modesty" that Addison had applied in the case of men.[25] When Portia explains how true modesty silences all improper talk, she characteristically writes not of unconscious vibrations but of "such a dignity and majesty . . . as never fails to command respect . . . confounds and abashes even the most profligate, and makes them either ashamed or afraid of giving vent to their low and obscene ribaldry." Such a truly modest woman subdues others as well as herself: "commanding" respect, inducing shame and even fear in the enemy, her virtue is at once an act of will, and, implicitly, at least, a claim to power. The "sheepish" young woman who "will hardly talk any at all . . . because she is afraid," on the other hand, sounds—or rather doesn't sound—all too much like the model young woman according to Dr. Gregory. Portia's modest daughter should not talk "too much or too high," but she herself should clearly speak, while Gregory will soon be informing his daughters that "this modesty, which I think so essential in your sex, will naturally dispose you to be rather silent in company."[26]

What *The Polite Lady* suggested obliquely, Mary Wollstonecraft argued boldly. *A Vindication of the Rights of Woman* presented itself not as a conduct book but as a critical commentary on such books, an effort to counter their celebration of instinctive feminine delicacy with an ideal of a more conscious and energetic virtue. Taking Rousseau, Fordyce, and Gregory as her principal targets, Wollstonecraft's "Animadversions on Some of the Writers Who Have Rendered Women Objects of Pity, Bordering on Contempt," also took them as representative: most of those who had written on female manners, she contended, had written to a similar effect. Yet if Wollstonecraft angrily disputed the conventional account of female modesty, she did so in modesty's name: her chapter on "Modesty.—Comprehensively Considered, and Not as a

Sexual Virtue" sought not to minimize the importance of the idea but to appropriate it for purposes of her own. Beginning with an apostrophe to "Modesty! Sacred offspring of sensibility and reason!—true delicacy of mind!" the chapter simultaneously defined and paid lavish tribute to such "true delicacy," while it contemptuously dismissed "Rousseau's and Dr. Gregory's advice respecting modesty, strangely miscalled!" as a mere "refinement on lust."[27] Like the writers she attacked, in other words, Wollstonecraft set out to discriminate true from false modesty in order to nurture the true—and in this connection, at least, her radical work belonged very much to the culture it criticized.

While Rousseau had dreamed of a woman "beautiful, innocent, and silly," as Wollstonecraft scornfully put it, she wished to argue that only the exercise of reason could make women genuinely virtuous. "It is a farce to call any being virtuous," an early chapter impatiently exclaims, "whose virtues do not result from the exercise of its own reason." Rather than deny that young women shrink from men instinctively, she chose to argue that blushing coyness was—and should be—a transitory phenomenon. "The downcast eye, the rosy blush, the retiring grace, are all proper in their season; but modesty, being the child of reason, cannot long exist with the sensibility that is not tempered by reflection." True "purity of mind," she declares, "is something nobler than innocence," and "so far from being incompatible with knowledge, it is its fairest fruit." Those women who have "most improved their reason," Wollstonecraft characteristically argues, "must have the most modesty." Though her book has often been read as a treatise on women's education, it has less to say about the specific knowledge they should acquire than about their continual need for such "improvement," "exercise," "effort," and "struggle." For Wollstonecraft ultimately rests her defense of women's equality on their "improvable" souls—and souls can only be improved, as she understands it, by a strenuous resistance to nature and bodies.[28] Against what she reads as Rousseau's regressive yearnings—his belief "that all *was* right originally"—she holds out the realization of a future ideal—"that all *will* be right" when women actively engage in exercising their powers. "The end, the grand end of their exertions," *The Rights of Woman* announces early in its argument, "should be to unfold their own faculties and acquire the dignity of conscious virtue."[29] And such an "end," the work as a whole makes clear, can only be imagined well beyond the plot of courtship and marriage.

Indeed, it is precisely because Wollstonecraft read the teleology of the conduct books so clearly that she resisted them so energetically. The representation of love as the end of women's lives, she believed, necessarily degraded them. "Love, considered as an animal appetite, cannot long feed on itself without expiring," *The Rights of Woman* asserts, and "as an animal appetite" the work will continue to consider it. Why raise a Sophie "only . . . to make her the mistress of her husband, a very short time?" Wollstonecraft demands, especially since "no man ever insisted more on the transient nature of love" than Rousseau himself—and she goes on to quote against him one of the passages from *Emile* that privilege the pleasures of the imagination over the satisfactions of fulfillment. Though Rousseau would prefer, therefore, to prolong the time of courtship, Wollstonecraft's own imagination focuses too firmly on the death of love—and of the body that inspires it—to console herself with a delaying action. "Youth is the season for love in both sexes," she acknowledges; but "love," she relentlessly reminds her readers, "from its very nature, must be transitory," and "friendship or indifference inevitably succeeds" it. Where other writers had chosen to blur love and friendship in the promise of marriage, Wollstonecraft insists on sharply distinguishing them. "Friendship is a serious affection . . . because it is founded on principle, and cemented by time. The very reverse may be said of love. In a great degree, love and friendship cannot subsist in the same bosom." She even ventures to suggest that "when two virtuous young people marry, it would, perhaps, be happy if some circumstances checked their passion" and thus inspired them to "look beyond the present moment, and try to render the whole of life respectable."[30] Wollstonecraft's hypothetical marriage plot should make clear by contrast how much the typical fiction of modesty evades the Christian sense of an ending.

"For what purpose were the passions implanted?" *The Rights of Woman* inquires in an opening catechism. "That man by struggling with them might attain a degree of knowledge denied to the brutes; whispers Experience."[31] The desires of the flesh exist to be overcome, or at least to be left behind rather hastily—and the woman who has "most improved her reason" is the one who knows best that the body is vulnerable and cannot be trusted. As both Mary Poovey and Cora Kaplan have demonstrated, *A Vindication of the Rights of Woman* may also be read as a defense against desire—a defense partly motivated by the author's fear lest her own strong passions leave her vulnerable to loss and betrayal. Though Wollstonecraft intended to write a sequel that would address the issue of women's legal oppression, the work that she did write focuses intensely, obsessively, on the dangers of feeling.[32] Taking for granted that the virtue of knowledge is to oppose the degradation of the body, she produces a book that can seem almost prudishly attentive to the body and its appetites.

The chapter on modesty, for example, seems to go out of its way to castigate the "nasty, or immodest habits" that girls acquire by mixing "indiscriminately" together in nurseries and boarding schools, the excessive familiarity that supposedly characterizes most women's relations with one another and leads to "that gross degree of familiarity that so frequently renders the marriage state unhappy." Though Wollstonecraft attributes these "nasty" habits to the fact that girls sleep in the same room or wash together at school, her account communicates nothing very clearly except the sense of her own disgust; while the diatribe ends by alluding mysteriously to "some still more nasty customs" that are common to the sex, customs she nonetheless hesitates to name. And though she repeatedly identifies true modesty with "purity" or "cleanliness" of mind, the idea remains almost as devoid of content as the mental vacancy she denounces: she never really explains how "purity of mind" differs from the mere blankness of innocence, nor how such a state of mind maintains itself without being hypocritically alert to every sign of the "impure" and the "dirty." "This desire of being always women," she argues, "is the very consciousness that degrades the sex," but the intensity with which she recoils from that desire means that her own text is everywhere suffused with the consciousness of what it would deny.[33]

For all the anxiety and conflict that the record of her own consciousness betrays, Wollstonecraft felt the vulnerability of her sex too sharply ever to suggest that any woman should prefer innocence to knowledge. She was among those writers on the woman question most keenly aware of the costs exacted by so many conventional differences between the sexes; and no one could be more alert to the dangers of courtship arrangements in which consciousness was male only, while women were possessed of a doll-like stupidity. Nonetheless, as we shall see, the rather more secular life histories envisioned by novelists—including women novelists—depended upon subtle transitions from unconscious to conscious attachments.

5

Modest Blushing

ꙮ

Even those who did entertain the dream of female innocence could not entertain it very long or consistently. The "true delicacy" of Bennett's Louisa might tremble at "the bare *apprehension*" of anything that could injure her, but if apprehension was not quite comprehension, the distinction was nonetheless not a very stable one. Though Bennett could sweepingly announce that "a girl should *hear*, she should *see*, nothing, that can call forth a blush, or even stain the *purity* of her mind," he could also assure his young lady that as long as hers was "the blush of *delicacy* and *reserve*," he would find "the crimson tint" on her cheek "ornamental."[1] Indeed, nothing sums up more vividly the culture's active worrying of the relations among the modest young woman's virtue, her sexuality, and her consciousness than the collective fascination with the sudden flow of blood to her cheek. While Bennett singled out "the blush of *delicacy*," others alluded to the "blush of modesty" or "the innocent blush," but there was scarcely a tribute to the modest woman that did not mention blushing, or that failed to identify both her virtue and her attractiveness with a certain transient coloring of her face.

When Richard Polwhele wished to caricature Wollstonecraft in his antifeminist verse polemic of 1798, *The Unsex'd Females*, he could imagine no more pointed way of doing so than to represent her—falsely—as an avowed opponent of blushing:

> See Wollstonecraft, whom no decorum checks,
> Arise, the intrepid champion of her sex;
> O'er humbled man assert the sovereign claim,
> And slight the timid blush of virgin fame.

"That Miss Wollstonecraft was a sworn enemy to blushes, I need not remark," he coolly added in a note to these lines. "But many of my readers, perhaps, will be astonished to hear, that at several of our boarding-schools for young ladies, a blush incurs a penalty." [2] There would seem no reason to think Polwhele more reliable as an historian of contemporary educational practices than as a reader of Wollstonecraft: that *The Rights of Woman* itself solemnly contrasted "the harlot's *rouge*" with "that celestial suffusion which only virtuous affections can give to the face" [3] was not the sort of evidence he was prepared to recognize, any more than he appears to have noted that Wollstonecraft ironically anticipated his view of female boarding schools as the breeding grounds of immodesty. Nevertheless, it is understandable that he should choose to represent *The Rights of Woman* as an attack upon blushing, for the young woman's blush had become the most familiar token of that seductive innocence Wollstonecraft deeply mistrusted. Polwhele saw himself as championing the "modest Virtue" of Hannah More against the "Gallic frenzy" of Wollstonecraft and her followers; and in the context of the political, sexual and literary battle he was fighting, "blushes of modest apprehension" testified above all to a desirable "diffidence" and "fearfulness" in the opposite sex, a diffidence that one note to the poem brazenly associates with their "consciousness of comparative imbecillity [sic]." "Yet, alas!" the same note concludes, "the crimsoning blush of modesty, will be always more attractive than the sparkle of confident intelligence." [4] Polwhele was writing vicious polemic, not advice on courtship, and few tributes to the blush were quite as shameless as his. But he was hardly alone in understanding the blush as a sign of submission, or in opposing it to more aggressive forms of mental activity. "It is not necessary to speak to display mental charms," the preface to *The Female Reader* typically advised young women in 1789: "the eye will quickly inform us if an active soul resides within; and a blush is far more eloquent than the best turned period." The *Reader*'s collection of miscellaneous pieces was issued pseudonymously, but the evidence strongly suggests that this recommendation that women blush rather than speak came from the pen of Mary Wollstonecraft. [5]

Whether or not Wollstonecraft consciously intended her "eloquent" blush to recall the celebrated lines from Donne's "Second Anniversary" ("her pure and eloquent blood / Spoke in her cheeks, and so distinctly wrought, / That one might almost say, her body thought"), the frequency with which those lines recur in the eighteenth and nineteenth centuries can make it seem as if Elizabeth Drury's articulate blood flowed in the veins of every model Englishwoman. Fielding's Sophia Western inherited it, for example, as did the heroine of *Coelebs in Search of a Wife*[6]—and so did a piously idealized Jane Austen in the "Bio-graphical Notice" affixed by her brother to the posthumous edition of *Northanger Abbey* and *Persuasion* in 1818: "It might with truth be said," Henry Austen wrote, "that her eloquent blood spoke through her modest cheek."[7] As Christopher Ricks has noted, Donne's lines do not in fact refer explicitly to blushing.[8] Blood rushes to the human face for many reasons—excitement or anger, for example, as well as shame or embarrassment—and merely to know that someone is blushing is scarcely to know what signals she is sending. But even as the conventional advice literature tended to reduce all possible directions for a good woman's life to a single plot of courtship and marriage, so it sought to imagine all possible suffusions in her face as forms of blushing, and all blushes, even, as testifying to her modesty and "innocence." "Who is she that winneth the heart of man to love?" the *New Lady's Magazine* inquired formulaically in 1791, only to answer in the same biblical cadences: "Lo! yonder she walketh in maiden sweetness; innocence in her mind, modesty on her cheek."[9] Elizabeth Drury's "pure and eloquent blood" simply "spoke in her cheeks," but when Henry Austen adopted the praise for another dead woman two centuries later, he typically remembered her cheeks as "modest."

No doubt a more or less tacit awareness of how equivocally the blood could speak lay behind so much insistence on a blush at once modest and innocent. Early in the century the *Spectator* had in fact argued quite explicitly that a woman's blushes were not a very reliable guide to her virtue, since she might well keep her sense of shame long after she had parted with her innocence. Steele offered in evidence the rosy cheeks of a certain Orbicilla—"the kindest poor thing in the Town, but the most blushing Creature living"—to argue, in effect, that true modesty would have had no cause to blush. "Modesty," in Steele's words, "consists in being conscious of no Ill, and not in being ashamed of having done it," while blushing he termed "that ambiguous Suffusion which is the Livery both of Guilt and Innocence." Though Steele's example illustrates only one of the ways in which a "Suffusion" in the cheeks can signal ambiguously, it raises a doubt that must have been particularly troubling to masculine lovers of a woman's blushes; and after carefully omitting the example of Orbicilla, at least one mid-century *Letter of Genteel and Moral Advice to a Young Lady* incorporated the passage into its instructions on modest behavior—as if to warn the reader that she had better demonstrate her virtue by more trustworthy signs.[10] But most authorities on female conduct, especially in the latter half of the century, seem to have found the young woman's blush irresistible.

"When a girl ceases to blush," Dr. Gregory informed his daughters, "she has lost the most powerful charm of beauty. That extreme sensibility which it indicates, may be a weakness and incumbrance in our sex, as I have too often felt," he acknowledged; "but in yours it is peculiarly engaging." So engaging did he apparently find this mark of vulnerability in the other sex that he gave it first place in his chapter on "Conduct and Behavior." Though blushes as he understood them hardly qualified as the sort of "conduct" even the most dutiful daughter could be taught to emulate, Gregory was more concerned with reassuring himself about the state of consciousness they reflected:

Pedants, who think themselves philosophers, ask why a woman should blush when she is conscious of no crime. It is a sufficient answer, that Nature has made you to blush when you are guilty of no fault, and has forced us to love you because you do so.—Blushing is so far from being necessarily an attendant on guilt, that it is the usual companion of innocence.[11]

As usual, Gregory appears to have spoken for many others—and not only those who plagiarized him directly.[12] In *Almeria: or, Parental Advice,* a didactic poem that Mrs. Cutts addressed "to the Daughters of Great Britain and Ireland" the year after *A Father's Legacy,* Almeria's father reminisced about the "blushing Modesty" with which her mother, Honoria, responded to his proposal of marriage:

> I spake my honest aim;
> And saw, howe'er decry'd, that virtuous Shame,
> When Purity, not Guilt, first took th'alarm,
> Glow'd on the cheek, and heighten'd ev'ry charm.[13]

Like Dr. Gregory, Almeria's father apparently knew the color of purity when he saw it; and no more than Gregory did he wish to distinguish between the moral and cosmetic attractions of the phenomenon.

Whether the glow of guilt on her cheeks would have heightened a young woman's charms just as effectively was not a question most authorities on female virtue had any intention of pursuing. When the first number of the *New Lady's Magazine* in 1786 informed its readers that "shamefacedness carries the very colour of virtue, and that blush which spreads itself over her face, is a mark of her abhorrence of vice," the magazine effectively chose to ignore the possibility of an Orbicilla.

A woman's "shamefacedness," by its account, could virtually be taken as proof that she had never done anything of which she might be ashamed. "Shamefacedness," the magazine continued, "is an innocent paint; women never seem more beautiful than when they are somewhat shame-faced; and there is no countenance, how taking soever, which receiveth not fresh lustre from an innocent blush."[14] So commonplace did such innocent blushes become in the conduct literature of the period that only the repeated need to specify their "innocence" acknowledged that not every crimson cheek testified similarly. "The vestal purity of heart / That glowing blush bespeaks," according to an anonymous poem on "The Blush of Innocence" that appeared in another magazine in 1816; while in 1824 *The New Female Instructor* was still paying fascinated tribute to the phenomenon in terms very much like Gregory's:

There cannot be a more captivating or interesting object than a young girl, who, with *timid modesty,* enters a room filled with a mixed company. The blush, which diffuses its crimson on her cheek, is not only the most powerful charm of beauty, but does honour to the innocence of her heart, and has a peculiar claim on the tender and generous feeling of every susceptible mind.[15]

In this representative account of the young girl's entrance into the world, an innocent blush predictably plays before a room filled with mixed company—and both the innocence and the beauty of that blush immediately exert a "peculiar claim" on the emotions of the "susceptible" observer. Whether or not Nature had "forced" men to love a blushing young woman, as Gregory contended, representations of the innocent blush are always thus promising to take on the colorations of a love story.

If Donne provided subsequent writers with the language of the "eloquent" blood, Milton supplied them with a type of the blush at once amorous and "innocent." *Paradise Lost* represents the cheek of the first woman as testifying variously to the state of her consciousness, but only on the threshold of the nuptial bower, significantly, does it describe her blushing. "No thought infirm / Alter'd her cheek," the poet tells us, when the naked Eve first welcomes her angelic visitor, Raphael; and "in her Cheek distemper flushing glow'd" when she later reports to Adam that she has eaten the forbidden fruit. If the flush of "distemper" in the latter line reflects both bad digestion and bad conscience, the unblushing cheek in the former merely reminds us that before the fall the naked hostess had no thought of shame. Though Milton imagines her anticipation of unfallen sexuality as "pure of sinful thought," however, he does not imagine it as free of blushing. A model of "Innocence and Vir-

gin Modesty," Eve follows Adam to their nuptial bower "blushing like
the Morn"—and something like her anticipatory blushes continued to
glow in the cheeks of the conduct-book woman as she hovered on the
threshold of marriage. When Dr. Gregory assured his daughters that
"nature has made you to blush when you are guilty of no fault," he may
have been recalling Adam's account of the blushing Eve: "Nature herself, though pure of sinful thought, / Wrought in her so, that seeing me,
she turn'd."[16] Yet after the fall, as Gregory's hasty dismissal of the question tacitly registered, it was a little more difficult to specify exactly how
and how far a blush was "innocent."

Why *should* a young woman blush when she is "conscious of no
crime"? Gregory's nervous hit at the "pedants, who think themselves
philosophers" was probably aimed at Mandeville, who had begun his
analysis of blushing in *The Fable of the Bees* by taking for granted that
consciousness of some sort—even in "innocent Virgins"—was inescap-
able. "The most Virtuous Young Woman alive," he insisted, "will often,
in spite of her Teeth, have Thoughts and confus'd Ideas of Things arise
in her Imagination, which she would not reveal to some People for a
Thousand Worlds." While Gregory rhetorically confounded the virgin's
inexperience with her lack of knowledge, and then attributed her mysterious unconsciousness to "nature," Mandeville significantly asked
why she should blush when she was "guilty" of no crime, and sought
his answer in the inevitable conflict between her thoughts and the modesty imposed by "Custom and Education":

Then, I say, that when obscene Words are spoken in the presence of an unex-
perienced Virgin, she is afraid that some Body will reckon her to understand
what they mean, and consequently that she understands this and that and several things, which she desires to be thought ignorant of. The reflecting on this,
and that Thoughts are forming to her Disadvantage, brings upon her that Passion which we call Shame; and whatever can fling her, tho' never so remote
from Lewdness, upon that Set of Thoughts I hinted, and which she thinks
Criminal, will have the same Effect, especially before Men, as long as her Modesty lasts.

"To try the Truth of this," he immediately suggested, "let them talk as
much Bawdy as they please in the Room next to the same Virtuous
Young Woman, where she is sure that she is undiscover'd, and she will
hear, if not hearken to it, without blushing at all, because then she looks
upon herself as no Party concern'd."[17] Though this young woman might
have only "confus'd Ideas" about the bawdy she had heard, Mandeville's
cynical representation of her self-consciousness was not likely to have

seemed very comforting to Dr. Gregory. From the perspective of the conduct books, that is, a virgin who listened to obscene talk willingly as long as she believed herself undiscovered would have touched all too closely on familiar anxieties about female calculation and hypocrisy. And even Mandeville's subsequent acknowledgment that a young woman might blush in private would have been far from consoling, since he continued to insist that her blushes would only signify her fear of exposure: "if in the same Place she hears something said of her self that must tend to her Disgrace, or any thing is named, of which she is secretly Guilty, then 'tis Ten to one but she'll be ashamed and blush, tho' no Body sees her; because she has room to fear, that she is, or, if all was known, should be thought of Contemptibly." [18]

Whether alone or in company, a blush by Mandeville's account remained too frankly a matter of face to have made most subsequent authorities on female virtue quite willing to trust it. By identifying a woman's blushes as a sign of shame, and shame as a wholly social phenomenon, *The Fable of the Bees* opened up the very division between her surfaces and depths that later writers anxiously sought to cover over. At the same time, however, the writers of conduct books clearly valued the efficacy of shame and praised the blush precisely as a sign of the young woman's responsiveness to the judgments—and feelings—of others. In the moral rhetoric of the period, the modest woman's blushes customarily figured as the "guard" or "defence" of her virtue; and though few writers chose to spell out the logic of this figure explicitly, such guardian blushes almost inevitably revealed themselves to be blushes of self-consciousness. While some commentators wishfully asserted that no well-bred man would continue to offend a blushing woman, most seemed implicitly to rely on the young woman's own desire not to blush too much—hoping, in effect, that her fear of betraying herself through blushes would serve to keep her immodest thoughts and actions in check. Among the harmful effects of attending a masquerade, for example, Marriott's *Female Conduct* specified the disappearance of blushes:

> There conscious Shame, fair Virtue's best Defence,
> Lost in a Mask, will yield to Impudence;
> Mask'd Virgins, when their Blushes are conceal'd,
> Grant Freedoms, which they would deny unvail'd;
> But Pow'r of Blushing, Nature's inborn Grace,
> Will soon forsake a masquerading Face;
> A shameless Bronce, each Feature, will invade,
> Whilst, in a Mask, the bashful Roses fade.

Alone in her room, Mandeville's unblushing young woman was at least not immediately in danger of losing her virginity; but behind a mask, and in a crowd, Marriott's runs all the risks and gains none of the benefits of mixed company. Even as Marriott associates the "Pow'r of Blushing" with "Nature's inborn Grace," the possibility of masking reminds him that nature's signaling system only operates under the gaze and judgment of others: "conscious Shame" is very much a social phenomenon. And without the restraint of shame, his verses suggest, he can imagine no female grace so natural or inborn that it will not soon be worn away—even this very "Pow'r of Blushing." According to an earlier passage of the poem, "True female Merit strives, to be conceal'd, / And only by its Blushes is reveal'd." [19] But when Marriott envisions those blushes covered up, he apparently recalls that the virtue of the other sex needs constant watching.

Like many tributes to the modest woman's blushes, Marriott's routinely identifies the beauty of her virtue with that of her complexion: behind a mask, he warns, the "bashful Roses fade," and a "shameless Bronce" replaces them—not the effect of the sun, presumably, but of constant brazening. Since habitual covering of the face would ordinarily be expected to induce a certain paleness, the latter may perhaps be viewed as a strictly moral coloration. But the Englishman's particular fascination with the coming and going of the blood to the cheek can never be wholly separated from a racial presumption about the visibility of the sign; and as this offhand association of a dark skin with shamelessness should remind us, the moralizing of the blush has always its potentially racist dimensions. Compared to an Anglo-Saxon red-and-white, a dark skin, like a mask, threatened to obscure vital truths about a person; [20] and when the English celebrated the superior modesty of their women to various Continental and Mediterranean types, they did not always trouble to distinguish too clearly between the advantages of a lighter complexion and a Protestant education. "On lily cheeks thy mantling charms / With treach'rous frankness truth betray," according to one poetic tribute to "A Blush" published by the *Lady's Magazine* in 1798, [21] and if this "treach'rous" blush appeared to speak of something less than innocence, it at least appeared to speak with candor. To the anxious Englishman, his countrywoman's "lily" cheeks helped to make the inner truth of her consciousness and emotions visible. Whatever she might try to pretend, the involuntary rush of blood betrayed her.

Indeed, from the standpoint of the men who observed her, the very fact that the young woman's blush was involuntary constituted a powerful attraction: unlike the other bodily signs of modesty—the downcast eyes, the head turned aside—her blushes were not subject to her will and could not, therefore, be affected. A woman who blushed might be innocent neither in thought nor deed, but as long as he saw her blushing, a man could see her as innocent of pretense or manipulation. In yet another tribute to blushing that appeared in the *Lady's Magazine* for 1825, an anonymous poet accounted for the phenomenon with a fable of origins—a brief allegory in which Heaven sends the Blush as the mark that distinguishes True Modesty from Affectation:

> When o'er the pure and blissful earth
>   Vice first her baneful influence shed,
> And gave those latent poisons birth
>   That through life's sweets infection spread;
>
> Bereft of home, her form to screen,
>   Meek Modesty deserted stray'd;
> Unnotic'd and unknown, when seen,
>   Pensive she droop'd her beauteous head.
>
> For Affectation, child of Guile,
>   Usurp'd the virgin's small domain;
> Assum'd her air, her artless smile,
>   And undisputed held her reign.
>
> Then Heaven benign bestow'd its aid,
>   The fiend's increasing pow'r to crush;
> Bore to the light the feeble maid,
>   And mark'd her presence with a blush.[22]

Note that Affectation can assume the air and even the "artless smile" of Modesty, but that she has no means of mimicking her blush. Any "child of Guile," of course, might try rouge, but while she could thereby feign a rosy cheek, she could never simulate the rapid coming and going of color that constitutes blushing. If a painted cheek provides an obvious metonym for falsehood when the natural complexion figures truth, then a blush seems truer still—since even natural coloring remains literally a superficial matter, while the sudden rush of blood reveals an inner reality.

Compared to rouge, then, "shamefacedness" *was* "an innocent paint," and the opposition between them figured repeatedly in the moral rhetoric of the period, from Wollstonecraft's lament that "till more understanding preponderates in society . . . the harlot's *rouge* will supply the place of that celestial suffusion which only virtuous affections can give to the face" to the pages of a contemporary fashion magazine, in which an essay "On the Use of Rouge" instead predictably commended blushing. "Who would not be more pleased . . . with the frequent suffusions of virtuous modesty, than with the brazen rouge of dissipated fashion?" the correspondent to *La Belle Assemblée* inquired in 1806, while conjuring his countrywomen "by all their hopes of a husband" not to persist in the practice. Like other immodest fashions, the writer was persuaded, the custom of rouging had been imported from France, where the already brazen complexions of the natives mysteriously re-quired it: "a French woman may use her rouge in order to relieve the sallow hue of her sun-burnt face," he explained, "and to brighten a complexion which has seldom any roses to boast." Since all the world acknowledged the natural beauty of the Englishwoman, on the other hand, she had no need of artifice—and besides, she was reminded, a painted cheek was a threat to the nation's moral superiority: "it is of course little better than a deceit, and on that account alone should be banished far, very far, from this land of integrity."[23]

Even as they celebrated the blush of innocence, the evidence sug-gests, what men saw in the blushing young woman was also modesty's other face—the implicit promise of her ardent surrender. In the court-ship of the first couple, as Milton imagined it, Eve's innocent blushes blurred imperceptibly into the first flushes of sexual desire; and when Dr. Gregory felt that Nature "forced" him to love a blushing woman, he already took her blushes, half-consciously, as a sexual signal. All blushes probably arouse speculation about the sensitivities that inspire them, prompting observers to imagine in the blushing person a susceptibility and responsiveness that extend beyond the present scene. But the con-ventions of a proper courtship understandably invested the woman's blush with an especial power, for such a courtship at once charged the atmosphere with erotic and emotional questions and severely restricted the means of answering them. The more ideally restrained her speech and gestures, the more revelatory a woman's sudden change of color could seem. Long before nineteenth-century science speculated openly about the physiological resemblance of a blush to other forms of sexual flushing and excitement, lovers of the modest woman read an erotic promise in her blushes—all the more so, no doubt, because so little other than her cheek was conventionally available for contemplation.

When the modest woman changed color, her lover could well see warm-bloodedness displaying itself in her suddenly glowing face, and find in her momentary surrender to emotion the evidence of an other-wise secret propensity to be overcome by feeling. In this sense, the young woman's red cheek was her heart—and other organs—made visible. Though these associations of her blush were rarely made explicit in the conduct literature and fiction of the period, they were usually present—and sometimes not very far from the surface. Here, for example, is the familiar topos of the blushing rose, as it appeared by contrast to the "gaudy tulip" in Moore's versified *Fables* of 1744:

> The gaudy tulip, that displays
> Her spreading foliage to the gaze;
> That points her charms at all she sees,
> And yields to ev'ry wanton breeze,
> Attracts not me. Where blushing grows,
> Guarded with thorns, the modest rose,
> Enamour'd, round and round I fly,
> Or on her fragrant bosom lie;
> Reluctant, she my ardour meets,
> And bashful, renders up her sweets.[24]

Both flowers seem strongly, almost anatomically sexualized, but while the tulip merely "yields" to every comer, the modest rose significantly "meets" the ardor of one. It is not just that the blushing flower saves herself for the poet, in other words, but that she alone can genuinely feel—or rather, that from the lover's point of view, she alone seems to respond. Though Moore called these *Fables for the Female Sex,* the erotic argument of his botany lesson more nearly anticipates Cobbett's advice to the "*ardent-minded*" young man.

That a blush might be read as a sexual sign did not, of course, mean that a blushing young woman had any interest in a particular young man—even if she changed color in his presence. As one "Harriet Diffident," a young woman who worried about her tendency to blush too much, complained to the long-running advice columnist of the *Lady's Magazine* in 1777, she could never find herself in company, especially that of young gentlemen, "without being in the greatest confusion." Once she had merely been teased about a young man, Harriet reported, "the very sound of his name ever after turns my face to crimson, though it is one that I look on with the greatest indifference, and never entertained a serious thought of him in my life." Despite Harriet's evident discomfort, the Matron, as the advice columnist called herself, was cautiously encouraging. Though she did remark the potential ambiguity of the sign—warning her correspondent that "blushes, too sudden and too frequent, undoubtedly tend to make a woman's real modesty suspected; they render her at least chargeable with the admission of indelicate ideas into her mind"—the Matron reassured her that it was better to blush too much than too little, and that "a moderate glow in the

cheeks of a young lady, upon many occasions, shews that she has a heart
susceptible of the most delicate feelings." While Harriet should strive to
conquer her excessive bashfulness,

> I would not, on any account, have her arrive at such a pitch of effrontery, as to
> bid defiance to *blushes;* for she who *colours* at every word she hears, or every
> time she opens her lips, will always appear in a more amiable light, than the
> bold, the intrepid female, who can listen to the most licentious conversation,
> without discovering the smallest trace of a "rosy pudency" in her countenance:
> such females are either totally void of feeling, or pride themselves in the exhibi-
> tion of sensations, of which they ought to be ashamed.

The woman who cannot blush has no feelings—or too much of the
wrong kind; while the moderately glowing young lady is courted at
once for her "heart" and her virtue. When the Matron later remarks that
"there was never a real lover who did not wish to have it in his power,
sometimes, to animate the face of his mistress with virtue's most beautiful vermilion," she distinguishes no more than does the lover himself
between his mistress's moral and her erotic attractions.[25]

Though the young woman's blushes always threatened to signify, as
the Matron put it, "the admission of indelicate ideas into her mind,"
for the duration of the blush, at least, she was more likely to feel herself,
like Harriet Diffident, "in the greatest confusion." When blushing, after
all, people are idiomatically said to be "covered with confusion"; and if
the frequent appearances of such "confusion" in the conduct literature
and fiction of the period are to be credited, the muddled state of mind
to which the idiom testifies may be said to have represented the ideal
state of the young female consciousness in courtship. Those who imagined the modest woman, as we have seen, generally imagined her as on
the way to marriage, and for all their talk of innocence, they were repeatedly compelled to acknowledge that a perfectly blank consciousness
was neither possible nor desirable. But so long as she was blushing, the
modest woman could be imagined as not yet knowing what had caused
her to change color—while the very warmth that marked her temporary
suspension between innocence and full consciousness aroused a corresponding warmth in the observer. Like her modesty itself, the modest
woman's blush appealed to conflicting wishes—its attraction not quite
that of female innocence or of innocence violated but of a seductive moment between, a moment in which innocent unconsciousness and erotic
knowingness seemed briefly to fuse, or to be "confused," together.

Extended into narrative, the moment of the blush becomes the time
of the courtship novel, that period between innocence and erotic expe-

rience that marks the modest heroine's entrance into the world. Not surprisingly, indeed, the cheeks of the modest heroine change color with a particular frequency and intensity: from the early scene of *Pamela* when the heroine responds to Mr. B's gift of his late mother's stockings and his mischievously self-defeating instruction, "Don't blush, Pamela," by "curt'sying and blushing . . . up to the ears," to the late scene in *Wives and Daughters* in which Roger Hamley returns from his long sojourn in Africa and Molly Gibson feels herself "colour all over with the consciousness of his regard,"[26] the modest heroine, as we shall see, is a woman often covered with blushes. And if the heroines of these novels exhibit a marked affinity for blushing, blushing has a marked affinity for narrative. Though a blush is a visible sign, the same qualities that make it a sign of truth mean that it can best be represented, paradoxically, not in the visual arts, but in language. An artist can imply a blush in painting, for example, by associating it with other gestures of modesty or embarrassment, but the very temporality of the phenomenon cannot be caught, and therefore it is difficult on canvas to distinguish among a blushing cheek, a naturally rosy one, and an artificially colored one; while the involuntariness of the sign makes the acting of a blush extremely difficult, if not impossible, on the stage—as the immodestly painted cheek of the actress conventionally testified.[27] Still more important, only narrative can finally verify a blush by testifying to the true state of the young woman's consciousness. As the novelists know very well, not every sudden flow of blood to the cheeks is a blush, and not every blush signifies what the observer imagines. To tell the story from her point of view is to make clear that even the modest young woman sometimes flushes with anger, and that even the slightest of her blushes may cover a rich and varied interior life.

❧

In 1899, the same year in which Havelock Ellis first published his "Evolution of Modesty," Henry James published his last nineteenth-century novel, a study of that period of confusion and muddle that he called *The Awkward Age*. James was not, so far as we know, a reader of female conduct literature, but when he came to reflect on his novel in the preface to the New York edition nine years later, he necessarily found himself reflecting on the bringing-out of daughters, and on the differences between the English and the Continental methods of doing so.[28] "Putting vividly before one the perfect system on which the awkward age is handled in most other European societies," James observed, "it threw again into relief the inveterate English trick of the so morally well-

meant and so intellectually helpless compromise." The problem, as he
saw it, was the difficulty of managing the inevitable transition between
girlish innocence and the adult knowledge of the married woman.
"A girl might be married off the day after her irruption, or better still
the day before it," James observed, but "even then, at the worst, an interval had to be bridged"—an interval whose awkwardness the English
characteristically compounded by their practice of exposing the unmarried young woman to the sophisticated conversation of the drawing
room. Though he sardonically remarked in passing on "the American
theory" of how to cope with the problem ("that talk should never become 'better' than the female young . . . are minded to allow it"), the
principal comparison he intended was with the French, whose "social
scheme absolutely provides against awkwardness" by rigorously excluding the young woman from adult conversation until she is married.
Ideally crossing without a break from the innocence of the convent to
the experience of married life, the *jeune fille* effectively avoided the awkward interval in the drawing room. From the perspective of *The Awkward Age,* on the other hand, she also afforded no opportunity for
narrative. Despite its allusions to the "perfect system" by which they
arrange these matters on the Continent, the Jamesian imagination
clearly preferred English confusion: "the consequent muddle, if the
term be not too gross, representing meanwhile a great inconvenience
for life, but, as I found myself feeling, an immense promise, a much
greater one than on the 'foreign' showing, for the painted picture
of life." [29]

"On the 'foreign' showing," of course, the woman's story came afterwards—not in the smoothly managed transition from girlhood to
marriage but in the risks and pleasures of adultery. Indeed, without
adultery, it would not be too much to say, the Continental novel would
scarcely be possible. "*L'honnête femme—n'a pas de roman*": so James
himself succinctly formulated the French creed when he entered into his
notebook for 1899 the germ of the tale he would later entitle, reso-
nantly, "The Story in It." To "a young, 'innocent,' yearning woman,"
with her "'Anglo-Saxon' clinging to the impossible thesis," in the notebook's phrase, the adulterous hero in James's original conception of that
story crisply lays down the narrative law: "if she's *honnête* it's not a
roman—if it's a *roman* she's not *honnête*." [30] By the time the story was
actually written, some three years later, the artist-hero had been transformed, oddly enough, into a colonel and an M.P. (though, significantly, one who "looked, as was usually said, un-English"), but the
secret affair he conducts and the narrative rules he articulates are essen-

tially unchanged. "Behind these words we use," according to Colonel Voyt, "the adventure, the novel, the drama, the romance, the situation . . . stands the same sharp fact"—an illicit relation. "The adventure's a relation; the relation's an adventure. The romance, the novel, the drama are the picture of one. The subject the novelist treats is the rise, the formation, the development, the climax, and for the most part the decline, of one. And what is the honest lady doing on that side of town?"[31]

Colonel Voyt states the ground rules of all the "lemon-coloured" volumes the heroine reads: like Tony Tanner, who has argued for an intimate connection between adultery and the novel by drawing chiefly on French and German examples, he offers a narrative theory that is actually an account of Continental fiction.[32] For Voyt there is only a "story in it" when a respectable woman crosses an implied border to that other, illicit, side of town; like Tanner's, his narratives really begin when the marriage contract is broken. But in the tradition of the English novel, the initial border crossing is not the married woman's transgression but the innocent young girl's awakening; and though the end is marriage, the whole "dilatory area" of the plotting, to borrow Roland Barthes's formula, is a function of her internalized capacity for erotic restraint and delay.[33] Though *The Awkward Age* makes a wonderful joke about a young woman raised on the Continental plan—from an innocence so absolute that conversation with her is virtually impossible, little Aggie immediately plunges, once married, into an equally mindless depravity, as she cheerfully takes possession of her aunt's toothy lover—James was clearly drawn to English "muddle" by the opportunities it offered to study consciousness, to locate a narrative crisis in a state of mind. If "'The Awkward Age' is precisely a study of one of these curtailed or extended periods of tension and apprehension," in the words of the preface,[34] so too was much English fiction before it: from those extraordinarily "extended periods of tension and apprehension" that are *Pamela* and *Clarissa,* through James's own poignant studies of adolescent girls in the 1890s, many an English novelist found story enough in the matter of the young woman's courtship and her consciousness.

Like other such novels, *The Awkward Age* explores what happens when "an ingenuous mind and a pair of limpid searching eyes" are introduced into the world: revealingly identifying the modest heroine with her organs of consciousness and observation, the preface's synecdoche for Nanda Brookenham might equally well characterize an Evelina, a Fanny Price, or a Molly Gibson.[35] By mockingly alluding to "the preposterous fiction, as it after all is, of Nanda's blankness of mind," James makes explicit the tacit premise of every novel that chooses to represent the world through the eyes and mind of a modest heroine. "There was never a time," as Nanda herself remarks, "when I didn't know *something* or other."[36] But *The Awkward Age* identifies a moment in social history as well as a critical "interval" in the young woman's coming-of-age; and in the corrupt atmosphere of fin-de-siècle London, the familiar courtship plot no longer proves tenable. As in "The Story in It"—the ironic point of whose title is that there is story enough for its innocent heroine in the mere "subjective satisfaction" of her love for the hero[37]—the virtuous young woman loves in vain. In the Brookenham drawing room, no modest vibrations forestall improper conversation, and Nanda's mere exposure to the free talk of her mother's circle suffices to ruin her. Fictions of modesty depend on the succession of generations, but in *The Awkward Age* Mrs. Brookenham refuses to give way to her daughter; at the close of the novel, she is still in possession of the handsome admirer who might otherwise have been Nanda's husband. For all his apparent sophistication, Vanderbank cannot reconcile his "old-fashioned" idea of female innocence with marriage to a girl so obviously tainted by knowledge. Indeed, there is a sense in which even James himself here abandoned the modest young heroine: though he was the supreme novelist of consciousness, he chose to keep *The Awkward Age* more or less strictly within the limits of dramatic dialogue—the province not of the earnest and somewhat humorless Nanda but of her perverse and witty mother.

But if *The Awkward Age* is not itself a modest fiction, James's extraordinary capacity to make high drama out of the fact that his heroines' minds are *not* blank nonetheless speaks to the power of the tradition. In the climactic scene of the novel, Mrs. Brookenham assures that Vanderbank will never propose to her daughter by making public Nanda's compromising acquaintance with a book: the young woman's mere admission that she has read a French novel brands her a sort of fallen woman. After nearly two centuries of modest consciousness, the *honnête* English heroine has her *roman* merely by reading about, knowing about, what French heroines do.

PART TWO

Narratives

Can any one by search through the works of
the six great English novelists I have named,
find a scene, a passage, or a word that would
teach a girl to be immodest, or a man to be
dishonest? When men in their pages have
been described as dishonest and women as
immodest, have they not ever been punished?
—Trollope, *Autobiography*

6

Pamela's Undesigning

ॐ

If modesty is the resistance that enables courtship, then Pamela is in some sense its prototypical heroine. She can say "yes" to Mr. B's offer of marriage *because* she has said "no" to his attempts at seduction: her resistance does not merely delay the consummation of B's desire but transforms its very nature, subliming his lust into marital love. Yet while it is customary to credit Richardson's novel with anticipating the pattern of much subsequent courtship fiction,[1] *Pamela* itself does not so much tell the story of a courtship as of an action that makes courtship possible. Before her own marriage, Pamela devotes most of her energy to fathoming and resisting what she idiomatically calls B's "designs"— and only by successfully holding out against them does she help to create a new kind of narrative, one that will no longer pose the question of the hero's "designs" on the heroine but his "intentions" toward her. Indeed, it is revealing that while Pamela and B frequently debate the question of whether or not he *has* any "designs" on her, only once, and then hesitantly and ambiguously, does B speak the new idiom of "intentions," an idiom whose beginnings the *Oxford English Dictionary* does not even acknowledge until the publication of Smollett's *Peregrine Pickle* eleven years later. Pamela has returned voluntarily to B after he has released her from captivity, and B has just assured her that at present he has "views quite different" from those which she "had once reason to be apprehensive of." "And yet," he cautiously adds,

to be sincere, I must own, that the certainty there will be, that I shall incur the censures of the world, if I act up to my present intentions, still, at times, gives me thoughts not altogether favourable to those intentions. For it will be said by every one, that Mr. B. a man not destitute of pride, a man of family, and ample fortunes, has been drawn in by the eye, to marry his mother's waiting-maid. Not considering, and not knowing, perhaps, that to her mind, to her virtue, as well as to the beauties of her person, she owes her well-deserved conquest: and that (as I firmly trust will be the case) there is not a lady in the kingdom who will better support the condition to which she will be raised, if I should marry her.[2]

As the talk of a lover to the woman who will soon be his bride, this hesitating speech may not seem very tactful. But as the talk of a landed gentleman to his mother's waiting-maid, of course, it already signals her triumph. To have turned the question from whether such a man will succeed in seducing such a maid to whether he will dare to marry her— to have persuaded him that her "mind" and her "virtue" weigh in the balance with his "family and ample fortunes"—is to have radically altered an old story.

If Pamela's case illustrates the paradox that modesty wins by resisting, however, it also illustrates the paradox that "true" modesty can only win by modestly not quite knowing what it is about. B's conversion suggests that men's designs on women may be subverted and transformed when they come to believe that women themselves are undesigning. But the subsequent reception of Richardson's novel suggests how difficult it is to sustain that belief. The suspicion that Pamela was not truly modest in this or any other sense has dogged her from the start. Richardson's more skeptical critics have always been eager to demonstrate that it is Pamela's "Skill in Intrigue," as one anonymous pamphleteer put it,[3] rather than her virtue that is rewarded, and that the upwardly mobile servant girl must essentially be a whore. Though the anti-Pamelists, as they were soon known, were quick to do away with the fiction of the heroine's sexual inexperience—Fielding's Shamela appears on the scene having already succumbed to the charms of Parson Williams, while Syrena Tricksy, the heroine of an *Anti-Pamela* (1741) usually attributed to Eliza Haywood, rapidly acquires both a lover and an abortion—they were even quicker to dismiss the premise of her innocence of mind. The title page of Fielding's satire announces that it will expose "all the matchless Arts of that young Politician," and Haywood redundantly subtitles her *Anti-Pamela* both *Feign'd Innocence Detected* and *Mock-Modesty Display'd and Punish'd*. By effacing the father and supplying their heroines with mothers who are themselves little more than prostitutes to advise and encourage them (Syrena's also doubles as her abortionist), the two satirists effectively foreclose the possibility of female innocence. A modest daughter is typically her father's child (though Pamela addresses both her parents, only Mr.

Andrews ever appears or speaks in the novel), while women born of women are apparently born to lust and knowingness. As their names obviously indicate, both Shamela and Syrena Tricksy are shrewd actresses, skilled at what Shamela repeatedly and openly calls "pretending." And what they pretend to, of course, are the tokens of modest resistance and other states of innocence:

and then he took me by the hand, and I pretended to be shy: Laud, says I, sir, I hope you don't intend to be rude; no, says he, my dear, and then he kissed me, 'till he took away my breath————and I pretended to be angry.

Mrs. Jervis and I are just in bed, and the door unlocked; if my master should come. . . . Well, he is in bed between us, we both shamming a sleep; he steals his hand into my bosom, which I, as if in my sleep, press close to me with mine, and then pretend to awake.

Pamela, said he, and takes me gently by the hand, will you walk with me in the garden; yes, sir, says I, and pretended to tremble.

Like falling asleep and waking, trembling is in large measure involuntary, and it is revealing that the anti-Pamelists make a special point of exposing as deliberately staged those motions of the heroine's body that are most closely associated with her innocent unconsciousness. Pamela's tendency to faint is a particular target: in Fielding's parody of the climactic scene in which B is seemingly discouraged from raping Pamela because of her fainting, Shamela of course "counterfeit[s] a swoon"—and while "poor Booby, frightened out of his wits," sits at her bedside genuinely "pale and trembling," she duly reports to her mother, "I kept my eyes wide open, and pretended to fix them in my head."[4] A month after the publication of *Shamela*, the author of some versified "Remarks on Pamela" summed up the apparent moral of this scene:

> The man it seems, was frightened fore
> At her pretended faint;
> So, when he might have had a w————e
> He took her for a saint.[5]

Syrena, too, has learned to faint at will, and manages a crucial encounter in which she first lures her victim to a settee and then "counterfeit[s] Faintings" so extreme that she appears to fall "dying on the Floor."[6] But perhaps the most arduous such exercise, if not the most violent, is Shamela's deliberate feigning of a bridal blush. "In my last I left off at our sitting down to supper on our wedding night," she begins her first letter to her mother after her marriage to Booby, "where I behaved with as much bashfulness as the purest virgin in the world could have done. The most difficult task for me was to blush; however, by holding my breath, and squeezing my cheeks with my handkerchief, I did pretty well." Comically defying the law that a blush is the one sign that cannot be faked, Fielding renders Shamela's pretense complete and insinuates that no mark of female modesty in the original is to be trusted.[7] Like the other anti-Pamelas, Fielding's persistently unmasks the new woman to reveal the old, drawing on a tradition of misogynist satire that long antedates Richardson's novel.

Of course the contradictions in that novel—and in the code it seemed to celebrate—were there to be exploited. A virtue whose reward is worldly wealth and status, a resistance whose end is giving in, a humility that repeatedly calls attention to itself—all these readily lend themselves to satire. Indeed, Richardson may be said to have compounded his own difficulties by confining his narrative of his heroine's triumph almost solely to that heroine's voice, thereby violating an implicit rule of feminine behavior that the *Lady's Magazine* would later spell out for its readers in one of its numerous essays "On Modesty": "take care you do not make yourself the heroine of your own story."[8] Yet what is notable is how often the impulse to attack *Pamela*'s design turns into an attack on Pamela as designing—and how persistent is this habit of coping with the contradictions of her narrative. Shamela's "I pretended" and "I counterfeited" are satiric reductions, but it was Richardson's novel rather than Fielding's satire that Arnold Kettle thought he was describing more than two hundred years later when he wrote dismissively of the girl's "hard-headed scheming."[9] Even a critic who rightly disputes the charge of conscious duplicity on Richardson's part can be strangely tempted to transfer the accusation to his imaginary female, as when Bernard Kreissman defends Richardson from the charge of "Specious Pretence" brought by the author of *Pamela Censured*. "The real point at issue is not pretense," Kreissman sensibly observes, "but Richardson's species of morality." Pamela "is not pretending to a certain kind of virtue," he also remarks, only to add, "This *is* her virtue—a good businesswoman's appreciation of the value of rejecting B.'s demands." That this amounts to a claim that Pamela does not pretend to virtue because her virtue is nothing but pretense becomes clear in Kreissman's later discussion of her "pretended modesty," his allusions to the importance of discovering "the scheming behind the 'virtue,'" and his advice to view Richardson's heroine as "the shrewd, scheming Shamela" in order to avoid the "mistake" of criticizing her as virtuous but unreal.[10]

The image of Pamela as a hardheaded schemer is very difficult to sustain on any close reading of her early letters and journal—but it appears to be very difficult to resist once that reading is over. For the logic of reducing Pamela to Shamela is partly teleological, the tendency to sort out all the contradictions and confusions in her account of herself in light of their end. Indeed, by calling attention to that end with his notorious subtitle, *Virtue Rewarded*, the author himself unfortunately encouraged the tendency; like Thomas Hardy's appending of the phrase *A Pure Woman* to the name of his *Tess of the d'Urbervilles* a century and a half later, Richardson's moralizing tag did more to harm the reputation of his heroine than to help it. "It is only when we get the final act of the marriage acceptance that the consistency of all her former deeds becomes clear," Kreissman revealingly observes at one point. "To try to 'improve' *Pamela* by removing this unifying element would bring down the whole structure." [11] But neither the reader's retrospective knowledge of this "unifying element" nor an anticipatory awareness that virtue will be rewarded is available to Pamela at the time of her writing. And the "whole structure" of her narrative is a function not only of its clarifying end but of a space of confusion and delay. If the dynamics of all narrative, as Roland Barthes has suggested, require enigma and delay—"a whole dilatory area whose emblem might be named 'reticence'" [12]— then in a certain kind of courtship fiction that reticence might well be named female modesty. It is Pamela's very unconsciousness of the end toward which she is moving—or at least her partially occluded consciousness—that makes that end possible.

❦

The fact that Pamela not only marries her would-be seducer but in doing so transforms herself from the lady's maid to the lady prompts an understandable cynicism in many of her readers—perhaps especially, as Fielding's case suggests, in those who read as upper-class men. Fielding's transformation of Mr. B into the hapless "Booby" who will be no sooner married than cuckolded signals his contempt for a man who lets down the standards both of his sex and his class. A gentleman who marries his mother's "chambermaid" when he could simply have had her is obviously a fool, as Fielding makes clear when he has his "Parson Oliver" denounce the pernicious effects of the book:

> Young gentlemen are here taught, that to marry their mother's chambermaids, and to indulge the passion of lust, at the expense of reason and common sense, is

an act of religion, virtue, and honour; and, indeed, the surest road to happiness.
. . . All chambermaids are strictly enjoined to look out after their masters;
they are taught to use little arts to that purpose: and lastly, are countenanced in
impertinence to their superiors, and in betraying the secrets of families.[13]

Significantly, Fielding refuses to credit Richardson's novel as a love story:
Booby's marrying Shamela is merely a stupidly expensive and self-
destructive way to "indulge the passion of lust." But within Richardson's
novel, Pamela's first reader apart from her parents is an upper-class man
whose "passion," as he puts it after the attempted rape scene, was "all
swallowed up" in his concern for her well-being (p. 244), and whose
sexual desire is mysteriously converted into marital love. Indeed, B's
changing relation to Pamela is marked by his gradual abandonment of
the sexual ethic that governs Fielding's parody. In the early portions of
the novel, B's principal means of defending himself against his growing
interest in the girl and his frustration at her resistance is by accusing *her*
of hypocrisy and "art": she is "a subtle, artful little gypsey" (p. 60), a
"little hypocrite," who has "all the arts of her sex; they were *born* with
her" (p. 67)—including, apparently, "the power of witchcraft" (p. 80).
One angry letter accuses her simultaneously of being a "*fool's plaything*,"
"*painted geegaw*," "*fair idiot*," and an "*artful creature*," a "*forward*" one,
a "*saucy designer*," and "this *plotting little villain of a girl*" (p. 201). The
latter outpouring is prompted by his jealous fantasy about her plan
to run off with Parson Williams—a fantasy which allows him to cast
Pamela in the predictable role of loose woman, a sort of Syrena Tricksy
avant la lettre:

The very first fellow that came in your way, you have practised upon, corrupted
too, and thrown your *forward* self upon him; after having by your insinuating
arts, and bewitching face, induced him to break through all the ties of honour
and gratitude to me. (P. 203)

In this sense B is the original anti-Pamelist, and the obvious sources of
his accusations in resentment and projection—if she resists my designs
she must herself be designing—may indirectly shed some light on the
motives of the entire company.[14]

But if B repeatedly tries to deal with his conflicting feelings about
Pamela by reducing her to a familiar stereotype, he is of course gradually converted to another way of seeing. Like the other satirists of this
new heroine, he begins with the premise that all female "innocence" is
really designing—a skepticism that takes one characteristic form in a refusal to believe in the genuineness of her unconscious states. The first of
Pamela's much-disputed fainting fits occurs after she has struggled in

vain against B's kisses, burst from him in "indignation," and locked herself in the nearest room, with B so hot in pursuit that he rips a piece of
her gown in the process (pp. 63–64). B, who has apparently looked
through the keyhole and "'spied" Pamela upon the floor before summoning the assistance of Mrs. Jervis, attempts to recover his dignity and
to guard himself from being moved by the spectacle by suggesting that
Pamela merely pretended to faint. "I have done her no harm," he protests to Mrs. Jervis. "But since she is so apt to fall into fits, or at least to
pretend to do so, prepare her to see me to-morrow after dinner, in
my mother's closet, and do you be with her as a witness to what shall
pass between us" (p. 64). Pamela next loses consciousness after B has
emerged from his hiding place in her closet to take her, half-clad, in his
arms, while Mrs. Jervis clings protectively to her feet:

> Mrs. Jervis was about my feet, and upon my coat. The wicked wretch still had
> me in his arms. I sighed, and screamed, and then fainted away.
> "Pamela! Pamela!" said Mrs. Jervis, as she tells me since, "O—h!" and gave
> another shriek, "my poor Pamela is dead for certain!"
> And so, to be sure, I was for a time; for I knew nothing more (one fit follow-
> ing another) till about three hours after. (P. 96)

Having held the insensible girl in his arms rather than merely observed
her through the keyhole, B no longer professes to doubt that she has
really fainted. His anxiety now takes a more subtle form—not that
Pamela's fits have been shammed but that she can induce them at will.
"As for Pamela," B memorably remarks to Mrs. Jervis, "she has a lucky
knack of falling into fits when she pleases" (pp. 97–98). He continues
to fear, in other words, that female hysteria is itself an art, a covert strategy of manipulation.[15]

   Not until he has briefly shared a bed with the unconscious girl does
B seem ready to abandon his skepticism. The turn comes in the climactic episode of attempted, or at least of threatened, rape, when he dis-
guises himself as Nan the maid, climbs into Pamela's bed, and pinions
her securely between himself and Mrs. Jewkes (who is also present in
the bed), and then reveals his identity by kissing her "with frightful vehemence" and announcing in a thunderous voice that "the time of reck-
oning" is come (p. 241). Demanding that Pamela swear acceptance
of his formal proposals to make her his mistress, he melodramatically
warns that if she continues to refuse, he "will not lose this opportunity."
When he accompanies his threats by putting his hand in her bosom,
Pamela swoons. "With struggling, fright, terror, I quite fainted away,
and did not come to myself soon," she later reports, "so that they both,

from the cold sweats I was in, thought me dying" (p. 242). Believing
that she was on the verge of being raped, Pamela herself subscribes to
the theory that only her providential loss of consciousness saved her.
"This, O my dear parents! was a most dreadful trial," she writes when
she recovers:

I tremble still to think of it. I hope, as he assures me, he was not guilty of indecency; but have reason to be thankful that I was disabled in my intellects. Since
it is but too probable, that all my resistance, and all my strength, otherwise
would not have availed me. (P. 243)

As it turns out, Pamela will have more reason to be thankful for her
timely swoon than she yet realizes, for this disabling of her "intellects"
not only forestalls any further "indecency" on B's part but helps sublime
his lust into love. This scene simultaneously marks B's most aggressive
attempt on her virtue and the beginning of his serious talk of marriage,
a transformation that seems obscurely related to his witnessing Pamela's
hysterical state. For the first time B seems thoroughly persuaded that
her unconsciousness is both genuine and entire—which is to say that
she neither shams her fainting fits nor willfully induces them. And only
after he comes to believe that Pamela is altogether innocent of such designs does he decide to make her his wife.

   Like Mrs. Jervis in the earlier bedroom scene, B too now interprets
Pamela's fainting fits as the signs of her dying. "I do assure you," he tells
her after she has recovered consciousness,

that the moment you fainted away, I quitted the bed, and Mrs. Jewkes did so
too. . . . and we both did all we could to restore you; and my passion for you
was all swallowed up in the concern I had for your recovery; for I thought I
never saw a fit so strong and violent in my life; and feared we should not bring
you to yourself again. (P. 244)

B's fear that Pamela might actually die testifies to his belief that her resistance is genuine—not the means toward another end but an end itself, definitive of her identity. If Pamela were in fact to die in this scene,
such a death would conclusively determine her innocence, not only by
enabling her permanently to elude B's advances but by unequivocally
divorcing her self from her body, that female body that while alive always remains under suspicion. Before the first fainting episode, she has
already disputed his attempt to take rhetorical advantage with the precedent of Lucretia, whose history B adduces to prove that rape leaves
the woman blameless, since the "shame" in Lucretia's case "lay on the
ravisher only." But Pamela knows that what certified Lucretia as blame-

less was the act that rendered her dead. "May I," she retorts, "Lucretia like, justify myself by my death, if I am used barbarously?" (p. 63). Lucretia's suicide after her rape by Tarquin thus becomes a type of the death that can even restore innocence lost or violated, retroactively certifying that the woman's "real" self had no complicity in the pollution of her flesh.[16]

But as Pamela also knows—and as she compels herself to remember when she later contemplates escaping her misery by drowning herself in the pond—the very act that would "justify" her as Roman would condemn her as Christian. Though she briefly fantasizes how after her drowning B will discover "the dead corpse of the miserable Pamela" and be forced belatedly to recognize that "she, poor girl! was no hypocrite, no deceiver; but really was the innocent creature she pretended to be!" (p. 212), she quickly reminds herself that to preserve her innocence in this sense would be to destroy it in another: "Hitherto, Pamela, thought I, thou art the innocent, the suffering Pamela; and wilt thou, to avoid thy sufferings, be the guilty aggressor?" (p. 213). It is thus crucial that B's conversion to a belief in Pamela's innocence be signaled not only by his momentary fear that she is dying but by the fact that he no longer accuses her of willfully inducing her fits.[17] Were Pamela indeed to die of her hysterical swooning, she apparently would perish by the grace of God and the novelist, a woman innocent in every sense of immodest designs. That Richardson does not allow her to die, however, means that she can never escape the imputation of having merely gone through the motions—that readers who know the outcome of her story will continue to suspect her of having plotted it all along. Only for that "dilatory area" of her narrative in which her worldly triumph is still in doubt—and only, therefore, on a first reading—can Pamela temporarily allay such suspicion.

❦

But B of course *is* a first reader, and not one who is privy to Richardson's ending. Or rather, the more he comes to believe that Pamela is innocent of design, the more he can regard the ending as his alone to write. Having intercepted her earlier letters to her parents and read through the portion of her Lincolnshire journal that Mrs. Jewkes has confiscated, B requests that Pamela turn over the pages that remain:

As I have furnished you with a subject, I think I have a title to see how you manage it. Besides, there is such a pretty air of romance, as you tell your story, in *your* plots, and *my* plots, that I shall be better directed how to wind up the catastrophe of the pretty novel.

Though he speaks of Pamela's "plots" and the exertion of her "wit," he
now alludes to these as "innocent exercises" (p. 268). For all of Pamela's
plots, as B has read them, have been strategies of resistance, attempts to
forestall the only sexual outcome of this struggle that she can consciously imagine. Because she has been writing to the moment—and
because she has been familiar only with the old story of a poor girl's
seduction—Pamela has been unaware of the direction in which her resistance is tending. In his very first letter, after all, Pamela's father warns
her that Mr. B's attentions may be the signs of a plot, but he can only
project one conventional alternative to the dreaded conclusion: the
Andrewses will prefer poverty and even their daughter's death to their
"dear child's ruin. I hope the good 'squire has no design," Mr. Andrews
piously continues (p. 45), but the rhetorical questions that quickly follow take for granted that B's interest in Pamela can only be explained by
such designing: "But then, *why should he smile so kindly upon you?* Why
should he take such a poor girl as you by the hand, as your letter says he
has done twice? Why should he deign to read your letter written to us,
and commend your writing and spelling?" (p. 46). Nancy Miller reads
these questions as evidence that the Andrewses are "good hermeneuts,"
who "know how to interpret," but surely the failure of their hermeneu-
tics to account for Richardson's plot is part of the deliberate surprise of
his novel.[18] Mr. Andrews's instruction that Pamela should come home
at once if she finds "the least thing that looks like a design" upon
her virtue (p. 46) is consonant with Richardson's own advice to be-
leaguered servant girls in his *Familiar Letters,* but it would abort his
plot—a plot which depends both on Pamela's delaying to take that advice and on her remaining modestly unconscious that any more satisfying conclusion will be possible. Though Richardson would later claim
in a letter to Aaron Hill that he had based Pamela's story on a real sequence of events that he had heard from an acquaintance about twenty-
five years earlier, both the letter to Hill and the novel itself treat hers as
an exceptional case.[19] "Well, my story, surely, would furnish out a surprising kind of novel, if it were to be well told," Richardson rather coyly
has Pamela observe at one point (p. 281); while Lady Davers later
speculates that her new sister-in-law's papers must tell "a rare, an uncommon story" (p. 474).

    Like her father, who arrives before the wedding still fearing that she
has been ruined and that B merely talks of marriage to make him "believe impossibilities" (p. 327), Pamela is far more conscious that she
might become B's mistress than that she might become his wife. Of
course, a fifteen-year-old servant girl, especially one deprived of her

mistress's protection, could not afford to be too innocently unaware of sex: if a girl of Pamela's class and situation were actually to preserve her virginity from men like B, she needed a certain consciousness—and Richardson is realist enough to show it. "Have I not heard you both talk enough of these subjects," she at one point addresses her parents, "and what false hearts these men have?" (p. 171). Certainly the girl who explains to Mrs. Jervis why she cannot be her master's "harlot" (p. 73), or reports to her parents that a neighboring squire "has had three lyings-in in his house" in as many months—"one by himself, and one by his coachman, and one by his woodman" (p. 103)—is sexually knowing in a way that Burney's heroines, for example, are not. Insofar as Pamela cannot imagine that she might marry Mr. B, however, she cannot allow herself to become conscious of her own attraction to him: one kind of modesty helps to create and enforce the other. In her early struggles with him, she typically attempts to preserve a modest space between them by reminding him of their remoteness in station: the proper "distance" between masters and servants becomes a figure for the proper distance between the sexes.[20] "But tell me truly," Lady Davers asks her after she has become B's wife, "did you not love him all the time?" This is the question that fictions of modesty must always both affirm and deny, for such fictions must simultaneously demonstrate that the heroine's erotic feelings do not come fast or easily and that they have never really been vulnerable to change—that in some sense she *has* loved the hero "all the time." The implicit promise of the heroine's future chastity depends on the retrospective continuity of her past, while the very possibility of the narrative has depended on subjecting the discovery of her changeless desire to uncertainty and delay. Pamela's reply to Lady Davers is a model of modest postponement and indirection:

I had always . . . a great reverence for my master, and thought highly of all his good actions; and, though I abhorred his attempts upon me, yet I could not hate him; and always wished him well; but I did not know, it was love. Indeed, I had not the presumption. (P. 472)

From her very first letters, ingenuously praising B as "the best of gentlemen" (p. 45), who looks like "an angel" when he gives her a suit of his late mother's clothes (p. 50), to her journal entry when he narrowly escapes drowning—her registration of relief typically modest in its double negations ("I cannot hate him," and "I could not in my heart forbear rejoicing"—p. 218)—the signs of Pamela's attraction to B have "all the time" been present in the text, but she has necessarily lagged behind in her capacity to decode them. Not until B frees her from captivity and sends her home with the pronouncement that "she *deserves* to go away virtuous, and she *shall*"—not until he puts this seemingly decisive distance between them—can Pamela begin to articulate to herself what she has "all the time" been feeling.[21] The receipt of his initial letter, generous and loving when she had "expected some new plot," prompts her first experience of conscious naming:

> But to be sure, I must own to you, that I shall never be able to think of any body in the world but him! Presumption! you will say; and so it is: but love, I imagine, is not a voluntary thing—*Love,* did I say! But come, I hope not: at least it is not, I hope, gone so far, as to make me *very* uneasy: for I know not *how* it came, nor *when* it began; but it has crept, crept, like a thief, upon me; and before I knew what was the matter, it looked *like* love. (P. 283)

"*Love,*" did she say? But not quite—for "*Love*" seems rather to have said itself before she "knew what was the matter." And before she quite does know what is the matter, consciousness is ready to hold it at a figurative distance: it only "looked *like* love." When love comes to such a heroine, it must come involuntarily and without her conscious "presumption": Pamela's "treacherous, treacherous heart" may have surrendered to love, but Pamela herself can still upbraid it for giving "no notice" of its mischievous intentions, for having yielded "without ever consulting" its "poor mistress in the least" (p. 284). When she receives B's second letter, professing himself unable to live without her and begging her to return, her "exulting heart" throbs, but Pamela immediately scolds it: "O credulous, fluttering, throbbing mischief! that art so ready to believe what thou wishest" (p. 287). Even as she decisively turns to go back to B—which is to say, even as she consciously chooses, for the first time, to come "forward"—it is still not quite Pamela who does the exulting. "Thus foolishly dialogued I with my heart; and yet, all the time, this heart was Pamela" (p. 287).[22]

"And can you return me sincerely the honest compliment I now will make you?" B asks of her the morning after her return:

> In the *choice* I have made, it is impossible I should have any view to my *interest.* Love, *true* love, is my *only* motive. And were I not what I am, as to fortune, could you give me the *preference* to any other person you know in the world, notwithstanding what has passed between us?

The "honest compliment" underlines an uncomfortable truth—that no motive but "love" can account for such a gentleman's marrying such a servant. Treat "love, *true* love" as mere mystification, as Fielding would gleefully do, and B becomes a motiveless Booby. But if his love poten-

tially lacks a motive, Pamela's—as the satirists were also quick to register—appears to have too many. B's desire that the servant girl "sincerely"
return his "honest compliment" reflects his lingering anxiety that her
"love" for him may conceal an embarrassment of "interest." Both explicitly and in the hesitations of her rhetoric, Pamela's response testifies to
her love by bespeaking her lack of "presumption":

> "Why," said I, "should your so much obliged Pamela decline an answer to this
> kind question? Cruel as I have thought you, and truly shocking and detestable
> as your attempts ever were to me, you, sir, are the only man living, my father
> excepted, who ever was more than indifferent to me. Yet allow me to add, that
> not having the presumption to raise my eyes to you, I knew not myself the state
> of my own heart, till your kindness to me melted away, as I may say, the chilling
> frost that prudence and love of virtue had cast about the buds of—What shall I
> say? Excuse, sir—"
> "My dearest Pamela," clasping me to his bosom, "I do excuse, and will spare
> your sweet confusion. I am fully satisfied. Nor am I now so solicitous as I was,
> about the papers that you have kindly written for to your father: and yet I still
> wish to see them." (P. 307)

Even at this climactic moment of "sincere" revelations, "sweet confusion" covers for and postpones the desire that cannot yet be named,
while Pamela's inability to identify the "buds" that have still to unfold
within her obscurely confirms that she is innocently unconscious of all
deliberation and design.

B's later boast that before he discovered Pamela "nobody was more
averse to the state" of matrimony than himself (p. 463) generalizes
his distrust of the sex—and suggests that only such a diligent and
unpresumptuous servant could ever satisfy him as a wife. As he also
tells her, his belief that Pamela would "conform" her will to his in all
things was one of the few inducements he had to marry (p. 462). Carol
Houlihan Flynn has tartly noted how B later presents this humble bride
as a model for the other ladies, including his own arrogant sister.[23] But
this difference in power and status that B finds so comforting is also the
source of considerable anxiety, for it arouses the disturbing suspicion
that he is not desired for himself at all. "*True* love," apparently, cares for
no other end than the beloved—and thus can only prove itself by proving undesigning. B's need to reassure himself that Pamela has no designs on his fortune is the masculine counterpart of her need to be
convinced that he has no sexual designs on her: Pamela's testimony that
she has never consciously entertained the fantasy of marrying B confirms that she is worthy of marrying him, her modest lack of "presumption" authenticating her love as genuine. Not every man who courts a

modest woman is literally a master who will marry his maid; but to the
degree that the difference between the sexes is always also a difference in
class, B may not be the only man to require this sort of reassurance.

❧

Though B takes Pamela's modestly inconclusive speech as a happy substitute for her "papers," his continuing solicitude about those docu-
ments suggests how closely his reading of them has been bound up with
the history of his conversion. For his repeated attempts to get at those
private records have originated in an obsessive need to reassure himself
that there is no *Shamela*-like subtext to her modest behavior, that her
seeming artlessness conceals no hidden designs. And the less she has intended her words for him, the more truly private they are, the more
vital it is that he see them. In Fielding's satire, Mrs. Jervis betrays the
merely instrumental modesty of her sex by speaking of "what we women
call rude, when done in the presence of others"; while Mandeville's hypothetical virgin, it may be recalled, will not blush if she thinks herself
alone.[24] In the context of this persistent belief in the secret immodesty
of women, it is crucial that Pamela writes not to her future husband but
to her parents and herself—and that by intercepting her letters and con-
fiscating her journal, B can thus test the truth of her innocence by surprising her most hidden thoughts. "But who can describe the tricks and
artifices, that lie lurking in her little, plotting, guileful heart!" he rhetorically inquires in disgust after the failure of the Lincolnshire escape
attempt (p. 225). But Pamela's record of that attempt will confirm what
her hysterical body has previously demonstrated—that what "lurks" in
her heart is not "tricks and artifices" but a modesty so deeply engrained
that she is willing to die to preserve it. Reading the journal entry that
transcribes her effort to escape and her narrowly averted suicide, B feels
himself so "sensibly" touched by her "mournful tale" that he pledges to
"defy the world, and the world's censures" and make her his wife—if
only, that is, his mind can "hold," and he sees no reason to alter his
good opinion when he reads her remaining papers (p. 276)! After Mrs.
Jewkes first seizes her journal, Pamela laments that now B "will see all
my private thoughts of him, and all the secrets of my heart" (p. 263);
but as she defiantly tells him before he begins to read, she is "not afraid"
that she will be found "guilty of a falsehood. . . . I remember not all I
wrote," she declares, "yet I know I wrote my heart at the time; and that
is not deceitful" (p. 266).

In *Clarissa* Lovelace will punningly define "*Cor-respondence*" as "writing from the heart"—a false etymology that is nonetheless often taken as

expressing good Richardsonian doctrine. But the structure of *Pamela*—
or, indeed, the tragic outcome of Clarissa's own "prohibited correspondence" with Lovelace—suggests that for Richardson the sincerity of the
heart is paradoxically best determined by obliquity and indirection, and
that the epistolary novel may most reliably turn into a "true love" story
if the lovers do not correspond too quickly or directly with one another.[25]
Coming as it does from a desiring lover, Lovelace's further claim that
there is "nothing of body, when friend writes to friend" is a dangerous
equivocation. In an extraordinary letter to one of his own young female
correspondents, Sophia Westcomb, the fifty-seven-year-old Richardson
struggled to articulate a defense of the modest woman's pen:

the Pen is almost the *only Means* a very modest and diffident Lady (who in
Company will not attempt to glare) has to shew herself, and that she has a
Mind. Set any of the gay Flutterers and Prattlers of the Tea-Table to write—I
beseech you, set them to write—And what will they demonstrate, but that they
do nothing but prate away?—And shall the modest Lady have nothing but her
Silence to commend her? Silence indeed, to me, is a Commendation, when
worthy Subjects offer not, and nothing but Goose-like Gabble-Gabble-Gabble
(begging their Flippancies Pardon) is going forward; For *Air* and *Attention,* or
Non-Attention, as Occasions require, will shew *Meaning* beyond what *Words*
can, to the Observing: But the pen will shew *Soul* and *Meaning* too.—Retired,
the modest Lady, happy in herself, happy in the Choice she makes of the dear
Correspondent of her own Sex (for ours are too generally Designers); uninter-
rupted; her Closet her Paradise, her Company, herself, and ideally the beloved
Absent; there she can distinguish Her Self: By this means she can assert and
vindicate her Claim to Sense and Meaning.—And shall a modest Lady then refuse to write? Shall she, in other words, refuse to put down her Thoughts, as if
they were unworthy of herself, of her Friend, of her Paper?—A virtuous and
innocent heart to be afraid of having its Impulses *embody'd,* as I may say? Tell it
not in Gath,—Lest the Daughters of the Philistines (The Illiterate, if you
please), rejoice!

For Richardson, obviously, this rather tortured defense of the good
woman's writing serves to rationalize her writing to *him*. Emphasizing
that he is "guarded by Years" and by the long established "Character" of
woman's instructor and friend, carefully distinguishing himself from all
those masculine "Designers" whose correspondence the modest lady
must shun, he makes himself virtually an honorary member of the sex—
a sex in turn declared to be both happier and better than men.[26]
    But it would be wrong to dismiss the rhetoric of this and similar
letters as merely self-serving. As in his fiction, Richardson characteristically strives here to imagine a space of female freedom, a space at once

physical and psychological ("her Closet her Paradise, her Company, herself"), in which a woman may transcend or at least evade any erotic "design." It is critical that one good woman write to another or to a man who stands in her father's stead because such correspondents are imagined as outside the sexual plot: corresponding in private with a female friend or with an "undesigning scribbler" like Richardson (the phrase is from another letter to Westcomb),[27] the modest lady can paradoxically "shew herself, and that she has a *Mind*." Like Pamela's "innocent" plotting, such writing is a means by which the modest lady can guiltlessly "assert and vindicate her Claim to Sense and Meaning." Indeed, Richardson's language suggests not merely that retirement frees a woman to show herself but that only she who modestly retires has a self and mind to show: among the "gay Flutterers and Prattlers of the Tea-Table" there is "nothing but Goose-like Gabble-Gabble-Gabble . . . going forward." Though the modest lady retires to her closet to address another, even another to whom she defers as a daughter, her correspondence becomes a means of defining and asserting herself. Like Pamela's letters to her parents, which she readily turns to the uses of a private journal, such writing enables a woman to "distinguish Her Self" in more senses than one.

While Richardson keeps struggling to imagine such a time and space for woman's innocent self-making, he also keeps imagining its being invaded: the fact of her body and the attendant hazards of "designing" are never absent from the scene. The letter to Sophia Westcomb is not of course a narrative, and its purpose is to urge her to write herself outside the courtship plot, but even its rambling passages inevitably lead to a hypothetical story of seduction, as Richardson warns against "an artful, a designing, a critical, an indecent Heart" quite likely to be discovered in a male correspondent—one capable of insinuating itself and distracting modest, worthy female hearts from "their Choice in the grand Article of Life." Nor is the story merely that of female innocence violated, but of the modest woman's own desire. As the same letter earlier put it, "The modest or diffident Person wants but to have her Bosom unlocked, as I may say, or her Lips open'd, by conscious, yet not gross, Praises, and she will surprise herself into Sentiments that she knew not she had in such Perfection."[28] As Richardson's characteristically erotic figures make evident, "the virtuous and innocent heart" can scarcely be thought without its being, in his revelatory phrase, "*embody'd,* as I may say."

In this sense the modest lady's letters also resemble Pamela's papers, which she attempts to conceal by sewing in her "under-coat" somewhere about her hips (p. 264)—and which thus themselves become the object of B's aggressively erotic play:

"Now," said he, "it is my opinion they are about you; and I never undressed a girl in my life; but I will now begin to strip my pretty Pamela, and hope I shall not go far before I find them." And he began to unpin my handkerchief.

I wept, and resisting said, "I will not be used in this manner. Pray, sir, consider! Pray, sir, consider!" "And pray," said he, "do *you* consider. For I *will* see these papers. But, perhaps," said the wicked wretch, (was ever any one so vile!) "they are tied about your knees with your garters"; and stooped. (P. 271)

As Lennard J. Davis has observed, this is a virtual parallel of the attempted rape scene. But if what Davis aptly terms "the metonymy of this scene of private letters in relation to private parts" helps to transmute "Pamela-the-heroine" into "Pamela-the-linguistic simulacrum," as he argues, it also tends the other way: the text that proves the modest woman other than a body keeps threatening to turn itself back into a body after all.[29] Richardson may have wished to believe that good women were "angels," as he contended to Sophia Westcomb,[30] but as *Clarissa* would later demonstrate, he knew that the only way they could unambiguously demonstrate that fact was to die and conclude the story.

❦

It is a commonplace of *Pamela* criticism that the heroine's marriage effectively ends *her* story—that when "the suspense of the seduction plot is relieved," in Carol Flynn's words, and "the novel gives itself over to incessant celebrations of Pamela's virtue," the reader's pleasure and excitement largely disappear.[31] Critics may speculate helpfully about Richardson's purposes in continuing *Pamela* I or composing *Pamela* II, but they still clearly prefer the premarital text.[32] As her wedding day draws near, even Pamela herself seems to have some suspicion that the best is behind her, and "can but wonder at the thoughtless precipitancy with which most young folks run into this important change of life" (p. 359). In Pamela's anxiety to delay the crucial event, Richardson sensitively registers the ambivalent desire and dread of the adolescent virgin[33] as well as an understandable apprehension of all the discipline and self-suppression that her marriage to B will obviously entail. There is, as she says, "something greatly awful . . . in the solemn circumstance, and a change of condition never to be recalled"; more than once she notes that a "strange" and "heavy" weight seems to hang about her mind and heart as the solemn moment approaches (pp. 359, 363, 364). When B urges her to move up the date, she hesitates and compromises, worrying lest she appear too "forward" (pp. 354, 357, 359). And on the appointed day itself, she begins to divide her journal not by days but by hours—entering separate lengthy accounts at 6:00 and 8:30 in the morning, another at 3:00, and still another at 10:00—as if she could prolong the delaying action still further by extending the record of her modest pen.

Though Richardson decorously makes clear that Pamela enjoys her wedding night ("How does this excellent man indulge me in every thing!" she exclaims in her journal the first thing the next morning— p. 380), there is a sense in which the end of her modest delaying action also marks the end of her record as an erotic narrative. Whatever pleasures the wedding night may have held for the sixteen-year-old virgin cannot be told—and not only because the modesty of Richardson's own pen prevents it. Like other forms of satisfaction, sexual fulfillment belongs to what D. A. Miller has called the "nonnarratable": [34] in the absence of desire, there can be no story. For all the clumsy aggression of B's attempts on Pamela's virtue and the tendency of the seduction scenes to play as farce, the history of his attempts and her resistance has an erotic tension that necessarily dissipates when that resistance is over. As the long-circuiting that produces narrative, Pamela's modesty has enabled her to keep her virtue and yet to have a story. Though she certainly retains her virtue after the wedding, what follows is more conduct book than narrative.

But there is still another sense in which readers' dissatisfaction with the later portions of the novel register a problem of modesty—a modesty defined not so much by the heroine's sexual innocence as by her humility. As the gap between her desires and her awareness closes, as the enigma of her own heart is unveiled to her and the enigma of her future is resolved, Pamela's text comes to sound increasingly self-conscious and complacent. That she is a first-person narrator who is also the heroine of her own story has meant that she has, of course, always been liable to this sort of immodesty; Pamela's scrupulous recording of her own virtue and what one critic has termed her "prehensile ear for praise" have constituted a moral and formal problem from the start.[35] Yet insofar as Richardson has successfully imagined for her a time of unconsciousness—insofar as some information is delayed or occluded—Pamela's early vanities still retain a kind of innocence. In the opening section of the novel, Pamela removes the finery she has acquired and dresses herself in the simple clothes of a country girl in order to return to her parents; admiring her image in the mirror, she looks about her "as proud as any thing," and then goes down to look for Mrs. Jervis, moralizing along the way about the pleasures of "an humble mind" (p. 88). But between this realistically proud-yet-humble girl and the married woman who composes four verses on the theme "My only pride's HUMILITY" (p. 514) is a subtle but telling difference. The didactic poem has a self-consciousness and an insistent teleology that the dramatic scene, contradictory and uncertain in its outcome, manages to avoid. Though "as it happened," B as well as Mrs. Jervis gets to view Pamela in her new costume and obviously finds this "tight smart lass" appealing (pp. 88, 89), she cannot be said deliberately to exploit the attractions of her sartorial modesty; unlike the later girl who delays naming her marriage date lest she "may *seem to be* forwarder" than her future husband might wish (p. 357, emphasis mine), she is not yet quite aware of the effects of her "humility" on B. The problem of *Pamela,* then, is not only that we know her virtue is rewarded but that Pamela comes to know and register it too. And the problem of rereading *Pamela*—or even of reading it for the first time with too much awareness of what is to come—is that it becomes especially difficult to distinguish our knowledge from hers. A modest heroine with too strong a sense of an ending, in other words, is in danger of undoing her story.

7

Fanny Hill's Virgin Heart

❧

Fanny Hill has scarcely acquired a reputation for modesty. The heroine and narrator of "that most licentious and inflaming book," as Boswell termed the *Memoirs of a Woman of Pleasure*,[1] seems to make both her living and her text out of repeated violations of female virtue. Unlike the heroines of more conventionally respectable novels, the fifteen-year-old Fanny loses little time in awakening to sexual desire: easily gulled into entering a brothel the morning after her arrival in London, she is rapidly "enflamed . . . beyond the power of modesty to oppose its resistance" by the "lascivious touches" of a whore practiced in the art of "break[ing]" young girls and by voyeuristic observation of the sexual encounters of others.[2] Cleland's fiction is premised on the masculine fantasy that the "woman of pleasure" pleases herself as well as her customers: having willingly surrendered her virginity to the first handsome young man she sees, Fanny soon embarks on a voluptuously varied career as kept woman and whore—a career to which she is initially driven by economic need when her lover abandons her, but in which she also takes an intensely conscious, if "merely animal," delight (p. 64). By the close of her relatively brief history, Fanny has described in detail more than ten lovers of her own—including a flagellant and a fetishist, and further extended the catalog of erotic possibilities by the interpolated stories of several other whores as well as by additional sophisticated exercises in voyeurism.

Though her story begins, like Pamela's, when she is an artless country girl of fifteen, Fanny's is no moment-to-moment record of confusion but the retrospective narrative of a highly knowing older woman, whose autobiographical recounting of her erotic experiences often appears a means of imaginative reindulging as well. Posing literally as pornogra-

102

phy—that is, as the writing of a whore—Cleland's novel is also pornographic in its extended sense, a text that clearly sets out to arouse the
desires of the reader. And insofar as it has such intentions, it resembles
other pornographic works in sacrificing linear development to the mo-
notonous rhythm of desire: rather than a modest long-circuiting, a prolonged space of reticence and delay, this heroine's narrative seems to
take the form of repeated short-circuits, her history governed by the
theoretically endless cycle of arousal, satisfaction, and the reawakening
of desire.[3] As the center of a pornographic fantasy, Fanny keeps finding
herself overcome by the longings her text seeks to evoke in the reader.
Whether the scene is that of the still virginal girl, whose "glowing
blushes" as she lies naked under the gaze of the lascivious Phoebe are
said to express "more desire than modesty" (p. 12), or of the experienced whore, who feels herself kindling with the fiery aftereffects of
flagellation until she is "devour'd by flames that lick'd up all modesty
and reserve" (p. 151), Fanny seems to possess only such modesty as
may be immediately—if over and over again—negated.

But the very fact that this modesty, which "began to melt away, like
dew before the sun's heat" simply under the influence of the conversation to which the virginal Fanny is exposed at the brothel (p. 23)—and
"all the remains" of which, she reports, were "soon strip'd" from her
under the tutelage of her second lover (p. 67)—is still being "lick'd up"
by the flames of passion so many pages and encounters later suggests
that matters are not so simple. Though Fanny Hill superficially appears
the antithesis of a Pamela Andrews—Lawrence Stone, for example,
speaks of "two contradictory theories about women's sexual nature"
finding "their most extreme expression in imaginative literature at just
the same moment" in Cleland's woman of pleasure and Richardson's
virtuous servant girl[4]—it is no coincidence that the two heroines should
make their appearance at virtually the same moment in literary history,
or that for all the dramatic differences in their fictive careers they should
each end their stories as happily married women. Nor is their resemblance merely a function of Fanny's notorious "tail-piece of morality"
(p. 187)—a last-minute conversion that allows her and her creator
cheerfully to indulge in a protracted career of vice while paying lip service in the concluding paragraphs to the superiority of virtue. Like
Pamela and so many of her fictional successors, Fanny is indeed the heroine of a love story that ends in marriage, but even her experiences of
what she calls "vice" are governed by a related economy: Cleland's representations of sexual pleasure do not so much subvert the conventions
of courtship fiction as render them physiologically immediate and vivid.

Though for more than two centuries following its publication in 1748–
49 the *Memoirs* remained effectively an underground text,[5] this most
famous work of prose pornography in English is essentially a modest
fiction.

Like all good heroines, Fanny Hill loves only once: the man whom
she eventually marries is the man who first takes her virginity and the
"dear possessor" of her "virgin heart" (p. 181). And like many such heroines, she first sees and falls in love with her future husband only after
she has already rejected the advances of another lover—an ugly and
brutish "old goat" named Mr. Crofts (p. 17). Crofts has given the owner
of the brothel a down payment of fifty guineas on Fanny's virginity, but
the repelled and frightened girl resists his attempts to penetrate her.
The scene in which the monstrous Crofts keeps "ogling" Fanny until
she is seized by a "sudden fit of trembling" ("I was so afraid, without a
precise notion of why, and what I had to fear") and then "squat[s]" beside her on the settee and nearly rapes her (p. 18) has reminded one
critic of the confrontation in Richardson's *Clarissa* between the trembling Clarissa and the "bold, staring" Solmes, who also "squat[s]" beside the heroine with his "ugly weight," so that he nearly presses upon
her hoop. As Edward Copeland observes, both Clarissa and Fanny "at
first tolerate the presence of these unwelcome suitors for the sake of
their 'families'": like "Mother" Brown, as the bawd at Fanny's first
brothel is known, the Harlowes are prepared to sell their daughter to a
man who disgusts her in order to aggregate the family estate.[6] Fanny's
own struggle with her odious suitor concludes with her "stretch'd on
the floor" after the fashion of a true Richardsonian heroine, her hair "all
dishevell'd," her nose "gushing out blood" (p. 20)—as Clarissa's nose
also does in the midst of a critical encounter with Lovelace; when
Crofts departs, Fanny temporarily averts any further attempts by falling
into a "violent fever" (p. 22). As so often in the *Memoirs,* Cleland seems
deliberately to parody another text (her nosebleed, Fanny parenthetically remarks, "did not a little tragedize the scene"—p. 20), even as he
makes more physically immediate its sexual implications: when Solmes
intrudes his repellant person on Clarissa's hoop, he, too, effectively
threatens rape.

But beyond the local resemblances to Richardson, the sequence by
which Fanny first violently struggles with the lecherous Crofts and then
awakens to "true" love when she sets eyes on the handsome Charles
makes vivid the erotic logic by which the disagreeable suitor—a Mr.
Collins, say, or even a Mr. Guppy—initiates the plot of so many court-

ship fictions. At once obliquely raising the possibility of the heroine's sexual awakening and drawing off, in effect, her initial hostility and revulsion, such a lover serves symbolically to manage the deep conflict between virginal resistance and desire. For as Freud would later argue in his analysis of the primitive "taboo of virginity," the intense emotions released by the virgin's surrender have at once a potentially civilizing and a dangerous power. In Freud's view, the "sexual bondage" that unites a woman to the man who first takes her virginity is "indispensable to the maintenance of civilized marriage":

Whoever is the first to satisfy a virgin's desire for love, so long and laboriously held in check, and who in doing so overcomes the resistances which have been built up in her through the influences of her milieu and education, that is the man she will take into a lasting relationship, the possibility of which will never again be open to any other man. This experience creates a state of bondage in the woman which guarantees that possession of her shall continue undisturbed and makes her able to resist new impressions and enticements from outside.[7]

The paradox, however, is that the same man also risks unleashing "an archaic reaction of hostility" toward him—a reaction that many primitive peoples seek to forestall, Freud suggests, by ritually employing a man other than the future husband to deflower a virgin.[8] Though even the *Memoirs* stops short of so physically direct a solution—the most Crofts can manage is premature ejaculation—the novel retains something of this "primitive" psychology. Like the disagreeable suitor of more conventionally respectable fiction, who first raises the question of marriage only to be vehemently rejected, the brutish Crofts works not merely to point up the appeal of the handsome and gentle hero but to enable the heroine to make the transition from virginity to love—all the while assuring that she technically preserves that virginity for the man she will marry. Falling in love with her "*Adonis*" (p. 39) as she comes across him for the first time sleeping off the effects of a drunken revelry, Fanny quickly agrees to run away from the brothel under his protection, her secret "elopement" (p. 48) from the house of "Mother" Brown resembling other heroines' flights from home to avoid the prostitution of forced marriage. Though she happily loses her virginity to Charles, Fanny, of course, does not elope to marry. Yet for all the unorthodox speed of her surrender, it is crucial that she does not literally "throw . . . herself into the arms of the first man she meets," as one reader claims,[9] but preserves—in this as in many other senses—some vestige of modesty.

And while she is passionately drawn to Charles the first moment that she sees him, Fanny's awakening to love significantly produces a heightening rather than a loss of modesty: "new-born love," as she calls it, "that true refiner of lust," opposes too sudden a surrender. Though she dwells with obvious longing on the sleeping Charles's "vermillion lips, pouting, and swelling to the touch, as if a bee had freshly stung them," she resists their attraction: "the modesty and respect," which "in both sexes," according to Fanny, "are inseparable from a true passion," check her "impulses." "Love," Fanny claims, makes her newly "timid" (p. 35); and when, after the elopement, the moment approaches at which she is to be alone with her "new sovereign," she reports herself feeling "a timidity which true love had a greater share in, than even maiden bashfulness":

I wish'd, I doated, I could have died for him, and yet I know not how, or why, I dreaded the point which had been the object of my fiercest wishes; my pulses beat fears, amidst a flush of the warmest desires: this struggle of the passions, however, this conflict betwixt modesty and love-sick longings, made me burst again into tears. (P. 38)

Such fear, Fanny's account suggests, proportions itself to the intensity of the desire: the more one "truly" loves, apparently, the more one modestly shrinks from the beloved. Perhaps because the lover longs so intensely for a return, true love makes her timid—the very extravagance of the hope arousing dread lest love not be forthcoming.

That these modest anxieties and fears are not merely a function of "maiden bashfulness"—that "true love is ever modest," as Elizabeth Gaskell would reiterate the doctrine in her own first novel exactly a century later[10]—is brought to the proof at the conclusion of Fanny's erotic adventures, when the return of Charles after their long separation brings with it a return of Fanny's modesty as well. Having recovered from the swoon with which she first greets the discovery of her beloved, Fanny begins to feel the revival of the "true passion . . . with all its train of symptoms":

a sweet sensibility, a tender timidity, love-sick yearnings temper'd with diffidence and modesty, all held me in a subjection of soul, incomparably dearer to me than the liberty of heart which I had been long, too long! the mistress of, in the course of those grosser gallantries, the consciousness of which now made me sigh with a virtuous confusion and regret: no real virgin in short, in view of the nuptial bed, could give more bashful blushes to unblemish'd innocence, than I did to a sense of guilt; and indeed I lov'd *Charles* too truly not to feel severely, that I did not deserve him. (P. 181)

Though she blushes with a consciousness of guilt rather than of "un-blemish'd innocence," hers are still modest blushes: Fanny's intervening history, one may say, has merely given her good and specific reasons— what she calls her "grosser gallantries"—for that sense of undeserving that always accompanies the experience of love. For Cleland as much as Gaskell, true love is ever modest because it is by its nature self-effacing, an intense consciousness of valuing the other more than the self.

As Fanny's guilty blushes testify, such love, of course, has hardly kept her faithful: Charles may have had her virginity, but in her case the civi-lizing effects of "sexual bondage" apparently did not take. True, the man who immediately succeeds Charles must first effectively assume possession by rape, since the shock of her beloved's coerced departure has reduced Fanny to a "death cold corpse" almost worthy of Clarissa: "I did not so much as know what he was about, till recovering from a trance of lifeless insensibility, I found him buried in me, whilst I lay passive and innocent of the least sensation of pleasure" (p. 60). But when Mr. H renews his attempts the same evening—after plying her with "at least half a partridge, and three or four glasses of wine"—he soon senses that there is already "more form and ceremony" than "good earnest" in her resistance (pp. 62, 63); and by the time they have retired to bed an hour later and he has penetrated her again, Fanny, in her own words, has "lost all restraint, and yielding to the force of the emotion, gave down, as mere woman, those effusions of pleasure, which in the strictness of still faithful love, I could have wish'd to have held up" (p. 64). Indeed, it is just this frank division between sexuality and love, the cheerful acknowledgement that women as well as men may feel merely sensual pleasure, that can make Cleland's novel seem attractively modern. Yet if Fanny's subsequent career gives scarce support to the masculine faith that taking a virgin guarantees her future chastity, there is one critical sense in which the rule nonetheless proves well-founded: once she has yielded her "virgin heart" (p. 181) to Charles, Fanny's most important organ can never be penetrated by any other lover. "Amidst all my personal infidelities," she writes on his return, "not one had made a pin's point impression on a heart impenetrable to the true love-passion, but for him" (p. 176).

Other men may variously attract and amuse her, but throughout the *Memoirs,* Fanny's heart remains chaste. "Yet! had not my heart been thus pre-ingag'd, Mr. *H*——might probably have been the sole master of it," she observes of the affair with her second lover, "but the place was full" (p. 65). Like Jane Austen later writing of another and very different heroine named Fanny, Cleland apparently subscribes to the doctrine that the "pre-ingag'd" heart renders itself impregnable to all subsequent advances. And like Austen, who so plots *Mansfield Park* that Fanny Price loves her cousin Edmund from virtually the beginning of the novel, Cleland helps to secure his heroine from further temptation by arranging for her heart to be rapidly occupied. (Fanny Price, too, has "a pre-engaged heart," and despite her consistent disapproval of Henry Crawford, Austen's narrator at one point suggests that even she could not "have escaped heart-whole" from his courtship, "had not her affection been engaged elsewhere" and her "heart been guarded in a way unsuspected by Miss Crawford.")[11] For Cleland, in any case, the fact that his Fanny's heart is "pre-ingag'd" seems to license the remainder of the fantasy—as if he could only indulge her in her cheerful promiscuity by thus assuring himself that she remains essentially untouched. And even as he seems sharply to distinguish love from mere sex, his metaphoric style characteristically tends to return the woman's psychological faithfulness to a function of her anatomy: once having surrendered to Charles, Fanny's heart is "impenetrable" and "the place is full"—as if the question were really whether two men (especially, one might mischievously suggest, two men with the enormous "machines" of Cleland's novel) could simultaneously occupy the same "place" in the woman's body. Indeed, it is worth noting—though perhaps merely as a sign that Charles alone was "born for domestic happiness" (p. 48)—that of all her lovers he appears uniquely capable of impregnating Fanny: between her miscarrying his illegitimate child as a consequence of her grief at their original separation and the birth of an unspecified number of "fine children" after their marriage (p. 187), the possibility that Fanny might be pregnant simply never arises. If this is evidence of judicious contraceptive practice, it is never mentioned; though Mrs. Cole, the experienced and prudent keeper of the second brothel, openly hints at the danger of venereal disease when she insists on investigating the background of all her customers and scolds Fanny for risking her health by engaging with a stranger, neither she nor anyone else ever suggests that sexual encounters might also issue in unwanted children. Insofar as the insistence on female modesty gathers much of its force from the patriarchal need to assure the legitimacy of the family, in other words, this unconscious management of children is another way in which Cleland's imagination allows him to suspend the rules while assuring that they are never seriously threatened. Like a fantastic version of the English heroine who is free to converse with men because she is unconsciously guarded by her modesty, Fanny's body is free to engage in its kind of conversation because it modestly knows when not to conceive.

𝕭

There is another sense in which even in the absence of her true love Fanny retains her modesty—and this despite (or perhaps rather because) she repeatedly describes herself as losing it. As the female resistance that enables male desire, modesty in some form is an attribute that no woman of pleasure can afford to go without. Of course, a hardened prostitute might be expected simply to fake it—substituting for the automatic shrinking and trembling of genuine innocence the affected coyness of a merely professional eroticism. As a successful whore, Fanny in fact does her share of faking—the most egregious instance of which is surely the gulling of Mr. Norbert, the debauched gentleman with the "taste of maiden-hunting" (p. 129) to whom she succeeds, aided and encouraged by Mrs. Cole, in selling herself as an innocent virgin. The elaborate scheme involves Mrs. Cole's device for secreting blood in the posts of the bed so that it can be released to simulate "virgin gore" (p. 136) at the crucial moment of penetration, and much vigorous dissembling of maiden fear and resistance on the part of Fanny. Though the deception of Norbert is more than justified by his own guilty history—according to Mrs. Cole's information, he has "ruin'd a number of girls" (p. 129)—Fanny is still troubled by the part she is playing; and it is characteristic of her erotic morality that between her lack of "taste" for Norbert and her unease at the deception, she should report herself as experiencing in the episode only a "faintish sense" of pleasure (p. 137). But it is also characteristic that even at this stage of her career Fanny's modesty is not all affectation, as her description of herself when she first meets Norbert in Covent Garden clearly indicates:

Now most certainly I was not at all out of figure to pass for a modest girl. I had neither the feathers, nor *fumet* of a tawdry town-miss; a straw hat, a white gown, clean linnen, and above all, a certain natural and easy air of modesty (which the appearances of never forsook me, even on those occasions that I most broke in upon it, in practice) were all signs that gave him no opening to conjecture my condition. He spoke to me, and this address from a stranger throwing a blush into my cheeks, that still set him wider off the truth, I answer'd him, with an awkwardness and confusion the more apt to impose, as there was really, a mixture of the genuine in them. But when proceeding on the foot of having broke the ice, to join discourse, he went into other leading questions, I put so much innocence, simplicity, and even childishness, into my an-

swers, that on no better foundation, liking my person as he did, I will answer
for it, that he would have been sworn for my modesty. (P. 127)

There is always this "mixture of the genuine" in Fanny's modest seem-
ings, as there is always some mixture of true shame in the most erotically
heated of her blushes. The rules at Mrs. Cole's orgiastic "ceremonial of
initiation" (p. 95), for instance, may officially require that "all modesty
and reserve" be "banish'd the transaction of these pleasures" (p. 120),
but Fanny significantly reports that she has "not, however, so thoroughly renounc'd all innate shame, as not to suffer great confusion"
when she finds herself stripped naked before the assembled company.
And though the "roving hands" of her partner will almost immediately
succeed in making "all shame fly before them, and a blushing glow give
place to a warmer one of desire" (p. 122), this very formula for arousal
suggests how the reawakening of desire always depends on there still
being some shame to surrender.[12]

   In Cleland's liberally eroticized world, either sex may apparently take
such pleasure in overcoming the modest reluctance of the other—as
when Fanny seduces the "modest and innocent" Will (p. 70), or Louisa
later arouses the bashful idiot, Dick. Both these episodes suggest how
closely the novel's eroticism is bound up with scenes of initiation,
even as they reverse the conventional roles of the sexes in the process.
Now the experienced women initiate the action, while the men—or
rather boys—are the hesitant virgins, "blushing, and almost trembling" (p. 72). Will "did not himself know," Fanny writes, "that the
pleasure he took in looking at me was love, or desire" (p. 70). The relative ease with which Cleland stages such reversals may owe something
to the fact that he is already engaged in a sexual masquerade: the position of aggressor, after all, can hardly seem foreign to the man who
speaks through Fanny's first-person. Even when the roles have been
thus reversed, in any case, Fanny/Cleland still seems to find something
particularly feminine about a virgin. Feeling that she is "no longer able
to contain" herself, as she puts it at a key moment in Will's seduction,
Fanny laments the "slower progress" of his "maiden bashfulness"—"for
such," she parenthetically adds, "it seem'd, and really was" (p. 72). And
though Fanny begins this scene playing the experienced aggressor to
Will's innocent "maiden," once the action is under way there appears to
occur yet another reversal—as the virginal boy proves to have so enormous a member that he manages to draw blood, and thus "triumph[s]
over a kind of second maiden-head" (p. 76).

   The modesty of inexperience may belong to either sex, in other words, but there is a kind of modest resistance that seems to belong peculiarly to the bodies of women. And one sign that Fanny is especially formed for male desire is her seemingly infinite capacity to renew that resistance. The morning after the seduction of Will, Fanny wakes with anxiety to think of "what innovation that tender soft system of mine might have sustain'd from the shock of a machine so siz'd for its destruction":

> Struck with this apprehension, I scarce dar'd to carry my hand thither, to inform myself of the state and posture of things.
> But I was soon agreeably cur'd of my fears.
> The silky hair that cover'd round the borders, now smooth'd, and reprun'd, had resum'd its wonted curl and trimness; the fleshy pouting lips, that had stood the brunt of the engagement, were no longer swoln or moisture-drench'd: and neither they, nor the passage into which they open'd, that had suffer'd so great a dilation, betray'd any the least alteration, outward or inwardly, to the most curious research, notwithstanding also the laxity that naturally follows the warm bath.
> This continuation of that grateful stricture which is in us, to the men, the very jet of their pleasure, I ow'd, it seems, to a happy habit of body, juicy, plump, and furnish'd towards the texture of those parts, with a fullness of soft springy flesh, that yeilding sufficiently as it does, to almost any distension, soon recovers itself so as to retighten that strict compression of its mantlings and folds which form the sides of the passage wherewith it so tenderly embraces, and closely clips any foreign body introduc'd into it, such as my exploring finger then was. (P. 79)

This "happy habit of body" is another gift of nature, like that "natural and easy air of modesty" that comes so readily to Fanny's aid when she first meets Mr. Norbert. Indeed, just as she finds it "incredible how little it seem'd necessary to strain my natural disposition to modesty" in order to pass herself off to Norbert as "a very maid" in their few social encounters, so she scarcely has need of Mrs. Cole's hidden blood supply to convince him in bed that she is a virgin—so "favour'd as I was by nature," as she reminds us, "with all the narrowness of stricture in that part requisite to conduct my designs" (pp. 131, 131–32).[13]

The natural gifts with which Cleland endows his heroine suggest that one ground for the culture's particular ascription of modesty to women may be the male's erotic experience of the female body: from the man's point of view, the woman's genitalia not only "modestly seem . . . to retire downwards" (p. 29)—unlike his own erect organ—but to offer a certain resistance to him even when she most unambiguously desires their encounter. And the more "narrowness of stricture," the more stimulating friction she supplies—which may be one reason why Cleland's imagination compensates for Fanny's avid interest in Will by fantastically enlarging his organ, while the vitiated Norbert seeks out virgins in order to stimulate a "machine" Fanny dismissively describes as "one of those sizes that slip in and out without being minded" (p. 133). Though in Fanny he in fact takes no virgin, both the natural conformation of her body and her pantomimes of modest resistance help him to achieve whatever pleasure he is able. Since "few men could dispute size" with her dear Charles (p. 40), Fanny's true love naturally has no need of such assistance, but his return nonetheless inspires in her a seemingly instinctive reaction:

But, ah! what became of me, when, as the powers of solid pleasure thickened upon me, I could not help feeling the stiff stake that had been adorned with the trophies of my despoiled virginity, bearing hard and inflexible against one of my thighs, which I had not yet opened, from a true principle of modesty, revived by a passion too sincere to suffer any aiming at the false merit of difficulty, or my putting on an impertinent mock-coyness. (P. 182)

Knowing what Fanny feels and wishes, we can be certain that her closed thighs signal no real resistance—or only, rather, that modest reluctance that always accompanies, and paradoxically intensifies, true love and desire. Sometimes, of course, such gestures signify quite different feelings; but the *Memoirs'* first-person narrative assures that the reader is in no danger of mistaking Fanny's loving response to Charles for her refusal to "unlock" her thighs, for example, in her struggle with Crofts (p. 18). By always speaking as and for his woman of pleasure, Cleland guarantees that no such anxiety-provoking confusions will trouble his blissful masculine fantasy of heterosexual desire.[14]

❦

It is not merely the ending of the *Memoirs* that succumbs to the teleology of romantic courtship: "pornographic" representations are so easily assimilated to a conventional fiction of marriage because the novel's eroticism is already encoded with the values of conjugal love. Though his heroine earns her living as a whore, Cleland manages to make virtually all the sex in the novel seem motivated by free choice rather than by compulsion: compared to Moll Flanders, for example—whose story at several points the *Memoirs* superficially resembles—Fanny pays far more attention to questions of feeling than of economic pressure.[15] As in so many novels of romantic love, money appears to be an incidental by-product rather than the end of heterosexual relations: the focus at any one moment is on the intimate association of two persons and the subtle adjustments of feeling between them. Even those relations that seem most nearly determined by mere calculation or use always entail a certain respect, even affection, for the partner. It is characteristic of Fanny that she should deliberately choose to call Norbert, for instance, her "lover" rather than a "cully" (a derogatory term for a man tricked by a strumpet—p. 132), or that she should feel herself "aw'd into a sort of respect" even for the idiot, Dick—seeing him as elevated rather than debased by his desire for Louisa (p. 164). Indeed, except for the repellent Crofts, to whom, of course, she refuses to surrender, Fanny describes all her men more or less sympathetically. Mr. H, for instance, who begins so unpropitiously, continues "kind and tender" and wins her "esteem" (p. 66); only when he casually betrays her with the serving girl does she decide to betray him in turn, acting more like an outraged wife avenging her husband's adultery than like a woman who regards sex merely as a financial proposition. As for the sensually so gratifying Will, Fanny recalls her "liking" as so "extreme" that "it was distinguishing very nicely to deny" that she loved him (p. 84). Even Barvile, the young flagellant—the one character in the novel who directly associates erotic pleasure with pain—turns out to be in an "habitual state of conflict with, and dislike of himself, for being enslav'd to so peculiar a gust," and otherwise to possess a "natural sweetness of . . . temper" (pp. 145, 146). Though Fanny not only agrees to beat him but submits to being beaten, neither sadism nor masochism inspires her role in the exchange—only curiosity and the honorable impulse never to refuse a dare. And while Barvile himself wishes to be tied up while being beaten, it is typical of the novel that he should courteously decline Fanny's equally courteous offer to reciprocate, insisting that her participation be "completely voluntary" and that she have "full liberty" to get up whenever she chooses (p. 149).

From one perspective, this pleasant catalog merely reminds us that the *Memoirs* is essentially an idyll: a nicer collection of sensualists and perverts one would be hard put to find. But it is also important to register how far the novel is from merely offering what one critic characterizes as a "succession of naked, churning bodies"—and how for all the illusion of polymorphous play and variety, it insistently channels erotic pleasure toward the voluntary engagement of an affectionate and heterosexual couple. Though a number of people are gathered on the scene, the initiation ceremonies at Mrs. Cole's significantly do not involve "group sex"[16] but the group's watching of an orderly sequence of couples. Indeed, the rules of the institution specifically enforce a kind of temporary monogamy: "it was an inviolable law," Fanny reports, "for every gallant to keep to his partner, for the night especially"—a law designed to preserve what she terms "a pleasing property" and "to avoid the disgusts and indelicacy of another arrangement" (p. 124). Thus the collective ritual concludes in dyadic withdrawal, as each man leads to bed the same woman with whom he has first publicly made love before the assembled company. The ceremonial displays of sex are designed to initiate Fanny into the group, but the end of the exercises is not some promiscuous intermingling: rather like a community gathered at a wedding, the spectators at once voyeuristically revel in and celebrate heterosexual union, while they pressure the as yet uninitiated to follow the example. As Fanny's designated partner explains to her, "the older standers were to set an example, which he hop'd I would not be averse to follow . . . but . . . still I was perfectly at my liberty to refuse the party, which being in its nature one of pleasure, suppos'd an exclusion of all force, or constraint" (p. 113). This gentleman proves, of course, a "noble and agreeable youth," with whom Fanny subsequently lives "in perfect joy and constancy," until he is sent off, like Charles before him, by his father (p. 126). Typically, it is not Fanny (nor, for that matter, even her lover) but some external person or force who breaks off the relation: with the exception of the love affair by which she avenges Mr. H's unfaithfulness, and her single act of intercourse with the sailor, Cleland's heroine clearly prefers serial monogamy. The "inviolable law" at Mrs. Cole's has only a limited extension, but when the other women's lovers approach her in search of variety, Fanny resists their advances. Moved by her attachment to her own lover and what she calls a "tenderness of invading the choice of my companions" (p. 127), Cleland's heroine effectively helps to enforce communal chastity.

But more than a certain habit of monogamy constrains the novel's eroticism. The indulgent Mrs. Cole may defend the unhappy flagellant by invoking the "infinitely diversify'd" and "arbitrary" nature of erotic appetite, but in fact even she has little tolerance for polymorphic experience. "For her part," Fanny reports in summing up Mrs. Cole's seemingly libertine doctrine, "she consider'd pleasure of one sort or other, as the universal port of destination, and every wind that blew thither a good one, provided it blew nobody any harm." Insofar as Fanny's "good temporal mother" speaks for the novel as well (p. 144), the latent teleology of its running metaphor betrays her—for "pleasure of one sort or other" essentially turns out to be pleasure of one sort only, and desire is always pointed in a single direction. Fanny's own desires, once aroused, "all pointed strongly to their pole, man" (p. 27)—and this by a natural magnetism that apparently operates despite the role that Phoebe plays in their awakening.[17] Recent theorists of gender have helped to explain why a masculine culture typically finds the homoeroticism of women far less threatening than that of men; and one sign of the relative ease with which such "deviance" may be accommodated is this persistent fantasy of the lesbian who is not an object of desire herself but an erotic agent and intermediary for the male.[18] Like *Pamela*'s Mrs. Jewkes, with her masculine kisses, Phoebe functions as a servant of the heterosexual plot—the immodest woman who works to break down another woman's defenses.[19] That the *Memoirs*' only scene of male homosexuality, in contrast, was cut from most editions of the novel for more than two hundred years (a censorship apparently originating in governmental pressure) [20] is an irony that merely confirms how little this "underground" text actually departs from the dominant values of its culture. For the most striking aspect of the episode itself is how abruptly the novel's otherwise genial warmth turns to "burning . . . rage, and indignation," the vehement disgust this "infamous passion" inspires in both Fanny and her mentor. Though Mrs. Cole alludes to "the common cause of woman-kind, out of whose *mouths* this practice tended to take something more precious than bread" (p. 159), the intense anxiety with which the issue is at once introduced and dismissed is clearly more masculine than feminine. Mrs. Cole's bawdy pun also recalls how much emphasis the novel has placed on the natural "fit" of male and female genitals—an anatomical teleology that the possibility of sodomy obviously threatens. Indeed, it is one more sign of what might be called the novel's monomorphic sexuality that the sodomizing of women is also, if less anxiously, rejected. Having disobeyed Mrs. Cole's advice never to consort with strangers, her "daughters" twice find themselves in the awkward position of having to redirect an errant male member. Emily attends a masked ball dressed as a shepherd, is picked up by a man who mistakes her for a boy, and narrowly manages to preserve "a maiden-head she had not dreamt of" (p. 155). In her casual encounter with the sailor, Fanny successfully averts a similar danger. Admonished that he is "going by the right door, and knocking desperately at the wrong," the easygoing sailor replies, "Pooh . . . my dear, any port in a storm"; but he dutifully alters "his course" (p. 141). The novel's prevailing winds, to extend its running metaphor, consistently blow in a single direction. Even poor Barvile, it might be noted, proves true to form, ending his scene in conventional (if rather acrobatic) intercourse. Only the elderly fetishist who is content merely to comb Fanny's hair and nibble at her white gloves might qualify as an exception, but this "most innocent, and most insipid trifler" would hardly be out of place in the most respectable of fictions: "all this led to no other use of my person," Fanny reports, "or any other liberties whatever, any more than if a distinction of sexes had not existed" (p. 153).

᭼

An erotic writer whose imagination focuses on the awakening of innocence, the scene of initiation, faces the problem of having to begin again and again. Settling Fanny in Mrs. Cole's "little family of love" (p. 93) at the beginning of the second volume of the *Memoirs* provides Cleland with a transparently artificial means of spinning out elegant variations on his theme—most obviously in the round-robin of rather specialized autobiographies with which one of the whores proposes that they wile away the time between Fanny's arrival and the official welcoming ceremonies of the evening. The artifice of Emily's proposal—"that each girl should entertain the company with that critical period of her personal history, in which she first exchanged the maiden state for womanhood" (p. 96)—is further compounded by the strict rules of the game, which prevent the narratives from passing beyond the scene of defloration. Summarily alluding to the events that followed her own loss of virginity, Emily announces that "these are all circumstances which pass the mark I proposed, so that here my narrative ends" (p. 99). And each of the subsequent speakers self-consciously keeps to that boundary, adhering to it as closely as a Frances Burney or a Jane Austen would adhere to the convention that concludes the young woman's history with her marriage. These tales, in other words, resemble less the typical whore-biographies of the period, with their loosely picaresque plotting,[21] than they do its courtship fiction. Beginning with the first stirrings of desire and ending with the loss of virginity, they provide the erotic subtext to all those histories of the young lady's entrance into the world. That the latent eroticism of such histories partly depends on their very limits is implicit not only in Emily's rules but in the many indirect ways in which Cleland keeps restoring to Fanny the hypothesis of a virginity, or at least a modesty, to lose. It is hardly coincidental that before the collective storytelling begins, Mrs. Cole specifically exempts both herself and Fanny from participating—herself on account of her age (she is too old, apparently, to be imagined as an erotic subject), and Fanny on account of her "titular maidenhood" (p. 96). Having supplied Fanny with a fictional virginity so that she may lose it twice again—first ritually at the initiation ceremonies and then for a profit with Mr. Norbert—Mrs.

Cole also helps to get the second volume of the *Memoirs* under way by artificially erasing the first, returning its narrator to the position of one who has no "story."

The account that each of the whores gives of losing her virginity defines her as a feminine type and places her on a scale at once erotic and moral. The complaisant Emily goes to bed with a young man in utter innocence but soon finds herself yielding easily; Harriet, who is "delicacy itself incarnate" (p. 99), meets her first lover in a scene of modest confusion, is initially taken in a swoon, and then with her "tacit blushing consent" (p. 105); while the lustful Louisa, herself an illegitimate child, furiously masturbates at twelve and eagerly searches out the first young man she can find. Not surprisingly, it is the modest Harriet—whose swoon, the narrative punningly suggests, is no "feint" (p. 104)—who most attracts Cleland's heroine. Harriet's lovemaking at the public ceremonies is accomplished with "a peculiar grace of sweetness, modesty, and yeilding coyness" that Fanny admires intensely (p. 114); as soon as it is over, Fanny rushes to embrace her, so that Harriet may "hide her blushes and confusion at what had past" in her new friend's bosom (p. 117). Unlike the rest of the company, Harriet and her partner—who happens to be a baronet—are of course in love; when Fanny later reports that the other men sought variety with her, she carefully excepts Harriet's faithful lover. Fanny's "great favourite" is obviously her author's as well, and she is rewarded accordingly: when we last hear of her she is living happily with the baronet, loving him with "tenderness and constancy," and possessed of a "handsome provision" for her and her dependents (p. 143). Less aristocratically delicate than Harriet, Emily nonetheless retains a certain "natural modesty" (p. 118), and Cleland frequently associates her lovemaking with the topoi of the virtue, even representing her at one moment in the posture of the *Venus pudica*.[22] "One of those mild, pliant characters, that if one does not entirely esteem, one can scarce help loving"—rather like Harriet Smith in Jane Austen's *Emma*—Emily is eventually married off to a sensible young man "of her own rank" and proves a model of domestic duty and affection (pp. 171, 172). Only Louisa's end remains appropriately unsettled, as she disappears "abroad" with a young man: as in the case of Lydia Bennet in Austen's *Pride and Prejudice,* her passion has proved stronger than her discretion (p. 166).

Before Fanny herself is allowed to marry, Cleland sees to it that she receives final training in the sort of erotic economy best suited to conjugal relations. To Mrs. Cole's "admirable lessons" in the "œconomy" of

her person and her purse (p. 125), Fanny's last lover adds instruction in
the capacity of the mind to "exalt and perfect" the delights of the body,
and the practical example of one who has mastered the reciprocal connection between sexual pleasure and restraint. While the debauched
Norbert was worn out at thirty, the "rational pleasurist" remains still
fresh and vigorous at sixty (p. 175). Like most of the figures in the
Memoirs, it should be said, this worthy gentleman is scarcely a realized
character: his entire history in the novel occupies little more than a half-
dozen paragraphs—just long enough to sketch in his doctrine and to
provide Fanny with a handsome settlement. Nor does all his care for his
health prevent him from conveniently dispatching himself before the return of Charles by standing so long near an open window to observe a
fire that he contracts a fatal cold from the damp night air. But as an
idealized token of "the power of age to please, if it lays out to please"
(p. 175), he seems a promising figure for the married couple to emulate, and a happy precursor of their long life together. The future author
of the *Institutes of Health* (1761) concludes his *Memoirs of a Woman of
Pleasure* in praise of the medicinal and erotic virtues of temperance—a
temperance that paradoxically works both to prolong life and vigor and
to intensify the experience of pleasure. As the *Institutes* would formulate the doctrine in one of Cleland's typically mechanical figures, nature
has so arranged matters that virtue "is to pleasure of the same service
that conduit-pipes, in a certain direction, are to water, confine it only to
raise it the higher."[23] Such virtuous moderation extends indefinitely;
and it is no accident that it should make its appearance toward the conclusion of the novel, as Cleland, like so many of his contemporaries,
seeks to accommodate the intensities of romantic love to the promise of
continuity in marriage.

᛭

Pornography as a form notoriously tends to repeat itself. "A pornographic work of fiction characteristically develops by unremitting repetition and minute mechanical variation," Steven Marcus has observed;
"the words that may describe this process are again, again, again, and
more, more, more."[24] At one point Cleland has Fanny herself wittily
acknowledge this generic liability: "I imagined indeed," she remarks to
her unnamed correspondent as she begins the second volume of the
Memoirs,

that you would have been cloy'd and tired with the uniformity of adventures
and expressions, inseparable from a subject of this sort, whose bottom or

ground-work being, in the nature of things, eternally one and the same, whatever variety of forms and modes, the situations are susceptible of, there is no
escaping a repetition of near the same images, the same figures, the same expressions, with this further inconvenience added to the disgust it creates, that the
words *joys, ardours, transports, extasies,* and the rest of those pathetic terms so
congenial to, so received in the *practise of pleasure,* flatten, and lose much of
their due spirit and energy, by the frequency they indispensibly recur with, in a
narrative of which that *practise* professedly composes the whole basis. (P. 91)

As most modern commentators on the novel have observed, Cleland's
own solution to this problem is above all rhetorical: rather than repeat
"the same images, the same figures, the same expressions," the *Memoirs*
elegantly varies them—producing close to fifty different tropes, by one
count, for the male organ alone, from the sublimely vague "grand
movement" to the bathetically concrete "conduit pipe," from the aggressive "furious battering ram" to the voluptuous "delicious stretcher"
and the domesticated "beloved guest." The variations on the female are
less numerous, but equally playful and hyperbolic—"theatre," "cock-
pit," "dark and delicious deep," "pouting-lipt mouth," "soft laboratory
of love," and "embowered bottom-cavity" among them.[25] Several critics
have argued that such stylistic play identifies Cleland's novel as parody
or burlesque;[26] and there seems little question that when Fanny describes Barvile, for instance, as exposing "some thing of the air of a
round fillet of the whitest veal," the immediate effect is less pornographic than comic (p. 148). But as the precedent of Jacobean and
Caroline poetry suggests,[27] verbal wit is not incompatible with erotic
intentions, and when Fanny herself defends her "figurative style," it is
the "poetry" of sex that she emphasizes—declaring her subject "properly the province of poetry, nay! . . . poetry itself, pregnant with every
flower of imagination and loving metaphors" (p. 171).

The author of the *Memoirs of a Woman of Pleasure* was, after all, the
man who reproved the author of *Tristram Shandy* because he found the
latter's "bawdy too plain": "if you had a pupil who wrote c—— on
the wall," he infuriated Sterne by demanding, "would you not flog
him?" Indeed, Cleland seems to have particularly prided himself on his
own euphemistic virtuosity: according to Boswell, he boasted that he
wrote the *Memoirs* in order to show what could be done without resort-
ing to the "plain words" of *L'École des filles*—a popular work of continental pornography.[28] Fanny, of course, never writes "c——" and
scrupulously avoids what she calls "the revoltingness of gross, rank, and
vulgar expressions" (p. 91). As Jean Hagstrum has remarked, "Cleland
is in his way as delicate as Henry MacKenzie."[29] But as with so many

forms of "delicacy," the motives behind all this euphemistic indirection seem notably double. For what was wrong with Sterne's "plain" bawdy, according to Cleland, was that it gave "no sensations" [30]—a verdict that makes one wonder whether the hypothetical pupil was to be flogged for vulgarity or for a failure of erotic invention. Recall how the problem of writing that Fanny poses sounds also like the problem of stimulating desire: the risk, she suggests, is that "the words *joys, ardours, transports, extasies,* and the rest" will "flatten, and lose much of their due spirit and energy." From this perspective, the style that avoids the "gross" and the "rank" is also a style that avoids the boredom of the "eternally one and the same." Like repeated changes of clothing whose function is at once to reveal and conceal, the rhetoric of the *Memoirs* serves as an elaborate tease—proliferating new figures in order to reawaken the erotic imagination.

Far from being at odds with the impulse to represent sex as the essential subject, the *Memoirs'* delicacy has the effect of encouraging the reader to find it everywhere, to make almost no phrase seem "innocent"—as the promptness with which critics identify puns even in passages that do not directly concern erotic encounters clearly testifies. If "what is peculiar to modern societies," as Michel Foucault has argued, "is not that they consigned sex to a shadow existence, but that they dedicated themselves to speaking of it *ad infinitum,* while exploiting it as *the* secret," [31] then the *Memoirs of a Woman of Pleasure* is a representative modern text. That pornography should have clearly emerged as a recognizable genre in Western Europe in the middle of the seventeenth century [32]—at roughly the same time that the culture began to elaborate what I have been calling its fictions of modesty—is neither coincidence nor evidence of repression and reaction, but a single phenomenon: both kinds of writing are part of that "discursive explosion" around and apropos of sex that Foucault has identified as one of the distinguishing characteristics of the modern period. [33] The very fact that the *Memoirs* can appear to occupy both categories simultaneously—at once pornography and modest fiction—only helps to clarify the singleness of the phenomenon. Though Cleland's relative conservatism may make his seem an exceptional case, all pornography, I would suggest, requires some boundary to violate, and thus always needs to postulate some fiction of modesty—just as such fiction always depends on the hypothesis, however arbitrary, of a "bawdy too plain."

But if Cleland's work may be understood as contributing to a new kind and intensity of erotic writing—and to a more general shift in the Western consciousness of sexuality—it is also important to recognize how this most famous work of English pornography immediately sets itself apart from its Continental predecessors. Unlike the more significant European representatives of the genre—*La Puttana Errante* (c. 1650), *L'École des filles* (1655), and Nicolas Chorier's *Satyra Sotadica* (1660)—the English novel imaginatively weds its eroticism to an ideal of conjugal love and concludes its narrative with a happy marriage.[34] While certain "*French* authors" had "given themselves the false air of turning conjugal love into ridicule," Cleland would declare in a review of Fielding's *Amelia* a few years later, "be it said, to the honour of the *English,* and to this writer in particular, that he never thought so ill of the public, as to make his court to it at the expence of the sacred duties of morality." Far from ridiculing marriage, "the chief and capital purport of this work is to inculcate the superiority of virtuous conjugal love to all other joys," and "to prove that virtue chastens our pleasures, only to augment them."[35] Though in comparison with Fielding's long-suffering heroine Cleland's had been in more than one sense a woman of easy virtue, her history had nonetheless been shaped to similar ends.

Fanny Hill presumably had no Latin, but if she had been able to read Chorier's amorous dialogues, what she would have found most unfamiliar was neither the sexual practices he represented nor those he condemned (the *Satyra,* too, rejects sodomy), but his fictional premise: though the worldly-wise Tullia begins by initiating her young cousin Octavia in the enjoyment of marital sexuality, she then continues her instruction with the pleasures of discreet adultery. *L'École des filles,* too, takes for granted that wedded love becomes routine, and concludes with the more experienced Susanne urging the young Fanchon to get married so that she can take a lover. But Cleland's heroine would have been very pleased to learn that when an adaptation of Chorier's work appeared in England in 1740, all signs of adultery (and of homoeroticism as well) had disappeared from the text. In English, the two women talk only of marital bliss, and the work ends with a night of wedded "Extasy." Fanny might also have been gratified to learn that when Octavia speaks English, she speaks often of her "Modesty."[36]

8

Evelina's Self-Effacing

⅌

For all narrative purposes, Fanny Hill has no father, only an adopted "mother" who is also a bawd. Evelina Anville's story, on the other hand, depends on her having not one father but two—and no sooner has she met her future lover than she is dreaming of the day when his "vivacity" will have "abated" and he will be old enough to resemble them.[1] If modest heroines are their fathers' daughters, then Fanny Hill's father-lessness—like her temporary childlessness—is one of the fantastic conditions that enable her immodest career: so long as she remains a woman of pleasure, the very possibility of paternity is banished from her narrative, which recounts a timeless idyll of peer relations, not a history of succession and inheritance. Though I have argued that the erotic success of Cleland's heroine nonetheless requires a kind of modesty, it is not a kind that the heroine of Burney's first novel—or that Burney herself, for that matter—could consciously recognize.

Indeed, in a narrative filled with scenes of embarrassment and confusion, perhaps none registers as more agonizing than the nightmarish episode in which Evelina finds herself walking the grounds of Maryle-bone gardens arm-in-arm with two women of the town, and twice manages to cross the path of Lord Orville. The first time, to her "infinite joy," he passes the group without distinguishing her (p. 234), but the second time she is not so lucky—and the awkward recognition scene that follows provides a paradigm of all the painful face-to-face encounters that keep threatening to mortify Burney's heroine:

And this was our situation,—for we had not taken three steps, when,—O Sir,—we again met Lord Orville!—but not again did he pass quietly by us,—

unhappily I caught his eye;—both mine, immediately, were bent to the ground; but he approached me, and we all stopped. I then looked up. He bowed. Good God, with what expressive eyes did he regard me! Never were surprise and concern so strongly marked,—yes, my dear Sir, he looked *greatly* concerned; and that, the remembrance of that, is the only consolation I feel, for an evening the most painful of my life.

What he first said, I know not; for, indeed, I seemed to have neither ears nor understanding; but I recollect that I only courtsied in silence. He paused for an instant, as if—I believe so,—as if unwilling to pass on; but then, finding the whole party detained, he again bowed, and took leave.

Indeed, my dear Sir, I thought I should have fainted, so great was my emotion from shame, vexation, and a thousand other feelings, for which I have no expressions. (P. 235)

As Margaret Doody has recently argued, the narrative form of *Evelina*, with its combination of public scene and personal record, is especially well-suited to studies of embarrassment.[2] Like Richardson, Burney exploits the modest woman's affinity for the private letter, but, as we shall see, she characteristically turns even that intimate record to purposes at once satiric and sociological.

Evelina is subtitled *The History of a Young Lady's Entrance into the World,* and the Marylebone scene emblematically stages the risk that every young lady runs who ventures "out" into public spaces—the risk of being seen to be one who belongs in them, a woman of the town, as the idiom has it, or one who walks the streets.[3] Having met Evelina several times before, Orville is scarcely in any real danger of mistaking her for a prostitute, but the mere fact that she is observed in such company, she rightly fears, is enough to taint her. The mental paralysis she describes is typical of one who suffers acute embarrassment: so confused is she that she cannot register what, if anything, is spoken—only the anxious experience of being looked at, or rather, of looking at one who looks at her and trying to read his "expressive eyes." Evelina's dread of being judged by the company she keeps, her obsession with watching herself being watched, and her striking propensity to land herself again and again in such exquisitely embarrassing predicaments all warrant closer study. But it is first worth noting that the intensity of Evelina's need to distinguish herself from her immodest associates is almost matched by her need not to distinguish too closely just what it is that she is avoiding. Finding herself alone in the crowd after having fled the noise of some fireworks, she seeks protection with the "two ladies" from a young officer who has violently accosted her—only to realize, as she later writes to her guardian, that "I had sought protection from insult, of those who were themselves most likely to offer it!" This notably oblique formula for describing a pair of prostitutes is the most explicit that Evelina ever offers, and surrounded by protestations of not-naming: in one sentence she "will not dwell" on their conversation, and her horror at her discovery is "inexpressible," while in the next she has "no words to describe" the terror she feels (p. 233).

That such modest obliquity in some sense covers for the young lady's immodest venturing forth into the world is suggested by a bit of manuscript history. In one of the early drafts of the novel—a draft written in secret for the amusement of Frances Burney and her sisters and not yet clearly intended for publication—Evelina had summed up her distress at the incident, exclaiming to "gracious Heaven!" at having been seen "in company with 2 women of the Town!" But when Burney came to revise the novel for the public eye, she apparently felt that her heroine could not afford to be so explicit: in the printed text, Evelina alludes only to "two women of such character!" (p. 237).[4] Though one might argue that Evelina's very inability to recognize the calling of the women at first glance is what gets her into trouble, to be more knowing would be to risk contamination: her true distance from the prostitutes with whom she is haplessly entangled is gauged by her inability even to articulate who they are.

A corresponding vagueness protects Evelina from too intimate relations with her own heart. Like so many fictions of modesty, Burney's depends on the premise that her heroine is long unconscious of her desire for the hero—though "desire" is perhaps too strong a word to name feelings that in Evelina's case remain properly sublimed to the end. While she has scarcely made her entrance into the world before she is ready to pronounce Lord Orville "the most agreeable, and, seemingly, the most amiable man" in it (p. 37), more than two volumes will have to pass before Evelina becomes formally acquainted with the state of her feelings. The speed with which her heart secretly engages itself guards her from emotional promiscuity—Orville happens to be her first partner at her very first ball—even as her ignorance about what has occurred absolves her from the charge of being too "forward" and enables the delaying action that constitutes her narrative. Like *Pamela*, *Evelina* prolongs the fiction of its heroine's innocence by temporarily displacing a part of her self—the heart that, as Pamela says, gives itself up without ever consulting its "poor mistress."[5] And as in Richardson's novel, there eventually comes a moment at which the heroine must discover her secret. But the greater distance at which erotic feeling is held in Burney's imagination means that the climactic knowledge arrives considerably

later in the narrative—and even when it comes, it comes not as the surfacing of buried awareness but as a message from outside the self, in the
form of a letter from the heroine's guardian and surrogate father. One
condition of Evelina's extended sojourn in the world has apparently
been that her consciousness of her own sexuality remain at home in the
safekeeping of the Reverend Villars:

> Hitherto I have forborne to speak with you upon the most important of all
> concerns, the state of your heart:—alas, I needed no information! I have been
> silent, indeed, but I have not been blind.
> Long, and with the deepest regret, have I perceived the ascendancy which
> Lord Orville has gained upon your mind.—You will start at the mention of his
> name,—you will tremble every word you read;—I grieve to give pain to my
> gentle Evelina, but I dare not any longer spare her.
> Your first meeting with Lord Orville was decisive. Lively, fearless, free from
> all other impressions, such a man as you describe him could not fail exciting
> your admiration, and the more dangerously, because he seemed as unconscious
> of his power as you of your weakness; and therefore you had no alarm, either
> from *his* vanity or *your own* prudence.
> Young, animated, entirely off your guard, and thoughtless of consequences,
> *imagination* took the reins, and *reason,* slow-paced, though sure-footed, was
> unequal to a race with so eccentric and flighty a companion. How rapid was
> then my Evelina's progress through those regions of fancy and passion whither
> her new guide conducted her!—She saw Lord Orville at a ball,—and he was *the
> most amiable of men!*—She met him again at another,—and *he had every virtue
> under Heaven!* . . .
> You flattered yourself, that your partiality was the effect of esteem, founded
> upon a general love of merit, and a principle of justice: and your heart, which
> fell the sacrifice of your error, was totally gone ere you suspected it was in
> danger. (Pp. 308–9)

Having long kept silent, Villars apparently decides the time has come
to speak because Evelina's feelings have risen dangerously close to the
surface of her awareness: in her last letter to him, she had declared herself "the happiest of human beings" at having been reconciled with
Orville after a misunderstanding (p. 307). So long as she remained unconscious, it seems, she could be trusted to remain in Orville's company, but once her feelings have been made known to her, she must
return home immediately. "Awake, then, my dear, my deluded child,"
Villars exhorts her: "awake to the sense of your danger, and exert yourself to avoid the evils with which it threatens you. . . . You must quit
him!" (p. 309). Though he never explicitly names the "evils" she must
flee, Villars presumably takes for granted that Orville will never marry
the propertyless and nameless Evelina, whose father has abandoned her

mother and refused to recognize their child—and that if the loving girl were to remain under these conditions she would necessarily be vulnerable to seduction. But in summoning Evelina home only after she has had two volumes in which to get to know Lord Orville—or at least to encounter him on virtually every public occasion—Villars unwittingly helps to make clear how the young girl's unconsciousness serves the uses of the courtship plot. "A thousand times have I been upon the point of shewing you the perils of your situation," he writes; "but the same inexperience which occasioned your mistake, I hoped, with the assistance of time and absence, would effect a cure" (p. 309). The "same inexperience" at once entangles her in a love story and delays its consummation; under the cover of innocence the heroine's heart is awakened, and under the cover of that same innocence she can stay out in the world long enough to be both courted and married. Had Evelina not been so unconscious of her own "weakness," her guardian claims, she would have taken the alarm much earlier. But had this heroine's consciousness thus kept pace with her feelings, there would have been no period of gradual friendship with the hero, no time for him to learn her merits—and very little narrative. A young woman who entered the world only to beat such a hasty retreat could scarcely have a story.

Of course, there would be no question of Evelina's taking the alarm were it not for the speed with which her heart leaps to commit itself. "Your first meeting with Lord Orville," Villars tells her, "was decisive." A young woman whose "fancy and passion" are so quick to carry her away, whose heart can be "totally gone" so rapidly, has full need of the delaying mechanism that her unconsciousness provides. The preternatural vulnerability of Evelina's heart may owe something to Burney's own remarkable sensitivity: at sixteen, one year younger than her heroine, she recorded in her diary her stepmother's verdict that she would "*never* be happy! *Never* while she live[d]!" because she possessed "perhaps as feeling a heart as ever girl had!"[6] But both the account that Burney gives of her heroine and the one she records of herself should remind us that the fiction of innocence has not so much replaced as covered over another, older, representation of the sex—a view of woman as all feeling "heart," all erotic body and desire.[7] Only the walls of her father's house—or perhaps a convent—would suffice to keep such a woman safe for marriage: were she to venture beyond its boundaries, she would soon be "totally gone" indeed. Though Evelina's heart proves vulnerable to virtually the first man she meets (the only partner she rejects before dancing with Orville is the fop, Lovel), her guardian can nonetheless permit her to cross his threshold because she has internalized the prohibition against knowing her own desire—or at least against knowing it until her future husband "speaks," and thus speaks it for her. The modest heroine's unconsciousness, in other words, substitutes for the father's protection and authorizes her temporary venture into the world.

Evelina's reply to Villars's letter registers the extraordinary dissociation of the self that such unconsciousness entails. While she has long been "doubtful" of her heart's "situation" and "dreaded a scrutiny," the fact that her guardian has said nothing has led her to believe that her fears were "causeless" and her "safety insured":

> You, Sir, relied upon my ignorance;—I, alas, upon your experience; and, whenever I doubted the weakness of my heart, the idea that *you* did not suspect it, reassured me,—restored my courage, and confirmed my error!

"Yet," she prudently adds, "am I most sensible of the kindness of your silence." She would be still more so were she aware that Villars has delayed almost long enough to bring Lord Orville to the point of proposing—and that her own modest retreat under the pressure of her "now conscious emotion" will do the rest (pp. 321, 322). Determining to avoid Orville whenever possible, she only succeeds, of course, in piquing his interest further. Though Evelina is merely trying to avoid exposing her own vulnerability—her sudden access of consciousness does not extend to the possibility of deliberately manipulating her lover—her abrupt coolness and withdrawal prompt the witty Mrs. Selwyn to accuse her of "rare coquetry" (p. 325). As Orville later confesses, he had not intended to propose until he had inquired into Evelina's background and connections, but his anxiety that she was about to leave without any commitment to see him again "put him quite off his guard" and inspired his proposal (p. 389).

The narrative works to absolve Evelina of responsibility even for the relatively brief time which intervenes between her guardian's speaking and her future husband's. That she does not immediately return home after she has received Villars's letter is owing to the timely intervention of her real father: Sir John Belmont's return to England after his long residence abroad provides the plot complications which keep his daughter "out" long enough to receive Orville's proposal, while his fortuitous arrival at the Hotwells enables him to authorize her marriage and to spare her the immodesty of disposing of herself. The wedding follows with unusual speed—but only to avoid shaming the young woman whom Belmont has mistakenly raised in the real daughter's place; no unseemly desire for haste can attach to Evelina herself. It is the "*mas-*

culine" Mrs. Selwyn (p. 268) who conspires with Sir John and Lord Orville to make the arrangement: "As to consulting *you,* my dear," Mrs. Selwyn pointedly remarks, "it was out of all question, because, you know, young ladies hearts and hands are always to be given with reluctance" (p. 377). Evelina only stipulates that she must obtain her guardian's formal approval as well—and when Villars's letter arrives, she characteristically finds herself unable even to read aloud its "aweful consent." To the end, Burney's modest heroine yields the naming of her desire to others: "having no voice to answer the enquiries of Lord Orville," she writes, "I put the letter into his hands, and left it to speak both for me and itself" (p. 404).

۞

The taboo on woman's speaking her love—even to herself—comes, of course, straight out of the conduct books. "It is even long before a woman of delicacy dares avow to her own heart that she loves," Dr. Gregory had written four years before *Evelina;* "and when all the subterfuges of ingenuity to conceal it from herself fail, she feels a violence done both to her pride and to her modesty."[8] It might be noted in passing that even Gregory's ideal woman proves secretly double—and that the "subterfuges of ingenuity" the woman of delicacy must employ may well call that delicacy itself into question. Unlike *Pamela,* however, with its claustrophobic focus on the consciousness of the isolated heroine, Burney's novel disperses the burden of such "subterfuges" among a number of other characters; though Evelina has often been accused of snobbery, the multiple voices of her narrative and its more crowded canvas have meant that she has largely escaped the charge of covert plotting. So thoroughgoing is Evelina's erotic delicacy where Orville is concerned that to most readers he scarcely comes alive at all; Hazlitt wittily dismissed him as merely "a condescending suit of clothes."[9] But while Burney's novels manage to convey very little sense of desire, they often effectively register a quite powerful feeling of anxiety; and it would be truer to say that when Evelina herself looks at Orville, what she sees is not so much a suit of clothes as a persistently scrutinizing pair of eyes. For if Burney's heroines successfully manage to avert their gaze from the body, it is only to concentrate all the more intently on the face, and to see in that face in turn a gaze that concentrates intently on them. Like Edgar Mandlebert in *Camilla,* Lord Orville appears above all a "watcher"[10]—though unlike Mandlebert, to whose deliberate intention of observing and judging the heroine the reader has separate access,

Orville seems largely a function of Evelina's first-person narrative, his watching less an activity of an independent character than a projection of the heroine herself.

When Lord Merton flirts with Evelina at the Pantheon, she writes that his attentions were "extremely disagreeable to me; and the more so, as I saw that Lord Orville had his eyes fixed upon us, with a gravity of attention that made me uneasy" (p. 111); when a servant openly announces before the assembled company in Mrs. Beaumont's parlor that he has been unable to deliver her note to Macartney, Evelina reports that she was "extremely ashamed of this public message; and meeting the eyes of Lord Orville, which were earnestly fixed on me, my confusion redoubled, and I knew not which way to look" (p. 301). Indeed, virtually every time Evelina ventures into public, she encounters Lord Orville; and virtually every time her gaze at once seeks his—not to meet his look but to check it out. From the letter in which she reports that Orville "looked all amazement" when Sir Clement Willoughby addressed him as her absconding partner at the ridotto (p. 46), to that in which she describes how she "saw, with concern, the gravity of his countenance" as he silently observed her talking with Macartney in the Hotwells pump room (p. 318), Evelina writes the history of her adventures in the world by recording their presumed reflections in her lover's eyes.

It might almost be said that the hero's chief function in this novel is not so much to court the heroine as to witness her embarrassment, so often do Evelina's reports of their meetings turn on "the ridiculous part I had myself played," as she writes of their very first encounter, "before so nice an observer" (p. 32). Orville looks "amazement" at being accused by Sir Clement of deserting his partner at the ridotto, for instance, because their engagement to dance has been simply the young woman's fiction—the pretense to which she has impulsively resorted in order to avoid Sir Clement's unwelcome attentions. Orville's look has its counterpart in Evelina's "unspeakable" sense of "shame and confusion," as she registers what she imagines to be his registering of the liberty she has taken (p. 46). Typically, an attempt at saving face— here, the lie about her previous engagement—only entangles Evelina in a further sequence of shame and embarrassment. So the "gravity" of Orville's countenance as he watches her talking with Macartney in the pump room more than two volumes later reflects a similar compounding of misapprehension and shame (p. 318)—a sequence begun when he previously chanced upon the pair engaged in a private conversation whose apparent intimacy Evelina has hesitated to explain because of her concern for Macartney's own delicate situation. To avoid further compromising herself in Orville's eyes, however, she has failed to keep a subsequent appointment with the young man, and now accosts him in the pump room to apologize for that failure—only to feel herself once again uncomfortably under observation. "But I did not find it very easy to excuse myself," she understandably reports, "as Lord Orville's eyes, with an expression of anxiety that distressed me, turned from him to me, and me to him, every word I spoke" (p. 317).

"To apprehend myself as seen," Sartre remarks in his phenomenology of shame, "is, in fact, to apprehend myself as seen *in the world* and from the standpoint of the world." And it is just such an apprehension of herself that Evelina repeatedly records when she makes what the novel idiomatically calls her "entrance into the world." Indeed, if shame is, in Sartre's formula, "the *recognition* of the fact that I *am* . . . that object which the Other is looking at and judging,"[11] it is only appropriate that the story of a young woman's coming "out," as the idiom also has it,[12] reads like an extended case history of the phenomenon. Given the conventional constraints on her role in courtship, for the woman to enter the world is largely for her to be exposed to the gaze of the Other, to be looked at and judged. Yet even as she comes out precisely in order to be seen, to stand out and be chosen, she remains subject to the contradictory injunction to keep herself modestly concealed, or at least to avoid any sign of aggressive self-display. All the anxious eyework of Evelina's narrative, all the accompanying blushing, wordlessness and confusions testify to the almost impossible double-bind of such a position.

It is striking how often Evelina's behavior is governed by her dread of exposure—of standing out as somehow different from the company she is in. Even when that company is itself both stupid and vulgar, as it typically is whenever her Frenchified grandmother is in charge, Evelina's fear of being seen to be out-of-context is almost more intense than is her fear of being seen to be vulgar. Or rather, the two fears, which are fundamentally one, come into strong and anxiety-inducing conflict, as Evelina is torn between the company to which she wishes to belong and the company she has been compelled to keep. When a bad cold prevents Madame Duval from accepting Mrs. Mirvan's invitation to the theater, Evelina confesses her relief in terms that register her anxiety of difference: "I was sorry for her indisposition, but I knew not how to be sorry she did not accompany us, for she is—I must not say what, but very unlike other people" (p. 77). The "other people" are of course the aristocratic company with whom Evelina, despite her vulgar relative, instinctively identifies. Yet when she is compelled to associate with her grandmother's vulgar unlikeness, Evelina struggles to suppress the marks of her own distinguishing superiority. Anticipating "great entertainment and pleasure" from joining the Mirvans at the opera, for example (p. 83), and fully dressed for the occasion according to the standards of the fashionable audience in the pit, Evelina finds herself dragged off by her penny-pinching and ignorant relatives to witness the performance instead from the gallery. Immediately worried that her attire is "very improper" for her company and "unwilling to be so conspicuous amongst them," she tries in vain to borrow a hat or bonnet so as at least to conceal her elegant headdress (p. 88). "If I had not been too much chagrined to laugh," she reports of her relatives' hapless wandering about the house on their arrival, "I should have been extremely diverted at their ignorance of whatever belongs to an opera." Conscious that she is the only knowledgeable member of the party, she professes indifference at their failure to consult her, but admits to feeling "not a little uneasy at finding that my dress, so different from that of the company to which I belonged, attracted general notice and observation" (p. 89).

So acute is Evelina's desire not to attract such notice that it overrides her sincere interest in the performance itself, an interest that for Dr. Burney's daughter clearly signals her heroine's sensitivity and taste. Despite her "delight" in the "sweet voice" of Signor Millico (p. 92), Evelina's wish not to call attention to herself in any way is stronger still:

> This song, which was slow and pathetic, caught all my attention, and I lean'd my head forward to avoid hearing their observations, that I might listen without interruption; but, upon turning round, when the song was over, I found that I was the object of general diversion to the whole party; for the Miss Branghtons were tittering, and the two gentlemen making signs and faces at me, implying their contempt of my affectation.
>
> This discovery determined me to appear as inattentive as themselves; but I was very much provoked at being thus prevented enjoying the only pleasure, which, in such a party, was within my power. (P. 93)

Perhaps only Burney could imagine a scene in which even attentive listening threatens to register as "forward." That the young writer recorded in her diary her own intense delight in Millico's singing ("Never have I known pleasure so exquisite, so heartfelt, so *divinely penetrating*")[13] merely underlines the poignancy of the situation in which she here places her heroine.

The coincidence of Evelina's entrance into the world with Madame Duval's return to England has a certain nightmarish logic, since the former tavern girl turned Frenchwoman appears on the scene like an exaggerated projection of her granddaughter's fear that to come out means to call improper attention to herself. Everything about Madame Duval—from the fractured language that identifies her as neither securely English nor French to her dressing "very gaily" and painting "very high" (p. 53)—marks her as a woman-out-of-place. The episode in which she demands that Evelina accompany her to the Hampstead ball and then makes what the latter tellingly calls "such an exhibition of her person" by attempting to dance the minuet herself is typical of the way in which she acts as a lightning rod for her granddaughter's own potential embarrassment on such occasions:

During this minuet, how much did I rejoice in being surrounded only with strangers! She danced in a style so uncommon; her age, her showy dress, and an unusual quantity of *rouge,* drew upon her the eyes, and, I fear, the derision of the whole company. Who she danced with, I know not; but Mr. Smith was so ill-bred as to laugh at her very openly, and to speak of her with as much ridicule as was in his power. (P. 222)

The numerous scenes in which Madame Duval serves as the butt of Captain Mirvan's practical jokes highlight her propensity to make herself the object of ridicule, often by intensifying her characteristic lapses in what Erving Goffman would call the "disciplined management of personal front."[14] When Evelina finds her after Mirvan's mock robbers have tied her up and abandoned her in a ditch, the older woman presents to the younger a front undisciplined in the extreme—a mess significantly compounded of her ordinary make-up as well as the filth in which she has been immersed:

Her dress was in such disorder, that I was quite sorry to have her figure exposed to the servants, who all of them, in imitation of their master, hold her in derision.

. . . Her head-dress had fallen off; her linen was torn; her negligee had not a pin left in it; her petticoats she was obliged to hold on; and her shoes were perpetually slipping off. She was covered with dirt, weeds, and filth, and her face was really horrible, for the pomatum and powder from her head, and the dust from the road, were quite *pasted* on her skin by her tears, which, with her *rouge,* made so frightful a mixture, that she hardly looked human.

The servants were ready to die with laughter, the moment they saw her. (P. 148)

It is as if Madame Duval's powder and paint were here revealed as already a kind of dirt, as if tossing her in a ditch did not so much unsettle her ordinary composure as call attention to her latent sluttishness and disarray. Though Evelina, of course, recognizes that her grandmother can hardly be blamed for her hapless condition in this scene, her acute discomfort at seeing Madama Duval exposed to the others' derision is very like that she will later register at the Hampstead ball—and very like that she perpetually fears to experience in relation to herself.

How is the young woman to enter the world, to display herself as marriageable,[15] without making what Evelina disgustedly calls "such an exhibition of her person"? Like so many of the double-binds governing the behavior of women in courtship, the contradiction can perhaps best be resolved by means of a fiction. In what is clearly Evelina's climactic public appearance in the novel, she enters the pump room at Bristol Hotwells and immediately feels herself the focus of "every eye" in the place:

> The first place we went to was the pump-room. It was full of company; and the moment we entered, I heard a murmuring of, "*That's she!*" and, to my great confusion, I saw every eye turn towards me. I pulled my hat over my face, and, by the assistance of Mrs. Selwyn, endeavoured to screen myself from observation: nevertheless, I found I was so much the object of general attention, that I entreated her to hasten away.
>
> . . . But we had not gone three yards, ere we were followed by a party of young men, who took every possible opportunity of looking at us, and, as they walked behind, talked aloud, in a manner at once unintelligible and absurd.
> "Yes," cried one, "'tis certainly she!—mark but her *blushing cheek!*"
> "And then her *eye,—her downcast eye!*" cried another.
> "True, oh most true," said a third, "*every beauty is her own!*"
> "But then," said the first, "her *mind,*—now the difficulty is, to find out the truth of *that,*—for she will not say a word."
> "She is *timid,*" answered another; "mark but her *timid air.*" (Pp. 326–27)

This scene enacts the fantasy of the modest heroine's triumph, publicly staging what the private proposal scene will soon confirm: Evelina stands out from the crowd precisely because of her attempts to efface herself. The tags that serve to identify her—the blushing cheek, downcast eyes, and timid air—derive from an anonymous set of verses that has been circulating in the pump room; though Evelina is not yet aware of the poem's existence, indeed cannot be aware of it if she is to make her entrance modestly unconscious of the stir she will create, the anonymous poet has drawn on the familiar topoi of female modesty in order to proclaim her, in effect, the *Venus pudica* of the wells. While all the local "beauties" are mentioned, Mrs. Selwyn later informs her, "*you* are the Venus to whom the prize is given" (p. 328):

> SEE last advance, with bashful grace,
>   Downcast eye, and blushing cheek,
> Timid air, and beauteous face,
>   Anville,—whom the Graces seek.
>
> Though ev'ry beauty is her own,
>   And though her mind each virtue fills,
> Anville,—to her power unknown,
>   Artless, strikes,—unconscious, kills! (P. 333)

Though the "killing" power of this Venus is a bit of conventional rhetoric, the latent violence in all her virtue is nonetheless worth noting: the relation between Evelina's modesty and her unconscious aggression is a matter to which I will return. But it is first of all crucial to observe how both the poem and the scene in the pump room work to transmute the signs of Evelina's embarrassment into the signs of her worth, so that the very confusion she manifests at being singled out for attention only serves to confirm her value. The scene works like the antitype of her grandmother's exposure in the Hampstead ballroom, where the "unusual quantity" of Madame Duval's rouge "drew upon her the eyes, and . . . the derision of the whole company" (p. 222). Here the more Evelina blushes and tries to conceal herself, and the more she hastens away, the more convincingly she identifies herself as the "bashful" star of the poem. A similar logic governs the subsequent scene in which she actually reads the verses in question—only this time Lord Orville is himself present to witness her blush. "What have you there, my dear?" asks Mrs. Selwyn, who interrupts the reading. "Nothing, Ma'am," replies Evelina, hastily concealing the paper. "And has *nothing*," demands Mrs. Selwyn, "the power of *rouge?*" Evelina reports that she "made no answer," but a "deep sigh which escaped Lord Orville at that moment, reached my ears, and gave me sensations—which I dare not mention!" (p. 334). The proposal scene itself swiftly follows.

    As that Other to whose gaze Evelina has been looking for judgment ever since she first entered the world, Orville has long stood in for her absent father(s), a role he can scarcely be said to leave behind him as he now prepares to be her future husband.[16] Of course, given the past history that Burney postulates for her heroine, there can be little wonder that she is so anxious for paternal approval, or so vulnerable to being shamed in front of men. Several analysts have observed how closely the fear of abandonment is associated with a particular susceptibility to shame[17]—and as the daughter of a man who has refused to acknowledge her, Evelina has good reason to fear abandonment. She has, after all, already once suffered the desertion of a father—while the consequent obscurity surrounding her birth heightens the risk that she will in turn be abandoned by others. Christened Evelina "Anville" by her guardian, the daughter of Sir John Belmont lacks a "real"—that is, a paternal—name. But for all "the peculiar cruelty of her situation" (p. 18), there is an important sense in which Evelina's circumstances do not so much serve to distinguish her from her peers as to exaggerate the anxieties that attend any young woman's entrance into the world. In a patriarchal culture the acquiring of husbands always entails the losing of fathers, and during the period of courtship the woman's fear of loss balances precariously against her imagination of gain. At once "in" and "out" of her father's house, such a woman is acutely vulnerable to the fear of finding herself nowhere—effectively, if not literally, as nameless as Burney's heroine. Indeed, as the courtship plots of *Cecelia* (1782) and *Camilla* (1796) will make painfully clear, whether a young woman bears no paternal name or too much of one,[18] whether the father himself is dead or alive, the sensation of being exposed and abandoned continues to shadow her story.

In this context, the fantasy that shapes *Evelina* is not merely that the young woman will be loved despite her perpetual embarrassments but that she will be loved because of them—that the more she blushes before the Other, the more she intensifies her beauty in his eyes. The very moments at which Evelina has felt herself to be most vulnerable prove to be the ones at which she has been covertly assuring her future safety. "It is very true," Orville will later admit, "that I did not, at our first acquaintance, do justice to the merit of Miss Anville."

She is not, indeed, like most modern young ladies, to be known in half an hour; her modest worth, and fearful excellence, require both time and encouragement to shew themselves. She does not, beautiful as she is, seize the soul by surprise, but, with more dangerous fascination, she steals it almost imperceptibly. (P. 347)

The fearfulness of such a heroine does not so much modify her excellence as define it: those modern young ladies who are known in half an hour are known not to be worth very much. Nor do such fast ones have the modest woman's erotic power—that "more dangerous fascination" by which an Evelina "imperceptibly" captures her future husband. Though all of Burney's heroines eventually manage in some degree to make their worth known, never again will their embarrassments and fears give way to so easy a dream of recognition by the male.

❧

But the story of this young woman's entrance into the world is not merely the story of her being exposed to the gaze, and possibly the ridicule, of others: it is also the story of her desire to look, and even to laugh, herself. It is no accident that when Evelina gets into trouble at the ridotto, she does so not by actually lying about Orville but by improperly looking in his direction. When Sir Clement denounces her fictitious partner as a "despicable puppy" for having deserted her, Evelina finds herself mysteriously impelled to turn her eyes toward Orville:

> I know not what bewitched me,—but my pride was hurt, and my spirits were tired, and—in short—I had the folly, looking at Lord Orville, to repeat, "*Despicable,* you think?"
> His eyes instantly followed mine; "why, is *that* the gentleman?"
> I made no answer. (P. 45)

It is, in other words, this initial misdirecting of Evelina's gaze that results in Orville's subsequently looking "all amazement" and her own "unspeakable" shame and confusion (p. 46). Indeed, the incident simply calls attention to a fact that is more or less evident throughout—that Evelina can only register Orville's look by first turning her own eyes upon him, and that her embarrassment at being seen is always caught up with her embarrassment at seeing.[19]

The incident at the opera, in which she sees the omnipresent Orville "unfortunately" seeing her as she attempts to extricate herself from Sir Clement's company (p. 95), suggests something of how looking compounds itself in this novel, and of how Evelina's own gaze is characteristically implicated in her confusion. The sequence has the disquieting reciprocity of the typical face-to-face encounters analyzed by Goffman— encounters in which, as he has suggested, the very act of looking feels like a form of exposure:

Ordinarily . . . in using the naked senses to receive embodied messages from others, the individual also makes himself available as a source of embodied information for them. . . . Here, then, is a second crucial communication condition of face-to-face interaction: not only are the receiving and conveying of the naked and embodied kind, but each giver is himself a receiver, and each receiver is a giver.
The implications of this second feature are fundamental. First, sight begins to take on an added and special role. Each individual can *see* that he is being expe-

rienced in some way, and he will guide at least some of his conduct according to the perceived identity and initial response of his audience. Further, he can be seen to be seeing this, and can see that he has been seen seeing this. Ordinarily, then, to use our naked senses is to use them nakedly, and to be made naked by their use.[20]

Understood in such terms, Evelina's constant sense of vulnerability derives not merely from her fear that she may be seen to be an object-out-of-place, but from her awareness that what may make her out-of-place is her own "naked" looking. And though Goffman does not stress the point, the consequent sense of being nakedly exposed to others' aggression is impossible to separate from an awareness of the aggression already implicit in the look—an aggression all the more socially proscribed when the observer was not Goffman's universal male but an eighteenth-century Englishwoman. Of course, the priority of Evelina's gaze throughout the novel is in part a function of the first-person narrative—of the fact that there is no third-person, in effect, to lift the burden of aggression from her, to report on Orville's expression while she averts her eyes. But to acknowledge this is only to say that the very adoption of the first-person conveys an immodesty that no account of "confusion" can wholly conceal.

The sexual aggression implicit in Evelina's own perpetual eyework is perhaps nowhere closer to the surface than in the scene in which she meets Orville in the Marylebone gardens while flanked by the two prostitutes—a scene in which, typically, Evelina sees him before he sees her. Only the second time their paths cross does she "unhappily" catch his eye (p. 235). The first time—"though I saw that, in a careless manner, his eyes surveyed the party"—she is greatly relieved to observe that he passed the group without distinguishing her. One of her companions, nevertheless, calls attention to the boldness of Evelina's own attentive looking at him:

> As soon as he was gone, one of these unhappy women said, "Do you know that young fellow?"
> Not thinking it possible she should mean Lord Orville by such a term, I readily answered, "No, Madam."
> "Why then," answered she, "you have a monstrous good stare, for a little country Miss." (P. 234)

At such a moment, more than their unfortunate proximity threatens to link the "little country Miss" to the women of the town. But if this "monstrous good stare" seems primarily charged with sexual aggression, the look Evelina much later turns upon her absconding father carries more nearly murderous implications: as Sir John exclaims, after having twice sunk to the ground before her, "Thy countenance is a dagger to my heart!" (p. 386). Of course, as so often in the novel, the dangers of looking here are imagined as reciprocal: Sir John is as fearful at their first meeting that his sight has "blasted" his daughter (p. 372) as Evelina subsequently is that the sight of her is "terrible" to him (p. 384). And Evelina's own aggression is further masked by the premise that what wounds Sir John is not his daughter's impulse to "look daggers," as the idiom has it, but her innocent resemblance to the wife he has wronged and abandoned: Mary Poovey has shrewdly argued that by standing in for her mother in this scene, Evelina manages to avenge both women "without really acting as either one."[21] As in the yet more oblique action by which her half-brother Macartney—Sir John's truly illegitimate child—draws his sword and wounds the man he does not then know to be their father, Evelina's own anger is still displaced and defused even as she, too, brings Sir John to his knees. Yet it is striking that her metaphorical dagger seems to have more power to hurt, and to produce change, than her brother's real one—and that the mere staging of a "*face to face*" confrontation (the emphasis is Evelina's) should be charged with such dangerous effects. No wonder that when Madame Duval initially proposes the meeting, Evelina finds the idea "terrible to think of" (p. 159), or that when she enters her father's presence for the first time she covers her face with her hands (p. 372).

As with its representation of looking, so with its representation of laughter, *Evelina* repeatedly allows a fiction of modesty to cover the impulses of a satirist. Note how the heroine no sooner enters the world than she embarrasses herself by her propensity to laugh at its inhabitants. By so arranging her narrative that the first man to approach Evelina in the novel happens to be the fop, Lovel, Burney designs her heroine's public career to begin with a burst of indecorous laughter.[22] Though the first time Lovel asks her to dance, Evelina turns aside to conceal her amusement, she cannot help laughing out loud when "with a most ridiculous solemnity" he accosts her again (p. 32). From her initial appraisal of the fop—"I really believe he even wished to be stared at" (p. 29)—to her abashed report that "Lord Orville actually stared at me" when she burst into laughter (p. 33), the dynamics of ridiculing and being ridiculed seem clear. Recall also that Evelina begins her account of her own "mortification" and "humiliation" at the opera (p. 94) with the admission that had she not been "too much chagrined to laugh," she would have been "extremely diverted" at the Branghtons' ignorance of all the conventions governing the occasion (p. 89). Not all of Evelina's laughter seems so obviously satiric in intent: when she twice protests that she "could not help laughing" at the "ridiculous" speeches with which Sir Clement seeks to amuse her at the private ball (pp. 41, 46), the impulse to which she surrenders seems closer to a childlike capacity for play—a capacity that also, however, marks her as potentially vulnerable to Sir Clement's teasing style of flirtation. That even as the comic novelist identifies with her heroine's laughter she knows it as a dangerous sign, associated by her culture with unacceptable impulses of aggression and sexuality, is further suggested by her representation of the Marylebone whores—whose sole distinguishing marks, it so happens, appear to be a "loud laugh" and a "drawling, ironical tone." What belatedly alerts Evelina to their calling, interestingly enough, is not any detail of gesture or dress but their insistent repetition of that "loud laugh" at "every other word" that she speaks. Indeed, given the women's noisy amusement at her expense, Evelina's formula for her discovery—that she had "sought protection from insult, of those who were most likely to offer it" (p. 233)—seems still more of a comment on their satirical than on their sexual license, and a covert reminder, of course, that to insult others by laughing at them is to risk being taken for a whore.[23]

If it is Evelina's immodest desire to look and to laugh that most closely allies her with the novelist, it may well have been Burney's need to conceal such impulses that prompted her to present her first novel through the letters of a modest heroine. When Richardson declared the pen "almost the *only Means* a very modest and diffident Lady . . . has to shew herself, and that she has a *Mind*," the instrument in question, we might recall, was engaged in private correspondence; he took for granted that in public she would often choose to be silent.[24] In the familiar letter, such a woman could write what she could not say, and Burney began her career as a novelist by exploiting that difference—exploiting it, one might add, far more daringly than Richardson. As Patricia Spacks has suggested, *Evelina* gives us a heroine whose exuberant, gossipy, and sometimes pointedly judgmental writing contrasts markedly with her quiet restraint in public.[25] In one letter Evelina records her first meeting with the Branghtons, neatly skewering each in turn, while in the next she reports that a compliment from Lord Orville left her blushing and silent: "I am inexpressibly concerned at the thought of his harbouring an opinion that I am bold or impertinent," she writes, "and I could almost kill myself for having given him the shadow of a reason for so shocking an idea" (p. 72). Yet even when she refrains from definitive judgment, the modest woman's account of events can serve the aims of the satirist—indeed, perhaps especially then, as the devastating "confusions" of Dickens's Esther Summerson in *Bleak House* would later suggest. When the idle young gentlemen at Clifton amuse themselves by betting on a footrace between two poor old women, the effect of careless brutality is intensified by Evelina's understated reporting of the scene. Like the violent practical joke that previously landed Madame Duval in the ditch, the old women's footrace leads directly to an incident in which Evelina herself suffers a related form of coercion: on the first occasion, the mock robbers attack the coach in which she has been traveling with her grandmother, and while Mirvan's men tie up the older woman, Sir Clement Willoughby takes advantage of the younger's isolation to importune her in private; on the second occasion, Lord Merton's candidate wins the race by default when the other old woman suffers a painfully immobilizing fall, and "giddy equally from wine and success," Merton grabs hold of Evelina—vowing not to release her, since "the *day was his own*" (pp. 312, 313). Evelina does not appear to register the logic of these sequences; perhaps even the novelist herself would not consciously have done so. Yet if it has taken contemporary feminist critics to make explicit the implications of the violence that so pervades Burney's fictional world,[26] such juxtapositions are there to be read, even in this most innocently optimistic of her fictions.

Though Evelina expresses pity for the old women in the race, in the represented action of the novel Burney typically works to deflect the responsibility of satire from her heroine, often by surrounding her with characters who act out her aggression for her.[27] Such displacement operates perhaps most openly in Evelina's relation to the clever Mrs. Selwyn, whose "*masculine*" understanding and manners the heroine can deplore, even as she innocently describes the older woman as "very kind and attentive to me" (p. 268). "Pray, Mrs. Selwyn, speak for me," Evelina cries when the drunken Lord Merton seizes her hand and refuses to release her (p. 313); and as the heroine's "satirical friend" (p. 284), that is precisely what Mrs. Selwyn does—here as elsewhere commenting with barbed irony on behavior that the younger woman suffers in silence or gently protests. Evelina reports that Mrs. Selwyn "is not a favourite with Mr. Villars, who has often been disgusted at her unmerciful propensity to satire" (p. 269), but like Mrs. Arlbery in *Camilla*, whose "spirit of satire" is correspondingly indulged and criticized,[28] she still seems something of a favorite with the author. Nor is it simply the heroine's latent hostilities for which her witty companion speaks: when Evelina finds herself unable to support her part in conversation with Lord Orville, Mrs. Selwyn characteristically "supplie[s] the

place of two" (p. 283), even as she also effectively takes the place of the
reluctant bride when she later names the day of her wedding.

The services performed for the heroine by the bullying Captain Mirvan, on the other hand, are at once more primitive and more screened
from conscious recognition: though there is scarcely a character in the
novel who seems more distant from Evelina than this crude ex-sailor, he
nonetheless has a remarkable tendency to aim his practical jokes at targets whom she herself has strong motives to attack. While her letters
duly lament his relentless persecution of Madame Duval, for example,
Evelina's striking reluctance to interfere more openly with his plans cannot altogether be attributed to her mistaken sense of propriety. In her
account of the incident in which she comes upon her grandmother after
Captain Mirvan has deposited her in a ditch, Evelina herself is all anxious concern, and only the servants are "ready to die with laughter"; but
it is not hard to imagine how the spectacle of her burdensome relative's
discomfiture should afford the heroine—or at least the novelist who
identifies with her—some secret satisfaction. A similar logic governs the
rather broad bit of farce that concludes the narrative, the scene in which
the Captain produces a monkey who in turn bites the hapless Lovel.
Though Evelina professes herself unable to account for the seemingly
gratuitous cruelty of the incident ("I was really sorry for the poor man,
who, though an egregious fop, had committed no offense that merited
such chastisement"—p. 401), the final punishment of the fop gains a
certain point when one remembers that it was Evelina's own desire to
laugh at him that first got her into trouble, and that he has persistently
sought to avenge her initial snub at every subsequent meeting. That it
should be the parodically effeminate fop who arouses both the uneasy
ridicule of the modest woman and the petty cruelty of the bullying man
is not really surprising: like the "*masculine*" Mrs. Selwyn, Lovel offends
by blurring distinctions that the culture strives anxiously to maintain, and on which the novel's own courtship plot partly depends.[29] As
Evelina tellingly writes when Orville comes to her rescue in the aftermath of the footrace, "Methinks I can never lament the rudeness of
Lord Merton, as it has more than ever confirmed to me the esteem of
Lord Orville" (p. 315). That the heroine should be partly complicit
with the bullying of a Mirvan or a Merton, even as she dreams of the
hero's "*feminine* . . . delicacy*" (p. 261), is still another contradiction of
modesty.

"In short, the joke is, the people speak as if they were afraid of me,"
the novelist wrote to her sister Susan not long after the publication of
Evelina, "instead of my being afraid of them."[30] The "joke"—if it can be

called that—conveys Burney's usual shyness but also her feeling for reciprocal action, for the responsive mirroring of self and others. Yet the reciprocity at work may have been still more complicated than she acknowledged, for if she was genuinely afraid of the ridicule of others—and much evidence suggests that she was[31]—that fear cannot finally be separated, I would urge, from her own impulse to ridicule them. If even the modest Evelina doubles as a satirist, it is precisely because her attention is so intently focused on the self as defined by the social field, on the conventions and expectations that govern people's immediate interactions with one another. The same heightened alertness to what Erving Goffman would call the "situational proprieties"[32] that renders her so sensitive to embarrassment and shame also helps to account for her sharp eye for the ridiculousness of others. Though the novelist never again adopted the cover of the modest first-person, her later fiction continued to focus intently on the double-binds that constrain women's action, and to render often nightmarish visions of what she saw. Despite her disclaimer, after all, people had very good reason to fear the potential satirist in their midst—"such a very nice observer," as one contemporary anxiously remarked, "that there would be no escaping her with safety."[33]

9

Fanny Price's Modest Loathings

ॐ

The heroine of *Mansfield Park* ends by marrying the man of her choice, but only after the familiar courtship plot has been deliberately entertained and subverted. When Fanny Price refuses her first admirer, Henry Crawford, "her modesty alone seemed to his sanguine and pre-assured mind to stand in the way of the happiness he sought." Indeed, such masculine assurance predictably finds a bit of modest opposition downright animating—a stimulus to pleasures at once erotic and narrative. "A little difficulty to be overcome, was no evil to Henry Crawford. He rather derived spirits from it. He had been apt to gain hearts too easily."[1] But "modesty alone" in *Mansfield Park* proves other than Crawford imagines, and the novel he inhabits finally resists his sense of an ending. Despite his "pre-assured mind," Austen assures that he will short-circuit his courtship plot when he surrenders to the temptation of adultery with Maria Rushworth. Though even the novelist's beloved sister urged her to "let Mr. Crawford marry Fanny Price," a niece reported, "Miss Austen stood firmly and would not allow a change."[2] Yet if *Mansfield Park* refuses such fictions of modesty as Crawford projects, there is nonetheless more than one sense in which it takes those fictions seriously. Austen's most deeply modest heroine belongs to her most problematic novel.[3]

When Elizabeth Bennet declines Collins's proposal of marriage in *Pride and Prejudice*, he, too, notoriously refuses to take "no" for an answer. Convinced that "it is usual with young ladies to reject the addresses of the man whom they secretly mean to accept, when he first applies for their favour; and that sometimes the refusal is repeated a second or even a third time," Elizabeth's suitor dismisses her repeated negatives as "merely words of course"—words that he memorably attributes to her "wish of increasing my love by suspense, according to the usual practice of elegant females." However her "natural delicacy" may lead her to "dissemble," as Collins revealingly puts it, he cannot imagine Elizabeth serious in rejecting him, both because he cannot imagine himself undesirable and because he knows quite well that her position as an impoverished gentlewoman otherwise renders her vulnerable. "Modesty" is the name he gives to her pointed attempt to avoid the encounter—"Believe me, my dear Miss Elizabeth," he hastens to inform her, "that your modesty, so far from doing you any disservice, rather adds to your other perfections"—and as "modesty" he persists in understanding her plain declaration that she would find such a marriage impossible. Yet when the rejected suitor reports that "he had every reason to be satisfied, since the refusal which his cousin had stedfastly given him would naturally flow from her bashful modesty and the genuine delicacy of her character," even the wishful Mrs. Bennet is appropriately "startled."[4] This is a man, we might recall, who reaches automatically for Fordyce's *Sermons* in preference to novels; and in his expectations as to "the usual practice of elegant females," his routine equation of "natural delicacy" with secrecy and dissembling, Austen gleefully sends up the familiar double-talk of the conduct books, even as she devastatingly identifies such rhetoric with the demands of masculine vanity and the complacent assumption of power.

But for all the energy of its satire, *Pride and Prejudice* manages to dismiss such fictions of modesty with comparative ease: everything about Collins's proposal, from its placement in the narrative to the characterizations of both wooer and wooed, helps to assure that the heroine is never in any serious danger. When Elizabeth protests that she is no "elegant female intending to plague you, but . . . a rational creature speaking the truth from her heart," she declares herself neither deceitfully manipulative nor unconscious of her own feelings but a woman capable of reasoned judgment—and what she easily judges, in this instance, is that the man who addresses her is a fool. Though Collins persists in his "wilful self-deception" to the end of the chapter,[5] only one more will elapse before her entanglement with him is over; by the opening paragraph of the next he has transferred his attentions to Charlotte Lucas. Whatever "the usual practice of elegant females," neither Elizabeth nor her creator has any intention of increasing this gentleman's "love" by suspense. Indeed, Collins talks of male "love" as mechanically as he does of female "modesty," and part of the joke depends on the reader's recognition of how little either term bears on the facts of the case.[6]

In Henry Crawford's courtship of Fanny Price, however, Austen tells a different story. Only one who speaks by rote could assume that Elizabeth's refusal would "naturally flow" from the "bashful modesty" of her character, but Henry clearly has the narrator's warrant for "the modest gentle nature" (p. 342) of the woman he addresses: if *Mansfield Park* dramatizes conflicting assumptions about what follows from such a "nature," it does so precisely by taking the fact of Fanny's modesty in some sense as a given. And while modern critics may insist that "nobody falls in love with Fanny Price,"[7] Jane Austen argues otherwise. Henry may begin only with "idle designs," but he soon finds himself "fairly caught" (p. 292)—and caught all the more effectively, the novel makes clear, because Fanny resists his advances. "He was in love, very much in love; and it was a love which . . . made her affection appear of greater consequence, because it was withheld, and determined him to have the glory, as well as the felicity, of forcing her to love him" (p. 326). Neither the note of sadistic excitement that the narrator registers here, nor the "freaks of a cold-blooded vanity" to which she later attributes Henry's swerving from his course (p. 467), need cancel her final verdict on his case—that in forfeiting "his best, most estimable and endeared acquaintance," he "so lost the woman whom he had rationally, as well as passionately loved" (p. 469).

To inspire a love at once rational and passionate is, of course, a principal function of the modest woman; and were Mary Crawford a little more acquainted with the conventional wisdom on such matters—or a little more persuaded that Henry is the "man of sense" he now proclaims himself—she might not be so utterly taken by surprise when her brother first announces his determination to marry. On the question of how Maria and Julia Bertram will respond to the news, Henry abruptly turns moralist: "They will now see what sort of woman it is that can attach me, that can attach a man of sense. I wish the discovery may do them any good" (p. 297). We might recall how another sententious brother in the 1793 *Lady's Magazine* dismissed the pleasures taken with "the companions of an hour, or of a day," while reminding *his* sister that men always choose "amiable diffidence" and "blushing timidity" when they choose to marry.[8] From Fanny's automatic habits of submissiveness to the promise of her continued chastity, Henry rehearses the familiar grounds for choosing such a wife:

The gentleness, modesty, and sweetness of her character were warmly expatiated on. . . . Her temper he had good reason to depend on and to praise. He had often seen it tried. Was there one of the family, excepting Edmund, who had not in some way or other continually exercised her patience and forbear-

ance? Her affections were evidently strong. To see her with her brother! What
could more delightfully prove that the warmth of her heart was equal to its
gentleness?—What could be more encouraging to a man who had her love in
view? Then, her understanding was beyond every suspicion, quick and clear;
and her manners were the mirror of her own modest and elegant mind. Nor
was this all. Henry Crawford had too much sense not to feel the worth of good
principles in a wife, though he was too little accustomed to serious reflection to
know them by their proper name; but when he talked of her having such a
steadiness and regularity of conduct, such a high notion of honour, and such an
observance of decorum as might warrant any man in the fullest dependence on
her faith and integrity, he expressed what was inspired by the knowledge of her
being well principled and religious. (P. 294)

Fanny, says Henry, "is exactly the woman to do away every prejudice
of such a man" as Admiral Crawford, his uncle, "for she is exactly such a
woman as he thinks does not exist in the world. She is the very impossibility he would describe" (p. 293). All this talk of the heroine's "honor,
decorum, faith, and integrity," Claudia Johnson has argued, "adds
up to the singularly important confidence that she will be above the
temptation of adultery"; and for a man raised by the adulterous Admiral Crawford, such a guarantee of faithfulness in a woman is no
small qualification.[9] Yet Henry also wants Fanny because he believes
"the warmth of her heart," in his formula, "equal to its gentleness":
were it not for the strength of her feelings, the modest woman's capacity for restraint would not appear such an attractive "impossibility."
The dinner at the Grants that marks Fanny's first real venture "out"
into the world also marks Henry's first discovery that "in that soft
skin of her's, so frequently tinged with a blush . . . there is decided
beauty"; and from that moment forward, he persists in reading the
language of her body for the promise of erotic responsiveness it obliquely betrays. The morning after this event, he tells Mary that he has
resolved to devote a fortnight to making "a small hole in Fanny Price's
heart" (p. 229): "I only want her to look kindly on me, to give me
smiles as well as blushes," he announces, though by the end of the
sentence he is "only" wanting that when he leaves Mansfield, "she
shall be never happy again" (p. 231). But as he observes the glowing cheek and bright eye with which she listens to the seagoing adventures of her brother, Henry finds himself more deeply involved
than he has expected. "It was a picture which Henry Crawford had
moral taste enough to value," the narrator remarks of the scene, while
going on to suggest that it was a picture that appealed also to his erotic
imagination:

Fanny's attractions increased—increased two-fold—for the sensibility which
beautified her complexion and illumined her countenance, was an attraction in
itself. He was no longer in doubt of the capabilities of her heart. She had feeling, genuine feeling. It would be something to be loved by such a girl, to excite
the first ardours of her young, unsophisticated mind! (Pp. 235–36)

Henry is still plotting a sort of psychological seduction of this virgin
rather than a marriage, but the temporal dimension of his plot significantly begins to extend itself, as the imagined intensity of the modest
woman's feelings produces a reciprocal effect on the lover: "She interested him more than he had foreseen. A fortnight was not enough. His
stay became indefinite" (p. 236). Already expert in the pleasures of an
erotic delaying action, this "most horrible flirt" (p. 43) is about to try
whether the courtship of the modest woman may prove more stimulating still.[10]

Such a courtship, of course, entails the usual fictions about the modest heroine's consciousness. When Sir Thomas Bertram first learns that
Fanny has apparently refused Henry's offer, he chooses to believe that
she has acted only from a proper sense of deference to himself. "I know
he spoke to you yesterday," he informs his niece, "and (as far as I understand), received as much encouragement to proceed as a well-judging
young woman could permit herself to give" (p. 315)—as much encouragement, he means, as a young woman may give a lover who has not yet
formally spoken to her uncle and guardian. If one would rather be
termed "a well-judging young woman" than an "elegant female" in the
manner of Collins, Sir Thomas nonetheless assumes, Collins-like, that
such a woman's refusal is largely a matter of form—that it testifies more
to what the occasion requires than to what Elizabeth Bennet would call
"the truth from her heart."[11] But Fanny's anxious denials soon prompt
the alternative hypothesis that she does "not quite know" her "own feelings"—that her no-saying signifies not merely a commendable "discretion," in other words, but a form of modest unconsciousness (pp. 316,
315). With this account of Fanny's resistance, the self-regarding Henry
predictably finds himself eager to agree. "He had vanity," the narrator
reports, "which strongly inclined him . . . to think she did love him,
though she might not know it herself." Even "when constrained at last
to admit that she did know her own present feelings," Henry still has
vanity enough to "convince . . . him that he should be able in time to
make those feelings what he wished"—such confidence in "time" having as its corollary the belief in a yet more thoroughgoing female unconsciousness, a still deeper burial of her desire:

He considered her . . . as one who had never thought on the subject enough to be in danger; who had been guarded by youth, a youth of mind as lovely as of person; whose modesty had prevented her from understanding his attentions, and who was still overpowered by the suddenness of addresses so wholly unexpected, and the novelty of a situation which her fancy had never taken into account.

   Must it not follow of course, that when he was understood, he should succeed?—he believed it fully. (Pp. 326–27)

Fanny's "present feelings" do not include love for Henry, according to the story Henry tells himself, because she does not yet even understand what talk of love might signify—while her understanding will necessarily be identical with the happy resolution of his plot. But "Fanny is not Henry Crawford's, she is Jane Austen's," as Margaret Kirkham crisply puts it.[12] And one measure of that difference is that the novelist has already granted her a complex interior life inaccessible to his view. As when his sister is several times shown "misinterpreting" Fanny's blushes, Austen underlines the difference between the modest fiction the Crawfords project and that which she is in fact engaged in telling: "Fanny was confused," she reports on one of these occasions, "but it was the confusion of discontent" (p. 277).[13] While Henry takes for granted that he will be the first to "excite" the modest woman's mind and her heart, we know that both these organs have been occupied in ways he scarcely troubles to imagine. Having long loved Edmund, and judged Henry, Fanny refuses the latter out of a full consciousness of that history. Yet precisely because she *is* a modest woman, those around her do not share the privileged knowledge of narrator and reader: love and judgment alike are constrained to silence.

   Mansfield Park repeatedly stages what might be called the trials of modesty, and it does so, in part, by dramatizing the conflict between Fanny's own consciousness of herself and the ways in which her virtue signifies for others. From the moment she first arrives at Mansfield, her "obliging, yielding temper" (p. 17) renders her remarkably convenient to others' uses: whether she is running errands for Mrs. Norris, or providing Tom Bertram with a timely dance partner, she modestly surrenders herself to the needs and desires of her relatives. The latter episode, in fact, provides a nicely ironic commentary on such compliance, as Tom indignantly protests the social pressure exercised by Mrs. Norris's request that he join in a game of whist, while managing his escape by exercising just this form of coercion on his cousin. "A pretty modest request upon my word!" he exclaims, as he abruptly leads Fanny off to the dance:

"And to ask me in such a way too! without ceremony, before them all, so as to leave me no possibility of refusing! *That* is what I dislike most particularly. It raises my spleen more than any thing, to have the pretence of being asked, of being given a choice, and at the same time addressed in such a way as to oblige one to do the very thing—whatever it be! If I had not luckily thought of standing up with you, I could not have got out of it." (Pp. 119–20)

"Fanny was led off very willingly," the narrator reports, "though it was impossible for her to feel much gratitude towards her cousin, or distinguish, as he certainly did, between the selfishness of another person and his own" (p. 119). Here as elsewhere in *Mansfield Park*, the "pretence" of choice is precisely what is offered the modest heroine, and here as elsewhere, she acquiesces quite readily[14]—though not without a certain awareness, as these lines suggest, that she thus participates in a fiction.

Only in two decisive episodes does this modest heroine actively put up any resistance: on the questions of performing in *Lovers' Vows* and of marrying Crawford, Fanny refuses merely to pretend that she is choosing. These episodes test the limits of her modesty and bring some implicit contradictions in the virtue openly into conflict. Fanny declines to play Cottager's wife, as she later declines to be Crawford's, and on both occasions the group at once pressures her to reverse her decision. Ever since Lionel Trilling first identified "the great fuss that is made over the amateur theatricals" with a traditional fear of dramatic impersonation,[15] the issue of the novel's antitheatricality has been much debated—and not only because of Austen's own delight in home performances. In his *Lettre à M. d'Alembert* on the theater, Rousseau had railed against a profession that required women to show themselves in public—and "what is worse, for money";[16] but despite Trilling's later suggestion that *Mansfield Park* contains its own "Letter on the Theatre,"[17] Edmund's preference for "good hardened real acting" over the amateur's kind stops well short of identifying the actress with the prostitute (p. 124). Yet there is little question that Fanny's refusal to act is grounded in her modesty, or that she particularly objects to *Lovers' Vows* because of the apparent casualness with which it treats female virtue.

In her preface to her English translation of Kotzebue's play, Elizabeth Inchbald explained how she had adapted it "to the English rather than the German taste," since "Amelia's love, by Kotzebue, is indelicately blunt," and "the forward and unequivocal manner in which she announces her affection to her lover, in the original, would have been revolting to an English audience."[18] Austen does not say whether her heroine's eager reading of *Lovers' Vows* included this preface, but Fanny would undoubtedly have agreed with her countrywoman—so troubling does she find even Inchbald's chastened version:

Agatha and Amelia appeared to her in their different ways so totally improper for home representation—the situation of one, and the language of the other, so unfit to be expressed by any woman of modesty, that she could hardly suppose her cousins could be aware of what they were engaging in; and longed to have them roused as soon as possible by the remonstrance Edmund would certainly make. (P. 137)

Unfortunately for Fanny, of course, Edmund's remonstrance proves more sober than lasting: though he "should not have thought it the sort of play to be so easily filled up, with *us*," as he scolds Maria (p. 139), he soon determines to fill up Anhalt's role himself rather than risk the part's going to a stranger. Austen's clergyman will stand in for Inchbald's, thus answering Mary's Amelia-like query, "What gentleman among you am I to have the pleasure of making love to?" (p. 143). As several commentators on the episode have noted, these obvious correspondences between the characters' roles offstage and on suggest that the novel testifies rather less to a Platonic fear of impersonation, as Trilling contended, than to an anxiety about the disruptive impulses that theatrical performance may put into play. When Mary takes the role of Amelia, and Maria, Agatha, it is not "the integrity of the real self" that is at risk, in Trilling's formula, but the discipline that otherwise keeps certain "real" desires prudently unspoken.[19] The line between the performers' own feelings and those they represent is already hopelessly blurred, and precisely because they are not "hardened" actors, in Edmund's phrase, the inhabitants of Mansfield Park will be less inclined to maintain firm distinctions between them.

"On a public theatre care is always taken to provide performers who are perfectly acquainted with the nature of the business they undertake," the *Lady's Magazine* had similarly argued in 1790, while warning women how private theatricals insidiously "blunted" the "fine edge" of modesty:

the modest miss, who would, previous to her commencing actress, have prudently resented every address that seemed to encroach beyond the bounds of modesty, submits to be treated with liberties which lay a foundation for her ruin. Sometimes she personates the coquette, and is regaled with all the *polite* double entendres of the refined libertine; they are familiar to her on the stage, and as *use* reconciles most *disagreeables,* she hears them with less dread every time they are repeated, even *off* the stage: thus by degrees the fine edge of her modesty is blunted, her morals are undermined, and the consequence is, that a feigned *Calista* may experience the perfidy of a real *Lothario*, and literally become *the Fair Penitent*.[20]

Austen would obviously question the force of modesty in this "modest miss," whose history closely resembles that of the unfortunate Maria Bertram. Indeed, even if acting were not "almost certain to prove . . . injurious" to the female sex, as Thomas Gisborne's 1797 *Enquiry* on that sex's duties contended, Maria's ambiguous situation during the theatricals would have rendered her vulnerable. Any engagement marks a period of transition, but the fact that she has been pledged to Mr. Rushworth while her father is absent means that she is even more precariously suspended than is customary between her father's domain and that of her future husband. The perils that Gisborne associated with any theatrical performance by a woman—the risks of "unrestrained familiarity with persons of the other sex, which inevitably results from being joined with them in the drama"[21]—could only be heightened for one tempted to flirt with the relative freedom of a woman who has committed herself elsewhere, even while she lacks the very protection that firm commitment affords. With its own shifting identities, its toying with sexual license and transgression, *Lovers' Vows* is hardly the play to minimize such dangers.

To be sure, few risks can attend Fanny in the role of Cottager's wife. As Tom rather brutally reminds her, "It is a nothing of a part," in which she may be as "creepmouse" as she likes. Though she disapproves of *Lovers' Vows* on her cousins' account, Fanny's own refusal to perform registers primarily as a modest shrinking from public exposure, even as her words also sound a note of Platonic resistance to the whole business of feigning. "No indeed," says Fanny, "I cannot act. . . . I really cannot act. . . . It would be absolutely impossible for me" (pp. 145, 146). But the heroine's absolutes here are not, and cannot be, the novelist's: as recent commentators on *Mansfield Park* have suggested, theatricality and antitheatricality, sincerity and insincerity, will not prove so easy to distinguish. "Shocked to find herself at that moment the only speaker in the room; and to feel that almost every eye was upon her" (pp. 145–46), Fanny must act even while refusing to do so.[22]

In short, even an antitheatrical novel is inevitably dramatic, and the novelist knows that modesty speaks on both sides of the issue. Alone in her room, Fanny begins to question whether the claims of others ought not to take precedence, whether her apparent self-effacement is not in fact self-indulgence. "Was she *right* in refusing what was so warmly asked, so strongly wished for? what might be so essential to a scheme on which some of those to whom she owed the greatest complaisance, had set their hearts? Was it not ill-nature—selfishness—and a fear of exposing herself?" Indeed, the very strength of such fear ironically testifies against her: "it would be so horrible to her to act, that she was inclined to suspect the truth and purity of her own scruples." Mrs. Norris, we might recall, has just publicly accused her niece of obstinacy and ingratitude; and the fact that in this case, as in that of Crawford's courtship, Fanny must confront the claims of those to whom she is seriously indebted only intensifies her dilemma, making all the stronger the voice that speaks for modest surrender: "as she looked around her, the claims of her cousins to being obliged, were strengthened by the sight of present upon present that she had received from them. . . . and she grew bewildered as to the amount of the debt which all these kind remembrances produced" (p. 153). Though Fanny survives her own cross-examination here, survives even the discovery that Edmund himself has decided to participate, the trials of modesty, Austen suggests, are neverending: the first volume of *Mansfield Park* closes with Dr. Grant's indigestion, Mrs. Grant's staying home, and Fanny once again "surrounded by supplications" to read the part of Cottager's wife (p. 171). This time Edmund, too, joins in the chorus, "and as they all persevered—as Edmund repeated his wish, and with a look of even fond dependence on her good nature, she must yield." Even Fanny's resolution, it seems, cannot hold out forever: "every body was satisfied—and she was left to the tremors of a most palpitating heart, while the others prepared to begin" (p. 172). Only the timely return of Sir Thomas obviates this reluctant yielding of modest resistance to modest compliance.

The trial by theatricals in *Mansfield Park* prefigures that by courtship. Performing in a play, of course, necessarily entails some surrender to the group, but so, as Austen ironically emphasizes, does choosing to marry: indeed, while the theatrical project threatens to founder in discord and confusion, the far more united front the group maintains on the issue of marriage suggests just how terrifyingly thorough a consensus that institution may command. On the question of the theatricals, Edmund openly urges the others to let Fanny "choose for herself" (p. 147), and even Mary tacitly supports her when Aunt Norris joins in the bullying; but on the question of marriage, everyone at Mansfield apparently concurs with Lady Bertram—"that it is every young woman's duty to accept such a very unexceptionable offer as this." Almost "the only piece of advice," as the narrator sardonically notes, that this aunt of Fanny's ever provides, Lady Bertram's single "rule of conduct"

(p. 333) rests on a conception of duty little different from Mary Crawford's. "Every body should marry as soon as they can do it to advantage" (p. 43), Mary announces when she first arrives at Mansfield, just as she later observes of the matrimonial prospects of the Miss Owens that "it is every body's duty to do as well for themselves as they can" (p. 289). Modern readers are inclined to view the owners of Mansfield and the city-bred Crawfords as ideological opponents, but in the matter of Henry's courtship their doctrines coincide. When Sir Thomas laments "that independence of spirit, which prevails so much in modern days, even in young women, and which in young women is offensive and disgusting beyond all common offence" (p. 318), he is referring not to the witticisms of Mary Crawford, as might be imagined, but to Fanny's refusal to marry Mary's brother. Now it is not merely Mrs. Norris but Sir Thomas himself who accuses her of "*ingratitude*" (p. 319) and labels her no-saying as "wilful and perverse" (p. 318). Fanny's resistance to *Lovers' Vows* may have been implicitly supported by the authority of the absent father, but her resistance to this lover's vows leaves her utterly isolated.

"Fanny knew her own meaning, but was no judge of her own manner," we are told of her struggle to convince Henry that their marriage is impossible: "her manner was incurably gentle, and she was not aware how much it concealed the sternness of her purpose" (p. 327). In fact, by confronting the "incurably gentle" and diffident Fanny with "a temper of vanity and hope like Crawford's" (p. 328), Austen deliberately subjects her heroine to the very sort of man most inclined to torment her—a man whose confidence in himself and the future merely intensifies his sex's usual assumptions about the direction of the plot. That Crawford has charm and intelligence enough to warrant his optimism only intensifies the conflict: even as *Mansfield Park* postulates a heroine whose "yielding temper" (p. 17) means that she is far less able to defend herself than the witty and outspoken Elizabeth Bennet, it presents her with a first suitor whose attractions prove far more difficult to dismiss.[23] While Mr. Bennet happily threatened never to see his daughter again if she accepted the foolishly complacent Collins, only poor Mr. Rushworth jealously confides that he "can see nothing in" Henry Crawford (p. 102).

The novel's final events, of course, will more than vindicate Rushworth's jealousy. Crawford's flight with Maria, Tony Tanner has argued, is "a reversion to his true self," proof that in courting Fanny the accomplished actor has merely been playing "the role of sincerity."[24] But this is a conclusion established only in, and by, retrospect: as long as

Fanny's suitor continues to move her by reading the parts of *Henry VIII* at Mansfield, or by speaking the part of a conscientious landlord in Portsmouth, he remains in more than one sense "truly dramatic" (p. 337). Austen makes him not only a good actor, in other words, but a man whose acting carries with it some real possibility of change. "I beleive *now* he has changed his mind as to foreseeing the end," she wrote of her own brother Henry when he was in the midst of the novel's third volume; "he said yesterday at least, that he defied anybody to say whether H. C. would be reformed, or would forget Fanny in a fortnight." [25] As for Fanny herself, even the dirt and disorder of Portsmouth have not inspired in her the wish to be mistress of Everingham. True, Sir Thomas's "medicinal project upon his niece's understanding" (p. 369) has effected a new appreciation of Mansfield, and of all that distinguishes a man like Crawford from her vulgar relations. "She thought him altogether improved since she had last seen him; he was much more gentle, obliging, and attentive to other people's feelings than he had ever been at Mansfield; she had never seen him so agreeable—so *near* being agreeable. . . . He was decidedly improved" (p. 406). Finding a suitor "so *near* being agreeable," however, is far from falling in love with him: indeed, Fanny ironically chooses to take this "wonderful improvement" in him as a sign that he will "not much longer persevere in a suit so distressing to her" (pp. 413, 414).

Yet if the resistance of this modest heroine holds out till the end, only the novelist's plotting of that end guarantees that it will do so. [26] As Sir Thomas opportunely returns at the close of the first volume to save Fanny from the theatricals, so Henry obligingly runs off at the last to save her from himself; and whether we compare these actions to the ringing down of a curtain or the short-circuiting of a plot, in both cases the novelist's hand can be felt behind the arrangements. Fanny has not yet agreed to be Henry's wife, as she had previously agreed to be Cottager's, but her continued resistance alone, it appears, would merely have delayed the usual progress of such a courtship. Or so, at least, the narrator herself seems to argue, when she moralizes over Henry's action in the final chapter of the novel:

Could he have been satisfied with the conquest of one amiable woman's affections, could he have found sufficient exultation in overcoming the reluctance, in working himself into the esteem and tenderness of Fanny Price, there would have been every probability of success and felicity for him. His affection had already done something. Her influence over him had already given him some influence over her. Would he have deserved more, there can be no doubt that more would have been obtained, especially when that marriage had taken place, which would have given him the assistance of her conscience in subduing her first inclination, and brought them very often together.

By the close of the passage, the "probability" of such an ending has become a certainty: "would he have persevered, and uprightly, Fanny must have been his reward—and a reward very voluntarily bestowed—within a reasonable period from Edmund's marrying Mary" (p. 467). Only by abruptly interposing a new action does Austen assure that her heroine's modesty will not yield this conclusion.

❦

Well before its heroine has reached marriageable age, *Mansfield Park* has begun to distinguish her modesty from the merely conventional kind, the sort to which even Mrs. Norris routinely pays lip service. "Remember that, if you are ever so forward and clever yourselves, you should always be modest," the latter exhorts the Bertram sisters at the same time that she flatters them. "For, much as you know already," she continues, "there is a great deal more for you to learn"—to which one nameless sister dutifully responds, "Yes, I know there is, till I am seventeen" (p. 19). By the time both sisters have passed that crucial barrier, the narrator dryly reports, "Their vanity was in such good order, that they seemed to be quite free from it" (p. 35). While true modesty struggles to resist the erotic plot, this is the sort of secret vanity, the novel will later make clear, that leaves Maria all too vulnerable to Henry's seductions. Indeed, insofar as it does reject such plotting, identifying true modesty rather with the activity of Fanny's consciousness—with inward efforts of self-suppression, discrimination, and judgment—*Mansfield Park* comes closer to Mary Wollstonecraft's account of the virtue than to that of the conduct books.[27]

Despite Nina Auerbach's suggestion that it is the bold and outspoken Mary Crawford who possesses Wollstonecraft's "pioneering sensibility," neither Mary's view of love and marriage nor her conception of sisterhood have much in common with *The Rights of Woman*.[28] Mary may persuade herself that she and Fanny "are born to be connected" and will one day be "sisters" (p. 359), but Fanny proves justified when she worries that "Miss Crawford, complaisant as a sister"—a brother's sister, that is—"was careless as a woman and a friend" (p. 260). Like the necklace that she pretends to offer as her own gift while actually pandering for Henry, Mary's professions of friendship have more to do with her loyalty to her brother and her interest in a husband than with her devotion to another woman. "I *should* have thought . . . that every woman must have felt the possibility of a man's not being approved, not being loved by some one of her sex, at least, let him be ever so generally agreeable," Fanny declares after refusing Henry's proposal, but Mrs. Grant and Mary appear to think differently (p. 353). On such questions, it is typically Fanny who keeps faith with her sex—choosing not to defend her rejection of Henry at the expense of betraying Maria and Julia, for example, or responding to Mary's boasts of her brother's previous conquests by asserting that she "cannot think well of a man who sports with any woman's feelings." While Mary argues for "the glory of fixing one who has been shot at by so many," convinced that "it is not in woman's nature to refuse such a triumph" (p. 363), Fanny comes closer to the Wollstonecraft who deplores such "perpetual rivalships." [29]

"Matrimony was her object, provided she could marry well," we are told on first meeting Miss Crawford (p. 42); and scarcely has she arrived at Mansfield before she has begun to weigh the attractions of elder and younger sons, even while she ponders the status of the potential competition:

"I begin now to understand you all, except Miss Price," said Miss Crawford, as she was walking with the Mr. Bertrams. "Pray, is she out, or is she not?—I am puzzled.—She dined at the parsonage, with the rest of you, which seemed like being *out;* and yet she says so little, that I can hardly suppose she *is.*" (P. 48)

"What can be more indelicate," Wollstonecraft had inquired, "than a girl's *coming out* in the fashionable world? Which, in other words, is to bring to market a marriageable miss, whose person is taken from one public place to another, richly caparisoned." [30] If Edmund Bertram does not speak as harshly, he nonetheless responds in terms that Wollstonecraft would have appreciated: "I believe I know what you mean," he replies, "—but I will not undertake to answer the question. My cousin is grown up. She has the age and sense of a woman, but the outs and not outs are beyond me."

From Mary's perspective, however, the "sense of a woman" settles nothing. "Till now," she continues, she "could not have supposed it possible to be mistaken as to a girl's being out or not," since "manners as well as appearance are . . . so totally different," and the moment many a girl crosses that imaginary threshold she abruptly abandons all semblance of modesty. In fact, "they sometimes pass in such very little time from reserve to quite the opposite—to confidence!" (p. 49). Though Mary deplores the awkwardness of such abrupt transitions, she confesses herself unable to determine "where the error lies." But Edmund responds that "the error is plain enough . . . such girls are ill brought up. They are given wrong notions from the beginning. They are always acting upon motives of vanity—and there is no more real modesty in their behaviour *before* they appear in public than afterwards." If modesty can be thrown off, apparently, it is not "real": true modesty is a form of consciousness, not merely of behavior, and the proof of its genuineness is that it does not change.[31] Mary, however, significantly fails to understand him:

"I do not know," replied Miss Crawford hesitatingly. "Yes, I cannot agree with you there. It is certainly the modestest part of the business. It is much worse to have girls *not out,* give themselves the same airs and take the same liberties as if they were, which I *have* seen done. *That* is worse than any thing—quite disgusting!" (P. 50)

By presuming that the only alternative to the girl who abruptly alters her behavior when she comes out is the girl who acts immodestly from the start, Mary unwittingly reveals that she finds a modest consciousness unimaginable. All she can recognize is the difference in manners and appearance, the distinction between acting with or without restraint. The inwardness of "real modesty" does not exist for her, and when she insists on returning to the problem of Fanny at the close of the conversation, it is only to settle the question in the most conventionally external of terms: "Does she go to balls? Does she dine out every where, as well as at my sister's?" The answer to both queries being negative, the "point" for Miss Crawford "is clear": "Miss Price is *not* out" (p. 51).

The narrator herself will later put the issue differently, when she remarks that "Miss Price had not been brought up to the trade of *coming out*" (p. 267). Like *The Rights of Woman, Mansfield Park* worries about the ends to which women are conventionally educated; and like the earlier work, if more obliquely, it implies that a young woman "brought up to the trade" is effectively a young woman prostituted—so at least Edmund will momentarily picture Mary Crawford, when he recalls his last vision of her "saucy playful smile," soliciting him from a doorway (p. 459). As for Maria and Julia, "such girls," as Edmund might say, have been "ill brought up," and only too late will their father come to recognize "the most direful mistake in his plan of education": they "had never been properly taught to govern their inclinations and tempers, by that sense of duty which can alone suffice. . . . and of the necessity of self-denial and humility, he feared they had never heard from any lips that could profit them." Just as Edmund has argued that those who

abandon modesty must never really possess it in the first place, so Sir
Thomas will conclude of his own daughters that "something must have
been wanting *within*"—a "something" he identifies with "principle, active principle" (p. 463). In more than one sense, Fanny will supply the
daughters' lack: "sick of ambitious and mercenary connections, prizing
more and more the sterling good of principle and temper," Sir Thomas
comes to realize that "Fanny was indeed the daughter that he wanted"
(pp. 471, 472).

"For what purpose were the passions implanted?" Wollstonecraft
had inquired rhetorically, only to answer "that man by struggling with
them might attain a degree of knowledge denied to the brutes; whispers
Experience."[32] So it appears that passions have been similarly "implanted" in Fanny—as when we are told, for example, that "she had
been feeling neglected, and been struggling against discontent and envy
for some days past" in response to Edmund's horseback riding with
Mary Crawford (p. 74), or that "she was full of jealousy and agitation"
upon hearing of his decision to participate in the theatricals, but "reflection brought better feelings" (pp. 159, 160). No doubt the author of
The Rights of Woman would have been troubled by the "creepmouse" in
this heroine—not to mention her physical debility—but it is nonetheless crucial that Fanny's is never an unconscious shrinking and trembling. Unlike Pamela or Evelina, for instance, Fanny is represented as
conscious that she loves virtually from the beginning.[33] Indeed, for a
young woman in this novel to lack "knowledge of her own heart" is
necessarily to lack "that higher species of self-command . . . just consideration of others," and "principle of right" (p. 91). When Edmund intervenes on Fanny's behalf in the expedition to Sotherton, the narrator
reports that "she felt [his] kindness with all, and more than all, the sensibility which he . . . could be aware of"; while it is he who is typically
said to be "unsuspicious of her fond attachment" (p. 79). Rather than
"the coyness of ignorance," in Wollstonecraft's contemptuous phrase,[34]
Fanny's is the virtue of self-knowledge and self-discipline. On the eve of
the ball, this modest heroine does not so much awaken to love as work
to suppress it, though Fanny's struggles to master herself—and Austen's mastery of the indirect style—still protect her from naming her
feelings too explicitly:

It was her intention, as she felt it to be her duty, to try to overcome all that was
excessive, all that bordered on selfishness in her affection for Edmund. To call or
to fancy it a loss, a disappointment, would be a presumption; for which she had
not words strong enough to satisfy her own humility. To think of him as Miss
Crawford might be justified in thinking, would in her be insanity. To her, he

could be nothing under any circumstances—nothing dearer than a friend. Why did such an idea occur to her even enough to be reprobated and forbidden? It ought not to have touched on the confines of her imagination. (Pp. 264–65)

"She would endeavour to be rational," the passage concludes, "and to deserve the right of judging of Miss Crawford's character and the privilege of true solicitude for him by a sound intellect and an honest heart" (p. 265).

We shall return to the powerful sense of anxiety the narrative registers here, and to what may seem oppressive in the "confines" of such an imagination. But for now it is more important to note how the passage characteristically associates Fanny's "endeavour to be rational" with her "right of judging" and "privilege of true solicitude"—with Fanny's virtues, in other words, as a center of consciousness. If Stuart Tave somewhat exaggerates when he declares that "it is always Fanny who sees the entire process, who sees what others are doing when they themselves do not understand their own actions, sees the whole drama of their interaction," he is nonetheless right to suggest that Austen often focalizes her narrative through the vision of her modest heroine, and that she does so precisely because she identifies Fanny's self-effacement with the ability to concentrate lucidly and patiently on others.[35] Like many such fictions, *Mansfield Park* repeatedly makes its heroine "a quiet auditor of the whole" (p. 136), the one who "screened from notice herself . . . saw all that was passing before her" (p. 185), even as its third-person narrative helps to underwrite her modesty as genuine. "Fanny is little more than an observant stillness," Leo Bersani has written, "but because of that she is an excellent judge." But rather than "a stable, nondesiring center of judgment," as Bersani has called her,[36] the novel takes this modest heroine as a center of judgment to the degree that she actively struggles against desire: if Fanny "could not think of [Julia] as under the agitations of *jealousy*, without great pity," for example, it is because she herself has consciously wrestled with the same emotion (p. 136). And if she sees clearly and well because she consciously resists desire, so she resists desire—at least as identified with the Crawfords—because she sees clearly: when she remarks to Edmund that "as a bystander, perhaps I saw more than you did" (p. 350), she is speaking not only about how she observed Rushworth's jealousy during the theatricals but about all the reasons why she "cannot approve" Henry's "character" (p. 349). In this modest fiction, a modesty that "endeavour[s] to be rational" opposes the erotic plot.

"Manners and morals are so nearly allied that they have often been confounded," Wollstonecraft wrote in the dedication of *The Rights of Woman;* "but, though the former should only be the natural reflection of the latter, yet, when various causes have produced factitious and corrupt manners, which are very early caught, morality becomes an empty name. The personal reserve, and sacred respect for cleanliness and delicacy in domestic life . . . are the graceful pillars of modesty." [37] The "corrupt manners" to which Wollstonecraft alludes are, inevitably, French; but something very like the same relation between "manners" and "morals," this "sacred respect for cleanliness and delicacy in domestic life" sustains the modesty of *Mansfield Park* and bolsters its anxious rejection of the Crawfords. Immediately before the climax of the novel, in the last chapter of Fanny's exile at Portsmouth, comes a passage extraordinary for Jane Austen—extraordinary both in its concrete details and in the sense of revulsion it records:

She felt that she had, indeed, been three months there; and the sun's rays falling strongly into the parlour, instead of cheering, made her still more melancholy; for sun-shine appeared to her a totally different thing in a town and in the country. Here, its power was only a glare, a stifling, sickly glare, serving but to bring forward stains and dirt that might otherwise have slept. There was neither health nor gaiety in sun-shine in a town. She sat in a blaze of oppressive heat, in a cloud of moving dust; and her eyes could only wander from the walls marked by her father's head, to the table cut and knotched by her brothers, where stood the tea-board never thoroughly cleaned, the cups and saucers wiped in streaks, the milk a mixture of motes floating in thin blue, and the bread and butter growing every minute more greasy than even Rebecca's hands had first produced it.

The vulgar confusion that Fanny has registered ever since her arrival at Portsmouth is here brought vividly into focus. From the walls marked by the oil of her father's head, to the unclean utensils on the table marred by her brothers, to the motes in the milk and the greasy bread, Austen's heroine sees her family home as stained and polluted. Fanny may have dwelled too long amidst the comforts of Mansfield Park, or Austen may have been tempted to indulge in some conventional disparagement of town life. But neither explanation accounts for the intensity of this consciousness of dirt—nor for its surfacing at this particular moment, as if prescient of the moral revulsion about to come. The passage continues:

Her father read his newspaper, and her mother lamented over the ragged carpet as usual, while the tea was in preparation—and wished Rebecca would mend it;

and Fanny was first roused by his calling out to her, after humphing and considering over a particular paragraph—"What's the name of your great cousins in town, Fan?"

A moment's recollection enabled her to say, "Rushworth, Sir."

"And don't they live in Wimpole Street?"

"Yes, Sir."

"Then, there's the devil to pay among them, that's all." (P. 439)

Fanny's disgusted perception of dirt and spoilage among her immediate kin at Portsmouth thus directly anticipates her shocked verdict on the "too horrible . . . confusion of guilt" (p. 441) among her great cousins in London. The squalor of Mrs. Price's housekeeping is inevitably swallowed up in the horror of Mrs. Rushworth's adultery, and the scandalized Fanny is soon summoned back to Mansfield and away from the mess on the family table. Guilty confusion commands more attention than the homely Portsmouth kind, especially in a world so insistently moralized as Austen's: distracted by the climactic revelations, the rush back to familiar characters and to moral judgment, the reader, too, tends to forget the dirt. But if pollution ideas come strongly to the fore whenever the lines of a social system are especially precarious or threatened, as Mary Douglas has argued,[38] it is not surprising that in this interval of heightened anxiety and suspense Fanny Price should see dirt. Nor is it surprising that *Mansfield Park* should cut short the erotic plot, as it earlier interrupted the preparations for the theatricals, with a certain fastidious attention to housekeeping.

Imagined temporally, one might say, modesty is always in danger of acquiescing—which is why at moments of crisis the novel abruptly puts a stop to the action and focuses instead on the marking of spatial boundaries, of arbitrary lines between the dirty and the clean. At the close of the first volume, recall, Fanny had just reluctantly agreed to read a part in *Lovers' Vows* when Sir Thomas returned to eradicate the "infection" of acting from his house (p. 184).[39] The theater that had been temporarily erected in his billiard room was dismantled, the scene painter dismissed, and "Sir Thomas was in hopes that another day or two would suffise to wipe away every outward memento of what had been, even to the destruction of every unbound copy of 'Lovers' Vows' in the house, for he was burning all that met his eye" (p. 191). By wiping away every sign of the theatricals, Sir Thomas does not merely put an end to his children's acting scheme but ritually purges Mansfield of its dangers. He wants "a home which shuts out noisy pleasures" (p. 186), and his gesture firmly reestablishes those boundaries that "shut out," restoring a space that has been profaned. Trivial as the removal of Sir

Thomas's billiard table may seem, the "general air of confusion in the furniture" (p. 182) is the sign of a more profound disturbance, at once portent and cause of the "confusion of guilt" in London that eventually follows (p. 441). Though the dirt of Portsmouth has no such direct relation to the mess in London, both will be firmly repudiated by the general housecleaning at Mansfield with which the novel closes.

The modest Fanny has not yet reached the point of acquiescing when the action stops a second time, but she has never before seemed so anxious and uncertain, her state of mind so vulnerably suspended. Indeed, the sojourn at Portsmouth has been characterized from its beginning by a peculiar tension and disquiet. To be at "home" for the heroine of this novel has been in fact to be in exile, displaced from the only ground to which her history has attached her. "*That* was now the home. Portsmouth was Portsmouth" (p. 431). No firm period has been fixed for her stay, and in the days before the scandal breaks the term of her banishment threatens to lengthen indefinitely. If the noise and disorder of her father's house have not yet prompted in her the wish to be mistress of Everingham, Fanny's shame at her own family and Henry's persistent courtship have nonetheless proved seriously unsettling. Worried and estranged, she has at the same time been compelled to wait helplessly for the resolution of Edmund's own unsettled state, the outcome of his protracted, indecisive courtship of Mary Crawford. The Portsmouth mail has already brought the disturbing news of Tom Bertram's illness, when it brings yet another alarming letter, the hasty note in which Mary mysteriously alludes to a scandal she does not name. The troubled suspense that has marked Fanny's entire stay at Portsmouth culminates in yet another day of waiting, before Mr. Price's newspaper unexpectedly confirms the scandal, and anxiety gives way to "the shock of conviction" (p. 440).

Fanny's revulsion at the news is vehement and absolute. "She passed only from feelings of sickness to shudderings of horror." And the origin of the sickness is the discovery of people dangerously out of place, of accustomed categories blurred and confounded:

The event was so shocking, that there were moments even when her heart revolted from it as impossible—when she thought it could not be. A woman married only six months ago, a man professing himself devoted, even *engaged*, to another—that other her near relation—the whole family, both families connected as they were by tie upon tie, all friends, all intimate together!—it was too horrible a confusion of guilt, too gross a complication of evil, for human nature, not in a state of utter barbarism, to be capable of!—yet her judgment told her it was so. (P. 441)

D. A. Miller is surely not the only reader to find Fanny's "curious disbelief and excessive disgust" in this passage "inadequately served by the moral terms in which they are accounted for."[40] But if "too gross a complication of evil" seems closer to the "stains and dirt" in the Prices' parlor than it does to considered judgment, it also bears a striking resemblance to the language in which Wollstonecraft, too, records her own anxious resistance to the body—as when she deplores the practice of "mixing" young women "indiscriminately together," for example, or denounces those who are "grossly familiar" with one another.[41] Like *The Rights of Woman*, in other words, *Mansfield Park* does not always distinguish a modest consciousness from a conscious sense of loathing toward the body. Of course, the judgments of the modest heroine are not necessarily those of the novelist, and most readers will be inclined to take Fanny's idea of "utter barbarism," for example, with a measure of irony. Though Fanny may rashly conclude that "the greatest blessing to every one of kindred with Mrs. Rushworth would be instant annihilation" (p. 442), Austen is not about to litter Mansfield Park with corpses.[42] But to the degree that the novel's plot finally seems to share in its heroine's impulse to sort the clean from the dirty, the sacred from the profane, it also seems to endorse and confirm her anxiety. Permanently banishing Mrs. Rushworth and Mrs. Norris, forever dividing Crawfords from Bertrams, *Mansfield Park* draws its boundaries after the consciousness of its modest heroine.[43]

"Modesty," in Wollstonecraft's words, "must heartily disclaim, and refuse to dwell, with that debauchery of mind"; and it is for mental "debauchery" rather than for any more bodily immediate crime that Edmund Bertram finally refuses to dwell with Mary Crawford. Wollstonecraft suggests, in fact, that mental immodesty is worse than the other kind: "how much more modest is the libertine who obeys the call of appetite or fancy," she exclaims, "than the lewd joker who sets the table in a roar!" Though she appears to be thinking principally of the "indecent allusions, or obscene witticisms" of men, she goes on to extend the argument to her own sex; and whatever Wollstonecraft may have meant by women's "bodily wit,"[44] one is tempted to offer Mary Crawford's notorious joke about the navy's "*Rears, and Vices*" as an example (p. 60). "Sometimes," Edmund tentatively remarks on the corrupting effects of an education at the admiral's, "it appears as if the mind itself was tainted" (p. 269); and by the time that he reports to his cousin on the final parting in London, that tentative judgment has hardened to a certainty. He may have looked back when Mary smilingly called after him from the doorway—but then he walked on and gave no sign. "It was a smile," he later tells Fanny, "ill-suited to the conversation that had passed, a saucy playful smile, seeming to invite, in order to subdue me" (p. 459). If Mary's equivocal placement and expression, as Edmund recalls them, are the final emblems of her impurity, the impulse by which he cuts her seems a momentary instinct of revulsion, an effort to avoid contamination.[45] By her willingness to call seduction and adultery mere "folly" (p. 454), her hope that the guilty pair might still join in marriage, even live down the scandal with "good dinners, and large parties" (p. 457), she has betrayed her tolerance for unclean mixtures, the casual promiscuity of her mind.

What finally condemns Mary Crawford is no deed of her own but the fact that her "delicacy" is "blunted" (p. 456)—which is to say that her consciousness fails to draw sharp lines of revulsion:

> "She reprobated her brother's folly in being drawn on by a woman whom he had never cared for, to do what must lose him the woman he adored; but still more the folly of—poor Maria, in sacrificing such a situation, plunging into such difficulties, under the idea of being really loved by a man who had long ago made his indifference clear. Guess what I must have felt. To hear the woman whom—no harsher name than folly given!—So voluntarily, so freely, so coolly to canvass it!—No reluctance, no horror, no feminine—shall I say? no modest loathings!" (Pp. 454–55)

Edmund's broken syntax, his hesitation to "say," conveys its own modest reluctance. To allude to "poor Maria's" crime is difficult enough, but the guilt of the adulteress seems dwarfed by the failure of Mary Crawford to condemn her. What Edmund most hesitates to name is Mary's lack, that absence of "modest loathings," which has left her mind "corrupted, vitiated" (p. 456). Mary is "spoilt, spoilt!" (p. 455)—or "at least," as Edmund conscientiously adds when he describes that last dangerously seductive smile, "it appeared so to me" (p. 459). How Mary actually looked at him and how Edmund needed to see her cannot in the end be distinguished. Like the narrator's ironic allusion to Edmund's going over the story with Fanny again and again, that detail suggests something of the anxiety that may motivate such a vision, the very uneasiness that prompts one to see and reject the unclean.

When Fanny Price returns to Mansfield Park, it is no longer to the humble east room with the chilly hearth: the wicked aunt is vanquished, the two older girls disgraced, and "the lowest and last" (p. 221) assumes her rightful place in the house. If Fanny resembles Cinderella, as many have sensed, she is perhaps most Cinderella-like in this—that hers is not so much a story of growing up as a myth of recognition, a fantasy of being at last acknowledged for the princess one truly is. In most versions of the fairy tale, the heroine begins as an only and much-loved child; her rags and ashes are a temporary debasement, signs of the humiliation she is forced to endure when a stepmother and stepsisters invade her father's house. At the crucial moment, degraded appearances are cast off as dirt, and the heroine reveals herself to be worthy of a prince. Magic may transform rats into coachmen and dirty rags into dresses of gold, but hers is the inherent virtue and loveliness—and the small feet. When the glass slipper fits, even her stepsisters are compelled to recognize Cinderella as the beautiful lady of the ball. Cinderella may have dwelled among ashes, but the dirt has not really touched her; in retrospect, she seems to have been simply waiting to be discovered, her essential purity undefiled. Indeed, in a curious footnote to his lengthy discussion of the tale, Bruno Bettelheim laments that by mistranslating the French "Cendrillon," the English name for the heroine incorrectly associates her with cinders rather than ashes—the latter being a "very clean powdery substance" and not "the quite dirty remnants of an incomplete combustion."[46] Though Bettelheim's etymology contradicts his earlier stress on the importance of dirt in the tale, his insistence that the genuine Cinderella was never really dirty at all suggests how deep are the longings her story addresses.

Like "Cinderella," *Mansfield Park* associates its heroine with dirt only to deny the force of the association. But unlike the fairy tale, the novel establishes her purity not by an outward, symbolic transformation but by an inner response, the experience of revulsion. Fanny visits her parents' home and finds it unclean—discovers, in effect, that she is not her parents' child. She cannot even stomach the food of this "home," but must send out, covertly, for chaster fare: "she was so little equal to Rebecca's puddings, and Rebecca's hashes, brought to table as they all were, with such accompaniments of half-cleaned plates, and not half-cleaned knives and forks, that she was very often constrained to defer her heartiest meal, till she could send her brothers in the evening for biscuits and buns." As to whether nature or nurture has prompted such disgust, the text seems unable to decide. "After being nursed up at Mansfield," the narrator observes in the matter of the puddings and the hashes, "it was too late in the day to be hardened at Portsmouth" (p. 413). But only a chapter earlier, Fanny had felt a "thrill of horror" when her father invited Henry Crawford to partake of the family mutton, since "*she* was nice only from natural delicacy, but *he* had been brought up in a school of luxury and epicurism" (pp. 406, 407). The structure of the novel has made it impossible to determine whether

Fanny could ever have thrived at the family table: though Fanny's Portsmouth origins were reported, her represented history began at Mansfield, and it was at Mansfield that her appetites and affections were
given narrative life. Even mother-love has long been displaced: embrac-
ing Mrs. Price for the first time, Fanny sees features which she "loved
the more, because they brought her aunt Bertram's before her" (p. 377)!
As for Mr. Price, "he swore and he drank, he was dirty and gross. . . .
and now he scarcely ever noticed her, but to make her the object of a
coarse joke" (p. 389). Upon their reunion, he greets her with "an acknowledgment that he had quite forgot her"—and "having given her a
cordial hug, and observed that she was grown into a woman, and he
supposed would be wanting a husband soon, seemed very much inclined to forget her again" (p. 380). At Mansfield, Fanny had imagined
that "to be at home again, would heal every pain that had since grown
out of the separation" (p. 370), yet no sooner does she return to that
home than her modest loathings confirm her division from it: "Fanny
shrunk back to her seat, with feelings sadly pained by his language and
his smell of spirits" (p. 380).

If the modest heroine is a father's daughter, then in *Mansfield Park*
even that relation is finally defined by consciousness rather than biology. Fanny may be connected by blood to Mr. Price, but her revulsion
from Portsmouth confirms that in taste and judgment she belongs with
Sir Thomas. As for the patriarch of Mansfield Park, who has banished
one female child and reconciled himself to the effective loss of the other,
"Fanny was indeed the daughter that he wanted" (p. 472). Indeed, he
wants her all the more because he himself has failed as a father, and by
decisively excluding the unworthy from Mansfield Park, he merely confirms the lines already drawn by her consciousness. Rather than "ex-
plode" Fanny's "confidence in the dispositions of patriarchal figures," as
Claudia Johnson has argued,[47] the acts that close the novel bring modesty home to help shore up the patriarchy. To the degree that Sir Thomas
does not so much raise Fanny as belatedly acquire her values, *Mansfield
Park* subordinates even fathering itself to the "active principle" of its
modest heroine (p. 463).

❦

"His only fault indeed seems Modesty," Austen wrote of a certain
young man in 1814, as she urged the merits of his suit on her vacillating
niece, Fanny Knight. "If he were less modest, he would be more agre-
able, speak louder, & look Impudenter," the letter continues, "—and is
not it a fine Character of which Modesty is the only defect?"

And as to there being any objection from his *Goodness,* from the danger of his becoming even Evangelical, I cannot admit *that.* I am by no means convinced that we ought not all to be Evangelicals, & am at least persuaded that they who are so from Reason and Feeling, must be happiest & safest.—Do not be frightened from the connection by your Brothers having most wit. Wisdom is better than Wit, & in the long run will certainly have the laugh on her side.[48]

Though in the courtship of this Fanny the problems of modesty would seem to have attached to the young man, the "Wisdom" of the letter's brief allegory remains traditionally feminine, and it is not difficult to hear an echo of Fanny Price's secret triumph in her victorious laughter. "How her heart swelled with joy and gratitude," the narrator of the novel remarks, as Fanny's carriage passes the barriers of Portsmouth on the way back to Mansfield, "and how Susan's face wore its broadest smiles, may be easily conceived" (p. 445).[49] *Mansfield Park* had appeared in print only six months before Austen wrote her advice on courtship to Fanny Knight, and the letter's sympathy for Evangelicals, its firm subordination of wit to virtue, have often been cited as a gloss on the novel. But no sooner has Austen put the case for Wisdom than she cheerfully reverses direction—now reminding her niece not to ignore the claims of love: "And now, my dear Fanny, having written so much on one side of the question, I shall turn round & entreat you not to commit yourself farther, & not to think of accepting him unless you really do like him. Anything is to be preferred or endured rather than marrying without Affection; and if his deficiencies of Manner &c &c strike you more than all his good qualities, if you continue to think strongly of them, give him up at once."[50]

Whether or not her aunt's insistence on the claims of affection proved decisive, Fanny Knight eventually chose to marry someone else. But fiction allows for the satisfaction of wishes that in life often remain incompatible; and even as the modest heroine of *Mansfield Park* virtuously resists the erotic plot, her secret desires nonetheless govern her story. "Repressed desire turns out, after all, to *be* desire," as George Levine has put it,[51] though until the lover speaks and the father approves, the modest Fanny successfully conceals that fact from all around her. Only for a brief moment in the middle of the narrative do her feelings nearly betray her. "This requires explanation," Sir Thomas sternly informs her, when she persists in refusing Henry's offer. "Young as you are, and having seen scarcely any one, it is hardly possible that your affections—"

He paused and eyed her fixedly. He saw her lips formed into a *no,* though the sound was inarticulate, but her face was like scarlet. That, however, in so modest a girl might be very compatible with innocence; and chusing at least to appear satisfied, he quickly added, "No, no, I know *that* is quite out of the question—quite impossible. Well, there is nothing more to be said." (P. 316)

As so often in *Mansfield Park*, Fanny's blushing is misinterpreted. But if at other times the color of embarrassment or anger is falsely ascribed to erotic consciousness, here the scarlet that suffuses her face is wishfully misread as "innocent." In the midst of Fanny's genuine no-saying comes a "no" that really does cover a modest affirmative, and the novel that seriously questions the fictions of modesty contains just such a fiction.

Indeed, were it not for this heroine's secret attachment to one man, we are reminded at several points in the narrative, she could not have long held out against the other. "Had not Fanny's heart been guarded in a way unsuspected by Miss Crawford," as the narrator obliquely puts it at an early stage of Henry's courtship, her fate "might have been a little harder than she deserved,"

for although there doubtless are such unconquerable young ladies of eighteen (or one should not read about them) as are never to be persuaded into love against their judgment by all that talent, manner, attention, and flattery can do, I have no inclination to believe Fanny one of them, or to think that with so much tenderness of disposition, and so much taste as belonged to her, she could have escaped heart-whole from the courtship . . . of such a man as Crawford, in spite of there being some previous ill-opinion of him to be overcome, had not her affection been engaged elsewhere. (P. 231)

Only "a pre-engaged heart" (p. 326), this would appear to say, can assure that a modest young woman will not surrender to the pressures of courtship. Since at other times, as we have seen, the novel implies that only Henry's own fall prevents Fanny from succumbing, her successful resistance to his wooing seems conspicuously overdetermined. In fiction, Austen playfully implies, "young ladies of eighteen" might hold out forever, but her Fanny is too real to remain "unconquerable." Yet it might be truer to say that for a novelist like Austen, only one courtship plot can finally drive out another. "Let no one presume to give the feelings of a young woman on receiving the assurance of that affection of which she has scarcely allowed herself to entertain a hope," Austen exhorts her readers in the final pages of *Mansfield Park*; and with the self-conscious artifice of a novelist intent on closure, she consigns her heroine to a "happiness . . . no description can reach" (p. 471). She would have needed no telling that this happiness was another fiction of modesty.

10

Lucy Snowe's Keeping Down

In Charlotte Brontë's last novel, the fiction of modesty strains on the verge of breakdown. The heroine's own hysterical collapse, the curious gaps and evasions in her narrative, her elaborate doublings and displacements of feeling, even the ambiguous destruction of the hero at the close—all testify to libidinal and aggressive energies that seem scarcely to be contained by her belated story of courtship. Despite his impatient dismissal of *Villette* as "disagreeable," Matthew Arnold's memorable allusion to the novelist's "hunger, rebellion, and rage"[1] feels truer to the spirit of the text than do Lucy Snowe's own professions of calm, or others' characterizations of her as "inoffensive as a shadow."[2] Yet there is a sense in which Lucy Snowe is an exemplary modest heroine—a modest heroine, one might say, even to excess. It is precisely because Brontë imagines her as one of those "unguarded Englishwomen" whose inner restraints enable them to "walk calmly amidst red-hot ploughshares and escape burning" (p. 291) that she imagines her as burning so fiercely, even dangerously, within.

Arnold was not the only contemporary reader to register his unease—and to remark certain of the novel's immodest tendencies. "*Villette*," Thackeray observed to a correspondent, "is rather vulgar." Though he followed up his verdict by wryly suggesting that the decorum Brontë had violated was essentially a literary convention ("I don't make my *good* women ready to fall in love with two men at once"),[3] while Harriet Martineau was concerned to argue that "it is not thus in real life," both were struck by the apparent intensity of Lucy Snowe's need for affection and by her open acknowledgment of "a double love." For Martineau, the narrow obsessiveness with which Brontë's women dwelt on love appeared disturbingly to limit their participation in a wider sphere, and like other champions of women before her, she sought to counter such an association of women and desire by enlisting a form of modest unconsciousness in their defense. "There are substantial, heartfelt interests for women of all ages, and under ordinary circumstances, quite apart from love," she protested; "there is an absence of introspection, an unconsciousness, a repose in women's lives . . . of which we find no admission in this book."[4] A review in the *Christian Remembrancer* also protested *Villette*'s open representation of female desire as an injury to women—not, however, because it artificially limited their lives but because it threatened to do away with men's motives for courtship. "So long as *men* wrote romance," according to this review, woman's heart had been "described as an all-but-impenetrable fortress," but now female novelists like Brontë were showing "the invader greeted from afar—invited, indeed, within the walls." If women really did "give away their hearts unsought," the *Christian Remembrancer* worried, "would the prize won on such easy terms be thought so much worth the having? Would this 'more than willingness' satisfy the inherent love of difficulty and of achievement in men's nature?" For one so steeped in the conventional rhetoric of female modesty, the answer—like the question itself—proved, of course, "happily" rhetorical: "a restless heart and vagrant imagination, though owned by woman, can have no sympathy or true insight into the really feminine nature."[5]

The author of this review, Ann Mozley, happened herself to be a woman, and it is symptomatic of the contradictions that inevitably attend such efforts at defining the essential "nature" of the sex that in the very act of denouncing Brontë's heroine as unfeminine Mozley should reproduce one of the same heroine's own more striking experiments in gender—and pretend to speak with the voice of a man. Indeed, like Lucy Snowe when she takes the role of Ginevra's lover in the amateur theatricals, Mozley appears to throw herself into the part. "We want a woman at our hearth," she announces, whereas Brontë's heroines are "without the feminine element, infringers of modest restraints, despisers of bashful fears":

We will sympathise with Lucy Snowe as being fatherless and penniless . . . but we cannot offer even the affections of our fancy . . . to her unscrupulous, and self-dependent intellect—to that whole habit of mind which, because it feels no reverence, can never inspire for itself that one important, we may say, indispensable element of man's true love.[6]

But ironically, while Mozley speaks so thoroughly for a masculine view of woman as to risk the very femininity she defends, the heroine she indicts as "unscrupulous, and self-dependent" herself subscribes to a similar doctrine about female desire. Lucy Snowe, in fact, can be as vehement as the *Christian Remembrancer* on the question of women's role in courtship:

> once, for all . . . I disclaim, with the utmost scorn, every sneaking suspicion of what are called "warmer feelings:" women do not entertain these "warmer feelings" where, from the commencement, through the whole progress of an acquaintance, they have never once been cheated of the conviction that to do so would be to commit a mortal absurdity. (P. 363)

This was not the first time, of course, that Brontë had been attacked as an immodest and potentially subversive writer, nor was it the first time that she was denounced for violating values with which she, and her heroines, would have professed to agree. Elizabeth Rigby's famous attack on the "unregenerate and undisciplined spirit" of *Jane Eyre* in the *Quarterly Review,* in which she declared that "if we ascribe the book to a woman at all, we have no alternative but to ascribe it to one who has, for some sufficient reason, long forfeited the society of her own sex," had deeply wounded and angered the novelist, though she presumably had no way of knowing that her anonymous reviewer was another woman disguising herself as a man.[7] But far more than *Jane Eyre, Villette* is a novel divided against itself—riven by the fantasies it still wishes to entertain and the less consoling stories it is only partly able to tell.[8] If *Villette* is a novel less coherent, certainly less smoothly plotted than its predecessor, it is also one that helps to lay bare the contradictions that more consistently modest fictions work to conceal. Judging by the novel's own evidence, after all, Mozley was wrong to claim that Lucy Snowe could not inspire "that one . . . indispensable element of man's true love." But she was perhaps not altogether wrong—still judging by the novel's own evidence—to find herself doubting the story.

Though Brontë's imagination had always been drawn to the figurative extremes of fire and ice to represent the emotional temperatures of her characters, in *Villette* she came closest to mapping these onto the psychic topography of the modest heroine. "I can hardly express what subtlety of thought made me decide upon giving her a cold name," she wrote to her publisher: but "a *cold* name she must have; partly, perhaps, on the '*lucus a non lucendo*' principle—partly on that of the 'fitness of things,' for she has about her an external coldness."[9] Lucy's "Snowe," in other words, signifies a familiar paradox, at once naming her external coldness and testifying to the warmth within. Recall William Cobbett, for instance, advising his young male readers that "women of *light minds* have seldom any *ardent* passion," while exploiting the formulaic contrast between the sober English and the light-minded French to urge that "modesty pushed to the utmost extent" promises not only the most constant but the warmest of wives:

it is a truth which, I believe, no man of attentive observation will deny, that, as, in general, English wives are *more warm* in their conjugal attachments than those of France, so, with regard to individuals, that those English women who are the *most light* in their manners, and who are the *least constant* in their attachments, have the smallest portion of that *warmth,* that indescribable passion which God has given to all human beings as the great counterbalance to all the sorrows and sufferings of life.[10]

Having set down her cool *Anglaise* in an imaginary "land of convents and confessionals" (p. 138), Brontë can construct a similar female typology—emphasizing her heroine's English and Protestant difference by surrounding her with representative products of the Continental system. Unlike the other inhabitants of Madame Beck's *pensionnat de demoiselles*—its Labassecourienne mistress, who runs the establishment with jesuitical skill but has "no heart to be touched" (p. 101); Zélie St. Pierre, the coquettish Parisienne who lavishes her schoolteacher's salary on cosmetics, dress, and confections but is "a cold, callous epicure" (p. 176), "externally refined—at heart, corrupt" (p. 175); the assorted *jeunes filles* themselves, some Labassecourienne, some French, but all with "eyes full of an insolent light, and brows hard and unblushing as marble" (p. 109); even the English-born yet Continentally educated Ginevra Fanshawe, who despite her origins now scarce knows "the difference between Romanism and Protestantism" (p. 73) and whose "liking and disliking . . . love and hate" prove correspondingly "mere cobweb and gossamer" (p. 118)—the novel's fiercely Protestant and self-contained heroine is alone capable of deep feeling. Only the Scotch-French Polly Home, who is Lucy's openly acknowledged "double" (p. 398) and the novel's conventionally modest heroine, proves a partial exception: as Lucy will tell her, "Paulina, that gentle hoar-frost of yours, surrounding so much pure, fine flame, is a priceless privilege of nature" (p. 545).

Paul Emanuel may himself be a good Catholic and fervent chauvinist, but he knows true English warmth when he meets it. Compared to Lucy's buried ardor, the empty flirtatiousness of Zélie St. Pierre or the calculated advances of his ironically named kinswoman, "Modeste"

Beck, fail to move him. Indeed, in his confident knowledge that the Englishwoman's cool reserve is to be read as a sign of her hidden warmth, he might have taken a leaf from the pages of William Cobbett. And insofar as the novel represents his growing friendship for the heroine as the gradual melting of Lucy Snowe, eventually identifying her hitherto pent-up feeling as her love for him, it approximates to the narrative of a modest courtship. At least that is the story Lucy herself seems to tell when she finally gives an explicit name to her feeling:

The love born of beauty was not mine; I had nothing in common with it . . . but another love, venturing diffidently into life after long acquaintance, furnace-tried by pain, stamped by constancy, consolidated by affection's pure and durable alloy, submitted by intellect to intellect's own tests, and finally wrought up, by his own process, to his own unflawed completeness, this Love that laughed at Passion, his fast frenzies and his hot and hurried extinction, in *this* Love I had a vested interest. (P. 678)

"Venturing diffidently into life after long acquaintance," a feeling tested at once by indirection and delay, "*this* Love" has a familiar shape and story. Constituted by its very opposition to the "fast frenzies" of an evanescent "Passion," such a love conventionally promises to be both "pure" and "durable."

Or so the story goes. But it is not merely the impression that there is something willed in Lucy's rhetoric here, or even her troubling emphasis on the bracing virtues of pain, that calls the usual courtship story into question. The very fact that "the *real* action," as one critic wistfully terms it, only gets under way when the novel is more than half over is a measure of *Villette*'s resistance to this normalizing model of female desire. Rather than take for granted that the relation between Lucy and Paul is "clearly the heart of the book," but one whose awkward placement must be attributed to "faulty craftsmanship" and "poor proportioning,"[11] it seems more useful to ask why the novel's anatomical outlines appear so distorted. For what is finally most striking about *Villette,* if also most unsettling, is how multiple—and multiply incomplete—are its imagined trajectories of energy and desire. At once everywhere and nowhere, the "heart" of Brontë's last novel remains stubbornly difficult to locate.

It is not the self-effacement of the modest woman that *Villette* calls into question but her hidden confidence, the secret belief that she will eventually be recognized as an object of desire. Strictly speaking, of course, one should refer not to the heroine's confidence but to her creator's, since the fiction depends on such secrets being kept from the modest woman herself. The adult Fanny Price will have to "harden" herself "to the idea of being worth looking at," as Edmund teasingly tells her,[12] though Austen has presumably known from the beginning that her awkward and shrinking heroine would grow up into a pretty woman. That we believe in Lucy Snowe's plainness as we do not in Jane Eyre's, as Helene Moglen has shrewdly observed,[13] has less to do with any account of her form and features than with the entire tone and structure of her narrative, its deep distrust of the possibility that anyone will ever find *her* worth looking at. Indeed, Lucy's tendency to appear to others, the handsome Dr. John in particular, as nothing more than an insensate piece of background furniture reads like an ironic fulfillment of Cobbett's wish for a woman so perfectly modest that she would appear to "receive . . . no more impression than if she were a post"[14]— while her self-effacing position at the margins of her own story threatens to turn her into a mordant caricature of the modest heroine:

> He [Dr. John] laid himself open to my observation, according to my presence in the room just that degree of notice and consequence a person of my exterior habitually expects: that is to say, about what is given to unobtrusive articles of furniture, chairs of ordinary joiner's work, and carpets of no striking pattern. Often, while waiting for madame, he would muse, smile, watch, or listen like a man who thinks himself alone. I, meantime, was free to puzzle over his countenance and movements, and wonder what could be the meaning of that peculiar interest and attachment . . . which wedded him to this demi-convent, secluded in the built-up core of a capital. He, I believe, never remembered that I had eyes in my head; much less a brain behind them. (Pp. 135–36)

Critics of *Villette* have often been troubled by Lucy's strange displacement from the center of her own narrative, especially in the opening portions of the novel, as well as by her seemingly willful evasions of her implied contract with the reader—most notably by withholding for several chapters the revelation that she has recognized in the adult Dr. John of Villette her childhood companion Graham Bretton.[15] But what appear to be Brontë's violations of narrative convention can perhaps better be understood as her bitter exaggeration of tendencies already latent in much modest fiction. The Lucy who watches impassively while the little Polly Home weeps for her father and flirts with the adolescent Graham in the early chapters of the novel, or who later feels herself "free to puzzle" over the countenance and movements of the adult Graham, herself "unobtrusive" and unobserved, is not so different from the quietly self-effacing Fanny Price, as she registers the emotional entanglements of her cousins during the Mansfield theatricals, or from Esther Summerson and her "silent way of noticing what passed before" her—including the progress of Richard Carstone's courtship of Ada Clare in Dickens's *Bleak House*.[16] "Why does Brontë choose a voyeur to narrate a fictional biography when this means that the narrator insists on telling the tale as if some other, more attractive woman were its central character?" Sandra Gilbert and Susan Gubar inquire. But their answer—that "obviously, Lucy's life, her sense of herself, does not conform to the literary or social stereotypes provided by her culture to define and circumscribe female life"—is a half-truth at best.[17] For in this respect Lucy conforms with a vengeance: if her narrative does finally appear to call certain female stereotypes into question, it does so not by openly defying them but by pushing them to their breaking point. "Voyeurism," one might say, is only the suspicious name for that silent noticing that a Fanny Price or an Esther Summerson faithfully practices, the ocular corollary of the *Lady's Magazine* maxim that a modest girl takes care not to make herself the heroine of her own story.[18] Or perhaps it would be more accurate to say that "voyeurism" is the name that threatens to attach itself to such watching when the look seems in real danger of not being reciprocated. What distinguishes Lucy Snowe from Fanny Price or Esther Summerson—or from Evelina, for that matter—is not her self-effacing observation of others but the novelist's seriously entertaining the possibility that no one will return her gaze.

At least in the first half of *Villette*, Brontë substitutes for the secret confidence of the modest heroine Lucy Snowe's defiant attempts at her own self-suppression. Her seemingly perverse narrative strategy where Dr. John is concerned is not so far, after all, from Esther Summerson's coy evasions and after-the-fact disclosures about her own Dr. Woodcourt—the chief difference being that what Dickens represents as a half-unconscious forgetting ("I have omitted to mention in its place, that there was some one else at the family dinner party"),[19] Brontë imagines as a deliberate act of will. "There is a perverse mood of the mind which is rather soothed than irritated by misconstruction," Lucy writes in explanation of her refusal to tell Dr. John that she recognized him; "and in quarters where we can never be rightly known, we take pleasure, I think, in being consummately ignored" (p. 137). If Dr. John cannot "know" her, she will refuse to "know" him—and extend that refusal of knowledge to the reader as well: though she reports that her gaze has been "riveted" on the handsome young doctor by a new and "startling" idea (p. 136), several chapters will pass before she reveals that she had been transfixed by her sudden realization of Dr. John's identity. As in *Bleak House*, the narrator's strained relations with the reader both stand in for her relations to the hero and serve to remind us of how the taboo on the female's self-assertion in courtship is always threatening the very possibility of her narrative. "I don't know how it is, I seem to be always writing about myself," Esther Summerson protests: "I mean all the time to write about other people, and I try to think about myself as little as possible." Dickens's heroine typically negotiates the contradiction between her modesty and her narrative by vaguely suggesting that a will other than her own compels her writing—a solution that is no doubt facilitated by the real-life distance between her person and that of her creator: "if these pages contain a great deal about me, I can only suppose it must be because I have really something to do with them, and can't be kept out."[20] Partly because the distance between Brontë and her narrator is much narrower—because the taboo on woman's speaking, that is, menaces them both—the voice of *Villette* is at once more consistent in its modesty and far more radical. The delayed revelation about Dr. John's identity is not the only instance of Lucy's withholding information from the reader: in her oracular allusions to the figurative shipwreck by which she was orphaned, or to Paul Emanuel's drowning at sea, Brontë's narrator also manages to keep herself "out" of her narrative, or at least to draw an obscuring veil around crucial parts of her history. The woman who prefers to be "consummately ignored" where she "can never be rightly known" seems to anticipate that her readers will share in the conventional hero's failure of perception, that they will lack the terms in which to recognize and understand her. And by deliberately laying claim to her own effacement, she threatens to reclaim it as a form of power.[21]

᭞

"Modesty pushed to its utmost extent," in Cobbett's phrase, may be always about to deconstruct itself—but perhaps especially, as *Villette* begins to suggest, when its contradictions no longer clearly subserve the plot of courtship. Take away the promise of the lover's gaze and of his speaking, in other words, and the modest Englishwoman may dangerously resemble a buried nun. Brontë seems to predicate her heroine's difference from others of her sex, after all, on a recognizably English and Protestant fiction: whereas Catholics depend on external and institutional restraints to control the sexuality of their women, drawing a sharp line between the conventual innocence of the *demoiselle* and the consequent license, even adultery, of the *dame,* English Protestants raise their daughters to be at once self-controlled and free—modest young women and faithful wives. Indeed, it is precisely because the self-contained Lucy carries her internalized restraints around with her, as part of her very being, that the novel imagines her as at liberty to move about her world, free from the Continental system of "surveillance" and restraint. "Foreigners say that it is only English girls who can thus be trusted to travel alone," Lucy observes as she watches Mr. Fanshawe deposit his daughter on the *Vivid* and depart from the ship, "and deep is their wonder at the daring confidence of English parents and guardians." Though the subsequent amorous career of Mr. Fanshawe's daughter will prove that Lucy is right when she immediately doubts "whether this particular young lady was of the sort that can the most safely be left unwatched" (p. 72), Ginevra's case does not so much disprove as confirm the rule: not only has her extensive "foreign" education left her barely able to write English anymore, but "into the bargain," she confesses, "I have quite forgotten my religion; they call me a Protestant, you know, but really I am not sure whether I am one or not" (p. 73). Lucy, on the other hand, makes repeatedly, even painfully, clear that she herself has no need for a duenna: a cool *Anglaise* who wears her "staid manner" like a "cloak and hood of hodden gray" (p. 59), she can travel under its protection where the Continental *jeune fille* could never be trusted to venture. "Il n'y a que les Anglaises pour ces sortes d'entreprises," Madame Beck pronounces when she hears of the adventures by which her new employee has made her way to the pensionnat: "sont-elles donc intrépides ces femmes là!" (p. 89). And "il n'y a que les Anglaises," apparently, who can safely contemplate the voluptuous image of the Cleopatra: if Lucy can "sit coolly down, with the self-possession of a garçon, and look at *that* picture," according to Paul Emanuel, it is only because she is one of those "nurslings of Protestantism" who could be "thrown into Nebuchadnezzar's hottest furnace" and "would issue forth untraversed by the smell of fire" (pp. 287, 291).

Like *The Professor* before it, *Villette* seems to take for granted that a product of the Catholic system would prove, in contrast, all too easily inflammable. "How was it, then," Crimsworth rhetorically inquires about his Continental pupils in the former novel, "that scarcely one of those girls having attained the age of fourteen could look a man in the face with modesty and propriety?" For the English schoolteacher, the answer, of course, "is to be found in the discipline, if not the doctrines of the Church of Rome." [22] As the *Lady's Magazine* had summed up the conventional wisdom more than seventy years earlier, "Unnatural confinement in a convent makes a young woman embrace with avidity every pleasure when she is set free," while "to relish domestic life, one must be acquainted with it" [23]—a rule that continues to operate, it would seem, even when a mere school has come to occupy the conventual site. Like a sort of secular Mother Superior, Madame Beck patrols the premises and routinely spies on the inhabitants, though when it comes to her own daughters, interestingly enough, she prefers to import her educational methods from England: "she would have the women of no other country about her own children, if she could help it" (p. 99). Lucy has no sooner arrived at the pensionnat than Madame Beck's three girls are reciting their prayers to their new governess in English, while their mother effectively demonstrates her own shrewdness by paying tribute—in her native tongue—to the moral superiority of "les Anglaises":

she would talk to me . . . about England and Englishwomen, and the reasons for what she was pleased to term their superior intelligence, and more real and reliable probity. Very good sense she often showed; very sound opinions she often broached: she seemed to know that keeping girls in distrustful restraint, in blind ignorance, and under a surveillance that left them no moment and no corner for retirement, was not the best way to make them grow up honest and modest women; but she averred that ruinous consequences would ensue if any other method were tried with continental children—they were so accustomed to constraint, that relaxation, however guarded, would be misunderstood and fatally presumed on: she was sick, she would declare, of the means she had to use, but use them she must; and after discoursing, often with dignity and delicacy, to me, she would move away on her "souliers de silence," and glide ghost-like through the house, watching and spying everywhere, peering through every key-hole, listening behind every door. (P. 100)

In this respect as stern a critic of the Continental system as any Protestant, Madame Beck implicitly acknowledges herself caught in a vicious cycle: the more that surveillance and restraint breed licentious propensities in the young, the more that the young must be subject to surveillance and restraint. When Lucy in turn ventures into the classroom, she can only imagine breaking the cycle by awakening in the "swinish multitude" (p. 115) some capacity for "honest shame"—a capacity that is signaled when even their immodestly sized organs prove vulnerable to a blush: "if I could but once make their (usually large) ears burn under their thick, glossy hair, all was comparatively well" (p. 116).

The opposition between the women of England and their Continental counterparts is not, as one critic implies, merely Brontë's own, rather desperate, invention—her half-conscious strategy for discrediting "certain highly traditional attitudes toward genteel women" by projecting them onto the Catholic and the foreign[24]—but a familiar

part of her culture's rhetoric about itself; and it is just because the difference has become so deeply engrained in Protestant England's conventional wisdom that the novelist can draw upon it so routinely. "Il y
a . . . quelquechose de bien remarquable dans le caractère Anglais,"
Madame Beck concludes after inspecting Lucy's hoard of letters from
Dr. John; and though she cannot say exactly "how" it is so, she associates this remarkable difference with the attitudes of the English toward
love, and with the fact that there seems no need to keep them under
distrustful observation: "les Anglais ont des idées à eux, en amitié, en
amour, en tout. Mais au moins il n'est pas besoin de les surveiller"
(p. 420). Yet for all the insistence with which the novel dwells on the
idea of a peculiarly English and Protestant difference, the opposition on
which Lucy founds her identity continually threatens to collapse. According to legend, we are told, Madame Beck's house has once been a
convent, and its premises are still haunted by a shadowy nun—the
ghost of a girl, as Lucy puts it, "whom a monkish conclave of the drear
middle ages had here buried alive, for some sin against her vow"
(p. 148). To the Protestant imagination, the nun's unnamed "sin" testifies to the license bred by the Continental system, while her punishment
gothically exaggerates the living burial already implied by immurement
in a convent. But insofar as the shadowy nun serves also, even primarily,
as a double for Lucy herself, the distinction between Catholic confinement and Protestant self-restraint begins to look like a distinction without a difference. The mysterious "image like—a NUN" that haunts the
English schoolteacher at crucial moments in her emotional history
(p. 351) will eventually be explained as a sort of practical joke, but the
phantom will not be unmasked until the novel has thoroughly confounded its uncanny appearances with the potentially hysterical workings of Lucy's own psychology.

Indeed, it is characteristic of Brontë's "new Gothic," as Robert B.
Heilman long ago identified the mode, that rational explanations are
finally enlisted not against the threat of genuine ghosts but against the
possibility that the nun has been only a "spectral illusion" (p. 358) of
Lucy's overwrought brain.[25] Yet even the anti-Gothic revelation that
Lucy has merely been haunted by Ginevra Fanshawe's foppish lover, Al-
fred de Hamal, who has adopted the disguise of the nun in order to
gain access to the carefully guarded pensionnat and "could not resist"
giving the teacher a "start" when she first intruded upon him in the attic
(p. 686), works as much to confirm as to undo the doubling—and not
only because Ginevra and her lover pointedly leave a bolster dressed in

the nun's abandoned costume lying in Lucy's own bed. For to say that the nun "is" de Hamal is not to say that she is not Lucy, since Lucy has already been engaged in her own form of cross-dressing, identifying with de Hamal when she played the role of Ginevra's lover in the amateur theatricals.[26] The "ambiguous status" of the nun, as Mary Jacobus has described it—"at once real and spectral, both a deceit practiced on Lucy and her psychic double"—is evidence that the barrier between subjective experience and objective "reality" in Brontë's fiction remains permeable to the end.[27] If *Villette* seems to ground its heroine's identity on the differences between restraints imposed from without and those developed within, it simultaneously calls such distinctions into question. "And in catalepsy and a dead trance," Lucy announces very soon after she has recorded the legend of the buried nun, "I studiously held the quick of my nature" (pp. 151–52).

Instead of a gradual awakening from a trance, a "Protestant" narrative of the accommodation of desire to courtship and marriage, the first half of *Villette* registers abrupt alternations of release and repression, a "Catholic" history of convulsively oscillating extremes. When all the inhabitants of Madame Beck's pensionnat depart for the long vacation, leaving the English teacher with only the *crétin* for a companion, she effectively endures a kind of solitary confinement—a living burial that at once manifests and further intensifies her psychological state: "my heart almost died within me; miserable longings strained its chords" (p. 218). Lucy herself associates her suffering with her sense of utter plotlessness, her inability to imagine any future that might serve as an outlet for her energies:

Even to look forward was not to hope: the dumb future spoke no comfort, offered no promise, gave no inducement to bear present evil in reliance on future good. . . . The hopes which are dear to youth, which bear it up and lead it on, I knew not and dared not know. If they knocked at my heart sometimes, an inhospitable bar to admission must be inwardly drawn. When they turned away thus rejected, tears sad enough sometimes flowed; but it could not be helped: I dared not give such guests lodging. So mortally did I fear the sin and weakness of presumption. (Pp. 218–19)

Why Lucy "dare not" know her own impulses to hope, which she typically allegorizes here as alien visitors with wills of their own, is a question the novel never directly answers—unless we are meant to associate her "mortally" fearing her own "presumption" with the mortality of all whom she has ever dared to love in the past. But before her spiritual deadness manifests itself somatically in a nervous breakdown, and her figurative "trance" becomes an actual swoon on the streets of Villette, the Protestant schoolteacher will briefly seek relief for her suffering by pouring out her buried feelings at the Catholic confessional. As she later figures her psychic economy for Dr. John, the blocked currents of the heart find an "abnormal outlet":

I cannot put the case into words, but, my days and nights were grown intoler-able; a cruel sense of desolation pained my mind: a feeling that would make its way, rush out, or kill me—like (and this you will understand, Dr. John) the current which passes through the heart, and which, if aneurism or any other morbid cause obstructs its natural channels, impetuously seeks abnormal outlet. I wanted companionship, I wanted friendship, I wanted counsel. I could find none of these in closet, or chamber, so I went and sought them in church and confessional. As to what I said, it was no confidence, no narrative. I have done nothing wrong: my life has not been active enough for any dark deed, either of romance or reality: all I poured out was a dreary, desperate complaint. (P. 264)

That she had "no narrative" to offer the listening priest in one sense *was* her complaint—as if without the conventional channel of the court-ship plot her feelings could assume no articulate shape. Even now, she "cannot put the case into words," so much does the woman's telling of her story still await the Other's speech. By coming to the aid of the un-conscious woman he knows only as the English schoolteacher, Dr. John has unwittingly restored his old friend to life: when Lucy awakens from her trance to find herself amid the familiar objects of Mrs. Bretton's household, she also awakens to Graham Bretton's belated discovery of her identity. But Graham's capacity to recognize Lucy Snowe will re-main strictly limited, and whatever feelings his recognition might en-able her to express will therefore have to go unspoken. Though he does promise to write to her, Lucy's Reason sternly cautions her to say little in exchange: to Lucy's anguished cry, "But if I feel, may I *never* ex-press?" that "hag," her Reason, grimly answers, "*Never!*" (p. 327). With the reappearance of Polly Home—now metamorphosed into the Count-ess Paulina Mary Home de Bassompierre—the doctor's correspon-dence with Lucy is abruptly terminated. "The letter, the message once frequent, are cut off," and so, too, is their implicit promise of a story: where Graham is concerned, there falls instead "a stilly pause, a word-less silence, a long blank of oblivion" (p. 380)—"seven weeks as bare as seven sheets of blank paper" (p. 382). Lucy's figurative rebirth amid the familiar surroundings of her Bretton childhood leads only to a ritual confirmation of her living burial, as she seals up Graham's letters in an "air-tight" bottle and deposits them—together with "that grief over

which [she] had lately been weeping"—in the plot of ground associated
with the legendary nun (pp. 423, 424). Indeed, the figure of the nun
has presided over this relation from the beginning: even as Lucy sees
the image for the first time when she retires to read Graham's initial
letter, so she encounters the shadowy figure for the second time just
after she has consigned the correspondence to its grave. "The impulse
under which I acted, the mood controlling me, were similar to the impulse and the mood which had induced me to visit the confessional,"
Lucy writes of her visit to the old broker from whom she purchases the
burial vessel (p. 424)—a resemblance she has already anticipated by
representing the act of whispering into the ear of the old priest as the
"pouring out" of her pain "into a vessel whence it could not be again
diffused" (pp. 226, 227). While in one ritual she seeks to discharge her
feelings and in the other to seal them up, confession and burial, it
would seem, are mysteriously the same—functional equivalents for that
short-circuiting of the courtship plot that *Villette* symbolizes by the
living death of the nun.

❦

If women never entertain "warmer feelings" where they have received
no encouragement to do so, as Lucy insists (p. 363), then her own narrative at once confirms and subverts the rule. Though she emphatically
disclaims any such feelings for Graham Bretton, her previous conclusion that "if" she feels, she may "*never*" express, has already opened up a
hypothetical gap between feeling and expression that calls the disclaimer into question. Strictly speaking, of course, Lucy never acknowledges that she "loves" the handsome doctor. But her very inability to
give her feelings a familiar name, the repeated blocking of the accustomed channels for their expression, only intensifies their potential for
disruption. Desire in Lucy is buried alive, not dead; but so long as it
remains buried, so long as there is no courtship plot to express and contain it, such desire remains dangerously labile and uncharted. Indeed,
what Brontë's contemporaries would have subliminally registered as
most disturbing about Lucy's narrative, I would contend, is not her
half-admission that she might love a man without return, nor even that
she might love two at once, but her intimation of desires and energies
that threaten to exceed conventional measures and that might be plotted toward more than one "abnormal outlet" (p. 264). Or rather, the
possibility that Lucy might entertain "a double love," in Harriet Martineau's phrase, is merely the least "abnormal," and therefore most readily
specified, of these dangerously expansive tendencies—though, unlike

some of the novel's critics, its narrator chooses to the very end to approach the subject only by figurative indirection:

I kept a place for him, too—a place of which I never took the measure, either by rule or compass: I think it was like the tent of Peri-Banou. All my life long I carried it folded in the hollow of my hand—yet, released from that hold and constriction, I know not but its innate capacity for expanse might have magnified it into a tabernacle for a host. (P. 662)

Not surprisingly, the scene that comes closest to representing the potential disruptiveness of Lucy's desires is the scene of acting. As in *Mansfield Park*, the amateur theatricals in *Villette* mark an occasion of collective freedom and indulgence: like Austen, Brontë exploits the conventional associations of dramatic performance with the seductive transgression of boundaries, with psychic fluidity and self-display, and like Austen, she initially poses her modest heroine as a solitary "looker-on" at the spectacle (p. 181). Feeling herself "a mere shadowy spot on a field of light," Lucy characteristically affirms her own effacement by dressing in a dun-colored gown and seeking refuge from the holiday bustle in the deserted schoolroom (p. 182). But when Paul Emanuel breaks into her retreat and insists that she take a part in the play, Lucy, though "horror-struck," acquiesces (p. 186). Whereas Fanny Price's refusal to act signals her consistency with herself, her inability to represent any identity but her own, Lucy's performance draws its energies from the multiple, even contradictory, impulses of her psyche, and testifies to her own frightening powers of self-transformation. As in the performance of *Lovers' Vows* at Mansfield, emotional configurations on stage at once stand in for and threaten to subvert the characters' offstage relations: by throwing herself into the role of the de Hamal-like fop who struggles with his Dr. John-like rival for the favors of a coquette played by Ginevra, Lucy engages in a performance whose erotic and aggressive implications multiply and shift with vertiginous rapidity. That she should accept the part of the fop in the first place—despite her contempt for him as "a butterfly, a talker, and a traitor" (p. 187)—may be contrasted with the mockery by which Evelina attempts to keep her distance from another such equivocal figure; and Lucy's insistence on retaining her dress and costuming herself as a man only from the waist up merely intensifies the sexual ambiguity of the identification. In solitary rehearsal, she expresses her scorn for the fop by deliberately exaggerating his fatuousness; in public performance, however, she radically transforms the role—turning herself not into an effeminate doll but a manly suitor worthy of rivaling and even conquering Dr. John. Registering the peculiar emphasis with which Ginevra is carrying on their flirtation, Lucy becomes conscious that the coquette is aiming her shafts at a certain tall and silent figure in the audience, that she is "acting *at*" the handsome doctor:

The spectacle seemed somehow suggestive. There was language in Dr. John's look, though I cannot tell what he said; it animated me: I drew out of it a history; I put my idea into the part I performed: I threw it into my wooing of Ginevra. In the "Ours," or sincere lover, I saw Dr. John. Did I pity him, as erst? No, I hardened my heart, rivalled and out-rivalled him. I knew myself but a fop, but where *he* was outcast *I* could please. Now I know I acted as if wishful and resolute to win and conquer. Ginevra seconded me; between us we half-changed the nature of the *rôle*, gilding it from top to toe. Between the acts M. Paul told us he knew not what possessed us, and half expostulated, "C'est, peut-être plus beau que votre modèle," said he, "mais ce n'est pas juste." I know not what possessed me either; but somehow, my longing was to eclipse the "Ours:" *i.e.*, Dr. John. Ginevra was tender; how could I be otherwise than chivalric? Retaining the letter, I recklessly altered the spirit of the *rôle*. Without heart, without interest, I could not play it at all. It must be played—in went the yearned-for seasoning—thus flavoured, I played it with relish.

What I felt that night, and what I did, I no more expected to feel and do, than to be lifted in a trance to the seventh heaven. Cold, reluctant, apprehensive, I had accepted a part to please another: ere long, warming, becoming interested, taking courage, I acted to please myself. . . . A keen relish for dramatic expression had revealed itself as part of my nature. (Pp. 196–97)

Fanny Price, too, it may be recalled, once briefly attempts to play the lover of her own rival, but "with all the modest feeling" that the idea of standing in for Edmund inspires in her, she predictably proves a bad actress: even in private rehearsal with another woman, Fanny reads her part "with looks and voice so truly feminine as to be no very good picture of a man."[28] Unlike Fanny, Lucy performs in public; and the success of her performance entails her temporary abandonment of the very modesty that inhibits the other—her ecstatic transgression of those inner restraints by which Fanny keeps the lines of sexual difference, and of individual identity, clear. As Brontë imagines the scene, her heroine paradoxically animates one role by identifying with all, by speaking at once for and against each figure in the triangle. Indeed, even to refer to a "triangle" is artificially to stabilize the impulses of desire and resistance that Lucy's performance puts into play, to treat as a fixed set of erotic positions what is rather a highly charged and continually shifting field of possibilities. "Animated" by the look of a man to whom she herself is attracted, Lucy converts the part of his foppish rival into that of his double, identifying her own frustrated desires with his, even as she triumphantly discharges her aggression against him; wooing the woman who is her own rival in the offstage triangle, she at the same time makes love *to* Dr. John by making love *for* him—and to herself in Ginevra's place. As Joseph Litvak has astutely observed, "What is at stake here is not merely the reversal or reapportionment of traditional gender roles" but "a dizzying plurality of complications intimated by a polymorphous scenario"—a scenario "simultaneously autoerotic, homoerotic, and heteroerotic."[29] Indeed, the scene briefly puts in question not merely the nature of the subject's desires but the very stability of the subject herself—so thoroughly does Lucy's account of her performance multiply and confound the impulses of identification, hostility, and love. "I acted," Lucy says, "to please myself," and it is a rare moment in *Villette* when she says so much. Yet if the rest of her narrative gives us no reason to doubt the truth of her claim, it also gives us no grounds to distinguish that "self" from this scene of its momentary fracturing and dissolution.

Lucy represents her performance as a form of translation, but a translation of something she apparently cannot put into words: even as she professes to register the "language" in Dr. John's look and to draw from it a "history," she "cannot tell what he said." Though it is tempting to see the potential actress in Lucy as a figure for the artist who created her, it is important, I think, that Lucy's artistry here bears at best an oblique relation to the spoken or written word, that the effect she produces depends on altering only the "spirit" and not the "letter" of the script.[30] For even as she repeats the words of an altogether conventional text and yet somehow manages to evoke impulses that cannot be given a name, so does the novel as a whole manifest a related tension—hinting at energies and desires that it can neither speak directly nor express by the forward motion of its plot. Though the dramatic experiment concentrates these impulses with particular intensity, it is far from the only moment at which Lucy's account of herself obliquely gestures at such immodest possibilities, at disruptive forms of resistance and of love. Other passages evoke images of literal or figurative cross-dressing, for example, or vaguely recur to intimations of homoerotic feeling;[31] while the very evening of the theatricals finds Lucy "going beyond myself," in her words, "for the second time that night" and "speaking in an unpremeditated, impulsive strain," as she rallies Dr. John on his hapless courtship of Ginevra (p. 211). But like Lucy's "keen relish for dramatic expression" itself, these alternative and immodest desires seem to be realizable only in a scenic rather than a narrative mode; surfacing briefly only to be sealed up once again, they effectively lead nowhere. The morning after her theatrical experiment, Lucy characteristically locks away her newfound "strength and longing," vowing "never to be drawn into a similar affair": "I put them by, and fastened them in with the lock of a resolution which neither Time nor Temptation has since picked" (p. 197). In the violently oscillating rhythm that characterizes so much of *Villette,* emotional release is inevitably succeeded by repressive reaction—as if the thrills of the *fête,* the exhilarations of public display, were the proximate cause of the living burial and hysterical collapse during the long vacation that quickly follows.[32]

Like the moment at which the modest heroine belatedly realizes her hitherto secret desires and the hidden motive of her story, Lucy's discovery of her own dramatic powers is a kind of recognition scene—but here "strength and longing" apparently resist assimilation, cannot be made to serve as the driving energy of a narrative. As its representation of "Vashti" will make painfully clear, *Villette* can only figure the art of the actress as a violent and self-consuming spectacle, "an inordinate will, convulsing a perishing mortal frame" (p. 373): in Lucy's account of the famous star, neither the woman herself nor the role she plays comes attached to any narrative, only a set of vivid images and heightened abstractions, "wild and intense, dangerous, sudden, and flaming" (p. 372)—a figurative fire, "half lava, half glow" (p. 368), which finally realizes itself in the actual burning of the theater. At once fascinated and repelled by the spectacle, Lucy obviously sees in this "demoniac" figure (p. 369) the avatar of her own destructive appetites—an identification that has been ironically anticipated in her account of the modest consciousness with which she agrees to accompany Graham to the theater, unchaperoned:

And away I flew, never once checked, reader, by the thought which perhaps at this moment checks you: namely that to go anywhere with Graham and without Mrs. Bretton could be objectionable. I could not have conceived, much less expressed, to Graham such thought—such scruple—without risk of exciting a tyrannous self-contempt; of kindling an inward fire of shame so quenchless, and so devouring, that I think it would soon have licked up the very life in my veins. (P. 366)

Insofar as Vashti burns in Lucy's place, the conflagration in the theater at once figures this "inward shame" and puts an end to the unarticulated hypothesis that inspires it—the shameful possibility of Lucy's own erotic relation to Graham Bretton. For it is in the confusion that attends the fire that Polly Home opportunely makes her reappearance; and it is not Lucy but this modest double whom Graham rescues from the frightened crowd.[33] More precisely, he shares this honor, as he will later share Polly herself, with her father: the rapid sequence of events, which begins when the as yet unidentified young girl, who has been "very quietly and steadily clinging" to the latter gentleman, is "suddenly struck from her protector's arms by a big, butcherly intruder, and hurled under the feet of the crowd," only to be rescued "scarce two seconds" later by the combined forces of her father and her future husband, concisely sums up the limited trajectory of her plot (p. 375). While the mysteriously orphaned Lucy is, effectively, "nobody's daughter" (p. 203), this only child of a devoted widower is unmistakably her father's; and the opening chapters of the novel have already made clear that it is just because her affections have been so intensely trained on the one man that "Papa's little Polly" (p. 17) will eventually become the wife of the other. "She must be busy about something, look after somebody" (p. 29), and when her father temporarily abandons her at the Brettons, the little girl who took her greatest pleasure in serving his tea begins to console herself for his absence by carrying the teacup to Graham. "One would have thought the child had no mind or life of her own," Lucy remarks at the time, "but must necessarily live, move, and have her being in another: now that her father was taken from her, she nestled to Graham, and seemed to feel by his feelings: to exist in his existence" (p. 32). If there is a potential contradiction between such passionately exclusive love and the adult Paulina's belief that she can adore a husband without sacrificing a father, hers is the sort of modest fiction that glosses over such conflicts. "Papa, I love you both," she announces in the proposal scene (p. 629); and in Lucy's last vision of her, the bride-to-be sits serenely between father and lover on a pleasant park bench, her hands busily weaving an "amulet" of "mutual concord" from the locks of their hair (p. 631).

That Paulina replaces Lucy in the conventional plot is clear not only in their shared desire for Graham but in the form that desire takes: an idealized modest heroine, she passes from daughter to wife governed by an unproblematic version of Lucy's emotional economy. Like a milder Lucy, Paulina guards her warmth with a cool reserve—her "gentle hoar-frost . . . surrounding so much pure, fine flame" (p. 545)—and no more than Lucy, as she herself insists, would she ever be the first to speak her love: "if I liked Dr. John till I was fit to die for liking him, that alone could not license me to be otherwise than dumb—dumb as the grave—dumb as you, Lucy Snowe" (p. 540). Like Lucy, too, she secretly hoards the "treasure" of Graham's first letter (p. 542), refusing to

break the seal until she can lock herself alone with it in an upstairs
room, and then three times scrupulously rewriting her response—
"chastening and subduing the phrases at every rescript," until the final
message resembles "a morsel of ice flavoured with ever so slight a zest of
fruit or sugar" (p. 544). Even her comparison of her sensations on reading the letter to those of a thirsty animal drinking from a well duplicates
the tropes in which Lucy typically represents her own experience—the
crucial difference, of course, being that in Paulina's case the waters
prove "full" and "gloriously clear" (p. 543).

Lucy herself understands their difference teleologically, as a function
of divine will or destiny. The happy lovers belong to nature's "elect," in
her terms (p. 632), and "must be united" (p. 545): in all that concerns
them there is "promise, plan, harmony" (p. 546). Paulina need only
leave the revelation of her love to "Time" and her "kind Fate," Lucy
instructs her, never doubting that the latter will "benignantly order the
circumstances, and fitly appoint the hour" (p. 545). That a number of
Brontë's contemporaries expected the novel to focus on the "girlhood,
courtship, and matrimony" of Paulina only emphasizes how closely her
character was attached to that familiar and consoling plot[34]—a plot that
in *Villette* has become not the heroine's story but merely a story that she
tells. And though Lucy herself strenuously insists that such a story is no
fiction, that "without any colouring of romance, or any exaggeration of
fancy, it is so" ("some real lives do . . . actually anticipate the happiness
of Heaven"), her very insistence underlines its fairy-tale-like remoteness. "I *do* believe there are some human beings so born, so reared, so
guided from a soft cradle to a calm and late grave, that no excessive suffering penetrates their lot" (p. 632), she protests; but the effort of wish-
ing—Lucy's, and perhaps Brontë's as well—is all too evident. As the
novelist herself later confessed, the character of Paulina lacked "the
germ of the *real*" and was "purely imaginary."[35]

᭜

In contrast to Paulina's, of course, Lucy's own history presents itself as
painfully sober. Yet insofar as even that history is eventually assimilated
to a courtship fiction, it too keeps threatening to betray itself *as* a fiction, everywhere testifying to the strain of its making. Indeed, we
scarcely need the well-known facts of the novelist's Brussels experience
and of her unrequited love for M. Héger to register how much of artifice and will is bound up with the resolution of her narrative. For it is
not merely that Brontë seems unable to believe in a happy ending to her

lovers' story—though this is a matter worth exploring further—but that she puts into question the very status of the feeling between them: during most of the novel, Paul seems less the object than the agent of Lucy's hidden desires, desires that he does not so much gradually awaken as forcibly exaggerate into being. Karen Chase only slightly overstates the case when she argues that "Paul *assumes* Lucy's deep passions and high aims, and in so assuming . . . creates them,"[36] for the line between what Lucy "really" feels and Paul's hyperbolic account of her is virtually impossible to determine. From the first, he proceeds by a method of what might be called deliberately antithetical interpretation: where others see in Lucy only "colourless shadow," Paul insists that she is one of those who "must be *kept down*"—a "petite ambitieuse" whose fiery glance bespeaks her "passionate ardour for triumph" (pp. 216, 215, 216). "This idea of 'keeping down' never left M. Paul's head," Lucy later remarks; "the most habitual subjugation would, in my case, have failed to relieve him of it" (p. 526). Given Paul's proto-Freudian mode of reading, in fact, the most habitual subjugation on Lucy's part would only confirm the diagnosis, for it is precisely the force of her self-suppression that serves as his measure of the energies she suppresses: the more she keeps herself down, the more he determines that hers is a "fiery and rash nature—adventurous, indocile, and audacious" (p. 432). And the more he insists on thus reading her, the more he brings out her fire and rashness: scolding her for trespassing the "limits proper" to her sex, Lucy later recalls, Paul "gave wings to aspiration . . . warmed the blood in my veins" (pp. 508, 509).

As the man who at once recognizes and elicits the heroine's hidden warmth—elicits it *by* recognizing and naming it—Paul performs the lover's familiar function. Of the young Paulina, Lucy observes that "her little character never properly came out, except with young Bretton" (p. 30), a remark that obviously prefigures their adult relation, even as Lucy's own character might be said never properly to "come out" except with M. Paul. Certainly it is he alone who enables her to speak, to come out with the words that have hitherto eluded her. "I want to tell you something," Lucy says, after he has presented her with the school in the Faubourg Clotide; "I want to tell you all":

"Speak, Lucy; come near; speak. Who prizes you if I do not? Who is your friend, if not Emanuel? Speak!"
I spoke. All leaped from my lips. I lacked not words now; fast I narrated; fluent I told my tale; it streamed on my tongue. . . . All I had encountered I detailed, all I had recognized, heard, and seen; how I had beheld and watched

himself; how I listened, how much heard, what conjectured; the whole history, in brief, summoned to his confidence, rushed thither truthful, literal, ardent, bitter.

Still as I narrated, instead of checking, he incited me to proceed; he spurred me by the gesture, the smile, the half-word. Before I had half done, he held both my hands, he consulted my eyes with a most piercing glance: there was something in his face which tended neither to calm nor to put me down. (Pp. 708–9)

The immediate reference of Lucy's speech is to her drugged wanderings on the night of the *fête* and her jealous misapprehensions about Paul's ward, Justine Marie; but to tell this story, her language suggests, is effectively to tell "all"—not merely in the sense that a confession of jealousy is indistinguishable from a confession of love but in the sense that a confession of love seems to become, in this context, "the whole history." And only from the retrospect of such an ending, it would appear, can her desires assume narrative form: "summoned to his confidence" and "incited . . . to proceed," Lucy has for the first time a "fluent" tale to tell. As in *Jane Eyre*'s central proposal scene, the woman's implicit declaration of love precedes the man's formal speaking,[37] but for all the risk of immodesty in Lucy's speech her narrative makes clear that she can now openly entertain warmer feelings because she receives ample encouragement to do so. Syntactically, her record of the moment makes self-discovery and the Other's loving recognition virtual equivalents:

Warm, jealous, and haughty, I knew not till now that my nature had such a mood; he gathered me near his heart. I was full of faults; he took them and me all home. For the moment of utmost mutiny, he reserved the one deep spell of peace. These words caressed my ear:—

"Lucy, take my love. One day share my life. Be my dearest, first on earth."
(P. 709)

In the end, as at the beginning, Paul enjoins her to speak; but unlike the theatrical experiment that inaugurates their relation, the proposal that closes it approximates to an orthodox recognition scene—the moment at which the heroine discovers herself by discovering a desire that is already reciprocated, a desire that is no sooner expressed than it is safely answered and contained.

"He meant to see through me," Lucy thinks when Paul reads her countenance at their first meeting: "a veil would be no veil for him" (p. 90). Professing to "see through" her, and to love what he sees, Paul eventually proposes marriage. But if *Villette* cannot quite bring us to believe in this conventional resolution of Lucy's story, it is in part because the very impulses he has helped her to name would appear to resist such accommodation, threaten to undo the fiction of coming out properly. When Lucy first publicly appears with Graham Bretton at the concert, the "pale pink" dress that she has reluctantly adopted at the urging of Mrs. Bretton immediately turns in Paul's eyes to a "*scarlet gown,*" a "flaunting" and "giddy" sign of the wearer's "degeneracy" (p. 480). That Graham scarcely notices the unaccustomed color, while Paul flamboyantly exaggerates it, only underlines the novel's engrained distrust of modest fictions—as if there were no alternative to Lucy's perpetual cloak of gray short of her blazoning forth as a scarlet woman. And though Paul's propensity to see red is made to seem partly comic,[38] it also confirms Lucy's secret fear that she has indeed been "decking myself out to draw attention" (p. 295), that she cannot come out at all, in effect, without coming out immodestly. The "pale pink" that might have suited Fanny Price at the Mansfield ball, or Evelina at the wells, signifies an impossible accommodation for Lucy Snowe. It is no accident that when she first glimpses a mirrored reflection of "a third person in a pink dress and black lace mantle" in the Bretton party, she fails to recognize her—or that she has no sooner done so than she feels "a jar of discord, a pang of regret" (p. 298).

Nor is it accidental that the only man who proves able to "see through" this heroine's "veil" comes equipped with unusual "skill in physiognomy" (p. 90). Even more than most love stories, *Villette*'s entails a fantasy of recognition—a fantasy all the more strenuously willed because its heroine is imagined as one who otherwise lacks all power to attract a gaze:

"Do I displease your eyes *much*?" I took courage to urge: the point had its vital import for me.

He stopped, and gave me a short, strong answer—an answer which silenced, subdued, yet profoundly satisfied. Ever after that, I knew what I was for *him;* and what I might be for the rest of the world, I ceased painfully to care. Was it weak to lay so much stress on an opinion about appearance? I fear it might be— I fear it was; but in that case I must avow no light share of weakness. I must own a great fear of displeasing—a strong wish moderately to please M. Paul. (P. 699)

For all the profound satisfaction Paul is said to provide, his answer significantly registers in the text as an absent negative, as if neither Lucy nor Brontë herself could quite believe in the full reciprocity it promises.

Between Lucy's "strong wish" and her hope of "moderately" pleasing, an excess of feeling remains—an excess that will not be assimilated even to this temporary dream of fulfillment.

᭟

By intimating Paul's death at sea, Brontë once again consigns the court-ship plot to the realm of consoling illusions. As in *Jane Eyre,* she associ-ates a proposal of marriage with a momentary return to Eden,[39] but by moving that moment from the center of the text to the penultimate chapter, she allows herself virtually no narrative space in which to mod-erate the fantasy. The lovers celebrate their brief hour of happiness by dining on an idyllic meal of chocolate, rolls, and a "plate of fresh sum-mer fruit" (p. 705), and say their farewells by "such moonlight as fell on Eden" (p. 709); the next morning, Paul sets sail for the West Indies, never to return. One need not take literally Kate Millett's notorious claim that a "sly and crafty" Lucy tricks Paul into providing her with the means of liberation, and then effectively does away with him, to recog-nize that his death cuts short an ending that would at once be too satis-fying and not satisfying enough—and that there is at least an oblique relation between *Villette's* representation of a labile excess of female de-sires and its resistance to the conventional fiction of their containment.[40]

And though it would wildly distort the tone of the narrative—not to speak of Lucy's conscious intentions—to suggest that she merely sub-mits to love as a cover for managing her "career," Paul's courtship does have its practical uses. The three years of his absence, Lucy tells us, were the "happiest years of my life"—a seeming "paradox" (p. 711) that she explains by recounting her success in establishing her school and the pleasures of working hard as the steward of another's property:

The secret of my success did not lie so much in myself, in any endowment, any power of mine, as in a new state of circumstances, a wonderfully changed life, a relieved heart. The spring which moved my energies lay far away beyond seas, in an Indian isle. At parting, I had been left a legacy; such a thought for the present, such a hope for the future, such a motive for a persevering, a laborious, an enterprising, a patient and a brave course—I *could* not flag. Few things shook me now; few things had importance to vex, intimidate, or depress me: most things pleased—mere trifles had a charm. (Pp. 712–13)

Like more conventional heroines, Lucy here comes to terms with her energies only by displacing the "spring" that moves them: the secret of her success, she insists, lies not so much in her own power as in her relation to another. But by refusing to realize that relation except in absence and in memory, Brontë finally requires us to understand it as part of the heroine's self. If this is still a sort of modest fiction, it is one that enables Lucy to survive and prosper alone.[41]

As we know from Elizabeth Gaskell's testimony, the novelist self-consciously resisted a plot shaped to paternal wishes. "Mr. Brontë was anxious that her new tale should end well," Gaskell reported, "as he disliked novels which left a melancholy impression upon the mind; and he requested her to make her hero and heroine (like the heroes and heroines in fairy-tales) 'marry, and live very happily ever after.'"

But the idea of M. Paul Emanuel's death at sea was stamped on her imagination till it assumed the distinct force of reality; and she could no more alter her fictitious ending than if they had been facts which she was relating. All she could do in compliance with her father's wish was so to veil the fate in oracular words, as to leave it to the character and discernment of her readers to interpret her meaning.[42]

Anticipating the metafictive turn with which her favorite novelist would soon invite the reader of *The Newcomes* to "settle your Fable-land in your own fashion" and conclude the novel with "the hero and heroine happy at last, and happy ever after,"[43] Brontë writes in her father's sense of an ending, but only as fiction. Having recorded the seven-days' storm at sea, the "thousand weepers," and the terrible silence that follows, Lucy refuses to specify further:

leave sunny imaginations hope. Let it be theirs to conceive the delight of joy born again fresh out of great terror, the rapture of rescue from peril, the wondrous reprieve from dread, the fruition of return. Let them picture union and a happy succeeding life. (P. 715)

As when she much earlier passed a mysterious veil over the eight years of her adolescence, merely "permit[ting]" the reader to "picture" her "as a bark slumbering through halcyon weather, in a harbour still as glass" (p. 46), so she again leaves it to "the character and discernment of her readers," in Gaskell's words, to question the picture. All Lucy would tell us of that previous time was that it ended with her as the sole survivor of a figurative shipwreck. But if the second storm at sea at once repeats the earlier disaster and literalizes it, the suggestion that Lucy's final solitude is somehow implicit in her earlier isolation has a certain logic. This heroine, after all, is "nobody's daughter" (p. 203).

11

Molly Gibson's Secrets

❦

As its full title suggests, Elizabeth Gaskell's last novel takes for granted what Brontë's unsettles—that "wives and daughters" are "an every-day story" and that narratives are made from the passing of somebody's daughter into somebody else's wife. When *Wives and Daughters* opens, Dr. Gibson is "startled into discovering that his little one was growing fast into a woman"; as it closes, he is reluctantly acknowledging that "losing one's daughter is a necessary evil." "'Lover *versus* father!' thought he, half sadly. 'Lover wins.'" [1] And though Gaskell did not live to complete her novel, no reader really needs her editor's assurance, customarily appended to the text, as to who the winner was to be: unlike the heroine's flighty stepsister, Cynthia, who likes her love "widely spread about; not all confined to one individual lover" (p. 595), and whose feelings for the men in her life are so casual that Dr. Gibson jokingly wonders which one of them she will invite to her wedding, the blushing Molly has spent virtually the entire narrative nurturing her deep, if largely unconscious, interest in the man she will marry. If Molly's "shy modesty" (p. 136) means that no one could be imagined to joke about *her* doing the inviting, it also means that hers unmistakably is a love "all confined to one," and that the very force of that confined and focused desire will eventually exert its own unconscious powers of attraction. For most of the novel Roger Hamley may be "bewitched" by the fascinating Cynthia, but he will end by denouncing himself as a "blind fool" for ever having preferred her to Molly (p. 677). Though the novel breaks off while he is still worrying whether Molly can ever be brought to listen to him "after seeing and knowing that [he] had loved a person so inferior to herself" (pp. 677–78), no reader could seriously doubt the outcome.

But it is, of course, a central premise of such a fiction that the heroine cannot share our confident awareness of where her history is headed. As Molly recovers from her illness in the closing chapters of the novel, the narrator associates her improved health and looks with "the faint fragrance of a new and unacknowledged hope" that "had stolen into her life" (p. 655)—the sense of an ending whose therapeutic and cosmetic effects still apparently outstrip the heroine's conscious knowledge. Molly will soon be awakened to fuller consciousness when she chances to overhear Mrs. Goodenough's gossiping speculation ("That Mrs. Gibson is a deep un. There's Mr. Roger Hamley as like as not to have the Hall estate, and she sends Molly a-visiting—"), but it is no accident that the words which first "put fancies into Molly's head" are spoken by another, or that it is only by accident that Molly happens to overhear them (p. 660). From the opening sequence of *Wives and Daughters*—in which Dr. Gibson intercepts a "flaming love-letter" to Molly from his young apprentice, Mr. Coxe, comforts himself with "the conviction of her perfect innocence—ignorance, I should rather say" (p. 48), and bundles her off to Hamley Hall lest that innocent unconsciousness be violated—the narrative has worked to preserve Molly's modesty by assuring that others will keep her secrets for her, even as it has also worked to demonstrate that her "perfect . . . ignorance" must inevitably give way. While Molly arrives at Hamley Hall for her first visit "perfectly unconscious" of her host's anxiety lest one of his sons fall in love with her (p. 81), she pays her last visit awkwardly constrained by the consciousness that Mrs. Goodenough's gossip has awakened. Molly's inability to suppress the words now "troubling her maiden modesty" clearly signals that her story is fast approaching its end (p. 668): like Evelina's abrupt coolness toward Lord Orville at Clifton, her unaccustomed constraint in Roger's presence is the sort of preceding backwardness that typically precipitates a lover's declaration.[2] But that the longest and most leisurely of Gaskell's novels has nearly run its course before the heroine's consciousness has quite awakened suggests just how thoroughgoing a fiction of modesty it has assimilated.

If Molly's "maiden modesty" seems less troubled than many of her predecessors', part of the reason is simply that her creator assigns her to carry less of the burden of the narrative. Because she does not record her own history in the first person, she is much less vulnerable than Pamela or Evelina to the appearance of false modesty. Molly is rarely in danger of calling attention to her own virtuousness or of seeming unduly alert to feelings she must not yet acknowledge. When Pamela writes, "I looked after [Mr. B] out of the window, and he was charmingly dressed: to be sure, he is a handsome, fine gentleman," she comes perilously close to admitting premature awareness of her own desire.[3] But when Gaskell's narrator notes that "Molly saw [Roger] in a minute when she entered the little drawing-room; but Cynthia did not" (p. 247), or remarks that "Molly knew the shape of the head perfectly," as "her eye was caught by the figure of a gentleman, sitting with his back to the light" (p. 255), she manages to convey her heroine's responsiveness to the hero without implicating Molly herself in the knowledge.

Of course, more than a difference of voice is at issue here: though the youthful Henry James would call Molly Gibson the novel's "central idea,"[4] she is far from the consistent center of consciousness—and the very freedom with which the novelist occludes the heroine's point of view helps to assure her comparative innocence. Dr. Gibson could hardly keep his daughter from knowing about his confrontation with poor Mr. Coxe, one might say, had not the novelist first conveniently removed her from the room. And even when Molly remains on the scene, as she does for most of the novel, Gaskell makes liberal use of the narrator and of other characters as momentary registers of the action.[5] When Richardson's heroine, already having recorded her intention of returning home to elude Mr. B, nonetheless determined to stay until she finished embroidering his waistcoat, she risked being charged as a hypocrite.[6] When Gaskell's heroine—who has been summoned to Hamley Hall to comfort its dying mistress—tearfully begs to remain a few days longer lest the invalid should want her, the narrator guards her from a similar charge by firmly assigning to Dr. Gibson all awareness of her potentially compromising situation: "her position (her father thought—the idea had not entered her head) in a family of which the only woman was an invalid confined to bed, was becoming awkward" (p. 211). The parenthetical quarantine of the negated thought undoubtedly has an awkwardness of its own, especially since it breaks abruptly into a passage whose indirect style has seemingly been rendering Molly's point of view. But the narrator's protective impulse toward the heroine is clear—as it is at a far more critical moment later in the novel, when Molly solemnly cross-examines her stepsister about the latter's feeling for Roger:

"Cynthia! you do love him dearly, don't you?"
Cynthia winced a little aside from the penetrating steadiness of those eyes.
"You speak with all the solemnity of an adjuration, Molly!" said she, laughing a little at first to cover her nervousness, and then looking up at Molly. "Don't you think I have given a proof of it? But you know I've often told you I've not the gift of loving; I said pretty much the same thing to him. I can re-

spect, and I fancy I can admire, and I can like, but I never feel carried off my feet by love for any one, not even for you, little Molly, and I am sure I love you more than—"

"No, don't!" said Molly, putting her hand before Cynthia's mouth, in almost a passion of impatience. "Don't, don't—I won't hear you—I ought not to have asked you—it makes you tell lies!"

"Why, Molly!" said Cynthia, in her turn seeking to read Molly's face, "what's the matter with you? One might think you cared for him yourself."

Since Cynthia is obviously about to declare that she cares more for her new stepsister than for the man to whom she has just engaged herself, Molly's rush to silence her is doubly self-effacing, a surrender of her own priority in Cynthia's affections as well as a more oblique surrender of any claim to Roger. Yet the very "passion" of her "impatience" nearly betrays her—and as the narrator's hasty defense of her heroine implicitly acknowledges, it is not the candidly unloving Cynthia but the self-denying Molly who comes close to a lie:

"I?" said Molly, all the blood rushing to her heart suddenly; then it returned, and she had courage to speak, and *she spoke the truth as she believed it, though not the real actual truth*.

"I do care for him; I think you have won the love of a prince amongst men. Why, I am proud to remember that he has been to me as a brother, and I love him as a sister, and I love you doubly because he has honoured you with his love." (Pp. 395–96; emphasis mine)

The contradictions managed by Gaskell's fiction of modesty are nowhere closer to the surface than in the swift reversals of this intimate exchange. Despite Cynthia's habits of deception, she often talks with appealing candor about her own failings; when she briefly trades places with her sister and in turn becomes the cross-examiner, she also engagingly fulfills her function as the heroine's immodest double, speaking the truth of Molly's desire at a moment when Molly herself must continue to deny it. At the same time, however, so open an exchange between the heroines threatens to call the continued unconsciousness of the modest one into question: when Molly declares that she loves Roger only "as a sister," the awkward redundancy with which the narrator hastens to distinguish "the real actual truth" from the truth as Molly "believe[s] it" understandably testifies to a certain strain. It is tempting to suggest that at such moments Gaskell does not so much resolve the contradictions of female modesty as sacrifice her narrator's reputation to save her heroine's. Yet so far as Molly herself is concerned, these quasi-maternal tactics are remarkably effective. Like other such fictions, *Wives and Daughters* makes of its modest heroine a father's child, conventionally opposing her, as we shall see, to a woman born of woman. But something like "the dear and tender tie of Mother and Daughter," as Gaskell termed it in the diary in which she recorded her loving observations of her own daughter Marianne (a child she on occasion called "Molly"), may nonetheless be felt in the narrator's relation to her heroine.[7] Here as elsewhere, Gaskell paradoxically helps to preserve her heroine's innocence by more or less acknowledging that it will give way in time.

❧

Though Molly's hapless first suitor has been easily defeated, her father's resistance to change is nonetheless futile, as the plotting of *Wives and Daughters* straightway makes clear. "Everything must have a beginning," Dr. Gibson himself remarks when Molly protests his decision to send her away from home for the first time without him (p. 57); and if the aborted courtship of Mr. Coxe keeps her history from abruptly short-circuiting, it also begins a series of actions whose end is already implicit—what Gaskell elsewhere calls "the natural and graceful resignation of parents to the prescribed course of things."[8] For the very gestures by which Dr. Gibson attempts to stave off the future effectively serve to bring it on, as when he tries to keep his daughter out of contact with the lovestruck apprentice only to send her off to the home of her future husband, or when he decides to remarry in order to provide her with a suitable duenna and thereby himself disrupts her childhood idyll. By intercepting Mr. Coxe's letter before it reaches its destination, Dr. Gibson temporarily succeeds in preserving his daughter's "perfect . . . ignorance" of the message of love it contains; indeed, not until his own offhand allusion to the matter near the close of the novel will Molly ever learn of Coxe's offer, a discovery so quietly anticlimactic that it barely registers on one "too tired to be amused, or even interested" (pp. 48, 591). But Molly has no sooner arrived at Hamley Hall than the squire's casual reference to the possibility that her father might marry again disturbs her perfect ignorance with "a troublesome Jack-in-the-box" of an idea that refuses to be suppressed once it has been articulated—an idea that keeps "popping up into her mouth" and threatening to pop out in the form of a question ("Who was it that people thought it was possible papa might marry?") when others are present (p. 70). The "new idea" of her father's potentially disruptive desire (p. 68), in other words, both substitutes for and anticipates her own, the consciousness of which will eventually surface when Mrs. Goodenough inadvertently sets going another mental jack-in-the-box in the final chapters of the novel. Yet if Molly's initial visit to Hamley Hall already resembles her last, the idea of her father's remarriage is also the first of a series of displacements and delaying actions that occupy the space between—a series of substitute representations that at once long-circuit the heroine's story and enable that story to be told.

Read *as* Molly Gibson's story, in fact, *Wives and Daughters* offers a virtual compendium of the strategies by which the English novel has traditionally managed to represent the young woman's courtship. As so often in such a narrative, the heroine's interest in the hero first appears under the cover of resistance and negation. While Molly likes the faces of both Hamley boys when she sees a portrait of them as children, she is easily "indoctrinated" in the parental faith that "nothing was too great or too good for 'the eldest son'" (p. 83); and when Roger arrives home bearing news of his older brother's failure at school, her "unconscious fealty" to Osborne turns to anger at the messenger, whom she greets for the first time "with anything but a welcome to him in her heart." The narrator introduces him as "a tall powerfully-made young man," with a "rather square, ruddy-coloured" face; but "to Molly, who was not finely discriminative in her glances at the stranger this first night"—and who has been vaguely dreaming of Osborne's elegance and refinement—"he simply appeared 'heavy-looking, clumsy,' and 'a person she was sure she should never get on with'" (pp. 86, 87). To any reader accustomed to the physiognomic code of English courtship fiction, however, it is clear that the "powerfully-made" Roger and not his effete older brother will be the sexually attractive figure. Indeed, by the conventions of such fiction, the mere fact of Molly's "mute opposition" to the young man marks him out for interest (p. 89), as does, of course, her turning "red as fire" when Miss Browning insinuatingly alludes to his kindness (p. 154), or the very intensity with which she later recalls and resists those insinuations: "'I would rather never be married at all,' thought she, 'than marry an ugly man,—and dear good Mr. Roger is really ugly; I don't think one could even call him plain.'" That Molly already has thoughts of marrying, one might say, is itself a telling sign, especially since Miss Browning never explicitly spoke of the possibility of marriage. Even the inability to call Roger plain looks rather promising—all the more so when the narrator follows up her heroine's mental disclaimer by remarking that the Miss Brownings, "who did not look upon young men as if their natural costume was a helmet and a suit of armour, thought Mr. Roger Hamley a very personable young fellow" (p. 170).[9]

Note, too, how the person Molly "was sure she should never get on with" has rapidly become "dear good Mr. Roger"—a transformation whose beginnings can be traced, appropriately enough, to the moment at which the young man first attempts to console her for the prospective loss of her father. When Molly responds with uncharacteristic bitterness to the news of his impending remarriage—"So I was sent out of the house that all this might be quietly arranged in my absence?" (p. 115)—Dr. Gibson leaves her to come to terms with her grief and anger alone; and it is Roger, of course, who opportunely steps into the father's empty place when he chances to interrupt Molly's solitary mourning. Indeed, with his "severe brevity," his impulse to lecture her about her duty, and his edifying tale of a daughter named Harriet—a model young woman "who thought of her father's happiness before she thought of her own," and might well have come straight from a conduct book by Dr. Gregory—he effectively steps into the father's place in more senses than one (p. 120). Like the heroes of other modest fictions, from Lord Orville to Edmund Bertram and Paul Emanuel, Roger Hamley begins in something of a tutorial relation to the heroine; and "it is pleasant to the wisest, most reasonable youth of one or two and twenty," as the narrator remarks, "to find himself looked up to as a Mentor by a girl of seventeen" (p. 140). As for Molly herself, the narrator tells us, she starts following Roger's advice almost at once, though she does not yet know it—bathing her eyes and struggling to keep from crying again so as to avoid inflicting her own pain on the ailing and already sorrowing Mrs. Hamley.

By the time her father returns home with his bride, even his requests are automatically mediated through the moral authority of the younger man. "What would Roger say was right?—that was the question that rose to Molly's mind" when Dr. Gibson asks that she call his new wife "mamma," and only after she has mentally submitted the issue to that tribunal does her initial resistance give way (p. 181). Insofar as *Wives and Daughters* recounts a struggle of "lover *versus* father" that the lover always "wins," as Dr. Gibson has it, the inevitable replacement of the older man has already begun—though insofar as the object of the struggle is worth winning because she in some sense remains a father's daughter, it is fitting that Molly imagines herself as pleasing the one by acquiescing in the wishes of the other. As Dr. Gibson implicitly acknowledges when he tells Roger in their final interview that "I'd rather give my child . . . to you, than to any man in the world!" (p. 678), the fiction of modesty arranges for less conflict in the passing on of daughters than at first appears. What cannot be so easily assimilated to the plot, the episode poignantly suggests, is the initial yearning of the daughter's "rebellious heart" toward another kind of love: Molly's momentary impulse of loyalty to "the name long appropriated in her mind to some one else—to her own dead mother" (p. 178).[10]

♥

Long before the modest heroine knows that she loves, her heart has thus secretly committed itself. Yet for most of *Wives and Daughters*, Molly spends her time consciously absorbed in the romantic secrets of others; and, as when she accidentally learns that Osborne Hamley has already been privately married, such innocent secret-keeping keeps her at a certain modest remove from the very matter of love that increasingly comes to occupy her attention. To read the novel for the romantic history of this self-effacing heroine, in other words, is necessarily to read for the histories that at once represent and displace it. "She had always wished to come into direct contact with a love-story," the narrator remarks when Molly inadvertently overhears Roger speaking of Osborne's wife; and the conjunction of "direct contact" with the mediated "love-story" nicely expresses the paradoxical means by which Molly's own story is conducted. Like the realization that her father might remarry, her discovery of Osborne's secret compels her to register a dimension of experience hitherto obscured from view—even as the need to keep the secret further cuts her off from the un-self-consciousness of childhood:

She would never have guessed the concealed romance which lay *perdu* under that every-day behaviour. . . . and she only found it very uncomfortable; there was a sense of concealment and uncertainty about it all; and her honest straightforward father, her quiet life at Hollingford, which, even with all its drawbacks, was above-board, and where everybody knew what everybody was doing, seemed secure and pleasant in comparison. (P. 220)

And like that earlier discovery, this new one proves impossible to erase from consciousness, permanently inscribing itself as a reminder of the inevitability of change. When Roger first realizes that she has overheard him, "Molly stood up in her corner, red, trembling, miserable, as though she were a guilty person" (p. 217), while after the fact her "interest and curiosity were always hovering over the secret she had become possessed of, in spite of all her self-reproach for allowing her thoughts to dwell on what was still to be kept as a mystery" (p. 243). The effects of her discovery, that is, prove something very like those which might accompany the adolescent's first encounter with the facts of sexuality itself: the defamiliarizing shock of perceiving that which has all along been hidden beneath "every-day behaviour," a sense of guilt at having been initiated into a secret that effectively alienates its possessor from the older generation, even an obsessive wish to dwell on the mystery "in spite of all her self-reproach" for doing so. Yet this guilty secret, we should remember, involves not a mistress but a wife, and a wife who will turn out to have been chosen from impulses more sentimental than erotic. Aimée herself may be French, but Osborne's "concealed romance" is clearly the work of an English novelist, and testimony to the indirection with which such a novelist gradually manages her heroine's awakening.

But it is above all the charming Cynthia, the new stepsister also conveniently imported from France, who serves the narrative as its principal double agent—whose multiple love stories at once delay and cover for Molly's own. When Dr. Gibson marries the widow Kirkpatrick, he also introduces into his household her only child, a young woman who proceeds to attract virtually every available man in the novel. "One of those natural coquettes" (p. 488) who "like to be liked" (p. 427) and possess the "exquisite power" of "'being all things to all men'" (p. 226), Cynthia is as changeable as the moon goddess for whom she is named—and unmistakably a mother's daughter. Of course, her automatic flirtatiousness and casual habits of deceit hardly make her a Shamela, any more than the fact that Mrs. Kirkpatrick "could no longer blush"[11] turns her into that woman of dubious honor, Shamela's only discernible parent. But the girl who arrives in the narrative to declare "I shall never be a good woman" (p. 229) is a girl who has long been deprived of a father—and in this, as in so many other ways, she is obviously to be contrasted with Molly. While Dr. Gibson's daughter has always remained at home until her father sends her away in the hope of preserving her innocence yet a little longer, Cynthia's mother has regarded her female child as both a burden and a future rival, and has arranged her life so as to keep the younger woman out of her way as much as possible.[12] When Cynthia first joins the Gibson household, she has just returned from the Continent, where, in addition to "trying to perfect herself in the French language" (p. 108), she seems to have been acquiring considerable experience in the arts of love—though she is scarcely older than Molly. Before the public revelation of Osborne's marriage, Mrs. Gibson imagines that he is paying court to her daughter, "but Cynthia had come across too many varieties of flirtation, admiration, and even passionate love, to be for a moment at fault as to the quiet friendly nature" of the young man's attentions (p. 325). Since Osborne already has a wife, Mrs. Gibson's wishful matchmaking proves of no more consequence than Squire Hamley's earlier fears lest his son might choose to marry Molly. Osborne is, however, hardly the last man to be romantically linked with both sisters in the course of the novel: with the exception of Mr. Henderson, the narrative nonentity whom she finally marries, each of Cynthia's other suitors is also associated with the courtship history of her modest relative. Even the unfortunate Mr. Coxe is briefly brought back to Hollingford, so that he may make a fool of himself over the "pretty airs" of Cynthia (p. 422), when he had originally intended to propose to Molly. But the critical roles in the sisters' interwoven love stories belong, of course, to the novel's hero, Roger Hamley, and, perhaps less obviously, to the blackmailing land agent, Mr. Preston—the nearest *Wives and Daughters* comes to a villain.

For a good part of the novel, Cynthia will turn out to have been ambiguously engaged to both men, while she has been further risking a reputation as "a flirt and a jilt" by cheerfully coquetting with Coxe and Henderson (p. 572). Yet even as the fatherless girl is busily supplying much of the novel's intrigue, she is also providing her stepsister with repeated occasions to demonstrate the true modesty of a heroine. So long as Cynthia takes Molly's place in the affections of Roger, Molly's generous encouragement of the affair testifies to "her humility and great power of loving" (p. 362); when Molly stands in for Cynthia in the intrigue with Preston, she proves that for all the intensity with which she loves, hers is the unconsciousness of "perfect innocence" (pp. 481, 484). Though Cynthia is quick to detect the difference between Roger's feelings for her and Osborne's, Molly, we are told, is still quicker—the modest woman's loving instincts apparently serving as at least the equal of the other's experience: "the first time they saw him after the ball, it came out to her observant eyes" (p. 325). Most of the progress of the affair is in fact filtered for us through Molly's sympathetic identification with both participants—an identification that silently bespeaks love as strong as it is self-effacing:

She would look at Cynthia's beauty and grace, and feel as if no one could resist it. And when she witnessed all the small signs of honest devotion which Roger was at no pains to conceal, she thought, with a sigh, that surely no girl could help relinquishing her heart to such tender, strong keeping as Roger's character ensured. She would have been willing to cut off her right hand, if need were, to forward his attachment to Cynthia; and the self-sacrifice would have added a strange zest to a happy crisis. (Pp. 362–63)

For Gaskell, the ultimate measure of such love is the mother's devotion to an infant; and it is not surprising that when Molly learns of the fever Roger has suffered while away on an expedition to Abyssinia, her prayer that "he may come home safe, and live happily with her whom he loves so tenderly" should be identified with "that of the real mother in King Solomon's judgment": "'O my Lord! give her the living child, and in no wise slay it'" (p. 434).[13]

Though Cynthia has hardly demanded that Roger be cut in two, her rather casual response to the news of his illness presumably associates her with the false mother in the biblical story. Indeed, Molly "did not believe that Cynthia cared enough for him; at any rate, not with the sort of love that she herself would have bestowed . . . if she had been in Cynthia's place" (p. 432)—a judgment that Cynthia will later confirm, when she breaks off her engagement to Roger in the aftermath of the Preston scandal on the grounds that she does not love him "well enough" to go through the shame of having to excuse her behavior to him (p. 576). "I don't like people of deep feelings," she characteristically remarks, when Molly speaks of how painful it was to observe his suffering. "They don't suit me" (p. 633). But before the revelation of her entanglement with Preston proves Cynthia unworthy of Roger, Molly's own participation in the affair serve to demonstrate just how different is "the sort of love" she would bestow in the other's place.

Molly's desire to protect Roger, in fact, first draws the unwitting girl into the scandal, as her red-faced denial that Cynthia is engaged to Preston leads the Browning sisters to suspect that she herself is the young woman who has been seen alone with him by the local gossip. Molly at this point knows nothing about Cynthia's relations with the land agent: "she thought only of Roger; and the distress any such reports might cause, should he ever hear of them . . . made her colour up scarlet with vexation" (p. 465). But because Roger and Cynthia have agreed not to make any public commitment until he returns from Africa, the Brownings have no way of knowing the grounds of Molly's vehement denial, or of recognizing that it is anger rather than sexual self-consciousness that colors her cheeks. As when Dr. Gibson previously misread his daughter's "crimson" blushes at a passing allusion to Osborne, Molly is innocent of any personal involvement, but her bearing of another's secret renders her vulnerable to misconstruction (p. 418). Or rather, her innocence in one direction serves to distract from and to cover for her unacknowledged attachment in another, even as it implicitly confirms that, for Molly, only one such attachment is possible. Dr. Gibson is not so wrong, after all, to wonder if his daughter has fallen in love with one of the Hamley young men, but that very fact guarantees that she is not blushing for her attraction to his brother. Having unconsciously given her heart to Roger, Molly will never transfer it "to the next comer" (p. 677).[14]

And this is the logic that continues to operate as Molly literally takes Cynthia's place in the clandestine meetings with Preston, bringing down upon herself the charge of having "disregarded the commonest rules of modesty and propriety" (p. 543). For even as her true role in the affair more than vindicates her of the charge, whatever immodesty might attach to her own secret is quietly buried under her innocent suffering for the secrets of others. "It was fine to see the fearlessness of her perfect innocence," the narrator proclaims when Molly first stumbles upon the private rendezvous of the former lovers, though Preston, significantly, cannot bear that innocent look (p. 484), just as he will be unable to bear up before her innocence when they, too, meet privately. Indeed, the land agent's crimes, such as they are, prove exactly the sort this modest heroine has been made to counter: as a sexual blackmailer, one who repeatedly boasts that he will "make" Cynthia love him after they are married (pp. 498, 505), he is potentially guilty of turning both "love" and secret-sharing into forms of selfish coercion. Having begun by extorting Cynthia's pledge to marry him in payment of a debt, he now threatens to expose her incriminating letters unless she fulfills her promise—letters, this mother's daughter confesses, in which she "said things . . . about mamma" (p. 498). Molly, however, is no sooner alone after Cynthia's confession than she characteristically "los[es] herself in thoughts of Roger" (p. 499), a formula whose identification of love and selflessness implicitly defines her story. When Molly alludes to Roger in the course of her confrontation with Preston, the latter's sexual alertness makes him quick to register the note of unconscious yearning; but by continuing to act for the others rather than herself, she effectively cancels out his "disagreeable" insinuations. "You said the other day that Cynthia was engaged," Preston reminds her. "May I ask whom to?"

"No," said Molly, "you may not. You heard her say it was not an engagement. It is not exactly; and if it were a full engagement, do you think, after what you last said, I should tell you to whom? But you may be sure of this, he would never read a line of your letters. He is too—No! I won't speak of him before you. You could never understand him."

"It seems to me that this mysterious 'he' is a very fortunate person to have such a warm defender in Miss Gibson, to whom he is not at all engaged," said

Mr. Preston, with so disagreeable a look on his face that Molly suddenly found herself on the point of bursting into tears. But she rallied herself, and worked on—for Cynthia first, and for Roger as well. (Pp. 505–6)

The selfless concentration on her task that quickly absorbs Molly's suspect "warmth" toward Roger apparently renders her otherwise all but invulnerable. Even Preston "for[gets] himself for an instant in admiration of her," when she nervily threatens to expose him to the Cumnors unless he gives up the letters. "And besides," the narrator adds, "there was something that struck him most of all perhaps, and which shows the kind of man he was—he perceived that Molly was as unconscious that he was a young man, and she a young woman, as if she had been a pure angel of heaven" (p. 507).

Such invocations of bodiless purity are comparatively rare in *Wives and Daughters,* whose customary vision of things seems much closer to that of its naturalist hero than to the sublime perspective of an "angel of heaven."[15] But it is not surprising that the narrator should insist most strenuously on Molly's perfect innocence just as her habit of carrying others' secrets reaches this compromising climax,[16] and in the very episode which works to undo Cynthia's engagement to Roger. The morning after the meeting with Preston brings not only the return of Cynthia's incriminating correspondence but an invitation for her to visit her uncle Kirkpatrick's house in London—the same place, as Mrs. Gibson is quick to recall, where "that young lawyer" with the "good private fortune" fell "over head and ears in love with her" the previous summer (p. 515). This is, interestingly enough, the first we have heard of that useful character, but Mrs. Gibson has no sooner reminded herself of his existence than Cynthia's commitment to Roger begins to undergo a marvelously comic dissolution, its substance rapidly dissipated into the thin air of the mother's wishful thinking. When Molly voices her regret that Cynthia did not tell the Kirkpatricks of her engagement the last time she stayed with them in London, Mrs. Gibson responds with an impromptu lesson in the philosophy of language and the requirements of female "delicacy":

> "It is not an engagement, my dear! How often must I tell you that?"
> "But what am I to call it?"
> "I don't see why you need to call it anything. Indeed I don't understand what you mean by 'it.' You should always try to express yourself intelligibly. It really is one of the first principles of the English language. In fact, philosophers might ask what is language given us for at all, if it is not that we may make our meaning understood?"

"But there is something between Cynthia and Roger; they are more to each other than I am to Osborne, for instance. What am I to call it?"

"You should not couple your name with that of any unmarried young man; it is so difficult to teach you delicacy, child. Perhaps one may say there is a peculiar relation between dear Cynthia and Roger, but it is very difficult to characterize it; I have no doubt that is the reason she shrinks from speaking about it. For, between ourselves, Molly, I really sometimes think it will come to nothing. He is so long away, and, privately speaking, Cynthia is not very very constant. . . . I fancy she inherits it, for when I was a girl I was beset by lovers, and could never find in my heart to shake them off." (P. 516)

With the amusing cross-purposes of this debate over pronoun reference, Gaskell makes a fine verbal comedy out of the substitutions and reversals we have been tracing—as once again Molly's modest loyalty and self-sacrifice are ironically misinterpreted as a failure of "delicacy." Indeed, if Molly's insistence on speaking of the others' "engagement" is the linguistic equivalent of her effort to preserve that relation by serving as Cynthia's go-between with Preston, Mrs. Gibson's rebuke comically anticipates the scandal to come, when the report that the doctor's daughter has been seen meeting "clandestine-like" with the land agent (p. 525) quickly turns into the gossip that "Molly Gibson has lost her character" (p. 535). And in both instances, of course, Molly stands in for her "not very very constant" stepsister.

But Cynthia is about to return the favor. So long as the Preston scandal makes Molly "the unconscious black sheep of the town" (p. 533), her stepsister stays away in London; but as soon as Lady Harriet publicly confirms her faith in Molly's innocence—as soon, that is, as the novel has once more entertained and dismissed a specious charge against the modesty of its heroine—Cynthia returns with a new "mystery," which "one day . . . burst its shell, and came out in the shape of an offer" from Mr. Henderson. Though she has refused his proposal, the effort, she reports, has "strained" her virtue "to the utmost" (p. 563)— so much so, apparently, that when the Gibsons belatedly learn the truth about her history with Preston, she has no moral energy to spare for a confrontation with Roger. For one who above all likes to be liked, the loss of Dr. Gibson's good opinion brings misery enough; and rather than stand before her future husband "like a chidden child to be admonished and forgiven," Cynthia abruptly breaks off the engagement (p. 577). Yet if she cannot bear the idea of Roger's paternalistic judgment, Cynthia derives more than comfort from Molly's gentle mothering:

[Molly] took Cynthia into her arms with gentle power, and laid her head against her own breast, as if the one had been a mother, and the other a child.

"Oh, my darling!" she murmured. "I do so love you, dear, dear Cynthia!" and she stroked her hair, and kissed her eyelids; Cynthia passive all the while, till suddenly she started up stung with a new idea, and looking Molly straight in the face, she said,—

"Molly, Roger will marry you! See if it is not so! You two good—"

But Molly pushed her away with a sudden violence of repulsion. "Don't!" she said. She was crimson with shame and indignation. "Your husband this morning! Mine to-night! What do you take him for?"

Once more the double-talk of modesty has been divided up between them, so that one speaker may affirm what the other, shamefaced, hastens to deny. But this time we are close enough to the ending to allow Cynthia the last word:

"A man!" smiled Cynthia. "And therefore, if you won't let me call him changeable, I'll coin a word and call him consolable!" (Pp. 578–79)

❦

In a contribution to the *Tatler* of 1709, Richard Steele had promised to assist a modest young woman caught in a love triangle very like that of Gaskell's novel. Writing to Isaac Bickerstaff, one "Diana Doubtful" confessed her predicament: she was in love with a young man named Fabio, but he had confided to her his affection for a certain Cleora, while Cleora, who also made Diana her confidante, had revealed that she in turn was waiting for the best offer. Though Diana was conscious of what she felt, she believed that a modesty both natural and conventional prevented her from disclosing her affection to Fabio. "I am a Woman in Love," she wrote, "and that you will allow to be the most unhappy of all Circumstances in human Life: Nature has formed us with a strong Reluctance against owning such a Passion, and Custom has made it criminal in us to make Advances." Indeed, "tho' I love him better than Life," she declared, "I would not gain him by betraying *Cleora*, or committing such a Trespass against Modesty, as letting him know I my self love him." Whether or not the *Tatler*'s correspondent was a real woman, her conflict was to be resolved by some creative writing: though Diana was informed that she could do nothing herself to remedy her situation, her happiness was effectively to be assured by the inventive manipulations of the journalist—a journalist who somehow both already knew and controlled the persons in question. Even as Bickerstaff acknowledged rather brutally that "a Female Lover is in the Condition of a Ghost, that wanders about its beloved Treasure, without Power to speak 'till it is spoken to," he instructed Diana to continue in

her ghostly condition while he arranged for "a couple of special Fellows" to pay their court to Cleora. Each of these gentlemen had a better
estate than Fabio, and both happened already to be taken with Cleora.
"All Persons concerned will appear at the next Opera, where will begin
the Wild-Goose Chase," he promised in conclusion; "and I doubt,
Fabio will see himself so overlooked for *Orson* or *Walter,* as to turn his
Eyes on the modest Passion and becoming Languor in the Countenance of *Diana.*"[17]

Gaskell does not say whether Cynthia first encountered Roger's replacement at the opera, but like Bickerstaff conveniently conjuring with
his "special Fellows," the novelist assures that the timely reappearance
of Mr. Henderson will prompt her hero to recognize that Cynthia does
not care for him, and "to turn his Eyes," in the *Tatler's* words, "on the
modest Passion" of the heroine. If the *Tatler's* treatment of Diana's
problem suggests that the double-binds of a modest woman's love can
only be resolved by means of an authorial intervention, its complacent
image of the young woman as ghost makes painfully clear how such
arrangements threaten to drain the woman herself of all effective life in
the process. "Thinking more of others' happiness than of her own was
very fine," Gaskell's heroine reflects bitterly, when she is assailed by a
pang of jealousy at the prospect of her father's marriage; "but did it not
mean giving up her very individuality, quenching all the warm love, the
keen desires, that made her herself?" (p. 138). There as elsewhere in the
novel, Molly's impulses are realistically imagined, but her pointed question receives no answer apart from the modest fiction that allows others
to do her living for her.

Indeed, to read all of *Wives and Daughters* for its metonymic displacements of the modest heroine's story may seem perversely to over-
look its finest achievement—the independent vitality and charm of
Cynthia and her mother. Henry James was only one of the earliest, if
most eloquent, of critics to have fallen under their spell: "the fact is that
genius is always difficult to formulate," he wrote, "and that Cynthia had
a genius for fascination." James singled out "Cynthia Kirkpatrick and
her infinite revelations of human nature" as the best thing in the book,
but he was almost as lavish in praise of her mother: "touch by touch,
under the reader's eye, she builds herself up into her selfish and silly and
consummately natural completeness." Though he wrote appreciatively
of the "modest domestic facts" by which the reader is "educated . . . to
a proper degree of interest in the heroine," James was quick to assert
that "Molly Gibson . . . commands a slighter degree of interest than the
companion figure of Cynthia Kirkpatrick."[18] To the extent that Molly

successfully effaces herself, of course, it is hardly surprising that she should command less interest than her willful sister: such is the liability—even the duty—of a modest heroine. We have seen how the Kirkpatrick women enable Molly's story to be told, yet there is a sense in which Gaskell seems to conceive of the relation as reciprocal, a sense in which the novel's representation of Cynthia in particular appears mysteriously dependent on the presence of her self-effacing sister. For a novelist, after all, one of the virtues of a modest heroine is precisely that she does think of others more than herself, that her consciousness can serve as the comparatively transparent medium for narrative. In a curious passage that comes about midway in the novel, Gaskell seems to suggest that it is Molly's very unawareness of her own feelings that enables her to see clearly into the heart of the self-absorbed Cynthia—a Cynthia who in the same passage is significantly said to have "no modest unconsciousness about her":

Molly did not know her own feelings; Roger had no overwhelming interest in what they might be; while his very life-breath seemed to depend on what Cynthia felt and thought. Therefore Molly had keen insight into her "sister's" heart; and she knew that Cynthia did not love Roger. (Pp. 371–72)

The logic of this syllogism seems wishful at best: why ignorance of one's own feelings should afford special insight into the heart of another is far from clear, though the narrator may rather mean to suggest that Molly penetrates to the truth about Cynthia because she cares so intensely about Roger. But however strained the argument, the conclusion is unequivocal—all the more emphatically asserted, perhaps, in proportion to the haziness of the premises: "therefore Milly had keen insight into her 'sister's' heart," a clear perception of the other that somehow derives from her own modest consciousness.

"I think you must observe what is *out* of you, instead of examining what is *in* you," Gaskell declared in a letter of advice to a beginning writer—a letter that explicitly associates the ideal stance of the novelist with something very like the self-effacement of a modest heroine:

It is always an unhealthy sign when we are too conscious of any of the physical processes that go on within us; & I believe in like manner that we ought not to be too cognizant of our mental proceedings, only taking note of the results. But certainly—whether introspection be morbid or not,—it is not a safe training for a novelist. . . . Just read a few pages of De Foe &c—and you will see the healthy way in which he sets *objects* not *feelings* before you. I am sure the right way is this. You are an Electric telegraph something or other,— [19]

To observe faithfully what is "*out* of you," then, it is first necessary not to be "too cognizant" of what is "*in* you," a rule that begins to suggest why a novelist might choose to focalize a narrative, especially a long and thickly populated one, through the self-effacing watchfulness of a Molly Gibson—or, for that matter, of a Fanny Price or an Esther Summerson. Like the ideally objective writer, such a heroine may be imagined as a kind of "Electric telegraph," a sensitive and reliable instrument for transmitting the messages sent by the world around her. "They were two solitary sufferers," Austen remarks as her own modest heroine watches and pities her cousin Julia during the Mansfield theatricals, "or connected only by Fanny's consciousness."[20] So long as Molly does not know her own feelings, her consciousness is even more thoroughly given over to the actions and feelings of others—including the amusing self-absorption of her female relatives. Of course, fictions of modesty have a tendency to contradict themselves, and Gaskell's theory of authorial effacement is no exception: as Margaret Homans has shown, the writer's own desires and fears keep intruding into her letter, even as she propounds the doctrine that excludes them.[21] By this token too, however, it is significant that Gaskell should allow her imagination to dwell so freely on the amoral vitality of a Cynthia Kirkpatrick or a Mrs. Gibson in the very novel that she has most securely anchored in the consciousness of a modest heroine.

✌

Austen is perhaps the predecessor with whom Gaskell is most frequently associated; and while the mismatched marriage of the Gibsons often inspires allusions to the Bennets in *Pride and Prejudice,* there are obvious reasons why *Wives and Daughters* should have reminded several critics of *Mansfield Park.*[22] Mary Crawford proved to be mistaken in her belief that she and Fanny were born to be "sisters,"[23] but in virtually every other respect the central triangle of Austen's novel anticipated Gaskell's. In both novels, a younger son begins as a mentor and near-brother of the heroine, falls temporarily in love with a charming and flirtatious outsider, and finally turns, chastened, to the modest young woman instead. Like Mary Crawford too, as we have seen, Cynthia Kirkpatrick has a history of seducing the novel's critics along with its hero. But even before the appearance of the antiheroine, *Wives and Daughters* recalls its predecessor: as in Austen's novel, its courtship plot begins when the modest young woman arrives in the home of her future husband, and as in Austen's novel, the resident patriarch immediately fears lest one of his sons fall in love with the humble visitor. Indeed, were it not for Gaskell's notorious casualness about the naming of her characters, one would be tempted to find a direct allusion to Austen's heroine in Mrs. Hamley's habit of sometimes confusing Molly with a dead daughter of her own called "Fanny" (p. 210).

Like *Mansfield Park, Wives and Daughters* is a Bildungsroman that chooses to concentrate on the period of courtship. Though Gaskell literally begins her novel with "the old rigmarole of childhood" (p. 1), her little girl grows up almost as rapidly as Austen's: Fanny Price is nine years old in the opening chapter of her history and has "just reached her eighteenth year" at the close of the fourth,[24] while it takes Molly until her fourth chapter to pass from twelve to "nearly seventeen" (p. 34). Yet unlike its predecessor, Gaskell's novel is thoroughly at ease with the passage of time. Though Gaskell never suggests that poor Mr. Coxe would have proved a suitable mate for her heroine, the terms in which she dismisses him are more temporal than moral: his is a "Calf-Love," as the chapter title has it (p. 47), an inappropriate, because unseasonable, attachment. Dr. Gibson may initially be "startled into discovering that his little one was growing fast into a woman" (p. 55), but it appears to be one of the unspecified duties of his apprentice to remind him that "everything must have a beginning" (p. 57); and what Coxe begins will eventually end with the father more or less gracefully giving way to his successor. By the closing pages of the novel, only Mrs. Gibson is still comically protesting the inevitable: "'It is such a pity!' said she, 'that I was born when I was. I should so have liked to belong to this generation'" (p. 681).

In *Wives and Daughters,* girls come out by growing up—and only Mrs. Gibson, revealingly enough, pays any attention to the ritual by which society arbitrarily distinguishes the girl from the woman. Mrs. Gibson likes to talk of her daughters' "coming out," the narrative suggests, precisely because the boundary between the outs and the not-outs is a complete fiction, a purely imaginary line that can be shifted at will wherever it suits her personal ambition and convenience. "'They are not out yet,' was her favourite excuse when either of them was invited to any house to which she did not wish them to go, or were invited without her." When she tries to prevent them from accepting an invitation to tea and a card game at the Brownings with the excuse that "they are not out, you know, till after the Easter ball," Cynthia is as quick as ever to mock her mother's artifice and pretension: "'Till when we are invisible,' said Cynthia. . . . [who] enjoyed the idea of her own full-grown size and stately gait, as contrasted with that of a meek, half-fledged girl in the nursery" (p. 246). For Cynthia—and for Gaskell—the natural progression of time makes a joke of the effort to draw such artificial distinctions: "'After Easter, Molly and I shall know how to behave at a card-party, but not before,' said Cynthia, demurely" (p. 247).[25]

And despite the real pain that Molly suffers during the Preston scandal, even that episode resolves itself in something of a comic anticlimax, as if Gaskell could not take altogether seriously Dr. Gisbon's Gregory-like warning as to "how slight a thing may blacken a girl's reputation for life" (p. 545). Few novelists are as sensitive to the pressures of small-town gossip as Gaskell, yet the ease with which Lady Harriet succeeds in quelling the rumor that "Molly Gibson has lost her character" (p. 535) suggests a vision of experience comparatively untroubled by the fear of taint or pollution. Molly is, of course, innocent of any crime, but to speculate for a moment on what Frances Burney might have made of the episode is to recognize how much anxiety could nonetheless attend the idea of an innocent heroine. Though Gaskell pays lip service to the possibility that the slightest mistake might "blacken" a reputation "for life," it is hard to imagine that she would dismiss even the adulterous Maria Rushworth to a retirement "which could allow no second spring of hope or character."[26] In the case of Molly herself, Gaskell quickly replaces her heroine's social ostracism with bodily illness—a form of suffering that at once completes her rehabilitation in the eyes of the community ("all the Hollingford people forgot that they had ever thought of her except as the darling of the town"—p. 618), and itself gives way to a "delightful spring of returning health" (p. 648) in the restorative course of time.

There is a crucial difference, in other words, between an antiheroine who has "no modest unconsciousness about her" (p. 371) and one who has—as Edmund says of Mary Crawford—"no modest loathings,"[27] and that difference goes to the heart of the difference between the two novels. Molly's modest unconsciousness will inevitably change with time, but in Edmund's future home a virtue that carries with it some modest loathings seems permanently required to keep the place free of pollution. While the close of *Mansfield Park* seems to collaborate with the Bertrams' final acts of housekeeping—shutting out the Crawfords along with Maria and Mrs. Norris from the "tolerable comfort" afforded the rest[28]—the end of *Wives and Daughters* resists the impulse to sort the ins and the outs too cleanly. Cynthia and Molly do somewhat drift apart in the aftermath of the Preston scandal, but the same imagination that can turn the conventionally opposed pair of heroines into genuinely intimate and affectionate sisters apparently feels no need to sever them radically at the end. Though the fact that the novel is unfinished necessarily leaves the final disposition of Cynthia in doubt, Molly is still "bright with pleasure" at the thought of seeing her again in the last paragraphs Gaskell wrote (p. 682). In an uncharacteristic moment of hyperbole, Roger declares to Dr. Gibson that Molly "must despise" him for "choosing the false Duessa," but he has no sooner spoken than Una's own father sensibly reproves his extravagance. "Come, come!" Gibson says, "Cynthia isn't so bad as that. She's a very fascinating, faulty creature"—a tolerant assessment with which her former lover hastens to agree. "If I called her the false Duessa it was because I wanted to express my sense of the difference between her and Molly as strongly as I could," he observes, reasonably enough. "You must allow for a lover's exaggeration" (p. 677).[29] Unlike Austen's clergyman when he speaks to Fanny of Mary Crawford's "corrupted, vitiated mind," or describes his last view of her, smiling Duessa-like in the doorway,[30] Gaskell's naturalist is quick to recognize that such anxiously inflated rhetoric has more to do with the psychology of choosing than with any independent reality. And unlike that of *Mansfield Park,* the plotting of *Wives and Daughters* unambiguously endorses this more tolerant view. For a "faulty creature" in a mid-Victorian novel, Cynthia gets off very lightly indeed—her only punishment to be married to a handsome and wealthy stick figure of her choosing. While we have every reason to trust Molly's secret belief that the gentleman in question is "rather commonplace," and to judge Cynthia's taste accordingly, the future Mrs. Henderson is "evidently as happy as she could be" (pp. 634, 635).

Having decided to marry Henderson, the "not very very constant" Cynthia suddenly starts to talk—if only for the moment—like a modest heroine, declaring that her future husband has been the man she has really loved all along. "I believe I cared for him when he offered all those months ago," she confides to Molly, "but I tried to think I didn't; only sometimes I really was so unhappy, I thought I must put an iron-band round my heart to keep it from breaking, like the Faithful John of the German story" (p. 634). As Edgar Wright has dryly observed, this speech is "out of character as well as being of dubious application to the agreeable, conventional lawyer we briefly meet"—though one might argue that in offering us this brief glimpse of a Cynthia busily sentimentalizing her past, Gaskell does not so much "sacrifice . . . realism on the sacred altar of marriage," in Wright's words,[31] as hint that the daughter of Hyacinth Clare is beginning to take after her mother.

But if it is hard to take seriously a Cynthia who has all this while been concealing a faithful heart, the arbitrariness of her love life only points up, of course, the teleological consistency of Molly's. The modest heroine's end is always implicit in her beginning, and in the case of *Wives and Daughters* that end expressly entails the profession of her future husband. Soon after the novel was first conceived, Gaskell seems to have known that her hero would "work . . . out for himself a certain name in Natural Science," and "go round the world (like Charles Darwin) as naturalist."[32] Whether Roger was modeled directly on Darwin, who was in fact a casual aquaintance, or on one Dr. Allman, a professor of natural science at Edinburgh with whom she had been staying in the months before beginning her novel,[33] the naturalist as Gaskell imagines him is, in effect, the natural husband of a modest heroine. Dr. Allman she pronounced "the most charmingly wise and simple man I ever met with," and "like a child for unselfconsciousness and sweet humility"[34]— and something of that same un-self-consciousness appears to have gone into her portrait of Roger. With his careful habits of observation ("his eyes are always wandering about, and see twenty things where I only see one," says his father—p. 73) and his respectful effacement before that which he observes, Roger's virtues as a scientist seem almost indistinguishable from the kind of modesty she celebrates in her ideal artist as well as her heroine. "He was so great a lover of nature that, without any thought, but habitually, he always avoided treading unnecessarily on any plant," the narrator tells us, as if naturalists were made by the same kind of unconscious instincts that produce modest young women: "who knew what long-sought growth or insect might develop itself in what now appeared but insignificant?" (p. 117). As the scientist who succeeds where the effete poet fails, the brother with the "thoroughly good constitution" (p. 386), who owes "half" his success—to say nothing of his ability to outlive the other—to "his perfect health" (p. 385), Roger seems to have been clearly marked out for survival. Even his growing friendship with the amateur scientist Lord Cumnor seems to put him on the side of history by pointing to a future in which professional bonds will prove more significant than those of class. Though one critic has argued that the matches in *Wives and Daughters* are governed by "the anarchic processes of sexual selection identified by Darwin,"[35] there is nothing "anarchic"—if much that is Darwinian—in Molly's instinctive selection of Roger.

Insofar as Gaskell takes her heroine's modesty as natural and quietly adopts the conventional strategies of English courtship fiction to manage the story, *Wives and Daughters* can seem the most conservative of the novels by women we have examined: compared to a work like *Villette*, this novel appears scarcely to question the familiar order of things. But the natural in *Wives and Daughters* is a process of change, not Rousseau's mystified absolute; and the hero who can see twenty things where his father sees only one is a hero with an eye for difference.

PART THREE

Postscripts

☙

Suit the action to the word, the word to the
action, with this special observance, that you
o'erstep not the modesty of nature. For anything so o'erdone is from the purpose of playing, whose end, both at the first and now, was
and is to hold as 'twere the mirror up to nature; to show virtue her feature, scorn her
own image, and the very age and body of the
time his form and pressure.
—Shakespeare, *Hamlet*

12

Modesty and Female Choice

❦

Natural science being a very human endeavor, often Nature herself appears to reflect what humanity takes for granted. Like a respectable Victorian novel, Charles Darwin's *The Descent of Man, and Selection in Relation to Sex* implicitly deferred the representation of sex in order to dwell on the story of choosing. Just as the English novel quietly subordinated the erotic impulses that drove its courtship plot, so did Darwin's theory. As a contemporary reviewer was pleased to remark when the book first appeared in 1871, Darwin treated his subject "in a way that entirely strips it of all offensiveness."[1]

Though its principal topics were not always kept wholly separate from one another, the book really consisted of two texts published as one: *The Descent of Man* extended the argument of *The Origin of Species* to the evolution of humans, while *Selection in Relation to Sex* advanced the hypothesis of what Darwin called sexual, as distinct from natural, selection. Despite the controversy surrounding human evolution, however—or perhaps because of it—Darwin devoted most of his attention not to the descent of man but to the courtship of animals, giving over the great bulk of his two-volume work to accounts of how insects, birds, fish, and mammals go about choosing their mates. And despite Darwin's reputation for depriving history of conscious and consoling intentions, these accounts of courtship are typically stories in which deliberate choice leads to a satisfying conclusion—stories in which modest females successfully exercise their peculiarly feminine powers of taste and discrimination.[2]

The assumption of female modesty, in fact, provided Darwin with a happy solution to an enigma left unexplained by the laws of natural selection. The problem, as he saw it, is that some animals possess striking features that seem to be of no use in the struggle for survival and which at times even threaten to make life more difficult, such as brilliantly colored or elaborately ornamented feathers that call attention to their owners rather than camouflage them. Indeed, for reasons that will soon become apparent, bird feathers and song were among Darwin's favorite examples of the phenomenon, though he also dwelled with particular attention on the gracefully curved antlers of certain deer. These striking features, he contended, typically belong to the male of the species and only appear when the animal reaches sexual maturity. While he was characteristically honest enough to acknowledge that both rules have a number of exceptions, Darwin seems to have had little doubt that together they point to the obvious solution of the problem: if the question is why males are more beautiful, the answer must be that females are at once less lustful and more discriminating. Male cardinals have scarlet coats, in other words, because for generations the female has coyly held out for a red uniform, while the male has eagerly taken any dull bird who wandered along. Or as Darwin himself puts it when considering the brilliant colors of the butterfly, "From the ardour of the male throughout the animal kingdom, he is generally willing to accept any female; and it is the female which usually exerts a choice." "The cause of this," he writes at another point, "seems to lie in the males of almost all animals having stronger passions than the females," while "the female . . . with the rarest exception, is less eager than the male." Darwin goes on to spell out the implications of this law with his customary mix of caution and sweeping generalization:

As the illustrious Hunter long ago observed, [the female] . . . generally "requires to be courted;" she is coy, and may often be seen endeavouring for a long time to escape from the male. Every one who has attended to the habits of animals will be able to call to mind instances of this kind. Judging from various facts, hereafter to be given, and from the results which may fairly be attributed to sexual selection, the female, though comparatively passive, generally exerts some choice and accepts one male in preference to others. Or she may accept, as appearances would sometimes lead us to believe, not the male which is the most attractive to her, but the one which is the least distasteful. The exertion of some choice on the part of the female seems almost as general a law as the eagerness of the male.[3]

When Edward Moore spelled out the rule of female choice more than a century earlier, he had in mind the rights of daughters as against parents rather than the difference between male lust and female discrimination, but his tetrameter line might nonetheless serve as a refrain for Darwin's account of the wooing of animals: "To choose, belongs to her alone."[4]

Like most nineteenth-century naturalists, Darwin relied heavily on the reports and testimonials of others, many of whom were indeed "able to call to mind instances of this kind"—or at least to represent animal behavior in ways that could be more or less assimilated to the theory. Sometimes, though, the evidence proved a little recalcitrant. "It is obviously difficult," as Darwin candidly remarks, "to obtain direct evidence with respect to female fishes selecting their partners." The account that follows suggests that the difficulty he has in mind is not merely the effect of the watery depths at which their sex life is conducted—nor even, strictly speaking, the sort of crowded conditions to which his source initially alludes:

An excellent observer, who carefully watched the spawning of minnows . . . remarks that owing to the males, which were ten times as numerous as the females, crowding closely round them, he could "speak only doubtfully on their operations. When a female came among a number of males they immediately pursued her; if she was not ready for shedding her spawn, she made a precipitate retreat; but if she was ready, she came boldly in among them, and was immediately pressed closely by a male on each side; and when they had been in that situation a short time, were superseded by other two, who wedged themselves in between them and the female, who appeared to treat all her lovers with the same kindness."

"Notwithstanding this last statement," Darwin immediately adds, "I cannot, from the several previous considerations, give up the belief that the males which are the most attractive to the females, from their brighter colours or other ornaments, are commonly preferred by them; and that the males have thus been rendered more beautiful in the course of ages" (2:15–16).

Darwin's relative willingness to record evidence that tells against him constitutes one of his principal attractions as a writer: though he passes rather hastily over the reported boldness and kindly promiscuity of the female minnow, he implicitly acknowledges the challenge she poses to his theory. While his representations of animal coyness in courtship sometimes recall Rousseau's account of *pudeur* among the pigeons, the naturalist has little of the philosopher's tendentiousness—and far more tolerance for observations that resist the drift of the argument. Elsewhere he openly acknowledges the existence of some cases in which "there has been a complete inversion of the usual attributes of the two sexes" and "the males have selected the more attractive females" (2:22); later on, he mentions "some few cases" in which the female "courts the male, or even fights for his possession" (2:120).[5] Sometimes, however, the text registers almost no awareness of the disparity between the behavior being observed and the fiction in which it is encoded. Notice, for example, what happens to female modesty among the spiders—a species in which, as Darwin tells us, "the males are generally much smaller than the females, sometimes to an extraordinary degree" (1:338):

Mr. Blackwall has sometimes seen two or more males on the same web with a single female; but their courtship is too tedious and prolonged an affair to be easily observed. The male is extremely cautious in making his advances, as the female carries her coyness to a dangerous pitch. De Geer saw a male that "in the midst of his preparatory caresses was seized by the object of his attractions, enveloped by her in a web and then devoured, a sight which, as he adds, filled him with horror and indignation." (1:339)

Dangerous coyness of this order is scarcely coy. What is remarkable here is not the obvious terror and disgust that the devouring female inspires in her male observers, but their almost touching reluctance to abandon the fiction of modesty even at the moment of imagined engulfment. In fact, the abruptly terminated courtship of the spider-woman suggests that the masculine imagination may dwell with a particular insistence on the assumption of female modesty to counter or cover over something very like this terrifying alternative scenario.

In the first edition of *The Descent,* this paragraph ends on the dramatic note of "horror and indignation." When he came to revise and expand the work three years later, however, Darwin muted this terrifying climax by continuing the paragraph with a consoling theory that the small size of the male had evolved in order to facilitate his escape from the devouring female:

The Rev. O. P. Cambridge accounts in the following manner for the extreme smallness of the male in the genus Nephilia. "M. Vinson gives a graphic account of the agile way in which the diminutive male escapes from the ferocity of the female, by gliding about and playing hide and seek over her body and along her gigantic limbs; in such a pursuit it is evident that the chances of escape would be in favour of the smallest males, while the larger ones would fall early victims; thus gradually a diminutive race of males would be selected, until at last they would dwindle to the smallest possible size compatible with the exercise of their generative functions,—in fact probably to the size we now see them, i.e., so small as to be a sort of parasite upon the female, and either beneath her notice, or too agile and too small for her to catch without great difficulty."[6]

But if male fears of being swallowed up or devoured by women lie beneath the courtship narrative that Darwin has inherited, it must be admitted that they are for the most part very well buried. In Darwin's world, female animals rarely manifest spider-woman's alarming appetite—Nature having already seen to it, in effect, that most of them will be too well bred. One would have to go back to a writer like Rousseau to find texts openly fractured by the anxiety that female restraint may not be securely naturalized—texts which strenuously insisted that woman is modest by nature even as they everywhere betrayed their inability to take Nature for granted and their terror of the consequences. For if Rousseau's Nature had not happily provided women with modesty, we may recall, their unrestrained lust would quickly have produced a scene of apocalyptic destruction, as men, their "senses" endlessly aroused though their "amorousness" was "nearly extinguished," would "finally become [women's] victims, and would all see themselves dragged to their death without ever being able to defend themselves."[7]

That Darwin seems comparatively free of such terrors surely owes something to individual psychology and vocation as well as to the assumptions he shares with his culture. But the very fact that he can take the lesser desire of the female serenely for granted, that he thinks so little of her appetite and so much of her sensitivity and perception, depends on a story about sexual relations that Rousseau himself had helped to construct and that had been made comfortably familiar by more than a century of English fiction. Because women are naturally modest, they need to be courted, and because they are naturally modest, they are more discriminating, turning the interval before they surrender into an exercise in cultural improvement. Such tasteful choosing, it should be said, does not account for every case of sexual selection in Darwin's argument: in some instances, he speculates, males habitually battle with one another for possession of the female, and the traits of the victor in the struggle are then inherited.[8] And human history, as we shall see, ironically seems to him to pose a particular problem for the theory. But it is the sensitive female on whom *The Descent* dwells longest and most sympathetically—and it is her story, I believe, that the author most wants to tell.

As Darwin well knew, the theory of female choice presupposes rather fine perceptions on the part of the chooser, even—or perhaps especially—when she need only decide which of her available partners happens to be, in Darwin's tactful phrase, "the least distasteful" to her (1:273). "No doubt this implies powers of discrimination and taste on the part of the female which will at first appear extremely improbable," he admits early on in the discussion; "but I hope hereafter to shew that this is not the case" (1:259). Many of his critics, then and now, have not been altogether persuaded. For the argument mainly appeals to the reader's capacity for imaginative identification: the female must have an ability to discriminate, because she obviously shares our standards of taste.[9] So it would seem, at least, when Darwin comes—as he so often does—to the birds, whom he calls "the most aesthetic of all animals, excepting of course man." That "they have nearly the same taste for the beautiful as we have" can be shown, he argues, by our enjoyment of their singing, and "by our women, both civilised and savage, decking their heads with borrowed plumes" from certain species and "using gems which are hardly more brilliantly coloured than the naked skin and wattles" of others (2:39). Even as "love is still," in Darwin's words, "the commonest theme of our own songs," so "nearly the same emotions, but much weaker and less complex, are probably felt by birds when the male pours forth his full volume of song, in rivalry with other males, for the sake of captivating the female" (2:336). And while it may not be that the female "consciously deliberates" when she chooses a mate, or that she "studies each stripe or spot of colour,"

Nevertheless after hearing how carefully the male Argus pheasant displays his elegant primary wing-feathers, and erects his ocellated plumes in the right position for their full effect; or again, how the male goldfinch alternately displays his gold-bespangled wings, we ought not to feel too sure that the female does not attend to each detail of beauty. (2:123–24)

As for "female birds feeling a preference for particular males, we must bear in mind that we can judge of choice being exerted, only by placing ourselves in imagination in the same position" (2:122). After all, Darwin exhorts us later, "We should remember the fact given on excellent authority in a former chapter, namely that several peahens, when debarred from an admired male, remained widows during a whole season rather than pair with another bird" (2:400).

Those widowed peahens are scarcely the only animals whom Darwin represents in the language of human marriage, and we should indeed remember them—though not merely for their touching devotion. Sexual selection can only work if males who happen to possess the traits females admire manage to produce more offspring than the others—an effect that Darwin sometimes tries to explain by speculating that the most attractive males happen also to be the most "vigorous" (and therefore, presumably, the most fertile), or by suggesting that because the more attractive ones would be chosen first, they would have a headstart in the mating season. He also devotes much attention to the hypothesis that sexual selection comes into play whenever the males of a species significantly outnumber the females—the idea being that the redundant males would simply have no offspring—though he is compelled to admit that he can find little evidence to support this conjecture. What he cannot see, or at least prefers not to see clearly, is the solution generally offered by modern biologists—that sexual selection is largely confined to polygynous or so-called promiscuous species.[10] Attractive males have more opportunities to pass on their attractions, by this account, because more females choose to mate with each one. Though Darwin does briefly entertain this possibility, he continues to insist that "many animals, especially birds, which are strictly monogamous" nonetheless display the marks of sexual selection (1 : 266). But by focusing attention on the selective choosing of the female rather than the sexual activity of the male, most of *The Descent* effectively manages to evade the issue: the story it tells appears to end, and end happily, when the female "accepts one . . . in preference to others" (1 : 273).

By concentrating not on what he calls the animals' "marriage arrangements" (1 : 271) but on their courtship, in other words, Darwin quietly shapes their history after the plan of the novels he appears to have loved so well—those "works of imagination," as he testified in his *Autobiography,* which "have been for years a wonderful relief and pleasure to me . . . [so that] I often bless all novelists":

A surprising number have been read aloud to me, and I like all if moderately good, and if they do not end unhappily—against which a law ought to be passed. A novel, according to my taste, does not come into the first class unless it contains some person whom one can thoroughly love, and if it be a pretty woman all the better.

"He was extremely fond of novels," his son later confirmed, though "he could not enjoy any story with a tragical end. . . . Walter Scott, Miss Austen, and Mrs. Gaskell, were read and re-read till they could be read no more."[11]

To argue that Darwin's account of sexual selection owes something to the language and plotting of the novelists, or that it relies on textual evidence as well as direct observation, is not to deny its explanatory power. Indeed, the recent revival of a modified form of the theory—after a long period in which it was customary to argue that natural selection alone would account for most of the relevant evidence—suggests that Darwin's courtship stories may have clarified more than they obscured. And the very fact that a majority of Darwin's scientific con-

temporaries remained more or less skeptical about the importance of
female choice indirectly testifies to his originality: if the female-centered
courtship plot was familiar, his extension of it to insects and birds was
not. But while most modern biologists seem to believe that sexual selection in general, and female choice in particular, have at least a limited
evolutionary role to play, a fiction of modesty no longer governs the
story. Insofar as they seek to explain the apparently greater discrimination of the female, recent students of the subject write not about differences in the passion or ardor of the two sexes but about different
degrees of so-called parental investment: because the female produces
fewer and larger gametes, or because she devotes more time and effort
to nurturing the offspring, she needs to be more discriminating as to
how she "invests" her reproductive energies.[12] With the advent of modern genetics, in other words, an explanatory model based on reproduc-
tion has replaced the nineteenth-century model of desire.

As contemporary students of evolution often observe, Darwin did
not have the advantage of modern genetics. But for him, it would seem,
the theory of female choice produces the sort of happy ending written
out of history by *The Origin of Species*. "I know of no fact in natural
history more wonderful," he writes in the final pages of *The Descent*,
"than that the female Argus pheasant should be able to appreciate the
exquisite shading . . . and the elegant patterns" of the male's feathers
(2:400). And this wonderful fact is at once the end of the story and its
actively shaping force, since we owe the very making of the pheasant's
beauty to many generations of females choosing—their "aesthetic capacity," in Darwin's words, "having been advanced through exercise or
habit in the same manner as our own taste is gradually improved"
(2:401). At its happiest, the exercise of female taste even impels the
other sex actively to join in the aesthetic work: that male birds sometimes
sing out of the mating season, Darwin earlier suggests, does not disprove the thesis but confirms it, since "nothing is more common than
for animals to take pleasure in practising whatever instinct they follow
at other times for some real good," and "singing is to a certain extent
. . . an art, and is much improved by practice" (2:54, 55).[13]

For all his evident delight in this pacific and feminized narrative,
Darwin nonetheless feels compelled to recognize that human societies
have for a long time seemed to arrange matters differently. Though *The
Descent* has relatively little to say about sexual selection among men and
women—and that little is rather vague and confusing—it seems to argue that male dominance has caused human courtship patterns to undergo a striking reversal, men having seized the privilege of choice for

themselves and having exercised that privilege to select women for their beauty. "Man is more powerful in body and mind than woman," Darwin writes in one of the few passages to address the subject directly, "and in the savage state he keeps her in a far more abject state of bondage than does the male of any other animal; therefore it is not surprising that he should have gained the power of selection" (2:371). And not only in the savage state, apparently, have men been doing the choosing: while male birds have been selected for their beauty, we may recall that "our women, both civilised and savage" have been borrowing their plumes, or that Darwin himself prefers novels that supply him with a "pretty woman" to love. Yet to say that those same novels have also taught him to empathize with the pretty woman even as he loves her, or that his animal narratives obliquely pay tribute to her civilizing influence, is not quite the contradiction it might seem. For the life of savages, as *The Descent* everywhere makes clear, represents to Darwin a falling away from animal instinct, a fall into "immorality," "unnatural crimes," and "utter licentiousness" (1:97, 96) from which human civilization has only gradually and imperfectly recovered.[14]

Two centuries earlier, Richard Allestree had painfully sought to distinguish women from the "Brutes" in order to argue for a modesty that Darwin now finds natural even in female animals. But like Allestree when he simultaneously tried to argue for the naturalness of female modesty by ranking the "Impudent woman" as "a kind of Monster"— "as far beneath" the Brutes "as an acquir'd vileness is below a native"— Darwin effectively excludes "savages" from the naturally civilized company.[15] Insofar as Darwin seems implicitly to associate the instinctive modesty of the female animal with the civilizing influence of Victorian woman, then, William James was not altogether wrong to conclude that *The Descent* had shown how female "coyness . . . has played a vital part in the amelioration of all higher animal types, and is to a great degree responsible for whatever degree of chastity the human race may show"[16]—though Darwin himself makes only a brief remark to this effect (1:96). Good Englishman that he is, he much prefers animals to "savages," and prefers them because he imagines them as instinctively imbued with the virtues of his own civilization.

In the famous concluding paragraphs of his book, Darwin ringingly defended his account of human evolution by proclaiming that he would just "as soon be descended from that heroic little monkey, who braved his dreaded enemy in order to save the life of his keeper . . . as from a savage who delights to torture his enemies, offers up bloody sacrifices, practises infanticide without remorse, treats his wives like slaves, knows no decency, and is haunted by the grossest superstitions" (2:404–5). Despite his wish to repudiate this wife-abusing relative, Darwin was surely his descendent too—a kinship he made all too evident, one is tempted to say, whenever he simply took the superiority of men for granted. But in imagination, at least, this nineteenth-century Englishman preferred to dwell in the higher civilization of animals and women. And though Darwin was hardly a typical man of his time, the evidence suggests that he was not the only middle-class Englishman to identify in this way with women. To speculate about the gradual feminization of middle-class consciousness in the nineteenth century is not to claim that consciousness in any immediate sense as feminist. Yet if the self-effacing heroines of English novels captured the imagination of readers of both sexes, such novels may have helped to break down the very gender distinctions that fictions of modesty had originally been constructed to maintain.

13

Modesty and Sex

෧

By understanding female modesty as the hidden motor of the plot, Havelock Ellis read erotic desire back into the modest woman's story. Unlike Darwin, who assumed that the female resists the male because her passions are weaker than his, Ellis saw her resistance as radically bound up with her desire: "modesty," as the *Studies in the Psychology of Sex* represent it, is at once "the sign of sexual emotion" in the woman, the force that arouses the ardor of the man, and the means of intensifying and subliming the passions of both.[1] While other nineteenth-century commentators had sometimes spoken as if the modest woman's desire was effectively absent, or asleep for good, Ellis insisted that the capacity for sexual feeling in women was always there to be awakened. Ellis had little of Freud's mastery of suspense, or of his strenuous drive for causal explanation, but the *Studies* speak for the same general impulse to uncover that which had seemingly been hid; and his work must share some of the responsibility for the twentieth-century practice of seeing sex, in Ellis's own words, as "the central problem of life" (p. xxx). Yet what most preoccupied the English student of the subject, as it had Darwin before him, was not the fulfillment of sexual desire but what Nature had achieved by its delay—the interval that female modesty apparently opened up for "courtship."

Ellis saw himself not as a pathologist of sex, like Freud, but as a naturalist, like Darwin; and like Darwin he had the naturalist's mania for collecting, his sheer delight in the variety of his specimens.[2] The *Studies* begin by defining modesty as "an almost instinctive fear prompting to concealment"—a fear which, "while common to both sexes," is at the same time "more peculiarly feminine" (1–1:1). Though the numerous examples that follow are presumably intended to demonstrate the uni-

229

versality of the phenomenon, the collection proves so engagingly miscellaneous as almost to call the thesis into question. In some cultures,
people expose the genitals but cover the face; in others, the evidence
suggests, women act as the sexual aggressors. But if Ellis was clearly
fascinated by human variety, he also insisted that "the original inspiration of my own work, and the guiding motive throughout, was the
study of normal sexuality," and that he had "always been careful to
show that even the abnormal phenomena throw light on the normal impulse" (p. xxi). And what is "normal," as "The Evolution of Modesty"
describes it, turns out above all to be a delaying action—an action associated with "peculiarly feminine" habits of withdrawal, covering, and
reticence. Throughout the world, it would seem, males are normally aggressive and bold; females—those who are sexually attractive enough to
be courted, at least—timid and shy. This fact has its origins, he goes on
to suggest, in the sexual cycle of the female animal: while the male animal is always eager and ready for sex, the female is not—and modesty
begins with her attempt to communicate this lack of interest to her im-
portunate lover. Or so it would appear that Ellis wishes to argue; despite his title, his evolutionary argument must be termed sketchy at
best, and virtually the sole evidence he offers on this point comes from
the sex life of dogs. Between the bitch when she is not in heat and that
"classical example of womanly modesty," as he calls the Venus de Medici, the evolutionary chain is apparently clear. "Anyone who watches a
bitch, not in heat, when approached by a dog with a tail wagging gal-
lantly, may see the beginnings of modesty," he writes; and he goes on to
argue (with rather less gallantry than he attributes to the courting dog)
that when the bitch "squats firmly down on the front legs and hind
quarters," her "attitude of refusal is equivalent" to the classic posture of
the Venus de Medici—one of whose hands appears to guard her genitals, the other, her breast. "The essential expression in each case," he
asserts, "is that of defence of the sexual centers against the undesired
advances of the male" (1–1 : 37, 38).

"The sexual modesty of the female animal," in Ellis's summary formulation, "is rooted in the sexual periodicity of the female, and is an
involuntary expression of the organic fact that the time for love is not
now" (1–1 : 39). Like other late-nineteenth-century thinkers—Freud's
correspondent and friend, Wilhelm Fliess among them—Ellis seems to
have been attracted to theories of periodicity; and later volumes of the
Studies speculate about possible sexual cycles in men and women alike.
But his account of "normal" sexuality also requires that the potential for
erotic feeling in the woman be continuously, if latently, present: as the

human female evolved from the lower animals, he wants to argue, her modest gestures somehow came to signify not an actual lack of desire but an instinctive impulse of retardation and delay—not a simple refusal, in other words, but a kind of promise. That "the time for love is not now," comes to mean that the time *will* be later—and beginning with modesty, as Foucault would have predicted, proves to be just another way of focusing all the more intently on sex, of seeing it, to quote Ellis again, as "the central problem of life" (p. xxx). Yet beginning with modesty, as Ellis understands it, is also what makes "love" itself possible: when the bitch is not in heat, she is presumably indifferent to sex, but the human combination of desire and delay at once intensifies desire and compels it to seek indirect and symbolic expression.

With the theory of sexual selection, Ellis later wrote admiringly, Darwin "made the whole becoming of life art and the secret of it poetry."[3] Though Ellis himself focused not on selection but on sex, he, too, insisted that "throughout nature" the female "is usually fastidious in the choice of a lover" (1–2:205). But rather than assume, as Darwin seemed to, that the weaker passions of the female enabled her to attend more to choosing, Ellis took woman's greater fastidiousness as good reason *not* to believe that she was inherently colder than man—only that desire in her was more deeply buried. Though some nineteenth-century commentators purported to discover widespread sexual anesthesia in women—as in Dr. Acton's notorious claim that "the majority of women (happily for them) are not very much troubled with sexual feeling of any kind"[4]—Ellis sensibly observed that "it is very much more difficult than most people seem to suppose, to obtain quite precise and definite data concerning the absence of either *voluptas* or *libido* in a woman" (1–2:204). "Some of the most marked characteristics of the sexual impulse in women," he continued, "—its association with modesty, its comparatively late development, its seeming passivity, its need of stimulation,—all combine to render difficult the final pronouncement that a woman is sexually frigid" (1–2:205). Even a woman's own denial of sexual feeling should not be taken as "conclusive and final" (1–2:204)—only as a sign, in effect, that her particular courtship narrative had not yet reached its conclusion. Indeed, a man who hastened to pronounce a woman cold, in Ellis's book, would merely confess to his own inadequacy as a lover. "The fact that a woman is cold with one man or even with a succession of men by no means shows that she is not apt to experience sexual emotions," he remarks rather sharply; "it merely shows that these men have not been able to arouse them" (1–2:205).

"Throughout nature"—Ellis articulates the customary rule—the female in courtship is "usually comparatively passive," though this familiar claim already carries a telling reservation: "except when the male fails to play his part properly." But if Ellis's Nature seems to have arranged the roles of the sexes very much as she did for Darwin, the interpretation of those roles undergoes a striking transformation. Here is an account of what Ellis takes to be the standard plot, his supporting evidence drawn, as usual, from a motley assortment of other texts:

> Courtship resembles very closely, indeed, a drama or game; and the aggressiveness of the male, the coyness of the female, are alike unconsciously assumed in order to bring about in the most effectual manner the ultimate union of the sexes. The seeming reluctance of the female is not intended to inhibit sexual activity either in the male or in herself, but to increase it in both. The passivity of the female, therefore, is not a real, but only an apparent, passivity, and this holds true of our own species as much as of the lower animals. "Women are like delicately adjusted alembics," said a seventeenth-century author. "No fire can be seen outside, but if you look underneath the alembic, if you place your hand on the hearts of women, in both places you will find a great furnace." Or, as Marro has finely put it, the passivity of women in love is the passivity of the magnet, which in its apparent immobility is drawing the iron toward it. An intense energy lies behind such passivity, an absorbed preoccupation in the end to be attained. (1–2:229)

Notice how female coyness in this account proves not the opposite of male aggression but its mirror image—and how soon the male seems to drop out of the picture. This passage comes, admittedly, not from Ellis's initial discussion of modesty but from his later study of "The Sexual Impulse in Women"—and it is the woman's desire, therefore, that is at issue. But the woman's desire is always very much at issue for Ellis: and it is her energy that secretly fuels the plot. Whether represented as the enclosed heat of the alembic or the magnet's invisible force, such energy is imagined as all the more powerful, in fact, for being hidden. Cobbett's advice to the "*ardent-minded* young man" here receives the sanction of science: men find modest women the most sexually attractive, Ellis repeatedly contends, because they instinctively know that such women are themselves the most desiring.[5] The fact that "it is the spontaneous and natural instinct of the lover to desire modesty in his mistress," in Ellis's words, simply goes to prove "that curious and instinctive harmony by which Nature has sought the more effectively to bring about the ends of courtship" (1–1:45).

Ellis begins his *Studies in the Psychology of Sex* with modesty, then, because that is how he imagines "normal sexuality" does begin—with the covert desire of the woman. But it is the very obliquity of the process that fascinates him: for all his seeming deconstruction of her modest reluctance, he has no wish to short-circuit the plot. Phyllis Grosskurth has shrewdly observed that the "great deficiency" of the *Studies* is their failure to come to terms with what might be termed normal male eroticism[6]—a failure that cannot be separated, I think, from Ellis's assumption that masculine desire is virtually plotless, or that coitus itself is a rather straightforward, even trivial affair. "The man's part in courtship, which is that of the male throughout the zoological series, may be difficult and hazardous," he writes, "but it is in a straight line, fairly simple and direct. The woman's part, having to follow at the same moment two quite different impulses, is necessarily always in a zigzag or a curve" (2–3:547–48). Though "detumescence," as he characteristically phrases it, "is the end and climax of the whole drama" (2–1:116), ends and climaxes seem far less interesting to him than narrative middles: he is much more preoccupied by the imagined indirections of female desire, the simultaneous impulses of arousal and delay that transform a crude biological urge into something worthy the name of "courtship."

Peter Brooks has recently described the dynamic tension that propels all narrative plots on a model derived from Freud's *Beyond the Pleasure Principle* (1920): like living organisms, as Freud conceives of them, plots are driven forward by a desire to reach the quiescence of the end, but like living organisms, they only exist by virtue of divergence and detour, and necessarily seek the "right" death rather than a premature one. Freud wrote of "the paradoxical situation that the living organism struggles most energetically against events (dangers, in fact) which might help it to attain its life's aim rapidly—by a kind of short-circuit";[7] and Brooks adopts the term "short-circuit" to represent the "danger of reaching the end too quickly" in a narrative. Plot, he suggests, is "a kind of arabesque or squiggle toward the end," its "deviance from the straight line" determined by the danger of collapsing into silence—or death—immediately.[8] In this theory of plots, as in Freud's account of organisms, the energies of desire are also, of course, to be understood as erotic; and Brooks's model has been criticized for presupposing an implicitly masculine psychology and physiology—as in his suggestion that "narrative desire" begins as "a condition of tumescence" or his formulation of plot as "a postponement in the discharge which leads back to the inanimate."[9] But as a model for fictions of modesty, at least, we might think less of the avoidance of "short-circuits" and more of what Ellis sometimes likes to call the "long-circuiting" of desire[10]—a long-circuiting that he characteristically associates with the delaying action of the woman.

It is no accident that the first physiological response on which Ellis dwells at length is a woman's blush—or that he should be drawn to the hypothesis that the blush carries a sexual meaning because it originates in a displaced genital flushing, a flow of blood mysteriously diverted up to the cheeks by an "inhibition of fear." "An erection," he quotes an anonymous source, "is a blushing of the penis" (1–1:73)—a remark that simultaneously manages to make the sexual associations of the blush unmistakable and to offer a pleasingly feminized interpretation of male physiology. As Ellis reads the woman's blush, it becomes a vivid image of the "long-circuiting" of desire and Nature's first work of erotic symbolism. The temporary rerouting of blood from the genitals to the face is imagined both as a delaying action and as a means of humanizing the sexual impulse, of subliming it into love. "For erotic satisfaction, in its highest planes," he writes in one of the last volumes of the *Studies,*

is only possible when we have secured for the sexual impulse . . . a wide diffusion through the whole of the psychic organism. And that can only be attained by placing impediments in the way of the swift and direct gratification of sexual desire, by compelling it to increase its force, to take long circuits, to charge the whole organism so highly that the final climax of gratified love is not the trivial detumescence of a petty desire but the immense consummation of a longing in which the whole soul as well as the whole body has its part. (2–3:170)

There is considerable evidence to suggest that the man who compared his adolescent self to "an ordinarily modest schoolgirl"[11] continued to identify with women. Phyllis Grosskurth, who calls him a "motherer" and thinks some of his sympathy for women may be traced to his early career as a midwife, calls attention to Ellis's own belief in his "womanly" strain.[12] In his autobiography, he characteristically described himself as "a dreamer, reserved and diffident and sensitive," and insisted on "that passivity which has never ceased entirely to be an element of my character." "My nature isn't of the passionately impetuous kind (though it's very sensuous)," he wrote to his future wife, "and my affections grow slowly, and die hard, if at all." Later, struggling to come to terms with her affair with another woman, he wrote to her: "I seem to be a mother, and you my fretful babe that I fold and smother in my breast." After an interval of wavering, Edith Ellis seems to have identified herself primarily as a lesbian, and this affair was followed by a number of others; by Ellis's own account, she eventually proposed that their "marital relationship in the narrow sense" come to an end, and he "made not the slightest objection."[13] Though he went on to have intimate relations with other women, most of these do not seem to have involved genital intercourse. Typically, the woman appears to have taken the emotional initiative, while Ellis himself stressed the importance of "love" or "affectionate friendship" over "passion." "I am not a bit like the virile robust men of the people in your dreams!" he warned Françoise Lafite-Cyron, the woman who became his principal companion after Edith's death.[14] The particular configuration of Ellis's sexuality necessarily remains both complicated and elusive, but it is an ironic tribute to certain conventions of gender that even as he identified such experience as his own, he represented it as the woman's "natural" story.

Of course, as even the heterogeneity of Ellis's own *Studies* could go to show, the long-circuiting of the modest woman's desire was not the only representation of female sexuality available to the English imagination. The historian who wishes to characterize what a particular culture believed about sex and gender will always confront the problem that at any one moment there are likely to be multiple and potentially conflicting stories in circulation. And the difficulty of sorting them out is inevitably compounded by their tendency to draw, at least in part, on a common set of images and vocabulary. Dr. Acton too spoke of the "modest woman," for instance, when he formulated the "general rule" that such a woman "seldom desires any sexual gratification for herself."[15] But in associating woman's modesty *with* her desire, in claiming that it is the apparently timid woman who is secretly the most ardent, Ellis was, I believe, reproducing as science one of the dominant stories of his culture—arguably a story in wider circulation than Acton's.[16] Or perhaps it would be more accurate to say that he was making relatively explicit the dynamics of a story whose wide circulation had depended on its being understood more or less implicitly.

Reviewing this story at the end of the nineteenth century, Ellis himself suggested that the past two hundred years had witnessed a particular "elaboration of its social ritual"—that "a new ardor of modesty," in his telling phrase, had begun to spread in the social life and literature of eighteenth-century England.[17] But he also insisted that it would be "a mistake to suppose that this process is an intensification of modesty." On the contrary, he argued, the practice of elaborating codes and rules represented "an attenuation" of the impulse itself: though people retained a "vague sense" of the "deep-lying natural basis" of modesty, modern civilization was increasingly engaged, as Ellis saw it, in making the "observances of modesty . . . merely a part of a vast body of rules of social etiquette" (1–1:69). Whether he thought of his own heightened attention to the subject as merely another stage in the attenuating process, he did not say. Even as the *Studies* spoke admiringly of the ways in which Nature had adapted modesty to serve the ends of courtship, they also spoke for an imagination more drawn to the byways and indirections of desire than to its conventional resolution. And even as they argued for the natural basis of modesty, they effectively contributed to more open and aggressive representations of female desire.

Certainly it should come as no surprise to anyone familiar with the conventional opposition between the modest and the immodest woman—an opposition that can be traced from the moralized allegories of the conduct books to the subtly paired heroines of novels like *Mansfield Park* or *Wives and Daughters*—that Ellis should represent the modest one as secretly the more loving. While his allusion to the modest woman as fiery alembic may seem to operate at a different emotional register from most nineteenth-century English narratives, the figure of the apparently motionless but powerful magnet captures very well the latent force of a Fanny Price or a Molly Gibson. And no reader of modest fictions should be surprised to find Ellis dwelling so intently on a woman's blush, a phenomenon whose "sexual relationships" he pronounces "unquestionable." Though Ellis goes on to claim that blushing "occurs chiefly in women," attains "its chief intensity at puberty and during adolescence," and is usually prompted by "some more or less sexual suggestion" (1–1:73), he offers no statistical confirmation of these points. Nor does he pause to distinguish very clearly between the contributions of physiology and those of culture, apparently because he takes the universality of the blushing young woman's appeal pretty much for granted. Reading him is a salutary lesson in the degree to which a well-intentioned scientific exposition may actually be indebted to a family of texts that distinguishes hardly at all between fact and fiction.

Had not Darwin reported that "in Turkish slave-markets, the girls who readily blushed fetched the highest prices" (1–1:74)? Ellis's reference is not to *The Descent of Man*, in this case, but to the nearly contemporaneous work, *The Expression of the Emotions in Man and Animals*, whose extended chapter on blushing did indeed place in evidence the prices commanded by the slave market. "No doubt a slight blush adds to the beauty of a maiden's face," Darwin wrote; "and the Circassian women who are capable of blushing, invariably fetch a higher price in the seraglio of the Sultan than less susceptible women." Rather more careful with his footnotes than Ellis, however, Darwin not only cited the text of one of *his* chief predecessors in the science of blushes—Dr. Thomas Burgess's 1839 treatise on *The Physiology or Mechanism of Blushing*—but indicated that Burgess had in turn given the information "on the authority of" the eighteenth-century English traveler, Lady Mary Wortley Montagu.[18] First published posthumously in 1763, Lady Mary's famous *Letters* did describe her visits to the Turkish harem— one letter home even promised to supply her correspondent with a facial irritant the local women used to redden their cheeks—but the anecdote about the Circassian slave girls is almost certainly apocryphal.[19] Whatever the price structure of Turkish slave markets, the modest woman's blush was already familiar English currency. Several years before Lady Mary even set off for Constantinople, Steele was already recording the same prevailing wisdom in the *Tatler:* "and I have heard it reported by the young Fellows in my Time, as a Maxim of the celebrated Madam *Bennet,* That a young Wench, tho' never so beautiful, was not worth her Board when she was past her Blushing."[20]

Thus a small point about human behavior is authorized—no one knows by whom—over time. Far more significant, in my view, was the authorization of modesty by novelists of the same period, who in writing their own fictions sought not only to comprehend but also to question and hence to remake those they shared with their culture. A conventional courtship plot, even an insistent love story, undoubtedly subjected its heroine to narrow constraints: though a naturalist like Gaskell might manage to suggest the continuities of life beyond the end of marriage, in most fictions of modesty, "all is over"—the concluding words of *Evelina*—when the "fate" of the heroine is "decided."[21] In the space between, nevertheless, even the *honnête femme* had her story. If the assumption of her modesty enabled the novelists to make her the subjective center of their narratives, to represent her as a subject was also to represent, however obliquely, her energies and her desires. We need not believe that her modesty was merely a cover to recognize that, under its cover, other kinds of stories could also begin to be told.

NOTES

Chapter One

1. As quoted in Arthur Calder-Marshall, *Havelock Ellis: A Biography* (London: Rupert Hart-Davis, 1959), p. 166.

2. For an account of the trial and its aftermath, see especially Phyllis Grosskurth, *Havelock Ellis: A Biography* (1980; reprint, New York: New York University Press, 1985), pp. 191–204. Of Ellis's relation to the mysterious de Villiers, the swindling publisher, Grosskurth observes that "his ingenuousness in this matter is almost beyond belief" (p. 199); his conduct in the trial, she concludes, was anything but heroic. See also Arthur Calder-Marshall's *Lewd, Blasphemous & Obscene* (London: Hutchinson, 1972), which judges Ellis's behavior throughout the affair to have been "evasive" (pp. 193–229).

3. Havelock Ellis, *Studies in the Psychology of Sex*, 2 vols. (New York: Random House, 1942), p. xxi. Further references to this edition (each volume of which includes a number of Ellis's original "volumes") will appear parenthetically in the text. The first number indicates the volume of the 1942 edition; the second, after the hyphen, indicates a part number. Each part is separately paginated.

"The Evolution of Modesty" actually first appeared under a Leipzig imprint in 1899—the prosecution of Bedborough for selling "Sexual Inversion" having prompted Ellis to seek publication of subsequent volumes abroad. But de Villiers had deceived Ellis as well as the public, and the volume had in fact been printed and published in England. When it, too, was seized by the Crown, Ellis turned to America; and in 1901 the Philadelphia firm of F. A. Davis issued "The Evolution of Modesty" as vol. 1 of *The Studies*. Later editions have preserved the 1901 order.

4. See especially Jeffrey Weeks, *Sex, Politics and Society: The Regulation of Sexuality since 1800* (London: Longman, 1981), pp. 96–121; and his earlier treatments of the subject in *Coming Out: Homosexual Politics in Britain from the Nineteenth Century to the Present* (London: Quartet Books, 1977); and "Havelock Ellis and the Politics of Sex Reform," in Sheila Rowbotham and Jeffrey Weeks, *Socialism and the New Life: The Personal and Sexual Politics of Edward Carpenter and Havelock Ellis* (London: Pluto Press, 1977), pp. 139–85.

5. For a related discussion of some of these contradictions, see Mary Poovey's shrewd account of "the paradoxes of propriety" in *The Proper Lady and the Woman Writer: Ideology as Style in the Works of Mary Wollstonecraft, Mary Shelley, and Jane Austen* (Chicago: University of Chicago Press, 1984), pp. 15–30.

6. [Richard Allestree?], *The Ladies Calling* (Oxford: n.p., 1673), 1:14, 15. The British Library catalog indicates that there were at least eleven impressions of *The Ladies Calling* between 1673 and 1720; a new edition appeared as late as 1787. Its title page identifies it as "By the Author of the *Whole Duty of Man, The Causes of the Decay of Christian Piety,* and the *Gentlemans Calling.*" Though in what follows I will allude to this author as Allestree, the *Dictionary of National Biography* suggests that there is some evidence he may have had a collaborator in Bishop Fell, his biographer.

7. "Modesty and Bashfulness," *Lady's Monthly Museum* 1 (1798), 42.

8. "On Shamefacedness," *New Lady's Magazine; or, Polite, Useful, and Entertaining Monthly Companion for the Fair Sex* 1 (1786), 27.

9. Hannah More, *Coelebs in Search of a Wife: Comprehending Observations on Domestic Habits and Manners, Religion and Morals,* 2d ed., 2 vols. (London: Cadell & Davies, 1809), 1:189. The first edition of *Coelebs* appeared in 1808.

10. In an early footnote to "The Evolution of Modesty," Ellis notes the confusion that arises from what he calls the "two distinct meanings" of the word in English—a confusion he maintains "it is possible to avoid" in French, "where *modestie* is entirely distinct from *pudeur.*" In the "original form" of the word, according to Ellis, modesty "has no special connection with sex or women, but may rather be considered as a masculine virtue"—and it is this "modesty," interestingly enough, that he associates with the virtue "eulogized" by Mary Wollstonecraft. As for his own study, Ellis concludes: "It is, of course, mainly with *pudeur* that I am here concerned" (*Studies in the Psychology of Sex,* 1–1:7).

Though Ellis's distinctions have their uses, they are, needless to say, overly neat. On some of the problems raised by *pudeur* alone, see Jean Claude Bologne, *Histoire de la pudeur* (Paris: Olivier Orban, 1986). Bologne argues that "l'histoire du sentiment . . . ne reduit pas à celle du mot" and that his is a history of the sentiment—the word *pudeur* having first appeared in France only in the sixteenth century, since when it has most often been used to designate something other than the *pudeur du corps* that is his subject (pp. 16, 12). The history Bologne traces, in other words, is that of the socially agreed-upon border between what one conceals and what one reveals to others—a border that always exists, he argues, but whose placement is largely arbitrary and continually shifting. Such a *pudeur* is, of course, related to the erotic concealment and promise that Rousseau, for instance, tends to signify by the term, but it is not merely sexual, nor is it as clearly identified with women rather than men.

11. Though variants like "pudic" and "pudibond" had some brief currency, by the late seventeenth century, according to the *Oxford English Dictionary,* they had become obsolete. The *OED* does cite later uses for some of the other English variants ("pudency," "pudendous," "pudibund," "pudibundous," "pudibundity," "pudicity," and "pudify"), but only "pudency" has survived into the twentieth century without being labeled as rare or pedantic.

12. "An Essay on Modesty," *Lady's Magazine; or, Entertaining Companion for the Fair Sex* 6 (1775), 377. Future references to this periodical will shorten

the title to the *Lady's Magazine;* the titles of other, less frequently cited, magazines for women will be given more fully in order to make evident the distinction.

13. Thomas Marriott, *Female Conduct: Being an Essay on the Art of Pleasing. To be Practised by the Fair Sex, before, and after Marriage. A Poem, in Two Books* (London: Owen, 1759), pp. 22–23.

14. *The Polite Lady; or, A Course of Female Education. In a Series of Letters, from a Mother to a Daughter* (London: Newbery, 1760), pp. 229, 227–28.

15. Marriott, *Female Conduct,* p. 23; *The Polite Lady,* pp. 223, 224, 229; Marriott, *Female Conduct,* p. 21.

16. Mary Wollstonecraft, *A Vindication of the Rights of Woman,* ed. Carol H. Poston, 2d ed. (New York: Norton, 1988), pp. 121, 126, 78, 125–26, 123. Poston follows the text of the second edition, issued the same year as the first (1792). Among the principal targets of *The Rights of Woman* were Rousseau's *Emile* (1762), Dr. James Fordyce's *Sermons to Young Women* (1765), and Dr. John Gregory's *A Father's Legacy to His Daughters* (1774).

17. Wollstonecraft, *The Rights of Woman,* p. 125.

18. John Armstrong, *The Young Woman's Guide to Virtue, Economy, and Happiness* . . . , 6th ed. (Newcastle upon Tyne: Mackenzie & Dent, [1817?]), quotes "a popular writer" (Gregory) on "indelicacy in conversation" (p. 417) and offers "extracts from a work written on the rights and duties of women" in a discussion of modesty on pp. 435–40. "Maxims and Sentiments, Culled from Various Authors for the Exclusive Benefit of the Fair Sex," *Lady's Magazine; or, Mirror of the Belles-Lettres, Music, Fine Arts, Drama, Fashions, &c.,* n.s. 3 (1822), includes a paraphrase of Gregory on p. 413 ("The finest woman in the world . . . conceal it") and a quotation from Wollstonecraft on p. 414 ("Purity of mind . . . its fairest fruit").

19. Jean-Jacques Rousseau, *Emile ou de l'éducation,* in *Oeuvres complètes de J.-J. Rousseau,* ed. Bernard Gagnebin and Marcel Raymond, Bibliothèque de la Plèiade, 4 vols. (Paris: Gallimard, 1959–69), 4:747: "Her dress is very *modeste* in appearance, very coquettish in effect; she doesn't show off her charms; she covers them, but in covering them, she knows how to make them imagined." (All translations of Rousseau are my own.)

For More's objections to Rousseau, see, e.g., her *Strictures on the Modern System of Female Education: With a View of the Principles and Conduct Prevalent among Women of Rank and Fortune,* 3d ed., 2 vols. (London: Cadell, 1799), 1:32–34. The anti-Jacobin More also, of course, objected fiercely to the "radical" Wollstonecraft—whom she therefore refused to read. For a very helpful discussion of the "female domestic heroism" the two women nonetheless shared, see Mitzi Myers, "Reform or Ruin: 'A Revolution in Female Manners,'" *Studies in Eighteenth-Century Culture,* vol. 11, ed. Harry C. Payne (Madison: University of Wisconsin Press, 1982), 199–216.

20. "It is, at all events, very evident that the eighteenth century witnessed a tremendous narrowing of the ethical scale, a redefinition of virtue in primarily sexual terms. . . . The same tendency can be seen at work on the ethical vocabu-

lary itself: words such as virtue, propriety, decency, modesty, delicacy, purity, came to have the almost exclusively sexual connotation which they have since very largely retained." See Ian Watt, _The Rise of the Novel: Studies in Defoe, Richardson and Fielding_ (1957; reprint, Berkeley: University of California Press, 1967), p. 157.

21. [Richard Steele], _Tatler,_ no. 86, 27 October 1709. All quotations from this work are taken from _The Tatler,_ ed. Donald F. Bond (Oxford: Clarendon, 1987). Future references to this edition are also by the number and date of individual papers.

22. Edmund Leites, _The Puritan Conscience and Modern Sexuality_ (New Haven: Yale University Press, 1986), pp. 71, 72.

23. [Steele], _Tatler,_ no. 52, 6–9 August 1709. Cf. also David Hume's equivocal treatment of the masculine virtue in his "Of Impudence and Modesty" (1741): despite the general rule that "prosperity is naturally, though not necessarily, attached to virtue and merit; and adversity, in like manner, to vice and folly," Hume writes, "I must, however, confess, that this rule admits of an exception with regard to one moral quality, and that modesty has a natural tendency to conceal a man's talents, as impudence displays them to the utmost." See _Essays Moral, Political and Literary_ (London: Oxford University Press, 1963), p. 547.

24. [Steele], _Spectator,_ no. 484, 15 September 1712; [Joseph Addison], _Spectator,_ no. 458, 15 August 1712; [Addison], _Spectator,_ no. 231, 24 November 1711. All citations are to _The Spectator,_ ed. Donald F. Bond (Oxford: Clarendon, 1965). As with the _Tatler,_ future references to this work will be by number and date of individual papers only.

25. For the relation between the language and sentiments of _The Polite Lady,_ pp. 222–24, and _Spectator,_ no. 458, see below, ch. 4, p. 61.

26. See, e.g., "To the Hon. Mrs. Stanhope," _Lady's Magazine; or, Polite Companion for the Fair Sex_ 1 (1760), 253; "Female Virtues" (ch. 11 of "The Friend to the Fair Sex"), _Lady's Magazine_ 5 (1774), 201; and "Maxims and Reflections," _Lady's Magazine_ 6 (1775), 414. The first and last of these discussions of modesty are virtually identical, while the second alters the wording slightly— e.g., by calling it "the most indispensable" rather than "the most necessary" virtue.

27. [Allestree], _The Ladies Calling,_ 1:5. Substantial extracts from Allestree's discussion of modesty appear, among other places, in _The Whole Duty of a Woman; or, A Guide to the Female Sex. From the Age of Sixteen to Sixty, &c._, 3d ed. (London: Guillim, 1701); _The Ladies Library_ (London: 1714); _The Whole Duty of a Woman; or, An Infallible Guide to the Fair Sex_ (London: Read, 1737); and _The Lady's Companion,_ 4th ed. (London: Read, 1743). A brief selection, including the lines quoted, surfaces as an "Essay on Modesty," in _Lady's Magazine; or, Polite Companion_ 6 (1764), 114–15. All of these appeared anonymously, though _The Ladies Library,_ which purports to be "written by a Lady" (or rather "collected" by her "out of the several Writings of our greatest Divines"), was published by Richard Steele. By 1751, the Steele collection was in its sixth edition.

28. Hannah More, *Essays on Various Subjects, Principally Designed for Young Ladies,* 3d ed. (London: Wilkie & Cadell, 1778), pp. 107, 108. More's *Essays* were first published in 1777.

Chapter Two

1. [Robert Gould], *Love Given O're; or, A Satyr against the Pride, Lust, and Inconstancy, &c. of Woman* (London: Andrew Green, 1682), pp. A2, 11, 5–6. A photoreproduction of this work may be found in [Anon.], *Satires on Women (1682, 1687, 1691),* Augustan Reprint Society, publication no. 180 (Los Angeles: Clark Library, 1976).

2. As Felicity A. Nussbaum observes, Robert Gould, the author of *Love Given O're,* also wrote several panegyrics to women as well as a generally misanthropic *Satyr against Man.* See her introduction to *Satires on Women,* p. iii.

3. [Gould], *Love Given O're,* p. 3.

4. [Allestree], *The Ladies Calling,* 1:14–15.

5. Henry Fielding, *Amelia* (1751), ed. Martin C. Battestin (Middletown, Conn.: Wesleyan University Press, 1983), pp. 318–19.

6. "Female Virtues," ch. 11 of "The Friend to the Fair Sex," *Lady's Magazine* 5 (1774), 201.

7. Quotations are extracted from pp. iii–iv, ii–iii, ii, and iv of the preface to *The Ladies Calling;* pages unnumbered in the original.

8. See Norbert Elias's repeated comparisons between the 1729 edition of La Salle's *Les Règles de la bienséance et de la civilité chrétienne,* with its detailed and specific instructions on such matters as the use of the fork or the touching of body parts in public, and the considerably briefer and vaguer exhortations to appropriate behavior in the 1774 edition of the same work, when "much that could be and had to be expressed earlier," as Elias remarks, is "no longer spoken of." *The Civilizing Process,* Vol. 1: *The Development of Manners,* trans. Edmund Jephcott (New York: Urizen Books, 1978), p. 133; originally published in German in 1939.

9. [Allestree], *The Ladies Calling,* 1:3–4.

10. I quote here from [Addison], *Spectator,* no. 81, 2 June 1711. But compare the slightly different translation that appears in Thomas Gisborne, *An Enquiry into the Duties of the Female Sex,* 2d ed. (London: Cadell & Davies, 1797), p. 327; and *The Female Aegis; or, The Duties of Women from Childhood to Old Age . . .* (London: Sampson Low, 1798), p. 122. Published anonymously the year after Gisborne (the first edition of whose work, like the second, appeared in 1797), *The Female Aegis* plagiarized him almost word-for-word, including the citation of Pericles. But either its "author" or its typesetter misread "instinctive" as "instructive" modesty—yet another sign that the advice givers were busy copying one another rather than reading the Greeks.

Cf. also [Richard Polwhele], *The Unsex'd Females: A Poem, Addressed to the Author of the Pursuits of Literature* (London: Cadell & Davies, 1798), p. 30: "that the ancients entertained notions of female delicacy not very dissimilar from our own, may be inferred from the sentiments of Pericles, who 'advises the

Athenian women to aspire only to those virtues that are peculiar to their sex, and to follow their natural modesty.'" Polwhele, who heavily annotates his own poem, here comments on his lines: "Mark, where the sex have oft, in ancient days, / To modest Virtue, claim'd a nation's praise." The "unsex'd females" of Polwhele's poem are Mary Wollstonecraft and her followers; see below, ch. 5, pp. 65–66.

I am grateful to Ann Bergren for interpreting the Greek of Pericles' funeral oration, as recounted in Thucydides, *History of the Peloponnesian War,* Book 2.45.

11. On conduct literature before Allestree, see especially John E. Mason, *Gentlefolk in the Making: Studies in the History of English Courtesy Literature and Related Topics from 1531 to 1774* (Philadelphia: University of Pennsylvania Press, 1935); and Ruth Kelso, *Doctrine for the Lady of the Renaissance,* with a foreword by Katharine M. Rogers (1956; reprint, Urbana: University of Illinois Press, 1978). Though the authors of Renaissance courtesy manuals also appear to have claimed "modesty" as one of the principal virtues for women, they seem generally to have viewed it as a form of self-restraint rather than as a natural "instinct." As Kelso notes, "Most writers assumed . . . that women are naturally libidinous and no less inclined to venery than men" (p. 87). The great bulk of advice literature in the Renaissance, of course, was directed at aristocratic men rather than middle-class women. In their introduction to *The Ideology of Conduct: Essays on Literature and the History of Sexuality,* ed. Nancy Armstrong and Leonard Tennenhouse, (New York: Methuen, 1987), the editors assert that "the triumph of the modern middle classes took place at least in part through the triumph of the female conduct book over courtesy literature." For Armstrong and Tennenhouse, who follow Foucault in arguing that writing does not so much reflect history as make it, "this change in the representation of desire" in turn "produced" the gendered spheres that continue to define modern culture—"the primary difference between 'masculine' and 'feminine' then creating the difference between public and private, work and leisure, economic and domestic, political and aesthetic" (p. 15).

12. More, *Essays . . for Young Ladies,* title page.

13. [Bernard Mandeville], *A Modest Defence of Publick Stews; or, an Essay upon Whoring, as It Is Now Practis'd in These Kingdoms* (London: Moore, 1724), p. 49. The title page simply identifies the *Defence* as "Written by a Layman," but Mandeville's authorship of the pamphlet is now generally accepted.

14. See, e.g., William Edward Hartpole Lecky, *History of European Morals from Augustus to Charlemagne,* 2 vols. (London: Longmans, Green, 1869), 2:299–300, which says of the prostitute: "Herself the supreme type of vice, she is ultimately the most efficient guardian of virtue. But for her, the unchallenged purity of countless happy homes would be polluted. . . . On that one degraded and ignoble form are concentrated the passions that might have filled the world with shame."

15. [Mandeville], *A Modest Defence,* pp. 43–44.

16. Watt, *The Rise of the Novel,* p. 171.

17. John Cleland, *Memoirs of a Woman of Pleasure* (1748–49), ed. with an introduction and notes by Peter Sabor (New York: Oxford University Press, 1985), p. 79.

18. Rousseau, *Lettre à M. d'Alembert sur son article Genève* (Paris: Garnier-Flammerion, 1967), p. 172; Sigmund Freud, *New Introductory Lectures on Psycho-Analysis* (1933), in *The Standard Edition of the Complete Psychological Works of Sigmund Freud*, ed. and trans. James Strachey et al., 24 vols. (London: Hogarth Press and Institute of Psycho-Analysis, 1953–74), 22:132.

19. Bernard Mandeville, *The Fable of the Bees; or, Private Vices, Publick Benefits*, with a Commentary Critical, Historical, and Explanatory by F. B. Kaye, 2 vols. (Oxford: Clarendon, 1924), 1:65, 71–72. Though *The Fable* first appeared in 1714, the Clarendon follows the edition of 1732, the last issued during Mandeville's lifetime.

20. [Mandeville], *A Modest Defence*, pp. 42, 41, 42, 43, 45, 47.

21. Mandeville, *The Fable of the Bees*, 1:70, 71.

22. Ibid., pp. 70–71.

23. David Hume, *A Treatise of Human Nature* (1739), ed. L. A. Selby-Bigge (Oxford: Clarendon, 1967), 3:570.

24. Ibid., pp. 570–71.

25. Ibid., p. 571.

26. Ibid., pp. 571, 572.

27. Ibid., p. 573.

28. In the anthropologists' terms, the line in question defines gender rather than sex: it marks the division between culturally constructed maleness and femaleness, that is, not the biological difference of bodies. While there is widespread agreement that the distinctions of gender are in some measure arbitrary, that measure is much disputed. In their introduction to *Sexual Meanings: The Cultural Construction of Gender and Sexuality* (Cambridge: Cambridge University Press, 1981), Sherry B. Ortner and Harriet Whitehead assert that the majority of known cultures, though not all, conceptualize the differences between men and women as "sets of metaphorically associated binary oppositions" (p. 7); the essays collected by Ortner and Whitehead take up the varying ways that gender and sexuality have been constructed in a number of "simple" cultures. For further discussion of some of the issues involved, see Edwin Ardener, "Belief and the Problem of Women" (1972) and "The Problem of Women Revisited," in *Perceiving Women*, ed. Shirley Ardener (London: Malaby, 1975), pp. 1–28; Sherry B. Ortner, "Is Female to Male as Nature Is to Culture?" in *Women, Culture, and Society*, ed. Michelle Z. Rosaldo and Louise Lamphere (Stanford: Stanford University Press, 1974), pp. 67–87; and the essays gathered in *Nature, Culture and Gender*, ed. Carol MacCormack and Marilyn Strathern (Cambridge: Cambridge University Press, 1980), most of which engage Ardener's and Ortner's arguments. The work of Claude Lévi-Strauss has, of course, broadly influenced this line of symbolic anthropology.

29. See Mary Douglas, *Purity and Danger: An Analysis of Concepts of Pollu-

tion and Taboo (London: Routledge, 1966), and the chapter entitled "Pollution," in her *Implicit Meanings: Essays in Anthropology* (London: Routledge, 1975), pp. 47–59. In their introduction to *The Nineteenth-Century Woman: Her Cultural and Physical World* (London: Croom Helm, 1978), Sara Delamont and Lorna Duffin suggest that Douglas's work provides a useful frame for understanding the stress on gender classification and the various "pollution ideas" surrounding gender in nineteenth-century England.

30. John Bowles, *Remarks on Modern Female Manners, as Distinguished by Indifference to Character and Indecency of Dress* (London: Rivington, 1802), p. 12.

31. Rousseau, *Lettre à M. D'Alembert*, p. 171.

32. Ibid., pp. 166–67. In *The Rights of Woman*, Wollstonecraft quotes and responds to *Emile*'s account of "the life of a modest woman" as "a perpetual conflict with herself" (p. 82); Wollstonecraft's "modest woman" here is Rousseau's "l'honnête femme" (*Emile*, p. 709).

33. Rousseau, *Lettre*, pp. 236, 237, 239–40.

34. Ibid., pp. 168–69, 168.

35. Ibid., pp. 169, 170.

36. Guetti also remarks what she calls Rousseau's "verbal embarrassment" here and observes that "it is impossible to distinguish between decorous circumlocution and deliberate irony when Rousseau employs this vocabulary of 'victory' and 'defeat' with reference to what he is in fact discussing—the possibility of masculine impotence." See Barbara Guetti, "The Old Régime and the Feminist Revolution: Laclos' 'De l'Éducation des femmes,'" *Yale French Studies* 63 (1982), 153.

37. Rousseau, *Lettre*, p. 170. Cf. *Emile:* "If woman is made to please and to be subjugated, she ought to make herself agreeable to man instead of making advances to him: her own violence is in her charms; it is by these that she ought to compel him to find his strength and make use of it. The surest art for animating that strength is to make it necessary by resistance. Then self-respect joins with desire, and the one triumphs in the victory that the other has made him win. From this there arise attack and defense, the audacity of one sex and the timidity of the other, and finally the *modestie* and the shame with which nature armed the weak in order to subdue the strong" (pp. 693–94). Note how woman's weakness characteristically proves a secret strength and her resistance just another way of advancing—how female modesty both generates and sustains the erotic plot. Mary Wollstonecraft would understandably attack "this ingenious passage" for its "philosophy of lasciviousness"; indeed, she quotes and denounces it twice (*The Rights of Woman*, pp. 48n, 78.)

38. Rousseau, *Emile*, p. 694.

39. Rousseau, *Lettre*, pp. 174–75. When he records how the male pigeon "se défend" from her advances, Rousseau seems momentarily to have forgotten that Nature by his account assigned that verb to women ("qu'elle destinait à se défendre"—p. 170).

40. Cf. Jonas Barish's similar observations on the sexual aggressiveness of

Rousseau's female pigeon in *The Anti-Theatrical Prejudice* (Berkeley: University of California Press, 1981), pp. 285–86.

41. Rousseau, *Emile*, pp. 694, 695. Cf. Havelock Ellis, *Studies*, 1–1:39. Though Rousseau necessarily lacked the Darwinian language available to Ellis, something like the temporal dimensions of an evolutionary narrative could, in fact, help to clarify his otherwise contradictory account of a Nature that supplements Nature: as an evolutionary theorist, in other words, Rousseau could have argued that female modesty slowly developed as nature's way of checking a desire hitherto naturally boundless. To accept a nature in the process of evolution, however, Rousseau would have been forced to admit into his world far more chanciness and imperfection of design than he seems prepared to tolerate.

42. Rousseau, *Emile*, p. 695.

43. Rousseau, *Lettre*, p. 173. The passage from *Emile* quoted in ch. 1, n. 19 above continues: "In seeing her, one says: 'Here is a young girl, *modeste* and discreet'; but as long as one remains near her, his eyes and his heart wander over her whole person without his being able to remove them; and one would say that all this very simple attire was put on only in order to be taken off piece by piece by the imagination" (p. 747).

44. Rousseau, *Lettre*, pp. 176–77. Cf. Montesquieu, whose brief treatment "Of Natural Modesty" [*la Pudeur*] in *The Spirit of the Laws* (1748) anticipates this paradoxical turn: "All nations are equally agreed in fixing contempt and ignominy on the incontinence of women. Nature has dictated this to all. . . . It is then far from being true, that to be incontinent is to follow the laws of nature; since this is, on the contrary, a violation of these laws, which can be followed only by modesty [*la modestie*] and discretion. . . . When therefore the physical power of certain climates violates the natural law of the two sexes, and that of intelligent beings, it belongs to the legislature to make civil laws, to oppose the nature of the climate, and to re-establish primitive laws." Montesquieu is oddly reticent about the immodest climates in question, but like Rousseau's, they are presumably hot. Note that when the idea of "natural" modesty is combined with the metonymic definition of immodesty as excessive "warmth," it produces the paradox that the nature of some climates is to violate "nature"— and that civil laws must be introduced to reestablish natural ones. Rousseau must have known Montesquieu's account, though there is no evidence that he deliberately intends to recall it. I quote from the first English translation of *The Spirit of the Laws*, published in two volumes by J. Nourse and P. Vaillant in 1750, 1:369.

45. Rousseau, *Lettre*, p. 172.

46. Ibid., p. 175.

47. See Susan Moller Okin, *Women in Western Political Thought* (Princeton: Princeton University Press, 1979), p. 122.

48. Rousseau, *Lettre*, p. 171. Somewhat more obliquely, *Emile* also offers a social explanation of modesty, when it evokes the "frightful state" of the man who doubts his wife's honor and thus cannot be sure that his own offspring will

inherit his property (p. 698). Mary Poovey uses this passage to argue that the defense of male property rights was among the most fundamental causes of the extreme pressure brought to bear on female propriety in the period. See *The Proper Lady*, pp. 5–15.

Chapter Three

1. [Anon.], "The Bachelor's Choice," *Lady's Magazine* 35 (1804), 157–58.
2. Rousseau, *Emile*, pp. 862, 865–66.
3. See Pierre Burgelin, "L'Éducation de Sophie," *Annales de la Société Jean-Jacques Rousseau* 35 (1959–62), esp. 123–30. As Burgelin observes, *Emile*'s attitude toward marriage departs not only from the dominant strain of Continental literature ("qui oppose amour et mariage") but from Rousseau's own assumptions in *La Nouvelle Héloïse* (p. 126). When Sophie reads Fénelon's *Télémaque*, she identifies not with Antiope, the chaste future wife, but with the amorous nymph, Eucharis. "Certes la passion pour Eucharis n'est pas compatible avec les sentiments pour Antiope," Burgelin remarks. "Mais comme Emile doit être l'homme d'une seule femme, son éducation ne sera complète que si Eucharis est en même temps Antiope. C'est la synthèse paradoxale que Rousseau tente en la personne de Sophie, qui doit être à la fois objet amoureux et épouse" (p. 128). Cf. also pp. cxxv–cxxvii of Burgelin's introduction to *Emile* and *Les Solitaires* in the Pléiade edition of Rousseau cited throughout.
4. Rousseau, *Emile*, p. 860.
5. The claim that most people did not marry for long-term personal affection until the latter half of the seventeenth century has been put most baldly and controversially by Lawrence Stone in *The Family, Sex and Marriage in England, 1500–1800* (New York: Harper & Row, 1977). In the sixteenth century and earlier, according to Stone, mates were typically selected "by parents, kin and 'friends,' rather than by the bride and groom" (p. 5), and choices were motivated chiefly by the economic or status advantage of the lineage as a whole rather than by individual feeling. Stone traces the origins of "the modern family"—with its strong emphasis on personal feeling, privacy, and autonomy and its intense bonding "at the nuclear core" (p. 8)—to the period between 1640 and 1750 and the rise of what he calls "Affective Individualism." Though Stone sometimes acknowledges that his evidence is severely limited at best, his habit of sweeping and careless generalization (e.g., "only a handful of children resisted parental dictation [of a marriage partner] before the end of the sixteenth century, and their rebellion was soon crushed"—p. 183), his tendency to ride over class distinctions in favor of the upper bourgeoisie, and his complacent teleology have all been deservedly criticized. For a witty summary of some of the major weaknesses in Stone's account, see E. P. Thompson, "Happy Families," *Radical History Review* 20 (1979), 42–50. Cf. also Steven Ozment, *When Fathers Ruled: Family Life in Reformation Europe* (Cambridge: Harvard University Press, 1983), which relies chiefly on sixteenth-century German and Swiss sources to defend the affective life of the early modern family; and John R. Gillis, *For Better, for Worse: British Marriages, 1600 to the Present* (New York:

Oxford University Press, 1985), which focuses on the popular English history that Stone slights and significantly challenges the latter's monolithic account of "*the* family." For most people, Gillis argues, "the conjugal has always been more an illusive dream than an attainable reality" (p. 5). In *The Rise of the Egalitarian Family: Aristocratic Kinship and Domestic Relations in Eighteenth-Century England* (New York: Academic Press, 1978), on the other hand, Randolph Trumbach argues for a shift toward romantic and companionate rather than arranged marriages in eighteenth-century England, but he confines his argument to the aristocracy.

Despite these sharp differences, most commentators seem to agree that there was at least an increase of middle- and upper-class rhetoric about conjugal love and the wise choice of a mate in the eighteenth century, much of it in turn strongly influenced by Puritan conceptions of marriage. In addition to the above, see especially Watt, *The Rise of the Novel*, pp. 135–73; Christopher Lasch, "The Suppression of Clandestine Marriage in England: The Marriage Act of 1753," *Salmagundi* 26 (1974), 90–109; Jean H. Hagstrum, *Sex and Sensibility: Ideal and Erotic Love from Milton to Mozart* (Chicago: University of Chicago Press, 1980); Leites, *The Puritan Conscience and Modern Sexuality*, pp. 75–162; and Joseph Allen Boone, *Tradition Counter Tradition: Love and the Form of Fiction* (Chicago: University of Chicago Press, 1987), pp. 31–64.

6. [Steele], *Spectator*, no. 479, 9 September 1712. Cf. also [Thomas Salmon], *A Critical Essay Concerning Marriage* (1724; reprint, New York: Garland, 1985), especially his opening chapter on "Marriage Preferable to a Single State." While Salmon addresses both sexes, he implicitly recognizes that to argue against celibacy is also to argue against a long misogynist tradition: to persuade his male readers of the desirability of marriage, in other words, he needs simultaneously to raise their estimation of women. "The Design of these Papers is principally to shew," he announces in his dedication, "how aptly they are formed, to give us all that Joy that Heaven first proposed in their Creation, and vindicate them from the Aspersions that are thrown on them by the looser World, and made a Pretence for not entering into the married State" (p. iv, no pagination in the original). In the body of the text he argues, for example, that women are capable of "real Friendship" (p. 18) and thus of proving genuine helpmeets. Though Salmon's deliberate effort to improve men's view of women recalls Allestree's, it is worth noting that the earlier writer seems less inclined to assume that the virtuous woman should find her fulfillment in marriage: even as *The Ladies Calling* already acknowledges the growing pressure to marry by remarking that "an old maid is now . . . lookt on as the most calamitous creature in nature," it still expresses a certain wistfulness for the "voluntary Virginity" of the Roman Catholic nunneries (2:3).

7. [John Hughes], *Spectator*, no. 525, 1 November 1712; [Steele], *Spectator*, no. 490, 22 September 1712.

In setting out these "Discourses on Marriage," the *Spectator* was also engaged in a struggle of literary representations—an effort to counter the cynical picture of marriage in Restoration comedy and satire (when "a State of Wedlock was the common Mark of all the Adventurers in Farce and Comedy, as well as the Essayers in Lampoon and Satyr, to shoot at," as no. 525 complains) with an image of domestic happiness drawn largely from *Paradise Lost.* For the *Spectator,* as for much of the conduct literature that followed, Milton's lovers became the ideal conjugal pair, and his sweet, reluctant, amorously delaying Eve, the type of the modest woman. When it comes to "that natural Modesty in the Sex, which renders a Retreat from the first Approaches of a Lover both fashionable and graceful," Addison "would propose the Example of *Eve* to all her Daughters"—at least as Milton has represented her in the passage that begins with her "Innocence and Virgin Modesty" and ends with her "blushing like the Morn." (The practical rule that seems to follow from Eve's example, incidentally, is that while a "Virtuous Woman" should never play the coquette, she should always reject the first offer of marriage; see no. 89, 12 June 1711.) When Hannah More's Coelebs goes in search of a wife a century later, he finds a woman who cites Addison on Milton, and considers the innocent Eve "the most beautiful model of the delicacy, propriety, grace, and elegance of the female character which any poet ever exhibited"—thereby proving herself the ideal mate. "If any thing had been wanting to my full assurance of the sympathy of our tastes and feelings, this would have completed my conviction," Coelebs reports. "Our mutual admiration of the Paradise Lost, and of its heroine, seemed to bring us nearer together than we had yet been" (*Coelebs,* 2:285, 286). For a useful discussion of Milton's "portrayal of marriage as a joyous heterosexual friendship" and its powerful influence on eighteenth-century representations of the subject, see Hagstrum, *Sex and Sensibility,* pp. 24–49.

8. Rousseau, *Emile,* p. 825. The copy of *le Spectateur* belongs originally to Emile, but on the eve of his travels the lovers are instructed to exchange books: in return for Addison and Steele, Sophie is to give him her beloved *Télémaque,* so that her future husband can learn to resemble its hero. The *Spectator* had been translated into French in 1714, and Rousseau had known it since his youth.

9. [Addison], *Spectator,* no. 261, 29 December 1711; [Steele], *Spectator,* no. 479, 9 September 1712.

10. Rousseau, *Emile,* p. 822.

11. [Addison], *Spectator,* no. 261, 29 December 1711.

12. [Edward Moore], *Fables for the Female Sex* (London: Francklin, 1744), p. 31. According to Lawrence Stone, by 1660 the child's right to reject a parent's choice was generally conceded "in all but the highest ranks of the aristocracy." Between 1660 and 1800, he argues, the initiative shifted decisively to the children, with the parents retaining only the right of veto (*The Family, Sex and Marriage,* p. 272). The passage of Lord Hardwicke's Marriage Act of 1753 might seem to contradict this trend: by making marriages of persons under twenty-one illegal without the consent of their fathers or guardians, outlawing so-called clandestine marriages (those made in the absence of witnesses), and depriving the ecclesiastical courts of the power to enforce precontracts (the

practice of treating an engagement to marry, especially if followed by sexual intercourse, as binding on the parties), the act clearly sought to make it more difficult for young people to follow their own impulses. But as Christopher Lasch has shown, those who supported the act were not so much contending against love as for time to deliberate and in which to get acquainted: marriage should represent "a sedate and fixed love," in the words of one of the proponents, not "a sudden flash of passion which dazzles the understanding, but is in a moment extinguished" ("The Suppression of Clandestine Marriage," p. 100). The act, in other words, was another manifestation of the middle-class and Protestant effort to combine love and prudence that I have been associating with the paradoxical rhetoric of modesty. For a helpful analysis of the Parliamentary debates over the act and of the conservative function of the ideology of virtuous love, see Erica Harth, "The Virtue of Love: Lord Hardwicke's Marriage Act," *Cultural Critique* 9 (1988), 123–54. On aristocratic support of the act (and of marriages made for love, but slowly), see also Trumbach, *The Rise of the Egalitarian Family,* pp. 107–17.

13. [Allestree], *The Ladies Calling,* 2:20.

14. [Salmon], *A Critical Essay Concerning Marriage,* pp. 68, 69, 67.

15. Daniel Defoe, *Conjugal Lewdness; or, Matrimonial Whoredom. A Treatise Concerning the Use and Abuse of the Marriage Bed* (1727; reprint with an introduction by Maximillian E. Novak, Gainesville, Fla.: Scholars' Facsimiles & Reprints, 1967), p. 166.

16. The very fact that so much advice on courtship and marriage in the eighteenth century *is* addressed to daughters marks a significant shift from earlier periods. In the Renaissance, according to Ruth Kelso, "advice on the kind of husband to look for was usually addressed to fathers, in whose hands lay complete power over the disposal of their daughters" (*Doctrine for the Lady of the Renaissance,* p. 92). Unlike the largely middle-class advice literature of the eighteenth and nineteenth centuries, of course, the Renaissance texts were principally addressed to an aristocratic audience.

17. Rousseau, *Emile,* pp. 754, 755–56. An English translation of the speech of Sophie's father appeared under the title "Advice from a Father to a Daughter Concerning the Choice of a Husband" in *Lady's Magazine* 8 (1777), 182–83.

18. Rousseau, *Emile,* p. 695.

19. Ibid., p. 758.

20. Ibid., pp. 746, 739.

21. Ibid., pp. 739–40.

22. "Peculiarities Respecting the Education of Females. Extracted from *Loose Thoughts upon Education,* by Lord Kamis," *Lady's Magazine* 13 (1782), 396. On the basis of this article at least, Lord Kames's "loose thoughts" would appear to have been more or less loosely adapted from Rousseau.

23. John Andrews, *Remarks on the French and English Ladies, in a Series of Letters; Interspersed with Various Anecdotes, and Additional Matter, Arising from the Subject* (London: Longman & Robinson, 1783), pp. 86, 254, 67, 66.

The opposition between the free-and-modest English and the constrained-and-immodest French had obviously become a set piece for commentators on both sides of the Channel. But it is worth noting how the late-seventeenth-century French moralist, the Marchioness de Lambert, praised the courtship practices of her own country at the expense of the Spaniards and Italians by means of a remarkably similar contrast, a contrast, of course, that necessarily made nothing of religious differences. Having first declared that the women of France are "allowed a great Liberty . . . and are restrained by no other Checks than their own innate Modesty, and the Laws of Decorum," she goes on to explain how this combination of freedom and modesty works to produce a genuine art of love. "'Tis from the Desires and Designs of Men, and from the Shyness and Modesty of Women," she asserts, "that results that delicate Commerce which polishes the Mind, and purifies the Heart; for Love improves a virtuous Soul. And it must be confessed that the *French* are the only Nation that have refined Love into a delicate Art. The *Spaniards* and *Italians* are utter Strangers to the real Joys of this Passion; as most of their Women, are immured, as it were, in their Houses; the Men bend their whole Application to the surmounting of exterior Obstacles; and when once these are removed, they meet with none in the Object beloved: But Love so easily obtained, can have but very few Charms; and it seems to be the work of Nature, not that of the Lover. In *France,* a much better Use is made of Time; as the Heart bears a Part in these Engagements." Among the Spanish women, she later goes on to say that "the Moment a Passion is satisfied, it dies away." Unlike most English and Protestant versions of this argument, however, de Lambert's speaks of love without linking it to marriage.

Anne-Thérèse de Lambert's *Avis d'une mère à sa fille* was first published in 1698. I quote from "The Advice of a Mother to Her Daughter," in *The Works of the Marchioness de Lambert,* 2d ed. (London: William Owen, 1756), pp. 164, 165. The earliest English translation now in the British Library appeared in 1729; the latest in 1885.

24. François de La Rochefoucauld, *La Vie en Angleterre au XVIII siècle ou mélanges sur l'Angleterre* (1784), texte original publié par Jean Marchand (Paris: Guy La Prat, 1945), pp. 80, 79. The translation is my own.

25. See, e.g., J. Hajnal, "European Marriage Patterns in Perspective," in *Population in History: Essays in Historical Demography,* ed. D. V. Glass and D. E. C. Eversley (London: Edward Arnold, 1965), p. 115; Lasch, "The Suppression of Clandestine Marriage," p. 103 (citing Hajnal); Jean-Louis Flandrin, *Families in Former Times: Kinship, Household and Sexuality,* trans. Richard Southern (Cambridge: Cambridge University Press, 1979), pp. 168–69; and Stone, *The Family, Sex and Marriage,* pp. 318, 329, 521–22, where the young aristocrat appears to be confused with his seventeenth-century ancestor, the author of the celebrated *Maxims.* Stone himself further complicates the picture when he suggests elsewhere in his book that late-eighteenth-century France also had its "intensive propaganda" in favor of "free marriage choice, marital love" and "sexual fulfillment within marriage," but that there remained "a yawning gap" between

French theory and practice (p. 390)—a gap that he apparently does not find on the other side of the Channel. Of all the historians cited here, only Hajnal takes care to characterize La Rochefoucauld's view of English marriage as "charmingly romantic" ("European Marriage Patterns," p. 115).

26. Dr. [John] Gregory, *A Father's Legacy to His Daughters* (London: Strahan & Cadell, 1774), p. 103. Though this immensely popular work was first published in 1774, the text quoted here announces itself as a "new edition." To judge by the frequency with which it was reprinted and plagiarized, especially in the fifty years after its initial publication, *A Father's Legacy* appears to have had much of the same currency for the late eighteenth and the nineteenth centuries that *The Ladies Calling* had for the late seventeenth and eighteenth. The British Library has close to thirty subsequent editions of the *Legacy*, the last issued in 1877.

27. Gregory, *A Father's Legacy*, p. 67. "Though a woman has no reason to be ashamed of an attachment to a man of merit," he explains, "yet nature, whose authority is superior to philosophy, has annexed a sense of shame to it."

28. Gregory, *A Father's Legacy*, pp. 82–83. Other conduct books and magazines frequently repeated Gregory's advice, usually without attribution. For the passage cited, see, e.g., *The New Female Instructor; or, Young Woman's Guide to Domestic Happiness* . . . (London: Thos. Kelly, 1824), p. 57; and *The Female Instructor; or, Young Woman's Friend & Companion* . . . (London: Henry Fisher, Son, & P. Jackson: 1830), p. 179, both published anonymously.

29. Gregory, *A Father's Legacy*, pp. 105, 126, 114.

30. Ibid., pp. 113, 112–13.

31. Ibid., pp. 35, 43, 37, 29–30. Similar sentiments, sometimes repeated word-for-word, can be found in [Anon.], *The Female Instructor; or, Young Woman's Companion* . . . (Liverpool: Nuttall, Fisher, & Dixon, 1815), pp. 112–14; *The New Female Instructor* (1824), p. 19; and Armstrong, *The Young Woman's Guide to Virtue, Economy, and Happiness* (c. 1817), p. 417.

32. John Bennett, *Letters to a Young Lady, on a Variety of Useful and Interesting Subjects, Calculated to Improve the Heart, to Form the Manners, and Enlighten the Understanding*, 2 vols. (Warrington: The Author, 1789), 2:43, 77, 44.

33. See Gisborne, *An Enquiry into the Duties of the Female Sex*, pp. 92–98, 225–26. Though Gisborne does not make the familiar allusion to the dangerous way in which the convent-raised *jeune fille* is abruptly introduced into society on the Continent, he severely criticizes those parents who permit their daughters to "step from the nursery and the lecture-room" and "plunge at once into a flood of vanity and dissipation" (p. 93). In order to minimize the risks, he advises, the proper introduction of a young woman into the world should be a very gradual process. "To accustom the mind by degrees to the trials which it must learn to withstand, yet to shelter it from insidious temptations . . . is the first rule which wisdom suggests with regard to all trials and temptations whatever," he argues; and "to this rule too much attention cannot be paid in the mode of introducing a young woman into the common habits of social intercourse" (p. 95). The same advice also appears without attribution in *The Female*

Aegis (1798), p. 34; *The Female Instructor; or, Young Woman's Companion* (1815), p. 166; and *The Female Instructor; or, Young Woman's Friend & Companion* (1830), p. 166.

    34. Bennett, *Letters,* 2:160.

    35. [Allestree], *The Ladies Calling,* 1:19.

    36. James Fordyce, *Sermons to Young Women, in Two Volumes,* 3d ed. (London: Millar et al., 1766), 1:107; [Anon.] *The Young Lady's Book of Advice and Instruction* (Glasgow: W. R. M'Phun, 1859), p. 29. The first edition of Fordyce's *Sermons* was published in 1765. Since Fordyce also warns "young ladies" against making the "sight of their beauty" too "cheap," *The Young Lady's Book* may have inherited its Allestree by way of Fordyce. Other passages on modesty in *The Young Lady's Book* are lifted freely from Gregory.

    37. *Lady's Magazine* 24 (1793), 264; 49 (1818), 279.

    38. [Moore], *Fables,* pp. 62–63, 61.

    39. Gregory, *A Father's Legacy,* p. 56.

    40. Fordyce's *Sermons* also argued that "Modest Apparel" was a "powerful attractive to Honourable love," at least partly because it stimulated the male imagination. "We are never highly delighted," he observed, "where something is not left us to fancy." Unlike the others, however, Fordyce seems to have realized that this was a rather dubious stance for an advocate of Nature; and in the comments that immediately followed he sought to forestall the contradiction, contending with magisterial vagueness that Art is "agreeable no farther than as it is conformed to Nature" and that "the one will not be wanted in the case before us, if the other be allowed its full influence." If a young woman is "deeply possessed" of the right values, Fordyce maintained, "it will lead to decorum spontaneously" (1:53, 55).

    41. Marriott, *Female Conduct,* p. 62.

    42. [Hughes], *Spectator,* no. 525, 1 November 1712.

    43. William Cobbett, *Advice to Young Men, and (Incidentally) to Young Women, in the Middle and Higher Ranks of Life* . . . (London: Mills, Jowett, & Mills, 1829), letter 3, para. 90, 100.

    44. Rousseau, *Emile,* pp. 751, 752. Rousseau never actually specifies Sophie's nationality: in a note to this passage, the editor speculates that she is probably "genevoise" (p. 1657).

    45. Ibid., p. 782.

    46. Ibid., p. 821.

    47. [Addison], *Spectator,* no. 261, 29 December 1711.

Chapter Four

    1. [Allestree], *The Ladies Calling,* 2:6.

    2. Ibid., 2:7.

    3. [George Savile, Marquis of Halifax], *The Lady's New-Years Gift; or, Advice to a Daughter* (London: Randal Taylor, 1688), pp. 35, 37. Even while delivering this relatively blunt advice, it should be said, Halifax manages to surround the issue with a certain modest vagueness, alluding only to that which is "in the

utmost degree *Criminal* in the *Woman*," and "which in a *Man* passeth under a much *gentler* Censure" (p. 33). "Next to the Danger of *committing* the Fault yourself," Halifax instructs his daughter, "the greatest is that of *seeing* it in your *Husband*" (p. 35).

4. Gregory, *A Father's Legacy,* pp. 36, 35.

5. [Steele], *Tatler,* no. 126, 28 January 1709.

6. [Addison], *Spectator,* no. 231, 24 November 1711. For other appearances of this topos, in addition to the passages cited from John Bennett below, see, e.g., The Rev. Mr. Wetenhall Wilkes, *A Letter of Genteel and Moral Advice to a Young Lady: Being a System of Rules and Informations; Digested into a New and Familiar Method to Qualify the Fair Sex to Be Useful and Happy in Every Scene of Life* (1740), 7th ed. (London: Hitch & Hawes, 1760), p. 101; *Lady's Magazine* 6 (1775), 378, and 13 (1782), 419; More, *Strictures on . . . Female Education* (1799), 2:40; and Bowles, *Remarks on Female Manners* (1802), p. 10. Wilkes repeats Addison almost word-for-word, but changes "Modesty" to "Chastity" (as he does again when he later incorporates passages from Allestree), going on to call this "quick and delicate Feeling in the Soul" a "great . . . Check to loose Thoughts," and to distinguish it from "an affected Modesty." The first piece in the *Lady's Magazine* ("An Essay on Modesty") quotes the *Spectator* directly, but only the second ("Essay V."), which paraphrases, names the source. Though the first of these essays, like the *Spectator,* largely draws its examples from the behavior of men, it ends with a verse "panegyric" to a modesty unmistakably feminized—a "thrice humble, lovely maid" with "virgin cheeks," etc. (p. 379, misnumbered 376). More argues that women are led "instinctively to shrink from all those irregularities to which the loss of character is so much expected to be attached"; while Bowles writes, with characteristic hyperbole, of "that nice and extreme sensibility, which instinctively shrinks from whatever can give the smallest offence to the most refined delicacy."

7. Bennett, *Letters to a Young Lady,* 2:43, 44.

8. Ibid., 2:77, 78.

9. Ibid., 2:79.

10. "Effects of Mistaken Synonymy," *Lady's Monthly Museum* 1 (1798), 42, 43. Signed "M.," this essay professes to be the work of a woman. By "mistaken synonymy" she seems to mean the confusion of words that are closely allied but which in fact signify quite differently: she instances "Meekness and Servility—Pride and true Dignity—Superstition and Piety—Modesty and Bashfulness." But "the first . . . that strikes me as peculiarly adapted to the notice of my sex," in her words, is—inevitably—"Modesty and Bashfulness" (p. 41).

11. Mrs. Wilmot Serres, *Olivia's Letter of Advice to Her Daughter* (London: Dean, 1808), p. 19. No sooner does Serres evoke a woman's need to protect herself from "the attacks of the Libertine," however, than the "mind naturally Pure" appears to manifest a certain aggressive consciousness: "for one glance from the eye of Modesty and real Virtue, will subdue even the most determined Seducer" (pp. 19–20).

12. Cobbett, *Advice to Young Men,* letter 3, para. 90.

13. Cf. Nancy F. Cott, "Passionlessness: An Interpretation of Victorian Sexual Ideology, 1790–1850," *Signs* 4 (1978), 219–36, which associates the belief that women lacked sexual feeling with the rise of Evangelical religion between the 1790s and 1830s, and speculates that the idea arose out of Evangelical efforts to reconcile the virtue of female modesty with that of sincerity. Cott focuses chiefly on America, but most of the prescriptive works she discusses are necessarily British. In the etiquette manuals of Halifax or Gregory, she argues, modesty was still largely a matter of "manipulated and affected tactics," of "demure behavior" rather than lack of feeling, while for the Evangelicals, "if women were to act modest and sexually passive, and also act without affectation, then, logically, they must be passionless" (pp. 224, 226). Though Cott is undoubtedly right to stress the contribution of the Evangelicals, she markedly oversimplifies the representations of modesty that appear in the earlier etiquette manuals and in Rousseau, ignoring the degree to which they already tend to internalize the virtue, even as she overlooks the degree to which the ambiguities of true and false modesty persist in Evangelical writers like Gisborne and More. I would argue that it was enough to imagine women unconscious of their feelings to believe their modesty "sincere"—and that such unconsciousness came closer to characterizing the ideal of most advice literature and fiction of the period than did "passionlessness," strictly speaking. But Cott's general account of the effort to reconcile modesty and sincerity is very helpful, and her speculations as to why women might have found themselves subscribing to Victorian sexual ideology are invaluable.

14. Cobbett nonetheless repeats this disconcerting tendency to associate the desirable woman with a wooden object when he writes of the young woman who would in fact become his wife: "from the day that I first spoke to her, I never had a thought of her ever being the wife of any other man, more than I had a thought of her being transformed into a chest of drawers" (*Advice to Young Men,* letter 3, para. 95). Given the proprietary claim the sentence makes, its hypothetical identification of a wife and an article of furniture is perhaps not so surprising.

15. See Cobbett, *Advice to Young Men,* letter 3, para. 100, and ch. 3 above, pp. 48–49.

16. Cobbett, *Advice to Young Men,* letter 3, para. 90.

17. Mrs. [Sarah Stickney] Ellis, *The Daughters of England, Their Position in Society, Character & Responsibilities* (London: Fisher, Son & Co., 1842), p. 347.

18. Wollstonecraft, *The Rights of Woman,* p. 63.

19. "Letter to Mrs. Stanhope," *Lady's Magazine; or, Polite Companion for the Fair Sex* 1 (1759), 16, 17. Almost half a century later, "Elenora's" letter was simply given a new date and title ("On Modesty") and reprinted in the *Lady's Magazine* 33 (1802), 619–20.

20. On the Marriage Act of 1753, see Lasch, "The Suppression of Clandestine Marriage in England," and ch. 3, n. 12, above.

21. *Lady's Magazine; or, Polite Companion* 1 (1759), 17.

22. Ibid.

23. *The Polite Lady,* pp. 219, 222–23, 223.

24. Ibid., p. 224.

25. [Addison], *Spectator,* no. 458, 15 August 1712. The falsely modest young gentleman with whom this essay begins, incidentally, "had not the Confidence to refuse his Glass in his Turn"—and consequently ended by drunkenly abusing the rest of the company, even flinging a bottle at the head of the man who had treated him. Though Addison did not necessarily intend his subsequent analysis of true and false modesty to apply exclusively to men—"this false kind of Modesty," he says of the drunken gentleman, "has, perhaps, betrayed both Sexes into as many Vices as the most abandoned Impudence"—the rest of the essay alludes consistently to "Man" and "Men" and draws all its examples from scenes of masculine life. What Addison called "false Modesty," *The Polite Lady'*s paraphrase calls "sheepishness."

26. *The Polite Lady,* pp. 225, 223, 222; Gregory, *A Father's Legacy,* p. 28.

27. Wollstonecraft, *The Rights of Woman,* pp. 121, 125, 126.

28. Ibid., pp. 89, 21, 131, 122–23, 123, 124. Cf. Mitzi Myers's account of the resemblances between Wollstonecraft and Hannah More, both of whom "preach," as Myers wittily remarks, "a genuine upward mobility—that of the soul" ("Reform or Ruin," p. 205).

29. Wollstonecraft, *The Rights of Woman,* pp. 15, 26.

30. Ibid., pp. 73, 89, 27, 30, 73.

31. Ibid., p. 12.

32. See Poovey, *The Proper Lady,* pp. 71–81, especially her subtle account of how Wollstonecraft's allusion to the union of Sin and Death effectively turns Milton's rape victim into the sexual aggressor (pp. 75–76); and Cora Kaplan, "Wild Nights: Pleasure/Sexuality/Feminism," in *The Ideology of Conduct,* ed. Armstrong and Tennenhouse, pp. 160–84. "Women's reason may be the psychic heroine of *A Vindication,"* in Kaplan's words, "but its gothic villain, a polymorphous perverse sexuality, creeping out of every paragraph and worming its way into every warm corner of the text, seems in the end to win out" (p. 173).

33. Wollstonecraft, *The Rights of Woman,* pp. 127, 128, 99. Cf. Poovey's account of the evasive rhetoric that appears whenever Wollstonecraft attempts to cope with intense emotion: "her language becomes both obscure and abstract; she shuns concrete nouns as if they were bodies she is trying to cover over." Poovey singles out the apostrophe to modesty as a particularly striking example of this tendency (*The Proper Lady,* p. 78).

Chapter Five

1. Bennett, *Letters to a Young Lady,* 2:77, 44; 1:198.

2. [Polwhele], *The Unsex'd Females,* p. 13.

3. Wollstonecraft, *The Rights of Woman,* p. 165.

4. [Polwhele], *The Unsex'd Females,* pp. 30, 6, 16.

5. [Mary Wollstonecraft], "Preface," *The Female Reader* (1789; reprint, with an introduction by Moira Ferguson, Delmar, N.Y.: Scholars' Facsimiles & Reprints, 1980), pp. xiii–xiv. The original title page of *The Female Reader*

identified its *Miscellaneous Pieces in Prose and Verse* as having been *Selected from the Best Writers, and Disposed under Proper Heads; for the Improvement of Young Women* by a supposed Mr. Cresswick, teacher of elocution, but there is clear evidence for identifying Wollstonecraft as the compiler of the anthology and the author of its preface as well as one of its contributors. For the grounds of attribution, see n. 34 to Ferguson's introduction, p. xxxiii. I wish to thank Mitzi Myers for calling this eloquent blush to my attention.

6. Though Sophia blushes frequently in the course of the novel, Fielding's use of the Donne allusion is nicely ambiguous: "when Exercise, or Modesty, encreased her natural Colour," the narrator remarks, "no Vermilion could equal it. Then one might indeed cry out with the celebrated Dr. *Donne,—Her pure and eloquent Blood / Spoke in her Cheeks. . . .*" See Henry Fielding, *The History of Tom Jones, a Foundling,* ed. Martin C. Battestin and Fredson Bowers (Middleton, Conn.: Wesleyan University Press, 1975), p. 157; and More, *Coelebs,* 1:186.

7. [Henry Austen], "Biographical Notice of the Author," reprint in *Northanger Abbey* and *Persuasion,* ed. R. W. Chapman, 3d ed. (1933; reprint London: Oxford University Press, 1954), p. 5. The "Biographical Notice" was originally published in 1818 as an introduction to the posthumous edition of *Northanger Abbey* and *Persuasion.*

8. Christopher Ricks, *Keats and Embarrassment* (London: Oxford University Press, 1976), p. 199. I am much indebted to Ricks's wonderfully varied account of blushing. When he identifies the blush of embarrassment as a phenomenon that belongs especially to the culture of nineteenth-century England, however, he is, I would suggest, attending chiefly to the social sensitivities of men. How the modest blush of the seventeenth- and eighteenth-century Englishwoman was diffused to both sexes in the nineteenth century—how, in this dimension of experience at least, men, too, were subtly "feminized"—would itself be a history well worth recounting.

9. "Maxims and Reflections for the Regulation of Female Life. An Imitation," *New Lady's Magazine* 6 (1791), 87.

10. [Steele], *Spectator,* no. 390, 28 May 1712; Wilkes, *A Letter of Genteel and Moral Advice,* p. 106.

11. Gregory, *A Father's Legacy,* pp. 26–27.

12. See, e.g., *The Female Instructor* (1815), p. 112, which repeats Gregory on the blush almost word-for-word. At least as late as 1859, *The Young Lady's Book of Advice and Instruction* was still echoing his concluding formula: "blushing is so far from being attendant on guilt, that it is generally the companion of innocence" (p. 12).

13. [Mrs. Cutts], *Almeria; or, Parental Advice: A Didactic Poem. Addressed to the Daughters of Great Britain and Ireland by a Friend of the Sex* (London: Rodwell, 1775), pp. 29, 30.

14. "On Shamefacedness," *New Lady's Magazine* 1 (1786), 27.

15. "The Blush of Innocence," *La Belle Assemblée; or, Bell's Court and Fashionable Magazine, Addressed Particularly to the Ladies* 14 (1816), 178; *The New Female Instructor* (1824), p. 17.

16. John Milton, *Paradise Lost* (2d ed., 1674), in *John Milton: Complete Poems and Major Prose*, ed. Merritt Y. Hughes (New York: Odyssey, 1957), 5:384–85; 9:887; 8:502–11. Milton's imagination of the innocent blush, we might recall, extends even to angels: when he responds to Adam's inquiry about their lovemaking, Raphael glows "Celestial rosy red, Love's proper hue" (8: 619). On blushing in Milton's Paradise, see also James Grantham Turner, *One Flesh: Paradisal Marriage and Sexual Relations in the Age of Milton* (Oxford: Clarendon, 1987), pp. 263–65.

17. Mandeville, *The Fable of the Bees*, pp. 64, 65.

18. Ibid., p. 66. Cf. Eustace Budgell's discussion of the modest man as solitary blusher in the *Spectator* two years earlier. "If I was put to define *Modesty*," Budgell wrote, "I would call it, *The Reflection of an Ingenuous Mind, either when a Man has committed an Action for which he Censures himself, or fancies that he is exposed to the Censure of others*. For this Reason a Man truly Modest is as much so when he is alone, as in Company; and as subject to a Blush in his Closet, as when the Eyes of Multitudes are upon him." Perhaps because he was not worrying the sexual virtue of women, Budgell could thus commend "true" modesty without apparently feeling compelled to argue that such modesty must be natural: the man who blushes in his closet need only have internalized the social consensus so thoroughly that he carries it always with him. See *Spectator,* no. 373, 8 May 1712.

19. Marriott, *Female Conduct*, pp. 178, 60. The covering up of blushes is, needless to say, only one of the dangers—and attractions—of masking. For a brilliant study of the various implications of the masquerade, see Terry Castle, *Masquerade and Civilisation: The Carnivalesque in Eighteenth-Century Culture and Fiction* (Stanford: Stanford University Press, 1986).

20. Cf. Thomas Jefferson on the difference between Negroes and whites in this respect, and on the aesthetic and moral superiority of skins in which the coming and going of the blood was easily visible: "And is this difference of no importance? Is it not the foundation of a greater or less share of beauty in the two races? Are not the fine mixtures of red and white, the expressions of every passion by greater or less suffusions of colour in the one, preferable to that eternal monotony, which reigns in the countenances, that immoveable veil of black which covers all the emotions of the other race?" *Notes on the State of Virginia,* ed. William Peden (Chapel Hill: University of North Carolina Press, 1954), p. 138. The text is based on the first regularly published edition of 1787. I wish to thank Richard Yarborough for alerting me to this passage.

21. "A Blush," *Lady's Magazine* 29 (1798), 280.

22. "The Birth of a Blush," *Lady's Magazine; or, Mirror of the Belles-Lettres, Music, Fine Arts, Drama, Fashions, &c.,* n.s. 6 (1825), 81. This is a new series of the magazine previously known as the *Lady's Magazine; or, Entertaining Companion*. . . .

23. Wollstonecraft, *The Rights of Woman*, p. 165; "On the Use of Rouge," *La Belle Assemblée* 1 (1806), 119.

24. [Moore], *Fables for the Female Sex*, pp. 64–65. As Mitzi Myers has

pointed out to me, the topos of the modest rose and the vulgar tulip also appears in still another of Wollstonecraft's pedagogical works for young women, her *Original Stories* of 1788, when the handsome but vain Caroline is instructed by the teacher, Mrs. Mason, in the deeper beauties of humility. According to this moralized botany lesson, the streaks of the tulip "please the eye for a moment" but the attractions of the rose prove more lasting: "even when the fine tints fade, the smell is grateful to those who have before contemplated its beauties." Caroline is advised to study the example of a certain Mrs. B.: "she is not like the flaunting tulip, that forces itself forward into notice; but resembles the modest rose, you see yonder, retiring under its elegant foliage." See *Original Stories, from Real Life; with Conversations, Calculated to Regulate the Affections, and Form the Mind to Truth and Goodness* (London: Johnson, 1788), pp. 53, 56, 57.

25. *Lady's Magazine* 8 (1777), 411, 412. "The Matron," who also signed herself "Martha Grey," appeared regularly in the magazine from 1774 through 1791; the feature was briefly revived, ostensibly by her granddaughter, in vols. 48 and 49 of the magazine (1817–18).

26. Samuel Richardson, *Pamela; or, Virtue Rewarded* (1740), ed. Peter Sabor with an introduction by Margaret A. Doody (Harmondsworth: Penguin, 1980), p. 51; Elizabeth Gaskell, *Wives and Daughters* (1864–66), ed. Angus Easson (Oxford: Oxford University Press, 1987), p. 624.

27. Cf. Ricks, *Keats and Embarrassment,* esp. pp. 180–84. "The painter's art," as Ricks observes, "is one which can distinguish between a blush and a flush only by showing a situation or even a story from which we deduce it to be the one or the other; in this respect, it is freed from both the powers and the constraints which go with language's ability to *say* that it was the one or the other" (p. 181).

28. The following five paragraphs are adapted from my "Podsnappery, Sexuality, and the English Novel," *Critical Inquiry* 9 (1982), 339–57.

29. Henry James, preface to *The Awkward Age* (New York: Scribner's, 1908), pp. x, ix, xi, x, xii.

30. Henry James, *The Notebooks of Henry James,* ed. F. O. Matthiessen and Kenneth B. Murdock (1947; reprint, New York: Braziller, 1955), pp. 275–76. The notebook entry is dated 15 February 1899.

31. Henry James, "The Story in It" (1902), *The Complete Tales of Henry James,* ed. Leon Edel, 12 vols. (London: Rupert Hart-Davis, 1962–64), 11:310, 319.

32. See Tony Tanner, *Adultery in the Novel: Contract and Transgression* (Baltimore: Johns Hopkins University Press, 1979): "Just as one could say that by entering into an adulterous relationship, a person introduces a new element of narrative into his or her life, initiates a new living 'story,' so for the novelist it is often not really marriage that initiates and inspires his narrative, but adultery. That *does* offer something to tell. . . . It would be tempting to suggest that without adultery, or the persistent possibility of adultery, the novel would have

been bereft of much of its narrational urge" (p. 377). Tanner's subject is "the bourgeois novel" in general, but two-thirds of his rich and provocative book is devoted to extended readings of three Continental novels: Rousseau's *Julie; ou, La Nouvelle Héloïse*, Goethe's *Die Wahlverwandtschaften*, and Flaubert's *Madame Bovary*. Though *Adultery and the Novel* does include a discussion of *Clarissa*, Richardson's celebrated novel is not in fact about adultery: unlike their Continental counterparts in Choderlos de Laclos' *Les Liaisons dangereuses*, for instance, Richardson's English letter writers are never in any danger of that marital crime. It is a striking fact that Lovelace first disrupts the peace of the Harlowe household not by threatening adultery or even seduction but by proposing marriage; and that the extraordinarily protracted ordeal Richardson's heroine endures has its origin not in any sexual misdeed on her part but in the simple act of leaving her father's house—or, as she herself often suggests, in her initial willingness to enter into the "prohibited correspondence." That Richardson could generate all seven volumes of his immensely complex and influential novel from such apparently slight transgressions is one measure of how powerfully felt was the ideal of virtue he helped form.

33. Roland Barthes, *S/Z: An Essay*, trans. Richard Miller and preface by Richard Howard (New York: Hill & Wang, 1974), p. 75. Cf. also Peter Brooks's suggestive account of narrative middles as constructed by simultaneous impulses of desire and delay in his *Reading for the Plot: Design and Intention in Narrative* (New York: Vintage, 1985), esp. pp. 3–61, 90–112.

34. James, preface to *The Awkward Age*, p. ix.

35. Ibid., p. viii.

36. James, *The Awkward Age*, pp. 285, 528. The remark about the "preposterous fiction" is Mrs. Brookenham's. Cf. also Mitchy's allusion to Nanda as "the young thing who is . . . positively and helplessly modern and the pious fraud of whose classic identity with a sheet of white paper has been—ah tacitly of course, but none the less practically!—dropped" (p. 312). Despite Mitchy's emphasis on Nanda's modernity in this respect, the "pious fraud" of which he speaks was effectively "dropped" at least as early as *Pamela*. Any novel that took the young woman for a center of consciousness inevitably subverted her "classic identity with a sheet of white paper."

37. "Her consciousness . . . *was*, in the last analysis, a kind of shy romance." James, "The Story in It," p. 326.

Chapter Six

1. Watt, *The Rise of the Novel*, pp. 135, 149. But cf. John Allen Stevenson, "'A Geometry of His Own': Richardson and the Marriage-Ending," *Studies in English Literature* 26 (1986), 469–83, which argues that Richardson consistently resists the marriage ending because he distrusts the erotic resolution and release the courtship plot entails. Though Stevenson's reminder that none of Richardson's novels actually ends at the moment of marriage is helpful, his reduction of "the 'courtship' phase of Pamela's and Mr. B.'s relationship" to

"overt sexuality" (pp. 472–73) seems to me to ignore the way in which Pamela's resistance gradually effects the sublimation of B's impulses.

2. Samuel Richardson, *Pamela; or, Virtue Rewarded,* ed. Peter Sabor with an introduction by Margaret A. Doody (Harmondsworth: Penguin, 1980), p. 297. Subsequent references to this edition, which is based on the 1801 edition that incorporates Richardson's ms. revisions, will appear parenthetically in the text. For B's "designs," see, e.g., pp. 45, 46, 47, 50, 52, 60, 115, 117, 119, 123, 127, 177, 212, 214, 241, 244, 246, 247, 257.

3. *Pamela Censured* (1741), Augustan Reprint Society, publication no. 175 (Los Angeles: Clark Library, 1976), p. 51.

4. [Henry Fielding], *An Apology for the Life of Mrs. Shamela Andrews,* in *Joseph Andrews and Shamela,* ed. Martin C. Battestin (Boston: Houghton Mifflin, 1961), pp. 309, 313, 326, 313.

5. "Remarks on Pamela. By a Prude," *London Magazine* (May 1741), as quoted in Bernard Kreissman, *Pamela-Shamela: A Study of the Criticisms, Burlesques, Parodies, and Adaptations of Richardson's "Pamela,"* University of Nebraska Studies, n.s. 22 (Lincoln: University of Nebraska Press, 1960), p. 23.

6. [Eliza Haywood], *Anti-Pamela; or, Feign'd Innocence Detected* (London: Huggonson, 1741), p. 82.

7. [Fielding], *Shamela,* p. 330. But even Shamela, interestingly enough, is not wholly unblushing. Less than forty-eight hours later, the same letter records, Shamela contrives a scene whose end result is that Squire Booby invites Parson Williams to replace him in the coach: "I gave him a charming kiss, and then he asked me questions concerning my wedding-night; this actually made me blush: I vow I did not think it had been in him" (p. 334). A blush is still the sign of truth: the difference, of course, is that Shamela is really aroused by Williams.

8. "On Modesty," *Lady's Magazine* 23 (1792), 130.

9. Arnold Kettle, *An Introduction to the English Novel,* 2 vols. (London: Hutchinson, 1953), 1:64. Cf. David Daiches: "she sets herself out to attract her master from the beginning, though she herself does not realize it and perhaps her creator does not." *Literary Essays* (Edinburgh and London: Oliver & Boyd, 1956), p. 39.

10. Kreissman, *Pamela-Shamela,* pp. 33, 42, 61, 51.

11. Ibid., p. 41. "So long as Pamela is solely occupied in schemes to escape from her persecutor, her virtuous resistance obtains our unqualified approbation," Anna Laetitia Barbauld wrote in 1804; "but from the moment she begins to entertain hopes of marrying him, we admire her guarded prudence, rather than her purity of mind. She has an end in view, an interested end, and we can only consider her as the conscious possessor of a treasure, which she is wisely resolved not to part with but for its just price." See *The Correspondence of Samuel Richardson . . . to Which Are Prefixed, a Biographical Account of That Author, and Observations on His Writings,* 6 vols. (London: Phillips, 1804), 1:lxiii–lxiv. Cf., however, Florian Stuber's account of the sympathetic responses both the book and its heroine elicited from his late-twentieth-century students at the Fashion

Institute of Technology in New York—"truly innocent readers, coming to the novel with no preconceptions." See "Teaching *Pamela*," in *Samuel Richardson: Tercentenary Essays,* ed. Margaret Anne Doody and Peter Sabor (Cambridge: Cambridge University Press, 1989), pp. 8–22, esp. p. 9.

12. Barthes, *S/Z,* p. 75.

13. [Fielding], *Shamela,* p. 338. Cf. Margaret Anne Doody, *A Natural Passion: A Study of the Novels of Samuel Richardson* (Oxford: Clarendon, 1974), pp. 71–74. As Doody aptly remarks: "In a curious way, Fielding unconsciously upholds something of the *droit de seigneur.* . . . Richardson's novel affronted the old Etonian in Fielding, and he registered the reaction of the Establishment" (pp. 73–74).

14. Cf. Michael McKeon's suggestion that the letter B sends to his tenant farmer, in which he accuses Pamela of being a headstrong young woman embarked on a dangerous affair, reads like "a miniature anti-*Pamela.*" *The Origins of the English Novel, 1600–1740* (Baltimore: Johns Hopkins University Press, 1987), p. 360.

15. B does not, however, altogether abandon the previous hypothesis. When Pamela is "ready to faint," as she describes herself in the confrontation scene over Parson Williams, B apparently registers the signs: "she is mistress of arts, I assure you," he announces to Mrs. Jervis, "and will mimick a fit, ten to one, in a minute" (p. 222).

16. See Ian Donaldson, *The Rapes of Lucretia: A Myth and Its Transformations* (Oxford: Clarendon, 1982). As Donaldson observes, "The ultimate act of physical violence administered by the woman to herself is intended to cancel the earlier act of physical violence, administered to her by another: an act which can apparently be digested or countered in no other way. Like a religious sacrifice, the suicide seems to cleanse the effects of pollution, and to restore lost purity and innocence" (p. 25).

17. Willfulness is also a charge brought against Clarissa by Lovelace. As Ian Donaldson cautions, to read Clarissa's death as deliberate is "to place oneself in dubious alliance with Lovelace, who considers that Clarissa's illness, like the sham illness which he himself once staged in order to play upon Clarissa's affections, is quite consciously induced. Women can make themselves sick at will, he believes, just as they can make themselves blush at will" (*The Rapes of Lucretia,* p. 67). Confronted by Clarissa's mysterious illness, Lovelace does resort to a *Shamela*-like fiction about the nature of women. A much harder case than B, of course, he requires a genuine tragedy to convert him. In the penultimate letter he writes before Clarissa's death, he is still bringing "comfort" to himself with the reflection that "if she recover not . . . her departure will be owing rather to wilfulness, to downright female wilfulness, than to any other cause." See Samuel Richardson, *Clarissa; or, The History of a Young Lady* (1747–48), ed. Angus Ross (New York: Viking, 1985), p. 1346.

18. Nancy K. Miller, *The Heroine's Text: Readings in the French and English Novel, 1722–1782* (New York: Columbia University Press, 1980), p. 39.

19. To Aaron Hill [1741], in *Selected Letters of Samuel Richardson,* ed. John

Carroll (Oxford: Clarendon, 1964), pp. 39–42. Margaret Doody notes several predecessors of the successful master/servant love plot in the drama of the period: Charles Johnson's *The Country Lasses* (1715), Lillo's *Silvia; or, The Country Burial* (1731), and Edward Phillips's ballad-opera, *The Chamber-Maid* (1730). But as Doody notes, each of these finally turns on the revelation that the "lowly" heroine is actually of high birth after all. See *A Natural Passion*, pp. 36–45.

20. Roy Roussel has also observed how "obsessively" the word "distance" appears in this novel, as a marker of both social and sexual space. See *The Conversation of the Sexes: Seduction and Equality in Selected Seventeenth- and Eighteenth-Century Texts* (New York: Oxford University Press, 1986), pp. 67–93, esp. pp. 71–73. Though Roussel writes that "the separation of the sexes, of masculine from feminine, is mandated by the same system of social conventions which determines the distance among classes" (p. 72), I would argue rather that *Pamela*, at least, takes the separation of the classes much more for granted and uses it rhetorically to build the case for sexual modesty and privacy.

21. Cf. Jacques Blondel, who also defends Pamela against suspicions of feminine trickery and manipulation: "La 'vertu,' la défense absolue de sa virginité, n'ont pas été des moyens délibérés de conquête." Of Pamela's declaration to Lady Davers that she did not know it was love, Blondel observes that "semblable aveu exclut, pour le lecteur attentif, tout soupçon de ruse féminine pour éprouver le partenaire." See "L'Amour dans *Pamela:* de l'affrontement à la découverte de soi," in *Études sur le XVIIIe siècle,* présentées par J. Ehrard (Association des Publications de la Faculté des Lettres, Université de Clermont II, 1979), p. 25.

22. Despite his mockery of *Pamela,* Fielding exploits the same convention in *Tom Jones,* as Sophia's delayed acquaintance with her own heart allows her to fall in love with Tom while preserving her modesty. Sophia, however, takes up less of Fielding's narrative doing so: from the moment at which the narrator reports that "her Heart was irretrievably lost before she suspected it was in Danger" (p. 167) to the moment at which "her Heart . . . at once, discovered the great Secret to her, which it had been so long disclosing by little and little" (p. 190), only six chapters have elapsed. By scarcely troubling to represent his heroine's consciousness, of course, Fielding also manages to avoid raising suspicions of her hypocrisy: we must simply take his word for it that she is characterized by "the highest degree of Innocence and Modesty" (p. 167).

23. Carol Houlihan Flynn, *Samuel Richardson: A Man of Letters* (Princeton: Princeton University Press, 1982), pp. 65–69.

24. [Fielding], *Shamela,* p. 315. For Mandeville, see above, ch. 5, pp. 70–71; and cf. Lovelace: "The modestest women, Jack, must *think,* and think deeply sometimes—I wonder whether they ever blush at those things by themselves, at which they have so charming a knack of blushing in company—if not; and if blushing be a sign of grace or modesty, have not the sex as great a command over their blushes, as they are said to have over their tears?" (*Clarissa,* pp. 691–92).

25. Lovelace's definition of *"Cor-respondence"* does not appear in the first edition of the novel, and is among the material Richardson added when he expanded the novel for the third and fourth editions of 1751. I quote from the fourth edition, 7 vols. (London: 1751), 4:77. Contending that Richardson agrees with Lovelace's letter-writing doctrine, Malvin R. Zirker, Jr., has argued that "he is as misleading as his villain when he tells his [own] young correspondents that openness characterizes letter-writing. . . . Common sense, and Dr. Johnson . . . tell us that one cannot, if he has the least bit of self-awareness, write a personal letter without calculating to some degree the figure he wishes to make." Common sense and Dr. Johnson are right, of course, but insofar as the "calculation" in question concerns the plot of courtship and seduction—as it so often does for Richardson—I would suggest that the persistent hope of his fictional lovers is somehow to surprise or forestall such calculation by intercepting letters *not* meant for them—and that Richardson's own positioning of himself outside the possibilities of courtship when he writes to young women is a related strategy of indirection. See "Richardson's Correspondence: The Personal Letter as Private Experience," in *The Familiar Letter in the Eighteenth Century,* ed. Howard Anderson, Philip B. Daghlian, and Irvin Ehrenpreis (Lawrence: University of Kansas Press, 1966), p. 78.

Though Roy Roussel sensitively describes the disquiet aroused by face-to-face encounters in *Pamela* and rightly emphasizes the way in which the distance between the lovers enables their union, his argument that the familiar letter is the principal means of resolving "the tension between distance and presence" in the novel is rather misleading. Claiming that "the couple who write to one another achieve the equality of complete understanding" (*The Conversation of the Sexes,* p. 81), Roussel seems to forget how little Pamela and B actually write *to* one another in the course of the novel.

26. To Sophia Westcomb [15 September 1746], *Selected Letters,* pp. 67–68, 69.

27. To Sophia Westcomb [1746?], *Selected Letters,* p. 66. "Writing to your own sex I would principally recommend; since ours is hardly ever void of design, and makes a correspondence dangerous:—Except protected by time, as in my case, by general character, by choice already filled up; where is the man that deserves to be favoured?—And were there the least room to suspect that there was any thing less than paternal in my views, I would not dare to urge the favour, or take the liberty."

28. To Sophia Westcomb [15 September 1746], *Selected Letters,* pp. 68, 69, 67.

29. Lennard J. Davis, *Factual Fictions: The Origins of the English Novel* (New York: Columbia University Press, 1983), p. 185. Cf. also Nancy Armstrong, *Desire and Domestic Fiction: A Political History of the Novel* (New York: Oxford University Press, 1987), esp. pp. 6 and 116. Insofar as Armstrong traces a general process by which the middle-class subject becomes psychologized and "feminized" in the period's conduct literature and fiction, her book shares many welcome points of contact with my own. In my view, however, her Foucauldian

identification of the triumph of the novel with "techniques of social control" (p. 98) accords an implausibly monolithic power to language. Unlike Armstrong, for example, I do believe that "sexual desire already existed before the strategies were devised to domesticate it" (p. 6), though not necessarily prior to all forms of representation. Similarly, I would argue that Richardson's transformation of Pamela from "an erotic and permeable body into a self-enclosed body of words" is far more tenuous than Armstrong would suggest, since Pamela is a fiction to begin with. To argue that "Mr. B's repeated failures suggest that Pamela cannot be raped because she is nothing but words" (p. 116) then denies the effectiveness of the representation. I tend to accept, as a reader of the novel, that Richardson's heroine is still very much vulnerable to rape.

30. To Sophia Westcomb [15 September 1746], *Selected Letters*, p. 69.

31. Flynn, *Samuel Richardson*, p. 20.

32. See, for instance, Ian Watt, who argues that in 1740 the middle-class concept of marriage was not yet completely established, and that Richardson needed therefore to work out in detail a model of conduct for his married couple (*The Rise of the Novel*, p. 149); or Margaret Doody, who contends that in *Pamela* I the heroine "has not achieved her complete fulfilment until she has won a place in society and found security in her relationship with her husband." Of *Pamela* II, Doody remarks that "the lack of a story to tell is an almost insuperable barrier to success" (*A Natural Passion*, pp. 65, 77). Mark Kinkead-Weekes writes that "with Pamela's marriage her 'story' ends" and describes the rest of *Pamela* I as a kind of "'Whole duty of Woman,'" but he nonetheless argues that the repeated scenes of choric praise in the latter "enact Richardson's hopes for the educative power of his story." *Samuel Richardson: Dramatic Novelist* (Ithaca, N.Y.: Cornell University Press, 1973), pp. 58, 59.

33. Even when the question is no longer one of illicit sexuality, Pamela is still apprehensive: "If one's heart is so sad, and one's apprehension so great, where one greatly loves, and is highly obliged," she wonders before her wedding night, "what must be the case of those poor young creatures, who are compelled, by their tyrannical parents, to marry the man they almost hate, and, perhaps, to the losing of the man they most love! That is a sad thing indeed!" (p. 377).

34. D. A. Miller, *Narrative and Its Discontents: Problems of Closure in the Traditional Novel* (Princeton: Princeton University Press, 1981). In *Pamela* II, Richardson does try to reintroduce an element of the "narratable" by entertaining the possibility of B's adultery with the countess. A comparison with Rousseau's attempt to reopen the story of Emile and Sophie, however, is instructive—both because the adulterous attraction is never actually consummated in the English book and because Richardson represents the man, and not the woman, as the one who is tempted. The idea of Pamela as an adulteress is virtually unimaginable.

35. The phrase is B. L. Reid's. See "Justice to Pamela," *Hudson Review* 9 (1956–57), 524. Kinkead-Weekes provides perhaps the best account of this formal problem and suggestively links Richardson's blindness to its dangers to

his own diffidence and deep need for praise (*Samuel Richardson,* pp. 88–103). See also Gerard Barker, "The Complacent Paragon: Exemplary Characterization in Richardson," *Studies in English Literature* 9 (1969), 503–19, which traces Pamela's capacity to "exalt her own conduct and still be humble" (p. 505) to the tensions and inconsistencies of seventeenth-century Puritanism.

Chapter Seven

1. Boswell's journals, 31 March 1772, in *Boswell for the Defense: 1769–1774,* ed. William K. Wimsatt, Jr., and Frederick A. Pottle, Yale Editions of the Private Papers of James Boswell (New York: McGraw-Hill, 1959), p. 81.

2. John Cleland, *Memoirs of a Woman of Pleasure,* ed. Peter Sabor (New York: Oxford University Press, 1985), pp. 11, 12. Subsequent references to this edition, based on that identified by David Foxon as the first (originally published in 1748–49), will appear parenthetically in the text.

3. Cf. Nancy Miller: "throughout the novel a tension between two competing poles—sentimental (Richardsonian) teleology and fantasmatic (Sadian) repetition—is maintained" (*The Heroine's Text,* pp. 55–56). Roy Roussel registers a similar tension but characterizes it quite differently. Arguing that the novel's rhythm "involves the interruption of a project of mastery and definition by an effect which not only dissipates but seduces," he associates this effect with the seduction of the feminine. Surrendering to such interruption and dissipation, he suggests, temporarily enables the masculine reader to "escape the tedious responsibility of definition and mastery which society has imposed on him" (*The Conversation of the Sexes,* p. 41).

I am adopting the term "long-circuiting" from Havelock Ellis. "Short-circuits" is a term that Peter Brooks adopts from Freud and uses in his *Reading for the Plot* to characterize the danger of reaching an end too quickly in a narrative. For both terms, see ch. 13, pp. 233–34, below.

4. Stone, *The Family, Sex and Marriage,* p. 676. "Cleland's Fanny Hill enjoyed an exuberant and inexhaustible appetite for all varieties of sexual pleasure," Stone writes; while "Richardson's Pamela fainted away at the mere hint of the most tentative of sexual advances. Fanny seemed to be winning in the eighteenth century, but thereafter, for the next hundred years or more, the future lay with Pamela and her rarefied sense of feminine 'delicacy.'" That there is less contradiction here than might at first appear is the argument of much of this book and of this chapter in particular. It might be noted in passing, however, that the myth of Pamela's fainting "at the mere hint of the most tentative" advances has a striking tenacity.

5. Written while Cleland was in jail for debt, the *Memoirs* was issued in two parts in 1748 and 1749. In November 1749—some nine months after the advertisement for the second half of the *Memoirs,* and almost that long after he had emerged from debtor's prison—Cleland and his publisher were arrested for producing an obscene work. Though they were soon released, the book itself was proscribed in England for more than two hundred years. In 1821, it had

the distinction of being the first book prosecuted for obscenity in the United States, where it remained officially banned until Putnam reissued the novel in 1963 and an American judge ruled in its favor. "It is quite possible that were Fanny to be transposed from her mid-eighteenth-century Georgian surroundings to our present day society," Judge Arthur Klein aptly noted in exonerating her, "she might conceivably encounter many things which would cause her to blush." Despite this verdict, the subsequent English trial of 1964 resulted in a ruling of obscenity—a ruling that has still not formally been lifted, though a 1970 reprinting was issued without government interference, and both Penguin and Oxford issued scholarly editions of the novel in 1985.

For accounts of the history of the *Memoirs*—as well as of the expurgated *Memoirs of Fanny Hill* that Cleland himself prepared for his publishers—see David Foxon, *Libertine Literature in England 1660–1745* (New Hyde Park, N.Y.: University Books, 1965), pp. 52–63; William H. Epstein, *John Cleland: Images of a Life* (New York: Columbia University Press, 1974), esp. pp. 3–8 and 183–84; and Peter Sabor's very helpful introduction to the Oxford edition of the novel, pp. vi–xxvii. For the twentieth-century English trial, see John Sutherland, *Offensive Literature: Decensorship in Britain, 1960–1982* (Totowa, N.J.: Barnes & Noble, 1982), pp. 32–40.

6. Edward W. Copeland, "*Clarissa* and *Fanny Hill*: Sisters in Distress," *Studies in the Novel* 4 (1972), 344. See Richardson, *Clarissa*, p. 87.

7. Freud, "The Taboo of Virginity" (1917), *The Standard Edition*, 11:193.

8. Ibid., p. 208. To this reaction, Freud also suggests, "We may ascribe the fact that second marriages so often turn out better than first." It is unclear to what extent this remark subverts his previous argument about the force of the woman's "sexual bondage."

9. Janet Todd, *Women's Friendship in Literature* (New York: Columbia University Press, 1980), p. 87.

10. Elizabeth Gaskell, *Mary Barton: A Tale of Manchester Life* (1848), ed. Stephen Gill (Harmondsworth: Penguin, 1975), p. 177.

11. Jane Austen, *Mansfield Park* (1814), ed. R. W. Chapman (London: Oxford University Press, 1960), pp. 326, 231.

12. As the encounter proceeds, Fanny hides her face "burningly flushing with my present feelings as much as with shame" (p. 123). Note how little has changed from the novel's opening, when Phoebe's touch and gaze first evoked Fanny's "glowing blushes [that] expressed more desire than modesty" (p. 12). The scenes also resemble one another, of course, in evoking desire through representations of exposure and initiation.

13. Cf. the verdict passed on Fanny after the company at Mrs. Cole's inspects what she calls her "most material spot": "nor was it but agreed, that I had not the least reason to be diffident of passing even for a maid, on occasion; so inconsiderable a flaw had my preceding adventures created there, and so soon had the blemish of an over-stretch been repair'd and worn out, at my age, and in my naturally small make in that part" (p. 122).

14. The novel's obsession with what Peter Quennell termed the "longitudinal fallacy"—or "phallacy," as Nancy Miller has appropriately updated it—is of course another sign that Fanny Hill speaks for a male fantasy. See his introduction to the Putnam edition (New York, 1963) of the novel, p. 15; and Miller, *The Heroine's Text,* p. 168, n. 10, and "'I's' in Drag: The Sex of Recollection," *The Eighteenth Century* 22 (1981), 53.

15. For comparisons of the two novels, see especially L. J. Morrissey and B. Slepian, "Fanny and Moll," *Notes and Queries* 209 (1964), 61; Myron Taube, "Moll Flanders and Fanny Hill: A Comparison," *Ball State University Forum* 9 (1968), 76–80; Malcolm Bradbury, "*Fanny Hill* and the Comic Novel," *Critical Quarterly* 13 (1971), 265–66; and Michael Shinagel, "*Memoirs of a Woman of Pleasure:* Pornography and the Mid-Eighteenth-Century English Novel," in *Studies in Change and Revolution: Aspects of English Intellectual History 1640–1800,* ed. Paul J. Korshin (Menston, Yorkshire: Scolar Press, 1972), pp. 212–13. "As *Fanny Hill* is a pornography of sex," Bradbury observes somewhat glibly, "*Moll Flanders* is a pornography of money" (p. 226). Cf. also Roussel, who comments on "the independence of pleasure from the economic" during the episodes at Mrs. Cole's (*The Conversation of the Sexes,* p. 58).

16. Raymond K. Whitley, "The Libertine Hero and Heroine in the Novels of John Cleland," *Studies in Eighteenth-Century Culture,* vol. 9, ed. Roseann Runte (Madison: University of Wisconsin Press, 1979), p. 395. Though Whitley seems to me wrong to suggest that the novel ever represents "unrestricted hedonism"—even to reject it—his effort to distinguish Cleland's more conservative fiction from the French libertine tradition is very well taken.

17. Roussel notes how Fanny's heterosexual desires are naturalized, or made to "seem part of the inevitable order of things," at her first sight of the male erection, as her eyes are automatically drawn to the spectacle and she reports that her "seat of pleasure" begins "furiously" to take an interest in what she sees (*The Conversation of the Sexes,* p. 46).

18. In *Surpassing the Love of Men: Romantic Friendship and Love between Women from the Renaissance to the Present* (New York: William Morrow, 1981), Lillian Faderman suggests that it was not so much lesbian sexual activity as "the attempted usurpation of male prerogative by women who behaved like men that many societies appeared to find most disturbing." As long as women "appeared feminine," she contends, lesbian "sexual behavior would be viewed as an activity in which women indulged when men were unavailable or as an apprenticeship or appetite-whetter to heterosexual sex" (p. 17). She, too, later cites the scene between Phoebe and Fanny Hill in evidence (p. 28). See also Peter Wagner, "The Discourse on Sex—or Sex as Discourse: Eighteenth-Century Medical and Paramedical Erotica," in *Sexual Underworlds of the Enlightenment,* ed. G. S. Rousseau and Roy Porter (Manchester: University of Manchester Press, 1987), p. 60.

19. Unlike Fanny, of course, Pamela resists her "wicked procuress," as she calls Mrs. Jewkes. But note how Mrs. Jewkes exploits the situation by interpret-

ing Pamela's rejection of homoeroticism as the positive sign of heterosexual desire: "Every now and then she would be staring in my face, in the chariot, and squeezing my hand, and saying, 'Why, you are very pretty, my silent dear!' And once she offered to kiss me. But I said, 'I don't like this sort of carriage, Mrs. Jewkes; it is not like two persons of one sex to each other.' She fell a laughing very confidently, and said, 'That's prettily said, I vow! Then thou hadst rather be kissed by the other sex? 'Ifackins, I commend thee for that!'" (*Pamela,* p. 145). On Phoebe, cf. Janet Todd, who argues that so far as Fanny is concerned, the encounter is "more narcissistic than lesbian" (*Women's Friendship,* p. 82).

20. The informal censorship persisted, in other words, even in many pirated editions. By identifying the first edition of the *Memoirs,* David Foxon established that the sodomitical description was in fact Cleland's own and not—as one nineteenth-century bibliographer had claimed—a later interpolation by another hand. The description was still missing from Quennell's 1963 edition of the novel for Putnam but has been restored to the 1985 Penguin and Oxford texts. See Foxon, *Libertine Literature,* pp. 59–63; and Epstein, *Images,* pp. 183–84. Ironically, as Peter Sabor observes, Cleland was himself later accused of homosexuality (*Memoirs,* pp. xiii and 201, n. 159).

21. For a description of the whore biographies, see John J. Richetti, *Popular Fiction before Richardson: Narrative Patterns 1700–1739* (Oxford: Clarendon, 1969), pp. 35–41.

22. Douglas Brooks-Davies, "The Mythology of Love: Venerean (and Related) Iconography in Pope, Fielding, Cleland and Sterne," in *Sexuality in Eighteenth-Century Britain,* ed. Paul-Gabriel Boucé (Manchester: Manchester University Press, 1982), p. 194, n. 36.

23. [John Cleland], *Institutes of Health* (London: Beckett & Davies, 1761), p. 32.

24. Steven Marcus, *The Other Victorians: A Study of Sexuality and Pornography in Mid-Nineteenth-Century England* (1966; reprint, New York: Norton, 1985), p. 279.

25. The count is Michael Shinagel's. See *"Memoirs of a Woman of Pleasure,"* p. 226.

26. The argument for Cleland's comic intentions was first advanced by B. Slepian and L. J. Morrissey, "What is *Fanny Hill?*" *Essays in Criticism* 14 (1964), 72–75. In *"Memoirs of a Woman of Pleasure,"* Shinagel endorses and elaborates this argument: Cleland's "strategy in such passages cannot be termed pornographic in intention, regardless of the subject matter, because the primary appeal to the audience is one of literary wit, designed to elicit a smile, not an erection" (p. 226). Cf. also Epstein, who argues that Fanny's exaggerated style enters "the self-conscious, undercutting realm of the burlesque" (*Images,* p. 106), and Bradbury, who describes the work, more accurately I believe, as a "comic sexual romance" (*"Fanny Hill* and the Comic Novel," p. 275).

27. See Peter Sabor's introduction to the Oxford edition of the *Memoirs,* p. xix. John Hollander, who also associates Cleland's rhetoric with the diction

of Caroline poets as well as with the erotic conceits of their Renaissance predecessors, argues that the "heroic, hyperbolic, and hieratic" world of "true pornography" is always closer to poetry than to prose fiction. See "The Old Last
Act: Some Observations on *Fanny Hill*," *Encounter* 21 (October 1963), 69.

28. Boswell's journals, 13 April 1779, in *Boswell, Laird of Auchinleck*, ed.
Joseph W. Reed and Frederick A. Pottle, Yale Editions of the Private Papers of
James Boswell (New York: McGraw-Hill, 1977), pp. 76 and 76–77. Cleland's
comparison of his work to *L'École des filles* is taken from a damaged ms. and is a
conjectural reconstruction of the editors. The circumlocutions of the novel may
also, of course, have been motivated by a desire to avoid prosecution for obscenity: defending his publishers from the charge, Cleland protested that "they certainly were deceived by my avoiding those rank words in the work, which are all
that they Judge of obscenity by, and made them think the Line was drawn between them, and all danger of Law whatever" (quoted in Epstein, *Images*, p. 77).

29. Hagstrum, *Sex and Sensibility*, p. 252.

30. Boswell's journals, 13 April 1779, in *Boswell, Laird of Auchinleck*, p. 76.
"You have furnished me with a vindication," Sterne reportedly replied. "It can
do no harm."

31. Michel Foucault, *The History of Sexuality*, Vol. 1: *An Introduction*, trans.
Robert Hurley (New York: Vintage, 1980), p. 35.

32. See especially Foxon, *Libertine Literature*. Foxon identifies as his "most
important and unexpected discovery" the way in which "pornography seems to
have been born and grown to maturity in a brief period in the middle of the
seventeenth century" (p. ix). Working independently of Foxon, Steven Marcus
seems to have reached essentially the same conclusion, though he locates the
"full meaningful existence" of the genre in the late eighteenth century. Arguing
that the growth of pornography is "inseparable from and dependent upon the
growth of the novel," Marcus associates both phenomena with the growth of
cities, the privatization of experience, and the tendency to "split sexuality off
from the rest of life" (*The Other Victorians*, pp. 282, 283).

33. Foucault, *The History of Sexuality*, p. 17.

34. For accounts of these works, see Foxon, *Libertine Literature;* and Peter
Naumann, *Keyhole und Candle: John Clelands "Memoirs of a Woman of Pleasure"
und die Entstehung des pornographischen Romans in England* (Heidelberg: Carl
Winter Universitätsverlag, 1976). Though written in Latin, the *Satyra Sotadica*
was first published in France. Barry Ivker, "John Cleland and the Marquis d'Ar-
gens: Eroticism and Natural Morality in Mid-Eighteenth Century English and
French Fiction," *Mosaic* 7 (1975), 141–48; and Whitley, "The Libertine Hero,"
pp. 387–404, do not discuss these earlier pornographic texts but contrast
Cleland's work with the writings of some "libertine" French contemporaries.

35. [John Cleland], Review of *Amelia, Monthly Review* 5 (1751), 511, 512.

36. I am very grateful to James Turner for this account of the 1740 English
adaptation of Chorier's amorous dialogues. According to Turner, the evidence
strongly suggests that this English adaptation of the *Satyra* was identical with

one prosecuted for obscenity in 1684, though the earlier English text has been lost, and only a single sentence was recorded in the trial transcript. A fuller discussion of the history of these texts and their relation to Cleland's *Memoirs* will appear in Turner's forthcoming study of libertine literature.

Chapter Eight

1. Fanny Burney, *Evelina; or, the History of a Young Lady's Entrance into the World,* ed. Edward A. Bloom and Lillian D. Bloom (Oxford: Oxford University Press), p. 72. Subsequent references to this edition, which is based on the first edition of 1778, will appear parenthetically in the text.

On the multiplication of fathers in the novel, see Mary Poovey's fine essay, "Fathers and Daughters: The Trauma of Growing Up Female," in *Men by Women,* ed. Janet Todd (New York: Holmes & Meier, 1981), esp. pp. 44–47; and Patricia Meyer Spacks's brief but pointed remarks in *The Female Imagination* (1972; reprint, New York: Avon, 1976), p. 165. For a reading of the ways in which the novel copes with the attractions and dangers of incest, see also Irene Fizer, "The Name of the Daughter: Identity and Incest in *Evelina,*" in *Refiguring the Father: New Feminist Readings of Patriarchy,* ed. Patricia Yaeger and Beth Kowaleski-Wallace (Carbondale: Southern Illinois University Press, 1989), pp. 78–107.

2. Margaret Anne Doody, *Frances Burney: The Life in the Works* (New Brunswick, N.J.: Rutgers University Press, 1988), p. 59. For the argument that Evelina is a self-conscious letter writer who deliberately "edits" the letters she addresses to her guardian, see Julia Epstein, *The Iron Pen: Frances Burney and the Politics of Women's Writing* (Madison: University of Wisconsin Press, 1989), esp. pp. 95–103.

3. Cf. Susan Staves, "*Evelina;* or, Female Difficulties," *Modern Philology* 73 (1976), 375–76. Staves aptly cites Fordyce's *Sermons to Young Women* on the dangers that attend female young persons who "will be always breaking loose through each domestic inclosure, and ranging at large the wide common of the world" (p. 374).

4. Joyce Hemlow, *The History of Fanny Burney* (Oxford: Clarendon, 1958), p. 83.

5. Samuel Richardson, *Pamela,* p. 284.

6. *The Early Diary of Frances Burney, 1768–1778,* ed. Annie Raine Ellis, 2 vols. (1889; reprint, London: Bell, 1913), 1:8.

7. Cf. Patricia Meyer Spacks, "Ev'ry Woman Is at Heart a Rake," *Eighteenth-Century Studies* 8 (1974), 27–46, esp. 36–37.

8. Gregory, *A Father's Legacy to His Daughters,* p. 67. In "Fanny Burney and the Conduct Books," *PMLA* 65 (1950), 732–61, Joyce Hemlow long ago made clear how much Burney's novels owe to the courtesy books, Gregory's among them. According to Hemlow, Burney had at least read *A Father's Legacy* by 1778, the year of *Evelina's* publication—and she would later become acquainted with the surviving Gregory daughter (p. 738).

9. William Hazlitt, "Why the Heroes of Romance Are Insipid" (1827), in *The Collected Works of William Hazlitt,* ed. A. R. Waller and Arnold Glover, 12 vols. (London: Dent, 1904), 12:65.

10. Fanny Burney, *Camilla; or, A Picture of Youth,* ed. Edward A. Bloom and Lillian D. Bloom (Oxford: Oxford University Press, 1983), p. 482.

11. Jean-Paul Sartre, *Being and Nothingness: An Essay in Phenomenological Ontology,* trans. Hazel E. Barnes (New York: Philosophical Library, 1956), pp. 263, 261. Other analysts of shame concur in Sartre's emphasis on the look. See, e.g., Helen Block Lewis, *Shame and Guilt in Neurosis* (New York: International Universities Press, 1971), whose case studies repeatedly demonstrate how "the experience of shame often occurs in the form of imagery, of looking or being looked at" (p. 37); and Carl D. Schneider, *Shame, Exposure, and Privacy* (Boston: Beacon, 1977), who insists that "the core of the shame experience is found in the sense of visibility and exposure" (p. 34).

12. The *Oxford English Dictionary* cites Burney's second novel, *Cecilia* (1782), for the first recorded use of the idiom to "come out" in the sense of "to make a formal entry into 'society' on reaching womanhood."

13. Burney, *Early Diary,* 1:197.

14. Erving Goffman, *Behavior in Public Places: Notes on the Social Organization of Gatherings* (New York: Free Press, 1963), p. 27.

15. Analyzing the role of the city in this and other novels of the period, Patricia Meyer Spacks has argued that it "provides a synecdoche for the 'public' realm"—a realm which for a woman offered a locale for the only "business" open to her, that of marrying as well as she could. "London did not allow women to sit in Parliament, but it provided abundant opportunities for female self-display: there a woman could go about her 'business' by showing herself at theatre and assembly, making herself an object of sexual commerce." See "Women and the City," in *Johnson and His Age,* ed. James Engell, Harvard English Studies 12 (Cambridge: Harvard University Press, 1984), pp. 488–89.

16. Cf. Judith Lowder Newton, who notes the similarity of Lord Orville's and the Reverend Villars's names, as well as the fact that Evelina returns at the novel's close to Berry Hill—"a fitting locus for the end of a journey which has taken her from protected minor to *femme couverte.*" *Women, Power & Subversion: Social Strategies in British Fiction, 1778–1860* (1981; reprint, New York: Methuen, 1985), p. 50.

17. In *Shame and Guilt in Neurosis,* Helen Block Lewis associates the etiology of shame with the child's internalization of the "beloved or admired" parent, who then "functions . . . as the referent 'in whose eyes' shame is experienced"; the loss of love experienced in shame is thus a loss of parental love, now internalized and experienced as a loss of self-love or self-esteem (p. 23). She also contends that in our culture, at least, shame is "probably a universal reaction to unrequited or thwarted love" (p. 16), and later suggests that for a number of reasons—including their higher threshold for aggression against others and their traditionally passive role in courtship—"women may experience the shame of unrequited

love even more strongly than do men" (p. 154). On the relation between shame and the fear of abandonment, see also Gerhart Piers and Milton B. Singer, *Shame and Guilt: A Psychoanalytic and a Cultural Study* (1953; reprint, New York: Norton, 1971), p. 29; and Helen Merrell Lynd, *On Shame and the Search for Identity* (New York: Harcourt, Brace, 1958), p. 67.

18. In *Cecilia*, the heroine's father is dead, and she herself is an heiress, but many of the agonizing turns in the courtship plot follow from the premise that she will forfeit her wealth on marriage unless her husband takes her family name. In *Camilla*, the heroine's father is both alive and sufficiently concerned for her welfare to provide her with an entire chapter of advice, a "Sermon" so close to the sentiments and language of the conduct books that it was subsequently extracted and bound with editions of Gregory's *A Father's Legacy*. Yet even as Camilla's father urges her never to violate the laws of "delicacy" and "modest propriety" by revealing her love (*Camilla*, p. 362), the hero's suspicious and misogynistic advisor urges him never to commit himself unless he is thoroughly persuaded that she loves him. As Margaret Doody has wittily demonstrated, the conflict between these rules produces the repeated impasses, at once painful and comic, that structure the novel's courtship plot. See *Frances Burney*, pp. 230–34.

19. Joyce Hemlow's account of the revisions of the manuscript suggests that Burney felt some need to restrain this propensity on Evelina's part: in the manuscript, when Evelina goes to the theater, she notices Lord Orville in a neighboring box but comments that "he did not see us the whole evening"; in the printed text, he is no longer present, and Evelina simply reports that "we did not see any body we knew." As Hemlow puts it, "There is less peering about for his lordship than in the manuscript and more attention to the entertainment at hand" (*The History of Fanny Burney*, p. 84).

20. Goffman, *Behavior*, pp. 15–16.

21. Poovey, "Fathers and Daughters," p. 47.

22. Cf. Staves's astute remarks on this and other episodes of laughter in the novel ("*Evelina*; or, Female Difficulties," p. 378).

23. See, for example, Gregory's warning against even "innocent" female laughter at the theater. "Sometimes a girl laughs with all the simplicity of unsuspecting innocence, for no other reason but being infected with other people's laughing: she is then believed to know more than she should do.—If she does happen to understand an improper thing, she suffers a very complicated distress: she feels her modesty hurt in the most sensible manner, and at the same time is ashamed of appearing conscious of the injury." The only solution, of course, "is never to go to a play that is particularly offensive to delicacy" (*A Father's Legacy*, pp. 59–60). Elsewhere in the *Legacy*, Gregory informs his daughters that wit is "the most dangerous talent" they can possess and, unless "guarded with great discretion and good nature," will create "many enemies." Wit is so "flattering to vanity," he continues, "that they who possess it become intoxicated, and lose all self-command" (p. 30). Though Gregory apparently re-

gards "humour" as a softer and hence more acceptable quality, he cautions that it, too, is "often a great enemy to delicacy, and a still greater one to dignity of character. It may sometimes gain you applause," he warns, "but will never procure you respect" (p. 31).

24. To Sophia Westcomb [1746?], *Selected Letters of Samuel Richardson*, pp. 67–68. See above, ch. 6, pp. 97–98.

25. Patricia Meyer Spacks, *Gossip* (1985; reprint, Chicago: University of Chicago Press, 1986), p. 162. Cf. also Epstein, *The Iron Pen*, pp. 47–51.

26. On Burney and violence, see especially Doody, *Frances Burney*, and Epstein, *The Iron Pen*. As Kristina Straub has pointedly observed, when Evelina attempts to come to the assistance of the fallen woman in the footrace episode, she is "literally stopped by the rules of the game": Lord Merton calls out, "No foul play! No foul play!" That Evelina says she sprang forward "involuntarily," Straub continues, suggests that the attempt at intervention is "not a move considered in social consciousness, but an unarticulated and unformulated impulse outside the rules governing social activity." See *Divided Fictions: Fanny Burney and Feminine Strategy* (Louisville: University Press of Kentucky, 1987), pp. 48, 49. See also Straub's subsequent remarks on the problem of distinguishing between "the keen observer" and "the social critic" in this and other eighteenth-century women's texts (p. 107).

27. In *Imagining a Self: Autobiography and Novel in Eighteenth-Century England* (Cambridge, Mass.: Harvard University Press, 1976), pp. 175–82, Patricia Meyer Spacks reads Burney's diary together with her novels in order to suggest that the writer exploited such characters "to articulate repressed aspects" of her own personality (p. 181). See also Staves, "*Evelina;* or, Female Difficulties," pp. 376–79, and Newton, who argues that Evelina begins as a satiric observer but that the "locus of satiric observation" shifts to Mrs. Selwyn in the third volume, as Evelina herself dwindles into a wife (*Women, Power & Subversion*, p. 48). Doody, on the other hand, reads the younger woman's relation to the older one more affirmatively, contending that Mrs. Selwyn "is associated with the heroine once the girl has begun to learn to stand on her own feet" (*Frances Burney*, p. 47).

28. Burney, *Camilla*, p. 89.

29. Given the masculine brutality of its agent and the effeminacy of its victim, Doody's interpretation of the monkey trick as "antimasculinist satire" seems more wishful than convincing (*Frances Burney*, p. 65). In a reading that is closer to my own, Epstein suggests that Mirvan's trick simultaneously avenges Evelina and enables her to feel compassion for the vulnerability she shares with its victim (*The Iron Pen*, pp. 107–8).

30. *Diary and Letters of Madame d'Arblay*, ed. Charlotte Barrett with a preface and notes by Austin Dobson, 6 vols. (London: Macmillan, 1904), 1:109.

31. On "the dynamics of fear" in Burney's life and art and the "strategies of concealment" that the writer adopted to cope with that fear, see Spacks, *Imagining a Self*, pp. 158–92. While Spacks stresses Burney's need to be loved, and I

would emphasize more the satirist's fear of her own power to hurt, Burney herself would recognize how difficult it is to distinguish between these.

32. Goffman, *Behavior,* p. 196. Both in what it emphasizes and in what it excludes, Goffman's account of human relations is extraordinarily close to Burney's in *Evelina.* Compare almost any scene in the novel in which three or more people are present with his discussion of what it means to be in "a situation": "When a situation comes into being, mutual accessibility of body signs is not the only contingency faced by those who are present. As already suggested, each person becomes a potential victim or aggressor in the potential occurrence of violent interpersonal actions, such as physical or sexual assault, blocking of the way, and so forth. Further, each person present is in a position to accost or be accosted by the others for the purpose of initiating a state of talk—a joint conversational engagement. And this, too, has its own dangers, for when persons are joined in this way they can command and plead with each other, insult or compliment each other, inform and misinform each other, or be seen (by others) as being on close terms, and the like. Further, when an engagement is sustained in the presence of bystanders, the participants open themselves up to being listened in on and interfered with, just as the bystanders become vulnerable to undesired distractions" (pp. 196–97).

33. Burney, *Diary and Letters,* 1:107.

Chapter Nine

1. Jane Austen, *Mansfield Park,* ed. R. W. Chapman (1934; reprint, London: Oxford, 1960), pp. 302, 327. The novel was first published in 1814, but Chapman principally follows the second edition of 1816. All further references to this work will be included parenthetically in the text.

2. The niece in question was Louisa Knight. See Park Honan, *Jane Austen: Her Life* (1987; reprint, New York: Ballantine, 1989), p. 343. Honan's source here is the 1980 report of the Jane Austen Society at Chawton.

3. For a useful summary of the traits that associate Fanny Price with the model woman of the conduct books, especially conduct books by Evangelicals like Thomas Gisborne and Hannah More, see Marian E. Fowler, "The Courtesy-Book Heroine of *Mansfield Park,*" *University of Toronto Quarterly* 44 (1974), 31–46. Fowler reads Austen's novel as straightforwardly didactic, however, and appears to see neither irony nor conflict in its portrait of Fanny.

4. Jane Austen, *Pride and Prejudice* (1813), ed. R. W. Chapman (1932; reprint, London: Oxford, 1959), pp. 107, 108, 105, 110.

5. Ibid., p. 109.

6. Cf. Stuart M. Tave, *Some Words of Jane Austen* (Chicago: University of Chicago Press, 1973), p. 133: "there can be no question of any 'affection' for or from Mr. Collins, a man to whom the word is known, and known only, as a word which it is customary to employ during a proposal."

7. Tony Tanner, *Jane Austen* (Cambridge, Mass.: Harvard University Press, 1986), p. 143. While Tanner himself appears to be thinking primarily of the

novel's readers when he denies that anyone falls in love with Fanny Price, Nina Auerbach in turn cites his remark only to add that "Jane Austen further confounds our emotions by making clear that none of the characters within the novel falls in love with her either, though most heroines exist to win love." *Romantic Imprisonment: Women and Other Glorified Outcasts* (New York: Columbia University Press, 1986), p. 30. Nineteenth-century readers may have been more inclined to sense the erotic possibilities in such a heroine. In support of the argument that to such readers Fanny Price's "apparent innocence and religiosity" were "an aspect of her sexiness," Margaret Kirkham aptly cites an anonymous article from the *New Monthly Review* of 1852: "what a bewitching 'little body' is Fanny Price." Kirkham herself suggests that Austen intends her "conduct-book heroine" as an ironic version of figures like Rousseau's Sophie. See *Jane Austen, Feminism and Fiction* (Brighton: Harvester, 1983), p. 102.

8. *Lady's Magazine* 24 (1793), 264. Cf. ch. 3, p. 45, above.

9. Claudia L. Johnson, *Jane Austen: Women, Politics, and the Novel* (Chicago: University of Chicago Press, 1988), p. 109.

10. For a subtle account of the relation between Henry Crawford's flirting and his "narratability," see D. A. Miller, *Narrative and Its Discontents*, pp. 20–27.

11. In a related argument about the ways in which Fanny's "no" is made to inform against her, Claudia Johnson also evokes the shade of Mr. Collins: "from the outside, Fanny's refusal of Henry looks like the coquettish 'no' Mr. Collins has learned to expect from 'elegant' females before hearing their inevitable, grateful 'yes'—in short, like another of the many acts people in *Mansfield Park* stage for propriety's sake" (*Jane Austen*, p. 106). As I argue above, however, the double-binds of modesty go even deeper than Johnson's remarks suggest, for those around Fanny have available another, and psychologically more subtle, model for choosing not to take her refusal as final. Rather than implausibly assume that she is merely playing coy—a theory that only Mary Crawford, on occasion, seems to entertain at all seriously—they can allow for Fanny's sincerity even as they keep up the pressure, by postulating her modest unconsciousness of desires that will nonetheless surface in time. To suggest that these are the dominant terms in which Fanny's relatives choose to understand her is not, of course, to argue that they ever wholly abandon the alternative model— or to deny how unstable are the distinctions between unconsciousness and consciousness in all such fictions of modesty.

12. Kirkham, *Jane Austen, Feminism and Fiction*, p. 105.

13. Compare this scene of "confusion" at the Mansfield ball with Fanny's related embarrassment a few chapters earlier, when she blushed over the gift of the necklace, and "Miss Crawford thought she had never seen a prettier consciousness" (p. 259). As Austen very well knows, the relation between blushing and misinterpretation on such occasions is reciprocal: in both scenes, Fanny's embarrassment is intensified by her consciousness of how Mary may mistake her—as well as by a sense of helplessness and anger at the situation. Compare also Edmund's later and far more cautious interpretation of the "encourage-

ment" that Henry might legitimately take from Fanny's embarrassment: "it was so little, so very very little, (every chance, every possibility of it, resting upon her embarrassment only, if there was not hope in her confusion, there was hope in nothing else) that he was almost ready to wonder at his friend's perseverance" (p. 336).

14. Sir Thomas "might mean to recommend her as a wife by shewing her persuadableness," when he later "advise[s]" his niece to quit another ball and go to bed immediately (pp. 281, 280), but as Henry's testimony to the excellence of her temper indicates, the would-be husband scarcely has need of this little demonstration: he knows very well that for most of her history Fanny has acquiesced in the demands of others quite willingly. On the behavior of both Thomas Bertrams in these scenes, see Johnson, *Jane Austen*, pp. 101–3. "The 'pretence' of choice Tom resents is essential to the paternalistic discourse represented in *Mansfield Park*," Johnson argues, "because it enables people to compel others without having to regard themselves as bullies" (p. 102).

15. Lionel Trilling, *The Opposing Self: Nine Essays in Criticism* (New York: Viking, 1959), p. 218. Trilling's essay on *Mansfield Park* was first published in 1954.

16. Rousseau, *Lettre à d'Alembert*, p. 179.

17. Lionel Trilling, *Sincerity and Authenticity* (Cambridge, Mass.: Harvard University Press, 1973), p. 75. The passage is preceded by the daring—but in context, at least, remarkably apt—suggestion that the Rousseau of the *Confessions* "wished, in short, to be Fanny Price in Mansfield Park, not, of course, in her creep-mouse days, but in her time of flowering."

18. I quote from the preface to the fifth edition of *Lovers' Vows,* appended by Chapman to the Oxford edition of *Mansfield Park,* p. 478. Elizabeth Inchbald's English adaptation of Kotzebue's *Das Kind der Liebe* first appeared in 1798.

19. Trilling, *The Opposing Self,* p. 218. Though Tony Tanner also associates the fuss over the theatricals with "the old Platonic objection to acting" (*Jane Austen,* p. 162), most recent commentators tend to agree with Marilyn Butler, *Jane Austen and the War of Ideas* (1975; reprint, Oxford: Clarendon, 1987), p. 232: "the impropriety lies in the fact that they are *not* acting, but are finding an indirect means to gratify desires which are illicit, and should have been contained." For similar arguments see also Thomas R. Edwards, "The Difficult Beauty of *Mansfield Park,*" *Nineteenth-Century Fiction* 20 (1965), 61; David Lodge, *Language of Fiction: Essays in Criticism and Verbal Analysis of the English Novel* (London: Routledge, 1966), pp. 98, 107–13; and Tave, *Some Words of Jane Austen,* pp. 184–94.

20. *Lady's Magazine* 21 (1790), 397, 398. A subsequent piece in the same volume extended the argument, evoking a scene of domestic discord very like those in Austen's novel: "the ambition, however, of acting private plays occupies the whole mind, and that for a very considerable time, interrupts all domestic concerns, induces levity, giddiness, improper vanity." Though this essay continued to distinguish between the risk of private and public performance, its indictment of acting, and of actresses, was far more sweeping. "The characters

of most plays, if entered into with spirit (and if they are not, the performance is childish) are at least highly improper for modest and virtuous persons of either sex, particularly the female, to assume. There are few, I had almost said no Comedies in which the female characters are not such as a lady of delicacy ought to be ashamed of in private; pert flippancy, levity of speech and manners, an affected copy of high life, generally beyond nature, or a vindictive and rash spirit, constitute the greater part of them; and I presume there are very few husbands who would wish their wives to throw off the delicate demeanour of the sex to enter into the rakish and indecent manners of Lady Townly, notwithstanding her repentance; nor are there I hope many fathers who would wish their daughters to be so very free, familiar and *advancing* towards the other sex as we find our Letitias, Charlottes, and other young heroines in comedies" (p. 426).

21. Gisborne, *Enquiry into the Duties of the Female Sex,* pp. 174, 175. Austen seems to have read "Gisborne," as she called it; in a letter to Cassandra of 30 August [1805], she thanked her sister for recommending it and pronounced herself "pleased with it." See *Jane Austen's Letters to Her Sister Cassandra and Others,* ed. R. W. Chapman, 2d ed. (Oxford: Oxford University Press, 1979), p. 169.

22. For subtle accounts of how the novel is inevitably implicated in the theatricality it would appear to oppose, see Joseph Litvak, "The Infection of Acting: Theatricals and Theatricality in *Mansfield Park,*" *ELH* 53 (1986), 331–55; and David Marshall, "True Acting and the Language of Real Feeling: *Mansfield Park,*" *Yale Journal of Criticism* 3, no. 1 (1989), 87–106. Marshall specifically remarks the way in which Fanny's refusal already places her on stage, "cast in a prelude that is itself theatrical" (p. 91).

23. To dismiss Collins as a fool is not to dismiss the fact that Charlotte Lucas nonetheless is constrained to take him seriously. In the circumstances of Charlotte's marriage and of Elizabeth's pained reaction to it, Austen registers some of the more disturbing effects of her culture's arrangements between the sexes. But even as she acknowledges such darker possibilities, the plotting of *Pride and Prejudice* strictly subordinates them to the pleasures of sophisticated wish fulfillment. As Mary Poovey has argued, Austen "introduces the specters of spinsterhood, dependence, and compromise less to explore the social strictures of Elizabeth's situation than to invoke the reality that makes her own consoling art necessary" (*The Proper Lady and the Woman Writer,* p. 206).

24. Tanner, *Jane Austen,* pp. 156, 169. For counterarguments, which emphasize the difficulty of distinguishing between role playing and sincerity, see Litvak, "The Infection of Acting," p. 345, and Marshall, "True Acting and the Language of Real Feeling," pp. 99–100. If Tanner oversimplifies by reading too retrospectively, Marshall, on the other hand, sometimes fails to take sufficient account of the implications of ending—as when he writes that "the novel leaves open the possibility that . . . Henry has really become the part he plays" (p. 99). For all that *Mansfield Park* seriously entertains such possibilities, leaving them "open" is precisely what it does not do. Henry's elopement with Maria is decisive.

25. To Cassandra Austen, 5 March [1814], *Letters*, p. 381.

26. While I share Claudia Johnson's view of the helplessness potentially entailed by a modesty like Fanny's, I think that the plotting of the novel thus refutes her claim that Fanny's "efforts to be modest are . . . every bit as frustrating and corrosive as Maria's efforts simply to appear so" (*Jane Austen*, p. 104). To say that *Mansfield Park* finally underwrites Fanny's virtue is not, of course, to argue that it does so realistically: like most comic novelists, Austen manages contradiction by indulging in a form of wish fulfillment—while the ironies with which she hedges this ending in particular call attention both to its artifice and to her ambivalence.

27. For arguments directly associating Austen and Wollstonecraft, see especially Lloyd W. Brown, "Jane Austen and the Feminist Tradition," *Nineteenth-Century Fiction* 28 (1973), 321–38; and Margaret Kirkham, *Jane Austen, Feminism and Fiction*, pp. 33–50. As Kirkham contends, "Our habit of thinking of Mary Wollstonecraft as a Jacobin, and Jane Austen as a Lady Novelist praised by Scott, makes it difficult for us to see connections between them" (p. 40). When it comes to sexual politics, the resemblances between Wollstonecraft and Austen—or between Wollstonecraft and Hannah More—often cut across these conventional distinctions. Indeed, precisely because the discourse of female virtue was already so available for conflicting uses, we need not even presume that Austen must have read *The Rights of Woman*—let alone contend that she would have endorsed it unequivocally—to recognize the values she and Wollstonecraft held in common. Cf. also Cora Kaplan's brief but very shrewd remarks on Austen's "conservative recuperation of Wollstonecraft" in "Wild Nights," pp. 174–75.

28. Auerbach, *Romantic Imprisonment*, p. 34. Writing of "the emotional spaciousness," as she terms it, "with which Mary reaches out to Fanny as her 'sister,'" Auerbach continues: "Mary's quest for sisters of gender rather than family, her uncomfortably outspoken championship of abused wives, her sexual initiative, and her unsettling habit of calling things by their names all suggest the pioneering sensibility of her contemporary, Mary Wollstonecraft; but Fanny cannot endure so universal an embrace, clutching only the shreds of kinship." Cf. also Janet Todd, who calls the rejection of Mary Crawford "one of fiction's most decisive defeats of friendship" (*Women's Friendship in Literature*, p. 274).

29. Wollstonecraft, *The Rights of Woman*, p. 187.

30. Ibid., p. 170.

31. Cf. Wollstonecraft on the "shameless behaviour" of prostitutes: "But these poor ignorant wretches never had any modesty to lose, when they consigned themselves to infamy; for modesty is a virtue, not a quality. No, they were only bashful, shame-faced innocents; and losing their innocence, their shame-facedness was rudely brushed off; a virtue would have left some vestiges in the mind, had it been sacrificed to passion, to make us respect the grand ruin" (*The Rights of Woman*, p. 122).

32. Ibid., p. 12. Compare the similar terms in which Edmund deplores "the

mind which does not struggle against itself," when he disputes with Mary Crawford in Sotherton chapel (*Mansfield Park*, p. 88). On "struggle" as a key term in the novel, see Jane Nardin, *Those Elegant Decorums: The Concept of Propriety in Jane Austen's Novels* (Albany: State University of New York Press, 1973), pp. 106–8.

33. Austen had mocked the premise of a modest unconsciousness at least as early as the opening chapters of *Northanger Abbey* (1818), when she mischievously refused to report whether Catherine Morland dreamed of Henry Tilney on the very first evening of their acquaintance. "Whether she thought of him so much, while she drank her warm wine and water, and prepared herself for bed, as to dream of him when there, cannot be ascertained; but I hope it was no more than in a slight slumber, or a morning doze at most; for if it be true, as a celebrated writer has maintained, that no young lady can be justified in falling in love before the gentleman's love is declared, it must be very improper that a young lady should dream of a gentleman before the gentleman is first known to have dreamt of her." The "celebrated writer" in question is Samuel Richardson, and the doctrine to which Austen alludes appears in his single contribution to the *Rambler*, an essay lamenting the contemporary decline of modesty in the fair sex. See Jane Austen, *Northanger Abbey* and *Persuasion*, pp. 29–30; and *Rambler* 97, 19 February 1751, in *The Yale Edition of the Works of Samuel Johnson*, vol. 4, ed. W. J. Bate and Albrecht B. Strauss (New Haven: Yale University Press, 1969), 156. According to Park Honan, the daughter of Austen's godfather was "shocked" by Fanny Price's initiative in love (*Jane Austen*, p. 347).

34. Wollstonecraft, *The Rights of Woman*, p. 123.

35. Tave, *Some Words of Jane Austen*, p. 194. I adopt the term "focalize" from Gérard Genette, *Narrative Discourse: An Essay in Method*, trans. Jane E. Lewin (Ithaca: Cornell University Press, 1980), esp. pp. 185–211. Though I can find little evidence for Marilyn Butler's suggestion that Fanny's "consciousness succeeds the Bertrams' as the *locus* of the important action" only in the second volume (*Jane Austen and the War of Ideas*, p. 245), there is no question that *Mansfield Park*, like most novels, is highly flexible in this regard; in Genette's terms, it frequently resorts to "variable internal" as well as "external" focalization. Fanny's consciousness is wholly absent, to choose only one example, when the narrator momentarily focalizes the prospect of Sir Thomas's return through the viewpoint of the soon-to-be-married Maria: "It was a gloomy prospect, and all that she could do was to throw a mist over it, and hope when the mist cleared away, she should see something else. It would hardly be *early* in November, there were generally delays, a bad passage or *something*" (*Mansfield Park*, p. 107).

36. Leo Bersani, *A Future for Astyanax: Character and Desire in Literature* (Boston: Little, Brown, 1976), p. 77. Cf. George Levine's more careful formulation: "Fanny has occupied the correct position, not because she has no desires, but because she has been able to discipline them in case they were not to be satisfied." *Darwin and the Novelists: Patterns of Science in Victorian Fiction* (Cambridge, Mass.: Harvard University Press, 1988), p. 67.

37. Wollstonecraft, *The Rights of Woman*, p. 4.

38. Douglas, *Purity and Danger*, p. 139. Dirt, Douglas elsewhere suggests, is not so much an idea in itself as a function of the need for order—"a kind of compendium category for all events which blur, smudge, contradict, or otherwise confuse accepted classifications" (*Implicit Meanings*, p. 51).

39. For an acute discussion of how the "fear of contamination" that pervades the novel anticipates the Victorian emphasis on the sanctity of the home, see Julia Prewitt Brown, *Jane Austen's Novels: Social Change and Literary Form* (Cambridge, Mass.: Harvard University Press, 1979), pp. 80–100, esp. p. 87.

40. Miller, *Narrative and Its Discontents*, p. 58.

41. Wollstonecraft, *The Rights of Woman*, p. 127. Wollstonecraft is here deploring the "gross" familiarities women allegedly take with one another rather than the indiscriminate mixing of the sexes, but she does so because she wishes to argue against the erotic understanding of modesty, and for a virtue that consistently opposes the indulgence of the body.

42. Of Fanny's belief in the blessings of "instant annihilation" for all the relatives of an adulteress, Park Honan has wittily observed, "On *that* principle some of the author's friends would have caused mayhem in their families" (*Jane Austen*, p. 344).

43. Claudia Johnson writes of the way in which "Austen inconclusively plays the improper Mary Crawford off against the proper Fanny Price in *Mansfield Park*" (*Jane Austen*, p. 23), but I would argue that despite its complex view of Mary, maintaining the balance "inconclusively" is just what the novel does not do.

44. Wollstonecraft, *The Right of Woman*, pp. 125, 128. By alluding to women's "bodily wit," Wollstonecraft may mean to distinguish the sorts of practical joking customary at boarding schools and the like from the verbal wit more characteristic of educated men. So she seems to imply, for example, when she goes on to say that "the jokes and hoiden tricks" in which young women engage among themselves are "almost on a par with the double meanings, which shake the convivial table when the glass has circulated freely" (p. 128). Such a distinction, however, would only seem to make more reprehensible the "double meanings" that Mary Crawford introduces at the Mansfield dinner table.

45. In *Narrative and Its Discontents*, pp. 85–90, D. A. Miller offers a shrewd analysis of the "closure practiced" (p. 89) on Mary Crawford in this scene. Miller notes the partial detachment of the narrator from Edmund and Fanny here and rightly observes that "in the narrator's final wrap-up" of Mary's subsequent history, she is allowed to regain some of her earlier complexity (p. 87). That Jane Austen could imagine Edmund departing without even a word or an answering gesture is still something of a problem, however: the awkwardness, even the unimaginability, of the scene remains.

46. Bruno Bettelheim, *The Uses of Enchantment: The Meaning and Importance of Fairy Tales* (New York: Knopf, 1977), pp. 253–54n. See also his subsequent note (pp. 254–55), which elaborates on the association of Cinderella with Vestal Virgins and once again stresses that ashes are a sign of purity as well

as of mourning. For a brief and useful account of the many versions of "Cinderella," see Iona and Peter Opie, *The Classic Fairy Tales* (1974; reprint, New York: Oxford, 1980), pp. 152–59.

47. Johnson, *Jane Austen*, p. 111. Though Johnson's account of the novel's unsettling ironies is the best I know, I think she finally exaggerates its status as "a bitter parody of conservative fiction" (p. 96). Her sharp analysis of the demonization of Mrs. Norris, for example (pp. 114–15), seems to me more persuasive as a feminist criticism of Austen than as an oblique argument for Austen's feminism. While I agree that "we need not read" the Bertrams' story "the same way they do" (p. 120), I don't think we can overlook the degree to which the Cinderella plotting and the use of Fanny as a central consciousness tend to encourage such a reading—especially when taken in conjunction with various passages of the narrator's comparatively unironic moralizing.

48. To Fanny Knight, 18 November [1814], *Letters*, p. 410.

49. As if to reassure us that Susan's smiles did not manifest her sister's joy too vulgarly, the narrator adds that "sitting forwards, however, and screened by her bonnet, those smiles were unseen" (*Mansfield Park*, p. 445).

50. To Fanny Knight, 18 November [1814], *Letters*, p. 410.

51. Levine, *Darwin and the Novelists*, p. 67. Cf. D. A. Miller: "is there any doubt, for all her humility and reticence, how much she *wants* Edmund?" (*Narrative and its Discontents*, p. 56).

Chapter Ten

1. To Mrs. Forster, 14 April 1853, *Letters of Matthew Arnold, 1848–1888*, ed. George W. E. Russell, 2 vols. (London: Macmillan, 1896), 1 : 34.

2. Charlotte Brontë, *Villette*, ed. Herbert Rosengarten and Margaret Smith (Oxford: Clarendon, 1984), p. 454. Subsequent references to this edition, which is based on the first edition of 1853, will appear parenthetically in the text.

3. To Mrs. Carmichael-Smyth, 25–28 March 1853, *The Letters and Private Papers of William Makepeace Thackeray*, ed. Gordon N. Ray, 4 vols. (Cambridge, Mass.: Harvard University Press, 1945–46), 3 : 248. Writing to another correspondent, Thackeray automatically identified Lucy Snowe with her creator: "it amuses me to read the author's naïve confession of being in love with 2 men at the same time; and her readiness to fall in love at any time. The poor little woman of genius! the fiery little eager brave tremulous homely-faced creature!" (To Lucy Baxter, 11 March 1853, *Letters*, 3 : 233).

4. [Harriet Martineau], Review of *Villette*, *Daily News*, 3 February 1853, p. 2. Cf. Margaret Oliphant on "the inevitable failure in dignity involved" in Brontë's "impassioned revelation" of female desire. "There is but one strain of intense sentiment in these books [Charlotte Brontë's novels]—the desire of a lonely creature longing for its mate" ("The Old Saloon: The Literature of the Last Fifty Years," *Blackwood's Edinburgh Magazine* 141 [1887], 757).

5. [Anne Mozley], Review of *Villette* and *Lady Bird* by Lady Georgiana Fullerton, *Christian Remembrancer*, n.s. 25 (1853), 443.

6. Ibid., pp. 442–43.

7. [Elizabeth Rigby], Review of *Vanity Fair* and *Jane Eyre, Quarterly Review* 84 (1848), 173, 176. Before casting slurs on the respectability of the novelist if she were in fact a woman, Rigby had speculated that Currer Bell was probably a man, citing "minutiae of circumstantial evidence which at once acquit the feminine hand": "no woman—a lady friend, whom we are always happy to consult, assures us—makes mistakes in her own *métier*" (p. 175). It should be noted that Anne Mozley had previously reviewed *Jane Eyre* in the *Christian Remembrancer,* n.s. 15 (1848), attacking it, too, as "unfeminine" (p. 396). For Brontë's response to Rigby and Mozley, see Elizabeth Gaskell, *The Life of Charlotte Brontë* (1857; reprint, London: Everyman, 1973), pp. 259–60; and Margot Peters, *Unquiet Soul: A Biography of Charlotte Brontë* (Garden City, N.Y.: Doubleday, 1975), pp. 240–41, 251–52, 371.

8. The best recent criticism of the novel, most of it feminist, has been concerned in one way or another to articulate this split. See especially Helene Moglen, *Charlotte Brontë: The Self Conceived* (1976; reprint, New York: Norton, 1978), pp. 190–229; Sandra M. Gilbert and Susan Gubar, *The Madwoman in the Attic: The Woman Writer and the Nineteenth-Century Literary Imagination* (New Haven: Yale University Press, 1979), pp. 399–440; Judith Lowder Newton, *Women, Power & Subversion,* pp. 86–124; Mary Jacobus, *Reading Woman: Essays in Feminist Criticism* (New York: Columbia University Press, 1986), pp. 41–61; and Joseph Litvak, "Charlotte Brontë and the Scene of Instruction: Authority and Subversion in *Villette,*" *Nineteenth-Century Literature* 42 (1988), 467–89.

9. To W. S. Williams, 6 November 1852, *The Brontës: Their Lives, Friendships and Correspondence in Four Volumes,* ed. Thomas James Wise and John Alexander Symington (Oxford: Shakespeare Head Press, 1932), 4 : 18; "*Lucus a non lucendo,*" a false etymology meaning "the grove is so called because it gives no light," has come to stand for things named for their opposite.

10. Cobbett, *Advice to Young Men,* letter 3, para. 100, 90, 100.

11. Melvin R. Watson, "Form and Substance in the Brontë Novels," in *From Jane Austen to Joseph Conrad: Essays Collected in Memory of James T. Hillhouse,* ed. Robert C. Rathburn and Martin Steinmann, Jr. (Minneapolis: University of Minnesota Press, 1958), p. 115.

12. Austen, *Mansfield Park,* p. 198.

13. Moglen, *Charlotte Brontë,* p. 212.

14. Cobbett, *Advice to Young Men,* letter 3, para. 90.

15. Complaints on this score began with Brontë's contemporaries. See, e.g., the anonymous *Athenæum* reviewer of 12 February 1853: "To adopt a musical phrase, the novel begins out of the key in which it is composed. In its first chapters interest is excited for a character who disappears during a large part of the story, and who returns to it merely as a second-rate figure. A character in truth, and not a caricature, is the little Paulina. . . . [W]e hoped that Currer Bell was going to trace out the girlhood, courtship, and matrimony of such a curious, elvish mite. Instead of this, towards the middle of the first volume the narrator steps into the part of heroine, with an inconsequence and abruptness that sug-

gest change of plan after the tale was undertaken" (p. 186). Perhaps the best-known protest against Lucy's treatment of Dr. John is E. M. Forster's: "As an example of mistaken triumph, I think of a slip—it is no more than a slip—which Charlotte Brontë makes in *Villette*. She allows Lucy Snowe to conceal from the reader her discovery that Dr. John is the same as her old playmate Graham. When it comes out, we do get a good plot thrill, but too much at the expense of Lucy's character. She has seemed, up to then, the spirit of integrity, and has, as it were, laid herself under a moral obligation to narrate all that she knows. That she stoops to suppress is a little distressing, though the incident is too trivial to do her any permanent harm." See *Aspects of the Novel* (1927; reprint, New York: Harcourt, Brace, 1955), pp. 92–93.

16. Charles Dickens, *Bleak House* (1853), ed. George Ford and Sylvère Monod (New York: Norton, 1977), p. 17. In "A Suggestive Book for Charlotte Brontë?," *Journal of English and Germanic Philology* 76 (1977), 363–83, Jean Frantz Blackall argues that Brontë's reading of the early parts of *Bleak House* "exerted a seminal influence on the novel *Villette* was to become" (p. 363). Blackall draws on evidence from the discarded ms. fragments of *Villette* as well as on the completed texts. Though some of the likenesses Blackall points to are striking, it may be more useful to attribute these to a common tradition than to the immediate influence of Dickens on Brontë. The latter's only recorded comment on *Bleak House* concerns the first number, where she complained that "an amiable nature is caricatured, not faithfully rendered, in Miss Esther Summerson" (To George Smith, 11 March 1853, in Wise and Symington, *The Brontës*, 3:322).

17. Gilbert and Gubar, *The Madwoman in the Attic*, p. 418.

18. "On Modesty," *Lady's Magazine* 23 (1792), 130.

19. Dickens, *Bleak House*, p. 163.

20. Ibid., pp. 102, 103.

21. For related accounts of how Lucy's narrative strategies entail a defiant reversal of her powerlessness, see Nancy Sorkin Rabinowitz, "'Faithful Narrator' or 'Partial Eulogist': First-Person Narration in Brontë's *Villette*," *Journal of Narrative Technique* 15 (1985), 244–55; and Karen Lawrence, "The Cypher: Disclosure and Reticence in *Villette*," *Nineteenth-Century Literature* 42 (1988), 448–66.

22. Charlotte Brontë, *The Professor* (1857), ed. Margaret Smith and Herbert Rosengarten (Oxford: Clarendon, 1987), p. 98. (*The Professor* was written before *Villette* but published posthumously.) Crimsworth later describes the "grave and modest countenances" and "general air of native propriety and decency" of his half-dozen "British English" [sic] pupils: "by this last circumstance alone I could at a glance distinguish the daughter of Albion and the nursling of Protestantism from the foster-child of Rome, the *protégée* of Jesuitry" (p. 103). Francis Henri, the novel's heroine, is of course Anglo-Swiss.

23. *Lady's Magazine* 13 (1782), 396. Recall also Andrews, *Remarks on the French and English Ladies* (1783), cited in ch. 3, p. 40, above.

24. Newton, *Women, Power & Subversion*, p. 94. Newton similarly fails to

recognize the ideological context on which the novel draws when she accuses Brontë of being so anxious "to qualify, justify, and in part deny the power of her heroine that she . . . very speciously assures us that Lucy's boldness is characteristic of English women and that only foreigners would find it strange" (p. 100). The freedom of the Englishwoman may finally have been "specious," but the fiction about that freedom was hardly Brontë's alone; indeed, just because it was *not* hers alone she was enabled to exploit it.

25. Robert B. Heilman, "Charlotte Brontë's 'New' Gothic," in *From Jane Austen to Joseph Conrad,* ed. Rathburn and Steinmann, pp. 118–32. At least since Heilman's article, critics have been sensitive to *Villette*'s Gothic trappings. But it has, of course, been Brontë's recent feminist critics who have explored most fully the significance of her heroines' covert identification with incarcerated madwomen and buried nuns. See especially Gilbert and Gubar, *The Madwoman in the Attic,* pp. 425–30; Mary Jacobus, *Reading Woman,* pp. 47–55; and Christina Crosby, "Charlotte Brontë's Haunted Text," *Studies in English Literature* 24 (1984), 701–15. Cf. also E. D. H. Johnson, "'Daring the Dread Glance': Charlotte Brontë's Treatment of the Supernatural in *Villette,*" *Nineteenth-Century Fiction* 20 (1966), 325–36, for an earlier, if less resonant, treatment of the relation between the nun's appearances and the "successive stages" of Lucy's own psychological progress (p. 325).

26. Though some critics have emphasized Lucy's refusal to relinquish her "woman's garb" on this occasion, her ambiguous compromise—she merely tucks up her long hair, adds "a little vest, a collar, and cravat, and a paletot of small dimensions" (p. 194)—makes her all the more effectively the mirror image of the effeminate but unmistakably heterosexual de Hamal.

27. Jacobus, *Reading Woman,* p. 51. Jacobus is more interested in exploring the ways in which such ambiguity calls into question the novel's mode of representation by subverting its "facade of realism" (p. 48).

28. Austen, *Mansfield Park,* p. 169.

29. Litvak, "Charlotte Brontë and the Scene of Instruction," p. 480. Litvak's rich account is the best reading of this scene I know. Cf. also Christina Crosby: "the excessiveness of episodes like the play and the gratuitous degree to which Lucy assumes a masculine stance, display a fascination with the 'natural' division of the sexes—and a repeated tendency to call this difference into question" ("Charlotte Brontë's Haunted Text," p. 708).

30. Even Litvak blurs this distinction by alluding (if only in metaphor?) to Lucy's "rewrit[ing]" the script ("Charlotte Brontë and the Scene of Instruction," p. 479).

31. See, e.g., Lucy's stubborn refusal to exchange the cigar case she wins at the lottery for the "lady's head-dress" worn by Dr. John (p. 317) or her baffled report of her strange desire to share food and drink with Ginevra (pp. 334–35). Tony Tanner comments briefly on these and other instances of "that odd transference of male and female characteristics and rôles which occurs intermittently throughout" the novel, in his introduction to *Villette* (Harmondsworth: Penguin, 1981), pp. 34–35.

32. Cf. Gilbert and Gubar, who remark that "the crisis of the play (when Lucy comes out on the stage) can be said to cause the confinement and isolation she experiences during the long vacation" (*The Madwoman in the Attic,* p. 414).

33. "I thought the same," Lucy writes after Polly has declared her belief in the continuity of their childhood identities, "but I wondered to find my thoughts hers: there are certain things in which we so rarely meet with our double that it seems a miracle when that chance befalls" (p. 398). A number of critics have commented on this doubling. See, e.g., Moglen, *Charlotte Brontë,* pp. 197–200; Gilbert and Gubar, *The Madwoman in the Attic,* pp. 404–5, 426–27; and Janice Carlisle, "The Face in the Mirror: *Villette* and the Conventions of Autobiography," *ELH* 46 (1979), 280–83.

34. The quoted phrase is from the *Athenæum* review of 12 February 1853, p. 186; see n. 15, above. See also the review of *Villette* and Gaskell's *Ruth* in *Putnam's Monthly Magazine* 1 (1853): "The difficulty with the book as a work of art is, that the interest does not sufficiently concentrate upon the two chief figures. Graham and Paulina are disproportionately interesting. In fact, we are not sure that most readers are not more anxious to marry Graham than to follow the destiny of Lucy Snowe. There is a pause over his marriage, and a glance into the future, which properly belong only to the close of the book, and which materially affect the sequence of interest" (p. 537).

35. To George Smith, 6 December 1852, in Wise and Symington, *The Brontës,* 4:23. For further evidence of Lucy's wish to tell such a story, see her persistent fantasies that Ginevra's resistance to Dr. John is really just a modest delaying action: "I imagined her grateful in secret, loving now with reserve; but purposing one day to show how much she loved: I pictured her faithful hero half conscious of her coy fondness, and comforted by that consciousness: I conceived an electric chord of sympathy between them, a fine chain of mutual understanding, sustaining union through a separation of a hundred leagues— carrying, across mound and hollow, communication by prayer and wish. Ginevra gradually became with me a sort of heroine." It is her recognition of the nervous "malady" implicit in this "growing illusion" of hers that prompts Lucy's famous question: "How shall I keep well?" (p. 222). See also p. 275.

36. Karen Chase, *Eros & Psyche: The Representation of Personality in Charlotte Brontë, Charles Dickens, and George Eliot* (New York: Methuen, 1984), p. 70.

37. I have in mind, of course, the well-known scene in the garden at Thornfield in which Jane delivers her impassioned speech—"Do you think I can stay to become nothing to you? Do you think I am an automaton?—a machine without feelings?"—and the already married Rochester responds by "summon[ing]" her to be his wife. Here, too, Brontë's break with the convention has its limits, since Jane makes clear that she speaks as boldly as she does only because she believes her parting from Rochester is inevitable. See *Jane Eyre* (1847), ed. Jane Jack and Margaret Smith (Oxford: Clarendon, 1969), pp. 318, 319.

38. Cf. Lucy's account of her repeated attempts to keep Ginevra interposed between herself and Paul, as they walk together on the school outing: "my private motive for this manœuvre might be traced to the circumstance of the new

print dress I wore, being pink in colour—a fact which, under our present convoy, made me feel something as I have felt, when, clad in a shawl with a red border, necessitated to traverse a meadow where pastured a bull" (p. 549).

39. "No nook in the grounds," Jane tells us, was "more sheltered and more Eden-like" than the orchard at Thornfield; before he proposes there, Rochester professes to feel as if he were tied to her by "a string somewhere under my left ribs" (*Jane Eyre,* pp. 276, 280).

40. "Escape is all over the book; *Villette* reads like one long meditation on a prison break." Millett does not name Lucy as Paul's killer, but the implication is clear: "the keeper turned kind must be eluded anyway; Paul turned lover is drowned." See Kate Millett, *Sexual Politics* (1969; reprint, New York: Avon, 1971), p. 146. By arguing that the witch-like Mme. Walravens is yet another of Lucy's doubles—her "darkest and most secret avatar"—Gilbert and Gubar attempt to specify the agency of the murder: "it seems likely, indeed, that it is Lucy's unconscious and unspeakable will that Madame Walravens enacts when she sends Paul on a typically witchy quest for treasure in (of all places) *Basse/ terre*" (*The Madwoman in the Attic,* p. 431).

41. I would like to suggest that these "happiest years" of Lucy's life bear a significant resemblance to that period in which the young child, according to D. W. Winnicott, develops the "ability to be truly alone" by having the "experience of being alone in the presence of someone." Happily working in a school of her own, secure in the knowledge of her lover's absent presence, Lucy in this sense inhabits a much belated and geographically extended version of Winnicott's transitional space—his standard account of which involves the child playing contentedly in one room while aware of its mother's loving presence in another. Like Lucy, Winnicott calls attention to the fact that "the basis of the capacity to be alone is a paradox." See "The Capacity to Be Alone" (1958), in *The Maturational Processes and the Facilitating Environment: Studies in the Theory of Emotional Development* (New York: International Universities Press, 1965), pp. 32, 30. See also Jessica Benjamin's suggestive attempt to marshal Winnicott's theory of development for a feminist account of female desire—"A Desire of One's Own: Psychoanalytic Feminism and Intersubjective Space," in *Feminist Studies/Critical Studies,* ed. Teresa de Lauretis (Bloomington: Indiana University Press, 1968), pp. 78–101.

Sketchily imagined as it is, Lucy's final capacity to be alone might be instructively compared with her earlier breakdown during the utter loneliness of the long *vacance.* Though her deliberate effacing of her own early history makes it impossible to specify the origins of her pain, the fact that she appears to suffer from a form of survivor's guilt is clearly relevant here: immediately before her breakdown, she dreams that "the well-loved dead . . . met me elsewhere, alienated" (p. 223). Insofar as Lucy's morbid depressions and her terror of her own destructive powers are intimately related to the traumatic loss of all her loved ones, Paul's loving capacity to "survive" her aggressions, as Winnicott would put it, restores her to herself. On Lucy's—and Brontë's own—"survivor's guilt," see Moglen, *Charlotte Brontë,* pp. 19–24, 197–200; and Robert Keefe,

Charlotte Brontë's World of Death (Austin: University of Texas Press, 1979), esp. pp. 149–84. In the context of the above argument, it is worth noting that both Moglen (p. 216) and Keefe (p. 182) sense something "maternal" in Paul Emanuel's affection.

42. Gaskell, *The Life of Charlotte Brontë*, p. 366. Cf. Nancy Rabinowitz, who also comments briefly on the novel's handling of what she calls "the plot of the father" ("'Faithful Narrator' or 'Partial Eulogist,'" p. 251).

43. W. M. Thackeray, *The Newcomes* (New York: Harper, 1903), pp. 805, 806. *The Newcomes* began to appear serially in 1853, the year of *Villette's* publication; the last number was issued in 1855.

Chapter Eleven

1. Elizabeth Gaskell, *Wives and Daughters: An Every-Day Story*, ed. Angus Easson (Oxford: Oxford University Press, 1987), pp. 55, 678, 679. Subsequent references to this edition, which is based on the *Cornhill* serial of 1864–66, will appear parenthetically in the text. Like other editions since the first, this one concludes with the afterword supplied by Frederick Greenwood, the *Cornhill* editor, summarizing "all that is known of her designs for the story, which would have been completed in another chapter" (p. 685)

2. Patricia Beer cites Molly's "woundingly off-hand" behavior on this last visit as a representative instance of Gaskell's "confusion" about the issue of female honesty, arguing that despite the novelist's frequent insistence on the importance of truth telling, she "has trouble in reconciling it with the devious behaviour necessary to the coquetry which was thought proper, even by herself, to marriageable young women." Though Beer rightly identifies a central contradiction in the code of female behavior, her complaint that "the maidenly modesty in which [Molly] has been trained makes her behave in this stupidly insincere and self-defeating way" seems to me doubly insensitive to the ways in which the temporal dimensions of a narrative like Gaskell's serve to manage such contradictions. Insofar as Molly is *not* yet fully conscious that she loves Roger, she is not "insincere," and insofar as her shrinking predictably inspires him to come forward, her behavior is hardly self-defeating. See *Reader, I Married Him: A Study of the Women Characters of Jane Austen, Charlotte Brontë, Elizabeth Gaskell and George Eliot* (London: Macmillan, 1974), pp. 171, 170, 171.

3. Richardson, *Pamela*, p. 235. It is precisely because Pamela does half-register what she has just admitted that she hastens to deny it. "What pity his heart is not so good as his appearance!" the passage continues. "Why can't I hate him? But don't be uneasy, if you should see this; for it is impossible I should love him; for his vices all *ugly him over*, as I may say."

4. [Henry James], Review of *Wives and Daughters*, *Nation* 2 (1866), 247.

5. Though Molly is the principal focal character, the narrative of *Wives and Daughters*, like that of *Mansfield Park*, frequently adopts what Gérard Genette calls "variable internal" as well as "external" focalization. For a helpful discrimination of the possibilities, see his *Narrative Discourse*, esp. pp. 185–211.

6. As Peter Sabor notes, when Richardson came to revise the novel, he at-

tempted to cope with anti-Pamelist mockery of this episode by having Mrs. Jervis rather than Pamela insist on the need to complete the embroidery. See *Pamela*, p. 519, n. 32.

7. Elizabeth Cleghorn Gaskell, *My Diary: The Early Years of My Daughter Marianne* (London: Privately Printed by Clement Shorter, 1923), p. 5. Gaskell kept the diary from 1835 through 1838.

8. The quotation comes from Gaskell's late tale, "A Dark Night's Work" (1863), and in context the emphasis falls on the painful consequences of resisting nature's course: "it was the usual struggle between father and lover for the possession of love, instead of the natural and graceful resignation of the parent to the prescribed course of things; and, as usual, it was the poor girl who bore the suffering for no fault of her own." I owe the use of the passage as a gloss on *Wives and Daughters* to Pauline Nestor, *Female Friendships and Communities: Charlotte Brontë, George Eliot, Elizabeth Gaskell* (Oxford: Clarendon, 1985), p. 65.

9. Cf. Patricia Meyer Spacks: "although she spins romantic fantasies about Osborne Hamley, the elder son whom she has never met, they lack physicality: two angels holding hands." Though the remark seems to me apt so far as Molly's feelings for Osborne are concerned, it should be obvious that I disagree with Spacks's contention that "Molly appears to have no sexual potential." See *The Adolescent Idea: Myths of Youth and the Adult Imagination* (New York: Basic Books, 1981), pp. 37, 40.

10. Marianne Hirsch does not discuss *Wives and Daughters,* but the novel here vividly confirms her argument about the ways in which nineteenth-century women's plots seem to depend on the repression of the mother. See *The Mother/Daughter Plot: Narrative, Psychoanalysis, Feminism* (Bloomington: Indiana University Press, 1989), esp. pp. 43–67.

11. "She could no longer blush," we are told when we are first introduced to Mr. Kirkpatrick's widow; "at eighteen [Cynthia's age, as it happens] she had been very proud of her blushes" (p. 98). The prospect of marriage, however, appears to bring a certain ambiguous restoration of her original innocence: when Mr. Gibson arrives to propose, "she felt herself blush, and she was not displeased at the consciousness" (p. 107). She even "manage[s] to get up a very becoming blush" (p. 136) a second time when Gibson joins her for an audience with Lady Cumnor. After she becomes Mrs. Gibson, we hear no more of her blushes.

12. Patsy Stoneman aptly cites Wollstonecraft on this rivalry between mother and daughter: "supposing . . . that a being only taught to please must still find her happiness in pleasing;—what an example of folly . . . will she be to her innocent daughters! The mother will be lost in the coquette, and, instead of making friends of her daughters, view them with eyes askance, for they are rivals—rivals more cruel than any other, because they invite a comparison, and drive her from the throne of beauty, who has never thought of a seat on the bench of reason" (*The Rights of Woman*, p. 49). Though Gaskell is a shrewd observer of such ri-

valry, her tone of course is more amused than censorious. See Stoneman, *Elizabeth Gaskell* (Bloomington: Indiana University Press, 1987), p. 187.

13. Gaskell presumably does not wish the reader to recall that both women in the biblical story are introduced as "harlots" (1 Kings 3.16)—despite her own treatment of the fallen woman's redemption by maternal love in *Ruth* (1853).

14. When Mr. Coxe returns, even he finds there can be "no mistaking" Molly's lack of interest in him: "I came here with a heart as faithful to your daughter, as ever beat in a man's bosom," he protests in his final interview with Dr. Gibson; "but really, sir, if you had seen her manner to me every time I endeavoured to press my suit a little—it was more than coy, it was absolutely repellent, there could be no mistaking it,—while Miss Kirkpatrick—" (p. 423). While the novel gives us no reason to believe that Molly would ever be attracted to this rather foolish young man, her resistance is presumably intensified by her heart's preengagement.

15. For an analysis of some other, more overtly political, uses of such rhetoric to characterize the heroine at moments of crisis, see my "Why Political Novels Have Heroines: *Sybil, Mary Barton,* and *Felix Holt,*" *Novel* 18 (1985), 126–44.

16. Though I obviously agree with Margaret Homans on the central importance of Molly's role as a "receiver of secrets" and a "selfless mediator," I would argue that the novel's emphasis falls more on problems of licit and illicit consciousness than it does on the thematizing of language. See her *Bearing the Word: Language and Female Experience in Nineteenth-Century Women's Writing* (Chicago: University of Chicago Press, 1986), pp. 251–76; esp. p. 256. Even in this climactic episode, Molly does not, strictly speaking, function as a "letter carrier" (Homans, p. 267), since Preston sends back the incriminating correspondence after their encounter. Though Mrs. Goodenough later thinks she sees Molly slipping Mr. Preston a letter at the bookseller's, what in fact passes between them is an envelope "carefully sealed up like a letter" (Gaskell, p. 522), containing the banknotes that will repay Cynthia's debt.

17. [Steele], *Tatler,* no. 98, 24 November 1709.

18. [James], Review of *Wives and Daughters,* p. 247. Though most subsequent critics of the novel have more or less echoed James's praise of the Kirkpatrick women, Marilyn Butler enters a qualified dissent by arguing that Cynthia's character is largely modeled on that of Cecilia in Maria Edgeworth's *Helen.* See "The Uniqueness of Cynthia Kirkpatrick: Elizabeth Gaskell's *Wives and Daughters* and Maria Edgeworth's *Helen,*" *Review of English Studies* 23 (1972), 278–90.

19. To "Herbert Grey" [after 15 March 1859], in *The Letters of Mrs. Gaskell,* ed. J. A. V. Chapple and Arthur Pollard (Cambridge, Mass.: Harvard University Press, 1967), p. 541. "Grey" had apparently asked for Gaskell's opinion on his first novel, *The Three Paths* (1859). The letter in Chapple and Pollard is headed to Marianne Gaskell, who was at this time acting as her mother's amanuensis. I have omitted passages in the manuscript that the editors indicate Gaskell herself as having deleted.

20. Austen, *Mansfield Park*, p. 163.

21. Homans, *Bearing the Word*, pp. 172–73. Though Homans asserts that the intended recipient of this letter, the novelist who published as "Herbert Grey," was in fact Gaskell's daughter Marianne, I can find no evidence to support this identification.

22. See, e.g., Lucy Poate Stebbins, *A Victorian Album: Some Lady Novelists of the Period* (London: Secker & Warburg, 1946), p. 126; Arthur Pollard, *Mrs. Gaskell: Novelist and Biographer* (Cambridge, Mass.: Harvard University Press, 1966), pp. 231–33; and W. A. Craik, *Elizabeth Gaskell and the English Provincial Novel* (London: Methuen, 1975), pp. 202–3, 247, 252. All three also allude to resemblances between the Gibsons' marriage and that of the Bennets.

23. Austen, *Mansfield Park*, p. 359.

24. Ibid., p. 40.

25. "As soon as the holidays came round," Cynthia later reminisces about Mrs. Kirkpatrick, "she was off to some great house or another, and I dare say I was at a very awkward age to have me lounging about in her drawing-room when callers came" (p. 493). When James came to write the novel he called *The Awkward Age*, something of Mrs. Kirkpatrick's "selfish and silly and consummately natural completeness," in his words (review of *Wives and Daughters*, p. 247), may well have gone into the portrait of Mrs. Brookenham—another mother of a marriageable daughter who prefers not to acknowledge the passage of time.

26. Austen, *Mansfield Park*, p. 464.

27. Ibid., p. 455.

28. Ibid., p. 461.

29. Though he seems to have forgotten it, an anxious Dr. Gibson drew on the same romance analogy—and in similarly extravagant terms—when he confronted Coxe at the beginning of the novel. "But remember how soon a young girl's name may be breathed upon, and sullied," he scolded the young man. "Molly has no mother, and for that very reason she ought to move among you all, as unharmed as Una herself" (p. 54).

30. Austen, *Mansfield Park*, pp. 456, 459.

31. Edgar Wright, *Mrs. Gaskell: The Basis for Reassessment* (London: Oxford University Press, 1965), p. 225.

32. To George Smith, 3 May [1864], *Letters*, p. 732. Though Gaskell had just begun to write the novel, her plot outline here deviates remarkably little from the finished text, as several commentators have noted. Names, however, are another matter: the letter refers to her scientist hero as Roger "Newton."

33. On the inspiration Gaskell may have drawn from her visit to Allman, see Winifred Gérin, *Elizabeth Gaskell: A Biography* (Oxford: Clarendon, 1976), pp. 276–78.

34. To Charles Eliot Norton, 1 February [1864], *Letters*, p. 724.

35. Stoneman, *Elizabeth Gaskell*, p. 189. Though I disagree with Stoneman's characterization of both Gaskell and Darwin here, her remarks on the

way in which Roger's chosen discipline unites "'science' and personal relations" are very much to the point (p. 177).

Chapter Twelve

1. *Dublin Review*, n.s. 17 (1871), 3, as cited by Gertrude Himmelfarb, *Darwin and the Darwinian Revolution* (1959; reprint, New York: Anchor, 1962), p. 357.

2. Cf. Gillian Beer, who has recently argued that Darwin is "telling a new story, against the grain of the language available to tell it in" (*Darwin's Plots: Evolutionary Narrative in Darwin, George Eliot and Nineteenth-Century Fiction* [London: Routledge, 1983], p. 5). As a way of accounting for certain animal characteristics, Darwin's theory of female choice was, so far as I can ascertain, a relatively "new story"; but I am, of course, arguing that culturally it was not— and that the "grain of the language" in this case facilitated its telling. Though Beer does discuss *The Descent*, her primary emphasis is on *The Origin of Species*. George Levine's *Darwin and the Novelists: Patterns of Science in Victorian Fiction* (Cambridge, Mass.: Harvard University Press, 1988) also focuses chiefly on *The Origin* and on natural rather than sexual selection. But I obviously agree with Levine's general emphasis on the mutual interaction of the scientific and the extrascientific cultures: compare especially his account of the assumptions that the theory of natural selection shared with natural theology and my own argument about the relations between the theory of sexual selection and English courtship fiction.

3. Charles Darwin, *The Descent of Man, and Selection in Relation to Sex*, with an intro. by John Tyler Bonner and Robert M. May (Princeton: Princeton University Press, 1981), 1:403, 272, 273. Further references to this work, which is a photoreproduction of the first edition of 1871, will appear parenthetically in the text.

4. [Moore], *Fables for the Female Sex* (1744), p. 31. As it happens, the line comes from an animal fable—"The Wolf, the Sheep, and the Lamb." See ch. 3, p. 37, above.

5. According to Stanley Edgar Hyman, Darwin sometimes suppressed evidence in conflict with the theory, including the statement from a correspondent in 1868 that "the common hen prefers a salacious cock, but is quite indifferent to colour" (*The Tangled Bank: Darwin, Marx, Frazer and Freud as Imaginative Writers* [New York: Atheneum, 1962], p. 55). The correspondent in question seems to have been a Mr. Hewitt of Birmingham: see Darwin's letter to J. Jenner Weir, 4 April [1868], in *More Letters of Charles Darwin: A Record of His Work in a Series of Hitherto Unpublished Letters*, ed. Francis Darwin, 2 vols. (London: John Murray, 1903), 2:72. Though the "salacious cock" does disappear from *The Descent*, the information from Hewitt obliquely surfaces when Darwin alludes to him as one of several authorities on the courtship of fowls who "do not believe that the females prefer certain males on account of the beauty of their plumage"—to which Darwin immediately adds: "but some allowance

must be made for the artificial state under which they have long been kept" (2:117). In a wild state, presumably, the common hen would have more modesty and better taste.

6. Charles Darwin, *The Descent of Man, and Selection in Relation to Sex,* 2d ed. (London: John Murray, 1875), p. 273. This second edition was originally published in 1874. Hyman suggests that because Darwin was less directly threatened when it came to the lower animals, he felt free to indulge in "the fantasy image of the dominating, passionate, aggressive female"; he compares this revised passage to Gulliver in Brobdingnag or Baudelaire's "La Géante" (*The Tangled Bank,* p. 55).

7. Rousseau, *Emile,* p. 694. See ch. 2, pp. 27–28, above.

8. Sometimes Darwin even writes as if male combat were mysteriously subordinated to the pacific ends of female choosing: "It is certain that with almost all animals there is a struggle between the males for the possession of the female. This fact is so notorious that it would be superfluous to give instances. Hence the females, supposing that their mental capacity sufficed for the exertion of a choice, could select one out of several males" (1:259). "The logic of this statement," Ernst Mayr remarks, "is not compelling." See "Sexual Selection and Natural Selection," in *Sexual Selection and the Descent of Man 1871–1971,* ed. Bernard Campbell (Chicago: Aldine, 1972), p. 94.

9. Among those who resisted such identification, somewhat surprisingly, was Havelock Ellis. Though he did not dispute the theory of sexual selection, he protested that Darwin's "too anthropomorphic" language misleadingly implied that the female consciously exercised her aesthetic sense, when, in fact, she merely responded, unconsciously, to stimulation (*Studies,* 1–2:24). Ellis seized on a "Supplemental Note" to *The Descent* (first published in *Nature* in 1876) as evidence that Darwin had backed away from his belief in animal consciousness. "I presume," Darwin wrote, "that no supporter of the principle of sexual selection believes that the females select particular points of beauty in the males; they are merely excited or attracted in a greater degree by one male than by another, and this seems often to depend, especially with birds, on brilliant colouring." Despite this apparent disclaimer, Darwin had, in fact, often seemed to suggest that the females did "select particular points of beauty in the males"; see, e.g., the passage on the Argus pheasant quoted later in this chapter. And since the note immediately continues, "even man, excepting perhaps an artist, does not analyse the slight differences in the features of the woman whom he may admire, on which her beauty depends," it is hard to conclude that Darwin has retreated very far. See "Supplemental Note on Sexual Selection in Relation to Monkeys," *Nature,* 2 November 1876, p. 19.

While Ellis somewhat sententiously explained Darwin's alleged confusion on the grounds that the latter "was not a psychologist, and . . . lived before the methods of comparative psychology had begun to be developed," there is a certain irony in the fact that the author of the *Studies in the Psychology of Sex* should in this case opt for a narrow biological reading of the evidence (1–2:24).

From the standpoint of subsequent evolutionary science, perhaps the most influential of Darwin's contemporaries to question the theory of sexual selection was A. R. Wallace, who began by according sexual selection a limited role but became increasingly skeptical. Though Wallace also raised the problem of animal "taste," his objections were more far-reaching. For a useful summary of the shifting positions in the debate, see Malcolm Jay Kottler, "Darwin, Wallace, and the Origin of Sexual Dimorphism," *Proceedings of the American Philosophical Society* 124 (1980), 203–26. Most recent evolutionary biologists who devote significant attention to female choice steer clear of the aesthetic question. But see Lee Ehrman: "one only wishes to correct the Master by setting off the adjective 'attractive' in either quotation marks or italics, so that it is not interpreted merely to mean beauty" ("Genetics and Sexual Selection," in Campbell, ed., *Sexual Selection*, p. 114).

10. For the modern association of sexual selection with animal polygamy and promiscuity, see, e.g., Mayr, "Sexual Selection," pp. 93–98; and John Maynard Smith, *The Evolution of Sex* (Cambridge: Cambridge University Press, 1978), pp. 183–87. In an essay on "Sexual Selection and Dimorphism in Birds," however, Robert K. Selander argues that "there is no justification for altogether ruling out sexual selection in monogamous species as some authors have done," though he also goes on to confirm that there exists a strong relationship between sexual dimorphism and nonmonogamous mating systems (Campbell, ed., *Sexual Selection*, pp. 184, 192–210).

11. Charles Darwin, *The Autobiography of Charles Darwin 1809–1882*, ed. Nora Barlow (1887; reprint, with original omissions restored, New York: Norton, 1958), pp. 138–39; and *The Life and Letters of Charles Darwin*, ed. Francis Darwin, 2 vols. (New York: Appleton, 1896), 1 : 102.

12. For some helpful discussions of these issues, see Mayr, "Sexual Selection," in Campbell, ed., *Sexual Selection*, pp. 87–104; and Robert L. Trivers, "Parental Investment and Sexual Selection," pp. 136–79 of the same volume; Michael T. Ghiselin, *The Economy of Nature and the Evolution of Sex* (Berkeley: University of California Press, 1974), pp. 175–91; George C. Williams, *Sex and Evolution* (Princeton: Princeton University Press, 1975), pp. 134–39; and Smith, *The Evolution of Sex*, pp. 168–87. For a sharp warning against contemporary sociobiologists' glib application of the "investment" model to human behavior, see Ruth Bleier, *Science and Gender: A Critique of Biology and Its Theories on Women* (Oxford: Pergamon, 1984), esp. pp. 16–21.

13. Cf. Hyman, who quotes a passage from *The Descent* in which Darwin pays lyrical tribute to the "graceful double curvature" of the horns of certain antelopes. "If . . . the horns," Darwin writes, "like the splendid accoutrements of the knights of old, add to the noble appearance of stags and antelopes, they may have been modified partly for this purpose"—a passage that prompts Hyman to comment, "Here, where he uses 'purpose' to mean 'no purpose,' Darwin completely transcends the world of nature of the *Origin* and accepts the world of culture" (*The Tangled Bank*, p. 58). Though Hyman does not remark the feminine agency of that culture, his reading of *The Descent* has a number of points of contact with my own.

14. Hyman quotes an anonymous review of *The Descent* in the *Spectator* of 12 March 1871: "Mr. Darwin finds himself compelled to reintroduce a new doctrine of the fall of man. He shews that the instincts of the higher animals are far nobler than the savage races of men, and he finds himself, therefore, compelled to reintroduce,—in a form of the substantial orthodoxy of which he appears to be quite unconscious,—and to introduce as a scientific hypothesis the doctrine that man's gain of *knowledge* was the cause of a temporary but long-enduring moral deterioration, as indicated by the many foul customs, especially as to marriage, of savage tribes." "As the reviewer brilliantly recognized," Hyman writes, "the *Descent* is precipitous, a Fall out of animal Eden to the savage condition, and then the slow painful climb back" (*The Tangled Bank*, p. 49).

15. [Allestree], *The Ladies Calling* (1673), 1:15. See ch. 2, p. 13, above.

16. William James, *The Principles of Psychology*, 2 vols. (1890; reprint, New York: Dover, 1950), 2:438.

Chapter Thirteen

1. Havelock Ellis, "The Evolution of Modesty" (1899), in *Studies in the Psychology of Sex*, 2 vols. (New York: Random House, 1942), 1–1:45. Further references to this edition will be given parenthetically in the text. For the complicated publishing history of the *Studies*, see ch. 1, n. 3, above.

2. Recall Ellis's preface of 1935 and its defense of the decision to substitute "The Evolution of Modesty" for "Sexual Inversion" as the first volume of the *Studies*: "I was pleased to be able to effect this change of order, for . . . I had not originally proposed to start the *Studies* with what was inevitably regarded as an abnormal subject, and to put it at the head served to excuse the not uncommon error of describing my *Studies* as 'pathological'" (p. xxi).

3. Havelock Ellis, *The Dance of Life* (Boston: Houghton Mifflin, 1923), p. 123.

4. William Acton, *The Functions and Disorders of the Reproductive Organs . . . ,* 3d ed. (London: Churchill, 1862), p. 101.

5. Cobbett, *Advice to Young Men* (1829), letter 3, para. 100. See ch. 3, pp. 48–49, above.

6. Grosskurth, *Havelock Ellis*, p. 226.

7. Freud, *Beyond the Pleasure Principle* (1920), *Standard Edition*, 18:39.

8. Brooks, *Reading for the Plot*, p. 104. "Incest," Brooks later suggests, "is only the exemplary version of a temptation of short-circuit from which the protagonist and the text must be led away, into detour, into the cure that prolongs narrative" (p. 109). I am indebted to Brooks's general discussion of the dynamics of narrative for my own understanding of the tension between desire and delay in modest fictions.

9. Brooks, p. 103. For the argument that Brooks's account of plotting follows an implicitly masculine model of desire, see Boone, *Tradition Counter Tradition*, p. 72, and Hirsch, *The Mother/Daughter Plot*, pp. 53–54. "If this is so," Boone writes, "the erotic dynamic of the traditional love-plot, however much it may play to female desire, nonetheless would seem to encode at the most ele-

mentary level of narrative a highly specific, male-oriented norm of sexuality fostering the illusion that all pleasure (of reading or of sex) is ejaculatory." But as Ellis's delight in feminine indirection may suggest, the pleasure of reading—or of sex—may be as much that of postponing the climax as of getting there. On the relation between the figure of the female and various senses of delay and dilation in the Renaissance, see Patricia Parker, *Literary Fat Ladies: Rhetoric, Gender, Property* (London: Methuen, 1987), esp. pp. 8–35. For a study that emphasizes the feminist implications of women's "self-postponement," see also Kathleen Blake, *Love and the Woman Question in Victorian Literature: The Art of Self-Postponement* (Brighton: Harvester, 1983).

10. There is some evidence that Ellis derived the term and several associated ideas from the American psychologist Stanley Hall, as in the quotation he attributes to Hall and Allin: "perhaps the reluctance of the female first long-circuited the exquisite sensations connected with sexual organs and acts to the antics of animal and human courtship, while restraint had the physiological function of developing the colors, plumes, excessive activity, and exuberant life of the pairing season" (*Studies,* 1–1:5).

11. Havelock Ellis, *My Life: An Autobiography of Havelock Ellis* (Boston: Houghton Mifflin, 1939), p. 81.

12. Grosskurth, *Havelock Ellis,* pp. 79, 17.

13. Quotations are from Ellis, *My Life,* pp. 249, 147, 277, 315, 342.

14. The letter to Françoise Lafite-Cyron is quoted in Grosskurth, *Havelock Ellis,* p. 281. Grosskurth points to a posthumously published essay on "The Problem of Sexual Potency" in which Ellis suggests that coitus as such is not especially important and that a sufficiently skillful partner may find other ways to satisfy a woman's erotic needs (p. 286); she herself speculates that he was impotent—a diagnosis that Freud, among others, appears to have ventured, though apparently on the grounds that Ellis was a man who made so few judgments! (pp. 421–22).

Grosskurth suggests that "the tolerance which is the key-note of the *Studies*" may be partly attributed to Ellis's comparative innocence of sexual experience. Without necessarily disputing this, I would also associate that tolerance with what might be termed his relatively nonteleological view of sexuality. Though Grosskurth seems uncomfortable with Ellis's defense of what he called "erotic symbolism" (p. 228), it seems to me consistent with his general sympathy for the devious routes desire may appear to take.

15. Acton, *Functions and Disorders,* p. 102. After declaring that "the majority of women (happily for them) are not very much troubled with sexual feeling of any kind," Acton set aside nymphomaniacs and other "sad exceptions," and went on: "there can be no doubt that sexual feeling in the female is in abeyance, and that it requires positive and considerable excitement to be roused at all; and even if roused (which in many instances it never can be) is very moderate compared with that of the male. . . . As a general rule, a modest woman seldom desires any sexual gratification for herself. She submits to her husband, but only to please him; and, but for the desire of maternity, would far rather be relieved

from his attentions" (pp. 101–2). Acton's book was first published in 1857, but these celebrated comments do not appear until this significantly enlarged third edition of 1862. Compare Acton's frequently quoted remarks with the following passage from an article by W. R. Greg in the *Westminster Review* of 1850: "Women's *desires* scarcely ever lead to their fall; for (save in a class of whom we shall speak presently) the desire scarcely exists in a definite and conscious form, till they *have* fallen. In this point there is a radical and essential difference between the sexes: the arrangements of nature and the customs of society would be even more unequal than they are, were it not so. In men, in general, the sexual desire is inherent and spontaneous, and belongs to the condition of puberty. In the other sex, the desire is dormant, if not non-existent, till excited; always till excited by undue familiarities; almost always till excited by actual intercourse. Those feelings which coarse and licentious minds are so ready to attribute to girls, are almost invariably *consequences*. Women whose position and education have protected them from exciting causes, constantly pass through life without ever being cognizant of the promptings of the senses. Happy for them that it is so!" (pp. 456–57). Since Acton relied heavily on Greg's essay in his own 1857 study of prostitution, and since, beginning with the second edition of 1858, he also cited the essay in *The Functions and Disorders* as well, it is difficult not to conclude that his celebrated comments owed more to his reading of Greg than to his medical observations.

16. Cf. Peter Gay, who vigorously disputes Steven Marcus's identification of Acton with the "official view of sexuality held by Victorian society." "But this," Gay argues, "is precisely what it is not. While Acton, a pleasing writer, enjoyed widespread popularity, responsible physicians in his day expressed grave reservations about his opinions, and indeed his competence." *The Bourgeois Experience: Victoria to Freud* (New York: Oxford University Press, 1984), p. 468.

17. Given the English fondness for distinguishing themselves from the French in these matters, it should be noted that Ellis thought the same "elaboration" of the rituals of modesty could be recognized as early as the seventeenth century in France. But since he went on to suggest that the simultaneous impulses to analyze and "dissolve" the conception of modesty arose "more especially" in that country, he had perhaps not altogether abandoned the conventional opposition (*Studies*, 1–1:65, 69).

18. See Charles Darwin, *The Expression of the Emotions in Man and Animals* (1872; reprint, Chicago: University of Chicago Press, 1965), p. 337; and Thomas H. Burgess, M.D., *The Physiology or Mechanism of Blushing* . . . (London: Churchill, 1839), p. 43.

19. Neither I nor Lady Mary's editor and biographer, the late Robert Halsband, could locate the blushing Circassians. Halsband suggested that this may be one of the many pseudo–Lady Mary anecdotes that have circulated since the eighteenth century.

20. [Steele], *Tatler*, no. 84, 22 October 1709. Madam Bennet was a notorious Restoration bawd.

21. Burney, *Evelina*, p. 406.

INDEX

Acton, William, 231, 235, 298 n.16; *Functions and Disorders of the Reproductive Organs,* 297–98 n.15
Addison, Joseph: *Spectator,* 243 n.10; courtship, 36, 37, 49–50; echoed by others, 10, 61, 255 n.6; male modesty, 9–10, 61, 257 n.25; Milton's Eve, 250 n.7; and Rousseau, 35, 250 n.8; sensibility, 53–54
Advice to Young Men. See Cobbett, William
Allestree, Richard, 28, 33, 56, 244 n.11; and Darwin, 227
—*Ladies Calling,* 5, 240 n.6, 253 n.26; echoed by others, 15, 242 n.27, 254 n.36, 255 n.6; marriage, 37, 249 n.6; modest reserve, 44–45; modest unconsciousness, 52; modesty as natural, 12, 13–16; shamefacedness, 10; women's nature, 14–15, 16
Allin, Arthur, 297 n.10
Andrews, John: *Remarks on the French and English Ladies,* 40, 285 n.23
Anti-Pamela. See Haywood, Eliza
Ardener, Edwin, 245 n.28
Armstrong, John: *Young Woman's Guide to Virtue, Economy, and Happiness,* 241 n.18, 253 n.31
Armstrong, Nancy, 244 n.11, 265–66 n.29
Arnold, Matthew, 169
Athenæum, 284–85 n.15, 287 n.34
Auerbach, Nina, 155, 277 n.7, 280 n.28
Austen, Henry, 67, 154
Austen, Jane, 67, 116, 225; *Emma,* 117; *Letters,* 154, 166–67, 279 n.21; *Northanger Abbey,* 281 n.33
—*Mansfield Park,* 143, 145–66, 167–68, 236, 278 n.14, 280 n.26, 283 n.49; anxiety, 159, 160–63, 164; blushing, 146, 148, 168, 277–78 n.13; and "Cinderella," 164–65, 283 n.47; coming out, 156–57; and conduct books, 276 n.3; Crawford's courtship, 108, 143, 145–48, 149, 152–55, 162, 167–68, 277 n.10, 277 n.11, 279 n.24;

dirt and cleanliness, 160–66, 282 n.39; Fanny Price, 79, 174, 175, 191, 211, 277 n.7, 278 n.17, 281 n.35, 282 n.42; Fanny's desire, 158, 167–68, 281 n.33, 281 n.36, 283 n.51; Mary Crawford, 145, 152–53, 155–57, 163–64, 280 n.28, 282 n.43, 282 n.44, 282 n.45; and *Memoirs of a Woman of Pleasure,* 107–8; modest consciousness, 157, 158–59; modest unconsciousness, 147–48, 277 n.11; preengaged heart, 107–8, 168; theatricals, 149–52, 153, 183, 184, 278 n.19, 278 n.20, 279 n.22, 279 n.24; true modesty, 155–59; and *Villette,* 183, 184; and *Wives and Daughters,* 200, 211–14; and Wollstonecraft, 155, 156, 157, 158, 160, 163, 280 n.27, 280–81 n.32
—*Pride and Prejudice,* 117, 143–44, 279 n.23; Elizabeth Bennet, 143–44, 145, 147, 153; Mr. Collins, 104, 143–44, 147, 153, 276 n.6, 277 n.11, 279 n.23; and *Mansfield Park,* 153; and *Wives and Daughters,* 211, 292 n.22
Awkward Age. See James, Henry

Barbauld, Anna Laetitia, 262 n.11
Barish, Jonas, 246–47 n.40
Barker, Gerard, 267 n.35
Barthes, Roland, 79, 87
Beer, Gillian, 293 n.2
Beer, Patricia, 289 n.2
Bell, Currer. *See* Brontë, Charlotte
Belle Assemblée, La: "The Blush of Innocence," 69; "On the Use of Rouge," 73–74
Benjamin, Jessica, 288 n.41
Bennett, John, 255 n.6
—*Letters to a Young Lady:* blushing, 65; conversation, 43, 54; model young woman, 43, 44, 54–55, 65; modest unconsciousness, 54; prudery, 54–55; true vs. false modesty, 54–55
Bergren, Ann, 244 n.10
Bersani, Leo, 159